ASIA
AND
AFRICA

LEGACIES AND OPPORTUNITIES
IN DEVELOPMENT

Edited by

DAVID L. LINDAUER AND
MICHAEL ROEMER

A copublication of the International Center for Economic Growth
and the Harvard Institute for International Development

ICS PRESS
Institute for Contemporary Studies
San Francisco, California

Publication signifies that the International Center for Economic Growth believes a work to be a competent treatment worthy of public consideration. The findings, interpretations, and conclusions of a work are entirely those of the authors and should not be attributed to ICEG, its affiliated organizations, its Board of Overseers, or organizations that support ICEG.

This book is a copublication with the Harvard Institute for International Development, which manages technical assistance to the developing world and brings that experience back into the teaching and research programs of Harvard University. HIID has resident teams in ministries of finance, planning, health, and education in more than a dozen countries in Europe, Africa, Asia, and Latin America.

Publication was funded by the United States Agency for International Development (AID). Preparation of the manuscript was sponsored by the United States Agency for International Development under the Consulting Assistance for Economic Reform Project, Contract PDC-0095-Z-00–9053–00. The views and interpretations in this publication are those of the authors and should not be attributed to AID.

Inquiries, book orders, and catalog requests should be addressed to ICS Press, Institute for Contemporary Studies, 720 Market Street, San Francisco, California 94102 USA. Telephone: (415) 981–5353; fax: (415) 986–4878; book orders within the continental United States: (800) 326–0263.

This book is set in Garamond type and was manufactured by Braun-Brumfield, Inc., Ann Arbor, Michigan. The project was managed at ICS Press by Tracy Clagett and Debbie Reece, and the index was prepared by Stephen Ingle. The cover was designed by Ben Santora.

0 9 8 7 6 5 4 3 2 1

Library of Congress Cataloging-in-Publication Data

Asia and Africa : legacies and opportunities in development / edited
   by David L. Lindauer & Michael Roemer.
        p.   cm.
   Includes bibliographical references and index.
   ISBN 1-55815-320-9
      1. Asia—Economic conditions—1945– 2. Africa—Economic
conditions—1945–1960. 3. Africa—Economic conditions—1960–
I. Lindauer, David L., 1952– . II. Roemer, Michael, 1937– .
HC412.A7183   1994
338.95—dc20   94-7211
                                                              CIP

Contents

Preface

Africa in the early 1990s is similar enough to Asia in the 1960s to learn valuable lessons from the spectacular commercial and industrial growth of Asian countries. It is not, however, the well-known four tigers of East Asian development—Korea, Taiwan, Hong Kong, and Singapore—which provide the most relevant model for development in African countries. A basic premise of *Asia and Africa: Legacies and Opportunities in Development* is that the three flourishing countries in Southeast Asia—Indonesia, Malaysia, and Thailand—share a significant number of features with many African countries and may therefore serve as the most useful model for African development.

Unlike Korea, Taiwan, Hong Kong, and Singapore, the countries of Indonesia, Malaysia, and Thailand are relatively rich in natural resources—minerals, forests, and productive farmland—and, at the beginning of their rapid growth, were relatively poor in human capital. Their most productive entrepreneurs have been ethnic Chinese minorities, not indigenous people. Indonesia and Malaysia have enjoyed stable governments, but neither they nor Thailand and the Philippines have had regimes that have successfully imposed widespread, disciplined, export-oriented interventions. These factors establish common ground with conditions in Africa and suggest that the advances and mistakes made in Asia may provide constructive guidelines for African development.

Asia and Africa offers new perspectives on regional development: It analyzes lessons learned in Asia with reference to the specific circumstances of Africa, and it concentrates on Southeast Asian examples rather than on those of East Asia. The authors of this volume are both scholars and practitioners of development economics. Because they have had many years of combined practical working experience in both Asia and Africa, they examine development problems from a real-world viewpoint. Rather than depending on theoretically preferred approaches, they look more to the capacity of governments to implement strategy choices.

The volume editors, eminent development economists David L. Lindauer and Michael Roemer, and their contributors offer as hope and guidance for Africa the economic success that Asian countries have achieved despite barriers to growth that included war, revolution, political instability, ethnic competition, corrupt regimes, and grinding poverty. Most of what has been accomplished in Southeast Asia beginning thirty years ago, they suggest, could be accomplished by several African countries today.

This book is a copublication of the International Center for Economic Growth and the Harvard Institute for International Development. Together we are pleased to offer this unique and useful comparative work to policy makers who seek to facilitate economic growth in Sub-Saharan Africa, whether they are working from within countries of the region or from afar as members of organizations devoted to world development.

Nicolás Ardito-Barletta	Dwight H. Perkins
General Director	Director
International Center for	Harvard Institute for
Economic Growth	International Development
Panama City, Panama	Cambridge, Massachusetts

June 1994

Editors' Preface
and Acknowledgments

Over the past thirty years, the rapid economic growth and industrialization of East Asia has been a dominant story in economics, so much so that Korea, Taiwan, Hong Kong, and Singapore are viewed as models for development in other countries. More recently, it has become apparent that three countries in Southeast Asia—Indonesia, Malaysia, and Thailand—have also achieved rapid income and industrial growth and offer a development legacy for other countries.

During the same thirty years, another story was taking place in Sub-Saharan Africa, where most countries, having won independence, experienced a decade or so of moderate growth and then suffered a decade or more of economic shocks, poor policies, and stagnation or decline. Since the mid-1980s, several of these countries have been trying to regain their economic balance and start growing again, with limited success.

This book has been written with the conviction that Africa, although it has missed opportunities over the past thirty years, has not completely closed the door on sustained development. African conditions have not favored development, but neither did those in Southeast Asia in the beginning. The difference in performance has been substantially, though not entirely, due to policy differences. We believe that African countries intent on changing their economic fortunes can do so and that Southeast Asia, rather than East Asia, would be a good model for Africa.

Many writers have analyzed and advocated Asian strategies of development. This book provides three perspectives that have not been emphasized previously. *First,* our analysis of the Asian experience is tailored not to the generic developing country but to specific circumstances of Africa. Each chapter includes at least one author with extensive research or policy experience in Africa. *Second,* we focus more on the Southeast Asian examples than those from East Asia, although we use one to highlight the different characteristics of the other. Most of the chapters are written by experts with extensive Southeast Asian experience. *Third,* many of the contributors have worked for years as policy advisers, in both Asia and Africa, and take the view of practitioners as well as students of development. The capacity of governments to implement strategy choices weighs more heavily in these pages than theoretically or hypothetically preferred approaches.

This book has been written for the Africa Bureau of the United States Agency for International Development, which financed the effort through the Consulting Assistance for Economic Reform (CAER) project. Lester Gordon of HIID encouraged us to propose this project to AID; Jerome Wolgin of the Africa Bureau gave his support and arranged the funding; and Jay Smith saw the project through to its conclusion.

Therese Feng compiled much of the data used in this volume during the summer of 1992; in the following year, Markus Goldstein and Alison Barrows helped us to complete the work. Ken Repp assembled the edited chapters into the manuscript. Nicolás Ardito-Barletta, with his usual enthusiasm, saw the merits of this volume and suggested we submit it to ICEG for publication.

The authors presented first drafts of the chapters at a two-day workshop in Cambridge in February 1993. In addition to those already mentioned, we received helpful comments from Henry Bruton, Paul Collier, Forest Duncan, Clark Leith, Donald Morrison, Abby Riddell, Roger Riddell, Lee Ann Ross, Don Sillers, and Dirck Stryker. Gerald Meier, Robert Rotberg, and Donald Snodgrass read the first draft manuscript and offered many penetrating observations. We wish it had been possible to pursue more of their suggestions.

We are grateful to all of these supporters and especially to the contributors, who made this book possible.

CHAPTER 1

Legacies and Opportunities

David L. Lindauer and Michael Roemer

Three decades ago, it made sense to speak of the "underdeveloped" countries in Asia, Africa, and Latin America as the "third world." By the mid-1990s, such terms make little sense. The "Third World" is no longer a mass of stagnant, poverty-ridden countries. Economies in East and Southeast Asia have been growing rapidly for a quarter of a century. The city-states of Hong Kong and Singapore are already classified as high-income economies, and if current growth rates persist, per capita income levels in Taiwan could overtake those in Belgium, Italy, and elsewhere in Europe by the end of the century. Korea and Malaysia are not far behind, and Thailand and Indonesia, although considerably poorer, are also growing rapidly. By the year 2000, China will probably no longer be a locus of world poverty, as it has been for most of the last hundred years.

There was nothing preordained about which regions would succeed. In the 1950s and early 1960s, Asia appeared to be caught in a low-level equilibrium trap, with large and growing populations, unstable governments, and in many cases a weak natural resource base. Many observers thought Asia's economies were destined for prolonged poverty. In contrast, as Africa gained independence in the late 1950s and 1960s, it held great promise. Although Africa started with limited educational attainments and experience in governance, it enjoyed relatively generous land and resource endowments. Destructive civil wars had been uncommon, and national independence brought a wave of optimism that anything could be done.

But Africa's promise has not been realized. Its spurt of postindependence economic growth could not be sustained. External shocks, poor policy responses, and ineffective development strategies brought economic stagnation to many countries, causing even front-runners such as Kenya and Côte d'Ivoire to lose momentum. As Table 1.1 shows, while per capita incomes in East and Southeast Asian countries increased by more than 5 percent a year from 1965 to 1990, African incomes were stagnant and in several countries were declining.

Why Has Asia Grown Faster than Africa?

The macroeconomic data of Table 1.1 suggest some broad explanations for the differences in African and Asian economic performance. One obvious possibility is that Asian countries invested a larger share of their income. The average rate of investment for Africa is 17 percent, below that of all Asian countries in the table. But investment is not the whole story. Several African countries—Cameroon, Côte d'Ivoire, Kenya, Tanzania, and Zambia—invested at least 20 percent of their GDP during the twenty-five-year period, however, without coming close to the growth performance of the Southeast Asian countries and Taiwan, which also invested 20 to 25 percent of their GDP. Only Hong Kong, Singapore, China, and Botswana have invested massively in their growth since 1965.

By rough approximation, we can measure the total contribution of investment and labor force growth to the growth in GDP, through the familiar sources-of-growth equation.[1] In the formulation used here, the residual includes all factors other than capital and labor force growth, including gains in human capital and productivity. The fourth column in Table 1.1 shows that for all Asian countries except Malaysia and the Philippines, the residual accounted for growth of 2 to 5 percent a year. In Africa, except for Botswana, the residual was small and, in several cases, negative, as it was for the continent as a whole. To understand Asia's legacy of accelerated growth, we need to understand why the residual has been so much higher in East and Southeast Asia.

One reason may be that Asian countries started with greater endowments of educated people, as Dwight Perkins and Michael Roemer document in Chapter 2. Asia's investment in education since 1960 has not, however, been greater than Africa's, as shown in Table 1.1. A second reason for Asia's higher residual is that pure productivity gains, not attributable to investment in human capital, have been central to Asian success and generally lacking in

TABLE 1.1

Growth, Resources, and Productivity, 1965–1990

	Annual growth rate, % p.a.					
	GDP per capita	Population	Exports: goods and nonfactor services[a]	Total factor productivity[b]	Years of schooling per adult[c]	Ratio (%) investment to GDP
East/Southeast Asia	**5.3**	**1.9**	**13.5**	**2.4**	n.a.	**30.6**[i]
Korea	7.3	1.7	18.9	4.9	3.5	26.7
Taiwan	6.9	1.9	15.2	4.9	n.a.	23.8
Hong Kong	6.1[j]	2.0[j]	11.0[d]	3.6[j]	1.0	29.7[d]
Singapore	7.0	1.9	12.1[p]	3.6	1.9	35.3
China	6.1[d]	2.2[d]	10.7[j]	3.2[d]	n.a.	31.5[j]
Indonesia	4.3	2.2	13.6	2.7	4.3	21.1
Malaysia	3.0	2.7	8.7	1.1	2.7	25.4
Philippines	1.4	2.7	7.2	0.0	2.1	20.7
Thailand	5.1	2.5	10.5	3.3	2.0	24.3
Sub-Saharan Africa	**0.2**	**2.9**	**4.5**	**−0.4**	n.a.	**17.3**[i]
Botswana	7.9	3.7	15.9[f]	6.4	2.4	28.0[f]
Cameroon	1.5[k]	1.8	4.4[n]	2.5[n]	5.3	20.2[n]
Chad	−0.6[j]	2.2	1.3[j]	n.a.	n.a.	n.a.
Côte d'Ivoire	−0.7[j]	3.9[i]	4.8[o]	−0.7[n]	n.a.	20.0[g]
Ghana	−0.7	2.7	1.5	−0.8	5.7	9.6
Kenya	1.3[h]	3.8	3.3[d]	0.2[j]	3.0	20.5[h]
Mali	1.8[j]	2.3	6.3[j]	1.2[j]	9.1	13.2[j]
Nigeria	2.1[i]	2.8	10.9[i]	1.3[i]	n.a.	17.4[i]
Senegal	−0.3[j]	3.2	2.5[m]	−0.6[m]	−1.3	14.1
Tanzania	0.3	3.2	3.0	−0.7	−2.6	19.7
Zaire	−3.0[i]	2.0	−4.5[i]	−4.3[i]	4.9	14.6
Zambia	−1.9[d]	2.7	−1.3[k]	−3.1[e]	2.9	21.1[e]
Zimbabwe	1.0[j]	3.0	3.8[k]	−0.5[l]	2.2	18.1[l]

a. Revenues from exports of goods plus nonfactor services in constant U.S. dollars.
b. Total factor productivity calculated by the approximation explained in footnote 1 of text. Regional averages are roughly indicative only, as they use figures in this table, which are not all for the same years.
c. Annual growth from 1960 to 1985 in the completed years of schooling per population over age 25 as computed by the World Bank (unpublished) in connection with World Bank (1993).
d. 1965–89.   e. 1965–88.   f. 1965–87.   g. 1965–86.   h. 1967–89.   i. 1970–90.
j. 1970–89.   k. 1970–88.   l. 1970–87.   m. 1970–86.   n. 1970–85   o. 1971–86.
p. 1975–89
SOURCES: For growth of GDP per capita, population, and investment ratio, International Monetary Fund, *International Financial Statistics Yearbook* (Washington, D.C., 1992). For summary data for regions (except productivity growth), World Bank, *World Development Report 1992* (Washington, D.C., 1992). For export growth, World Bank, *World Tables 1992* (Washington, D.C., 1992).

TABLE 1.2
Reductions in Poverty, East and Southeast Asia

Country	Share (%) in poverty			No. of poor (millions)	
	1970	1980	1990	1970	1990
China	33	28	10	275	100
Indonesia	60	29	15	70	27
Korea	23	10	5	7	2
Malaysia	18	9	2	2	0.4
Philippines	35	30	21	13	13
Thailand	26	17	16	10	9
East/Southeast Asia	35	23	10	400	180

NOTE: Poverty line is the cost of 2,150 calories per person per day, 90 percent consumed as grain.
SOURCE: Frida Johansen, "Poverty Reduction in East Asia" (World Bank Discussion Paper 203, Washington, D.C., 1993), 42.

Africa.[2] A central premise of this book is that productivity gains are associated with the outward-looking, market-friendly policies associated with East and Southeast Asian development.

This book is about economic growth. It is important to note that in every Asian country experiencing rapid and sustained growth in incomes, there was a striking reduction in poverty. Table 1.2 summarizes data on the incidence of poverty in six Asian countries from 1970 to 1990, taken from a study by Johansen (1993). The poverty line is defined as the income needed to purchase 2,150 calories per person per day, 90 percent consumed as grain. In China and Indonesia, the largest and poorest countries listed, rapid growth helped to cut the incidence of poverty in 1990 to a third and a quarter, respectively, of 1970 levels. Korea and Malaysia started with less poverty and had even greater reductions. Data provided by Fields (1991, 23–27) reveal that, over a twenty-year period beginning in the early 1960s, Thailand reduced its incidence of poverty by more than half, from 57 to 24 percent, and Taiwan enjoyed an even sharper drop, from 35 to 10 percent in only eight years (1964–1972). The development strategies employed by Asian countries to achieve rapid growth were consistent with, and may well have directly contributed to, significant improvements in living standards for the poorest members of society.

Comparable data are not available for African countries. However, based on partial evidence from a few countries, the World Bank (1990, 42) concludes that "poverty in Sub-Saharan Africa is severe and has been getting worse."

Asian Models of Development

How has Asia invested more than Africa and employed its resources more productively? By the early 1970s, as evidence mounted that economic growth in East Asia was rapid and could be sustainable, development practitioners began to look to these newly industrialized countries (NICs) for a model that might be transplanted to other, more slowly growing regions.

The early consensus among economists identified the NIC model as a market-based, outward-oriented development strategy supported by relatively low and uniform protection of imports, a stable real exchange rate, well-functioning internal markets with factor prices reflecting real scarcities, and private enterprise as the engine of growth.[3] In recent years, this neoclassical interpretation of East Asia's success has been challenged. Several observers of Korea and Taiwan have noted that considerable government intervention, import and investment controls, and highly differentiated price and tax incentives existed alongside neoclassical features of open economies.[4]

Enriched by these revisionist views, the emerging consensus now sees East Asia as a continuum of development strategies. At one extreme lies Hong Kong, perhaps the purest open, neoclassically managed economy in the world. At the other end lies Korea, where government did intervene, but within a matrix of sound macroeconomic policies, flexible factor markets, and export targets that forced firms to compete in world markets.

None of the four, however, appears to be a relevent model for most African countries.[5] All are resource-poor countries; Hong Kong and Singapore have no rural economies at all. Populations are well educated and ethnically homogeneous (although Taiwan is split between mainlanders and native Taiwanese, and Singapore has a significant, if politically weak, migrant population). Governments are managed by highly effective cadres of officials, capable of implementing interventionist policies and running competitive state enterprises.

A basic premise of this book is that the three countries in Southeast Asia that have achieved sustained, rapid income growth—Indonesia, Malaysia, and Thailand—have more in common with many African countries and may therefore offer more relevant development legacies than any of the four East Asian tigers. The three ASEAN[6] countries are relatively rich in natural resources—minerals, forests, and productive farmland—and, at the beginning of their rapid growth, were relatively poor in human capital. The most productive entrepreneurs in all these societies have been ethnic Chinese minorities, not indigenous people. Indonesia and Malaysia have enjoyed stable governments, but neither they nor Thailand and the Philippines have had regimes that have shown themselves capable of disciplined, export-oriented interventions.

All the Asian economies shared two features: sound macroeconomic management, including especially flexible exchange rate management, and flexible factor markets. They differed mainly in trade and industrial policy. Southeast Asian countries had highly protective trade regimes, but they did not have the political or bureaucratic discipline to use protection and subsidies as tools of export policy, as Korea did. Instead, the Southeast Asian countries promoted exports by establishing mechanisms, such as duty-free zones and drawback schemes, to insulate export firms from the high costs of protection and rent-seeking. This policy mix satisfies neither the old neoclassical orthodoxy nor the proponents of intervention, but it has worked extremely well.

Asian development strategies are rooted in patterns of governance, designed to take fullest advantage of factor endowments, and implemented through economic policies that have become identified with Asia. This chapter discusses each of these before considering Africa's prospects under a similar policy regime.[7]

Governance and Economic Strategy

Perhaps the central question in comparing the economic performance of Africa and Asia is this: why, over the past three decades, have Asian governments been more development oriented? Political stability has certainly played a role.

Park's eighteen-year reign in Korea, the Kuomintang's hold on Taiwan, Britain's colonial regime in Hong Kong, Lee's long dominance of Singapore, Suharto's twenty-seven-year rule in Indonesia, and the long-tenured prime ministers of the United Malays National Organization (UMNO) in Malaysia all coincided with rapid developments in those countries. Thailand is a special case: although prime ministers changed frequently until the recent political reforms, the popularly revered monarchy has been able to protect and entrench the high-ranking officials who make economic policy.

Although political stability may be necessary for sustained rapid growth, it is obviously not sufficient. The Philippines, despite long-lived regimes, has not developed rapidly. Africa also has had stable governments for a decade and often much longer in Côte d'Ivoire, The Gambia, Kenya, Malawi, Senegal, Tanzania, Zaire, Zambia, and Zimbabwe, none of which has maintained rapid development into the 1990s.

For a regime to become developmentally effective, the government must value economic development so highly that it is willing to risk political capital to achieve growth. Dwight Perkins and Michael Roemer observe in Chapter 2 that several Asian governments saw rapid development as essential to the survival of their regimes, as in Indonesia and Malaysia, or even of their countries, as in Korea, Taiwan, and Singapore.

The choice of long-term development over short-term political and personal gain manifests itself in different ways. Rent-seeking is a common feature of Southeast Asian and African countries. Yet leaders in Southeast Asia, with the notable exception of Marcos in the Philippines, have understood that growing rents require growing economies; when rent-seeking threatened sound economies, the rents were curbed. Leith and Lofchie (1993) observe that in Ghana before the reforms of the 1980s and in other African countries, leaders extracted rents without heed to sustaining growth in the economy that produces them. The result has been economic decline, much as if a renewable but limited natural resource had been overexploited.

The accommodation of entrepreneurial ethnic minorities is another choice for development over politics. Ethnic Chinese have played major, even dominant roles in commerce and industry in Indonesia, Malaysia, and Thailand, where governments have secured the political and economic rights of their Chinese minorities despite strong, sometimes violent, popular pressure for their suppression. The position of former colonial European residents in Africa, of Lebanese in West Africa, and of ethnic Indians in East Africa has been far more precarious, discouraging their investment. Even indigenous Africans are disadvantaged if they belong to an ethnic group that opposes the government or is unpopular with a more powerful group. Few African governments have pushed forcefully for accommodation among different racial or ethnic groups either explicitly, as in Malaysia, or implicitly, as in Indonesia and Thailand.

The insulation of economic policy making from politics is another important manifestation of Asia's development priorities. In Korea, Taiwan, and Singapore, where economic prosperity and national survival were linked inextricably, good economic policy was considered good politics. In Southeast Asia, however, where rent-seeking was inherent in the clientelistic style of governance, regimes made self-denying choices to establish planning commissions, finance ministries, and central banks as bastions of economic technocrats entrusted to manage the economy. These officials have enjoyed long tenure in their jobs. One Indonesian finance minister spent fifteen years on the job before he became coordinating economics minister for five more years. Protected by the monarchy, the leading economist in Thailand outlasted several governments. Malaysia's technocratic policy makers were less influential, but Malay political leaders acknowledged that rapid economic growth underlay their political and social goals. Although Africa has had a number of excellent economic policy makers, few of them were as influential over so long a period as their counterparts in Asia.

Where political aims conflict with and supersede development aims, governments are often hemmed in by the forces that have sustained their regimes, unable to reform either their administrations or their economies to promote growth. In Chapter 3, Jennifer Widner suggests that for determined leaders, there are paths out of this thicket. In Thailand, the reforming government of Prime Minister Prem Tinasulanond struck alliances with trade associations that had interests in reform, overcoming the barons who had supported previous clientelistic regimes. Indonesia's Suharto also appealed to business when he brought in a Swiss firm to perform many tasks of the customs administration, dramatically reducing costs and waiting times. Yet in Côte d'Ivoire, which also has active trade associations, Houphouët-Boigny did not take advantage of their potential to support reform.

Governments in Asia have been able to choose economic development and reform without sacrificing regime stability, and African regimes could do the same. The governments of Korea, Taiwan, and to a lesser extent Singapore, threatened by foreign enemies and anxious to spur growth, chose to intervene forcefully to push their economies faster than unaided markets would develop, although in the same general directions. Determined political leaders, well-educated and generally honest officials, and militaristic discipline combined to elevate public goals above private gain as officials interacted with businessmen to generate export-led growth.

These characteristics were not so strong in Southeast Asia. Disciplined intervention to promote public goals was almost certain to be thwarted by the clientelism and rent-seeking that were entrenched features of governance. Consequently, the governments of Indonesia, Malaysia, and Thailand left development more to the market than did Korea and Taiwan. They have actively managed their macroeconomies to establish stable and productive climates for investment; invested heavily in infrastructure and agriculture; and acted to insulate exports from the distortions of protection and rent-seeking by making inputs available to exporters at world prices, free of quantitative controls. Other interventions have occurred, especially public investment in large-scale industry, but for the most part these industries have not played a central role in export-led growth in Indonesia, Malaysia, and Thailand (the ASEAN three). Export growth in Southeast Asia came from multinational firms (especially in electronics); from medium-sized firms producing labor-intensive goods, many owned by East Asian investors; and from agriculture. Market incentives, not government intervention, played the major role in guiding export growth.

The application to Africa of Asia's experience with government seems clear. African regimes, like those in Southeast Asia, have limited capacity to intervene decisively in private decision making to accelerate development, as Korea once did. In both regions, clientelism and rent-seeking are characteristic of most regimes. In Africa, these regimes have weakened only where economies were largely destroyed, as in Ghana and Uganda. In contrast to Southeast Asia, Africa's low government salaries, declining standards of performance, and weak official leadership have eroded morale in the civil service and forced many of the most competent officers to seek jobs elsewhere, often overseas. Until these conditions can be overcome, African developers should choose strategies that are no more interventionist than those in Southeast Asia, where civil service capabilities have been improving. For many countries in Africa, policies even closer to those of open market economies, as described below, are likely to be more effective until the governments themselves are transformed.

Factor Endowments: Making the Most of What You Have

Each of the rapidly growing economies of East and Southeast Asia followed the dictates of comparative advantage. Korea, Hong Kong, and Singapore, with few natural resources and capital but abundant unskilled labor, based their early development strategies on labor-intensive manufactures. Relative to its population, Taiwan had more land than the other tigers and used it intensively in the early stages of growth, while emphasizing labor-intensive manufactures and eventually more skill-intensive exports.

The export mix was not entirely dependent on existing endowments and market forces. Korea, Taiwan, and Singapore did intervene to promote new exports. The most dramatic of these, Korea's heavy and chemical industry drive of the 1970s, probably pushed beyond the market and beyond Korea's comparative advantage at the time. But as economies develop, they accumulate physical and human capital that gradually shift comparative advantage toward the kinds of goods in which Korea invested in the 1970s. These and similar interventions in East Asia may have accelerated a process that was occurring in any case, but they did not take great leaps beyond the countries' evolving capabilities.

All the Southeast Asian countries are endowed with highly productive agricultural land and other natural resources, which determined their export base during the early stages of rapid growth. In addition, the ASEAN countries invested to maintain their cost advantage in traditional exports such as oil, natural gas, metals, timber, rice, palm oil, and rubber, and also diversified within primary products into exports of coffee, tea, cocoa, and fruit. As Thomas Tomich, Michael Roemer, and Jeffrey Vincent document in Chapter 5, the primary export share of gross domestic product in Indonesia and Thailand increased from 1970 to 1990, while in Malaysia it was maintained at nearly 40 percent of GDP, even as manufacturing and modern service industries flourished.

Thus the ASEAN three moved into manufacturing, for import replacement and for export, from a solid base of primary export earnings. This strategy helped the ASEAN nations avoid a chronic shortage of foreign exchange, which crippled manufacturing in Africa in the 1980s. Nor did the Southeast Asian countries succumb to the opposite problem, Dutch disease, which handicaps export industry and agriculture through exchange rate appreciation brought on by rising export earnings. Indonesia, for example, devalued its exchange rate despite booming oil revenues in order to protect agriculture, while investing its oil rents productively in agriculture (especially irrigation for smallholder rice production), education, public health, and infrastructure. Employing such policies, Indonesia and Malaysia converted their primary export wealth into sustainable development in other sectors. Nigeria, in contrast, allowed its exchange rate to appreciate, which destroyed export agriculture, and invested too much of its oil rents in projects with poor long-run returns.

In Southeast Asia, governments invested in research, irrigation, fertilizer subsidies, infrastructure, education, and health to raise productivity in food agriculture, which was consistent with their comparative advantage and essential to their development strategy. Richard Goldman reminds us in Chapter 6 that rising output of rice and other foods, especially in Indonesia and Thailand, freed workers for employment in industry, contributed to the relatively low real wages of urban workers, and minimized the need to use foreign exchange for imports of staple foods. Agricultural productivity gains also played a central role in the dramatic reduction of rural poverty in Indonesia and Malaysia. In Africa, neglect of agriculture is reflected in the decline of food production per capita since 1975 and the persistence of both rural and urban poverty.

During the 1980s, as agricultural productivity rose and world prices fell for many commodities, Indonesia and Thailand took advantage of their low-cost labor by moving with almost explosive force into labor-intensive export manufacturing, especially in textiles, clothing, and electronics. Malaysia had anticipated this development a good decade earlier and by the end of the 1980s was moving into more capital- and skill-intensive exports, notably in electronics. Although investments were made in chemicals, autos, aircraft, and other industries not justified by existing comparative advantage, the principal thrust of policy was to encourage industries in which the ASEAN countries could compete in world markets. In Africa, inward-looking policies lost sight of comparative advantage and created a high-cost industrial sector with little export potential, as Michael Roemer documents in Chapter 7.

Industrialization was immeasurably helped by the ability of Asian countries to utilize not only their natural resources, but all the human resources available to them. For Japan and Korea, with their homogeneous populations, this was no problem. The Kuomintang government of Taiwan encouraged small-scale industry, guided by market forces, at least partly because that strategy would tap the productive energies of the native Taiwanese without threatening the political control of the mainland Chinese who moved to Taiwan with the Communist takeover of China in 1949. We have already spoken of the accommodation of ethnic Chinese businessmen in Southeast Asia. Indonesia's Sukarno, although no development leader, did knit many ethnic groups into a nation, largely ending ethnic strife as a deterrent to development. African states generally have not been as successful in drawing on the talents and energies of all their ethnic groups; this is one of the choices of politics over development discussed in the previous section.

Southeast Asia in particular has supplemented its own resources with capital from abroad, including direct foreign investment. This has added not only capital but entrepreneurial and technological capacity. African countries that have limited entrepreneurial capacity or cannot easily accommodate ethnic minorities may wish to utilize foreign investment as a substitute for some period. Louis Wells warns us in Chapter 10 that, although useful, this approach cannot substitute fully for locally generated resources. To attract foreign investors, African countries will have to follow the ASEAN three in managing rather open economies, with export-oriented incentives and a minimum of controls.

African developers, like those in Asia, will have to follow the path of comparative advantage based on existing factor endowments, making full use of all their resources. Africa's comparative advantage continues to lie in its natural resources and unskilled labor—that is, in smallholder agriculture for food and export in most countries; in mineral exports for Algeria, Botswana, Cameroon, the Congo, Namibia, Nigeria, Zambia, and Zaire; and in tourism. Investment opportunities still exist in these often maligned industries. In light of the Southeast Asian experience, investments in primary industries ought to be pursued.

Labor-intensive manufacturing for export is presumably the next step for many countries in Africa, especially those facing population pressure on their land. Several of the chapters in this volume focus on the policies needed to take this next step. None of the Asian countries skipped over it and, despite attempted technological leaps into chemicals, autos, and aircraft, Southeast Asia's comparative advantage is still based primarily on labor-intensive manufactures. Neither factor endowments nor governmental capabilities suggest that leapfrogging into technologically advanced industries could work in Africa.

Components of Development Strategy

Asian governments followed a range of strategies to move their economies briskly along the path of changing comparative advantage. All managed stable macroeconomies that attracted investment, using similar approaches (although with some significant differences). All maintained flexible labor and capital markets. But they followed different industrial strategies. We examine each of these topics in the following sections.

Macroeconomic Management

The Asian economies seldom strayed from balanced macroeconomies, as Jeffrey Lewis and Malcolm McPherson describe in Chapter 4. Government *budget deficits* were generally low, ranging from Singapore's surplus of 3 percent of GDP over the 1980s to Thailand's deficit of 2.3 percent of GDP. Low deficits meant that governments were not seeking finance that would crowd private investors out of credit markets; they were not pressuring central banks to increase the money supply beyond private demand for balances; and they were not accumulating unsustainable foreign debt. The one exception was Malaysia, which ran deficits approaching 20 percent of GNP in the early 1980s and brought them under control only by the end of the decade. However, as the country saved over a third of its GDP, such deficits could be financed without unbalancing the economy. Several African countries ran high budget deficits during the 1980s. In Kenya, Senegal, Tanzania, Zambia, and Zimbabwe the deficits ranged from 5 to 14 percent of GDP, and in none of them was savings sufficient to provide noninflationary finance without crowding out private investors.

Supported by conservative fiscal and monetary policies, Asian countries also kept *inflation* under control. Higher-than-customary inflation, or the fear of it, distorts relative price signals, increases the uncertainty faced by investors, and consequently diverts entrepreneurial and managerial energies from productivity-enhancing activities to financial management. During the 1980s, all of the seven rapidly growing economies in Asia had inflation averaging 8.5 percent a year or less, and in all cases the rate was lower than over the previous decades. Of the African countries for which Lewis and McPherson have data, few kept inflation in the range of the Asian economies. In Ghana, Nigeria, Tanzania, Zaire, Zambia, and Zimbabwe, inflation was not only high during the 1980s, but markedly higher than during the previous ten years. These inflation rates were severe enough to disrupt investment and growth. In all six cases, investment was a significantly lower share of GDP during the 1980s than during the previous decades, although it cannot be certain that inflation was a major contributing factor.

From the standpoint of investment and industrialization, the most important price in the macroeconomy is the *exchange rate*. Exchange rate management has two development aims. First, managers need to establish a rate that is sufficiently rewarding to producers of tradable goods so that investment in exports and import substitutes will take place. Lewis and McPherson present data that starkly contrast Asian and African exchange rate management in this respect. For most of the period since 1965, the seven rapidly growing Asian countries had official exchange rates quite close to their free market rate; only the Korean won was moderately overvalued. Virtually all African countries, except those in the franc zone, had official rates that were, in comparison to the parallel market rate, overvalued by 10 to over 100 percent. The parallel market for currency can be thin and illegal, so it may not be a perfect indicator of the equilibrium rate; nevertheless, large deviations from that rate suggest a problem.

Once a sufficiently rewarding official exchange rate is achieved, macroeconomic managers need to maintain the real value of that rate over an extended period. Rapidly growing countries such as Korea, Malaysia, Singapore, Taiwan, and Thailand have been able to do this, but so have Kenya and the franc zone countries, though the latter suffered some appreciation. Wide fluctuations in the real rate, especially if they tend toward appreciation, have severely hurt development in Nigeria, Tanzania, Zaire, Zambia, and Zimbabwe. Indonesia also had a fluctuating real rate, however, largely because it used large devaluations until the mid-1980s to correct the appreciations of Dutch disease. In that case, productive investment of oil revenues overcame the exchange rate problem until oil prices fell in the mid-1980s, when Indonesia devalued again and began using a crawling peg to maintain the real value of the exchange rate. Since then, investment in exports has soared.

Hong Kong, Singapore, Indonesia, Malaysia, and Thailand have maintained fully or nearly *convertible currencies* and totally or nearly unrestricted capital flows for many years. This fact appears to have cemented sound macroeconomic management in place as a cornerstone of development policy. Without exchange controls, fiscal and monetary policies are the only tools available to protect reserves, avoid sharp devaluations of the exchange rate, and maintain economic stability. Convertibility also gives investors confidence that they can get their money out at will, reducing their risk and thus lowering the return they require to invest.

In Africa, The Gambia has made its currency convertible, and Ghana and Kenya are moving in that direction. The franc zone countries have, of course, had convertibility with the French franc since their independence. The consequence of French backing, however, is that value of the CFA franc is virtually unrelated to economic scarcities and conditions in franc zone countries. It appears, then, that for convertibility to promote investment and growth, it should be combined with flexible exchange rate management.

In sum, the experiences of both Asia and Africa strongly suggest that a stable macroeconomy and a politically stable and growth-oriented government are necessary conditions for rapid economic development. In East and Southeast Asia rapid growth was accompanied by macroeconomic management that maintained sustainable fiscal deficits and achieved balances in the current account. Africa will have to do the same.

Industrial Strategies

We have already described how industrialization in Asia followed the contours of comparative advantage determined substantially by existing and evolving factor endowments. Despite this, the policy measures supporting industrialization were far from neoclassical in all but Hong Kong and Singapore. As Michael Roemer discusses in Chapter 7, Korea, Taiwan, and the ASEAN three all employed protectionist trade regimes. Although the average rate of extramarket incentives was low in Korea and Taiwan,[8] its dispersion was not strikingly different from protectionist regimes in Latin America. Effective protection was higher in Indonesia and Thailand, and widely dispersed in all three ASEAN countries. In the 1970s Korea, and to a lesser extent Taiwan, also embraced import substitution through investment in and official promotion of large-scale heavy industries such as petrochemicals, steel, shipbuilding, and automobiles.

All five of these countries found ways to promote manufactured exports despite their protection of domestic markets. In Chapter 11, Catharine Hill stresses the macroeconomic policies that supported export growth, notably exchange rate management that avoided overvaluation and maintained a steady real exchange rate. Without an encouraging macroeconomic environment, other export promotion measures were likely to fail. But Korea, Taiwan, Indonesia, Malaysia, and Thailand went beyond macroeconomic support. Each took steps to insulate exporters from the disincentives of protectionist regimes, providing manufacturers with simulated free trade environments that offered easy access to inputs essentially at world prices.

In Korea the large-scale, heavy, import-substituting industries were promoted on the understanding that they would soon become competitive exporters, as several did. Korea employed an arsenal of weapons to encourage exports, especially by the conglomerates (*chaebol*), including subsidized credit from government banks, licenses for and duty drawbacks on imported inputs, protection in the domestic market to cross-subsidize export development, relaxed enforcement of income taxes, and moral suasion. Officials, meeting with the *chaebol,* established and enforced ambitious export targets on which continued subsidies depended. Targets and their enforcement were directly sanctioned by President Park.

Korea's pro-export interventions, which have been described as "market-conforming," speeded industrial development beyond the rate dictated by comparative advantage and market forces, though in the same general direction. But these measures required an extraordinary performance by

Korea's bureaucracy. President Park laid down and enforced export goals as a national imperative. Officials were sufficiently disciplined to manage these complex interventions without putting personal gain ahead of national goals. Firms that did not meet targets suffered the consequences, giving Korea's interventionist policies a credibility that few other governments have been able to achieve.

Southeast Asian countries tried nothing so ambitious. Malaysia used export processing zones extensively, especially but not only for electronics exporters. Indonesia established an agency to grant exporters both access to imports despite protective licensing restrictions and drawbacks of (or exemption from) duties on inputs. Thailand relied more on macroeconomic incentives to support exports but also granted duty exemptions to foreign investors who planned to export. In all three countries, the economic stresses of the 1980s impelled governments to institute gradualist but determined reform programs that have begun to reduce protection, turning all industries outward to face international competition. These well-established reforms have given investors clear signals about the direction and dependability of future policies.

In Africa, trade policies have been exclusively inward-looking, and government intervention has been pervasive in industry. The political culture of clientelism and rent-seeking and the declining effectiveness of bureaucracies have hindered industrialization. After two decades of industrialization, there is little evidence of internationally competitive manufacturing. One exception is Mauritius, which adopted open-economy policies similar to those in Asia. For Sub-Saharan Africa as a whole, intervention has been tried and has failed.

Export zones in Africa have foundered because officials try to control or extract rents from them; tax rebate schemes are so slow and uncertain that firms do not count on them. A few determined governments may make such programs work, and they could be helpful. But for the majority of countries, a mix closer to the open, market-based economy, with limited protection for infant industries, may be more effective in moving toward the manufacturing-based phase of comparative advantage.

Flexible Factor Markets

If outward-looking, market-based economies are to produce rapid growth, they must contain markets for labor, capital, and other factors of production that can generate appropriate price signals and respond to them, moving resources quickly toward the industries that are most profitable. At issue is whether Africa can be competitive with other economies. Since, by definition, all nations possess some comparative advantage, a key issue is whether Africa can be a low-cost producer of manufactured products. One view says no: relying on cultural stereotyping, this view sees Asia's labor force inherently as disciplined and hard-working, and Africa's as expensive and unproductive.

David Lindauer and Ann Velenchik, in Chapter 8, take exception with this view, arguing that unit labor costs and hence competitiveness depend on the relationship among wages, productivity, and exchange rates. To the extent that African wages are influenced by strict labor codes, productivity by low investments in physical and human capital, and exchange rates by deliberate overvaluation, Africa will suffer competitive disadvantages. But this is a statement more about policy directions than about the basic attributes of the work force.

Asia's lesson is to let wages be set by the market rather than by government regulation. Equally important, to enhance labor productivity, investments must be made in educational opportunities, acquiring new technology, and developing a complementary physical infrastructure. The macroeconomy must also be managed to permit realization of the economy's comparative advantage. This package produced rapid growth of real wages and employment in East Asia, and the ASEAN three are following a similar pattern.

Africa's economies may not have the identical experience, in part because they face different factor endowments, often with relatively greater land abundance. But a policy strategy similar to Asia's of letting the labor market, not government regulations, determine wage and employment outcomes will enhance competitiveness, growth, and the welfare of the workforce.

In contrast to labor markets, many national *financial markets* in Asia were dominated by government institutions and repressed by government controls over entry, interest rates, and credit allocations, as David Cole and James Duesenberry recount in Chapter 9. Korea was among the most interventionist countries in Asia, using directed, subsidized credit as a tool to encourage investment in new exports, especially by the *chaebol.* Taiwan had a similar approach. Indonesia's banking system has been dominated by state-owned banks that offered subsidized credit to large firms and clients of the regime. Only Hong Kong and Singapore adhered to neoclassical principles, developing open financial markets that have become international financial centers.

Despite pervasive government intervention, financial markets remained flexible in all seven Asian countries, although for different reasons. Korea and Taiwan each had a flourishing parallel or curb market that handled sufficient credit for the needs of small- and medium-size firms, which were among the most dynamic exporters in the early stages of Korean growth and remain so in Taiwan. Although nominal interest rates, at 30 percent or more, were much higher on curb market loans than on bank loans, many labor-intensive firms were able to pay these rates and still earn profits in export markets.

The three ASEAN countries did not develop informal credit markets capable of financing industrialization. But because these countries maintained convertible currencies, many investors, especially ethnic Chinese businessmen, had access to financial markets in Singapore and Hong Kong. This enabled firms to overcome the most stifling effects of financial interventions. During the 1980s, the Southeast Asian countries inaugurated financial reforms that started to release domestic financial markets from repressive interventions.

African financial markets have also been repressed by credit and interest rate controls. Governments have not, however, been able to direct credit into productive channels as in Korea and Taiwan. Informal credit markets remain fragmented and operate on a small scale, serving households, farmers, traders, and microenterprises, but not modern manufacturers. Foreign exchange controls have barred all but the largest firms from world financial markets. Financial reforms were not a prerequisite for outward-looking growth in Asia. In Africa, however, some reforms may be necessary to overcome the disadvantages of small, fragmented informal markets and the long absence of African firms from world credit markets.

Policies and Productivity

We observed earlier that rapid economic growth in Asia derived both from high levels of investment in human and physical capital and from rapid increases in factor productivity, and that rapid productivity growth more clearly distinguishes Asian from African performance. Here we will discuss how investment levels and productivity gains are affected by the policy environment we have been discussing: a stable and development-oriented government, a strategy that utilizes all of a country's productive resources, macroeconomic stability, an outward-oriented incentive structure, and flexible factor markets.

All investors, including small farmers, traders, entrepreneurs, and modern corporations, as well as households who educate their children, take the risk of committing capital in return for the potential of future gains. Political and macroeconomic stability, by reducing risks, alter the equation in favor of more investment. Governments and policies that encourage the full use of all productive resources bring more potential investors into play. However, the other two components of a constructive policy environment—an outward-looking strategy and flexible factor markets—may not be necessary for high investment levels. As the comparison between Asia and Africa and the experiences of communist Europe and Asia show, inward-looking economies with inflexible, distorted factor markets have also experienced high ratios of investment to national income.

Rapid productivity growth is more difficult to achieve. To some extent, productivity gains emanate from investment: investment in modern industry and services moves capital and labor from traditional activities into higher-productivity employment, and advanced, higher-productivity technologies are usually embodied in new capital equipment. Another important source of rising productivity, learning by doing, can be set in motion whenever investment creates new lines of activity. In these respects, the policy conditions for high investment and productivity growth are the same.

But the other two policy components, an outward-looking strategy and flexible factor markets, also contribute to productivity growth. Reform programs that reduce protection and market distortions can yield static (once-and-for-all) gains as investment and labor are reallocated to more efficient uses. As export markets are added to domestic demand, outward-oriented manufacturing grows more quickly, accelerating the shift of labor and capital into higher-productivity pursuits and gaining economies of scale that are not available in limited domestic markets. Firms that are newly exposed to more productive technologies in overseas markets may begin to adopt them. And the stimulus of competition from abroad forces managers to continuously seek lower-cost ways to produce and market their output. Some empirical support for the impact of outward-looking policies on productivity growth is offered in a recent study by the World Bank.[9]

Prospects for Africa

Three decades of independence have not produced a foundation upon which to build rapid growth in Africa. But three decades ago Asia's prospects seemed equally limited. Perkins and Roemer (see appendix to Chapter 2) show that in some ways Africa in 1990 was similar to Asia in 1965. In other respects, however, Africa today is behind Asia of the 1960s. Despite a comparable educational effort, it has some distance to go to match Asia's early levels of literacy and other forms of human capital. Nor has Africa developed many governments with the capacity and development focus needed to implement sustained programs of accelerated growth. African populations are growing far more quickly than did Asia's, and the persistence of endemic diseases has been exacerbated by the specter of AIDS.

The challenges are formidable, but there is reason for some optimism. African countries are putting considerable effort into developing their human capital. Meanwhile, an outward-looking strategy will take advantage of the human capital base that does exist. Accommodating policies can supplement indigenous human resources by encouraging a return of talented emigrants, the economic participation of ethnic minorities, and investment by foreign firms. Governments now riddled with clientelism and inefficiency can become more developmental, as those in Asia did. If governments adopt market-oriented strategies, limited bureaucratic capacity need not halt development.

Governments able to manage programs of accelerated growth need to adopt the following reforms, which will send clear signals to investors, at home and abroad.

- Macroeconomic stabilization, with realistic and flexibly managed exchange rates and reduced budget deficits, is the foundation for everything else. Currency convertibility should be considered as a discipline on macroeconomic policy that also signals government's determination to the private sector.

- Investment in primary production, especially smallholder agriculture, will directly contribute to growth and broaden the economic foundation for gradual industrialization.

- Investment in education, both to improve quality and to ensure universal primary education, will make possible the productivity gains needed to sustain development in the long term.

- Financial markets should be reformed by freeing interest rates to be determined by banks and the market, ending credit controls, and opening entry to new banks and other financial institutions to create competition. More developed and flexible financial markets may be necessary to finance investment in newly profitable export industries.

- Trade and investment reform should turn economies away from their exclusively inward focus. Import controls should be eliminated, tariffs reduced and made more uniform, and barriers to domestic and foreign investment brought down.
- Export promotion will be less important with these other reforms in place, but it may still be helpful. A range of instruments can be considered, including export zones, bonded warehouses, duty drawbacks, and exemptions. But it is more important to implement one of these mechanisms well than to have many of them available.

If African countries reform their policies, as The Gambia, Ghana, Mauritius, and recently Kenya have done, will the outside world respond? The NICs enjoyed rapidly growing world markets for at least two decades, entering markets for labor-intensive manufactures as Japan was abandoning them for more sophisticated exports during the 1960s and 1970s. The ASEAN countries repeated the process, albeit in less buoyant markets, during the 1980s. Foreign capital, whether as loans or direct investment, flowed readily to all these countries, whether from the industrial economies or from East Asia itself.

Conditions are less promising in the 1990s. The industrial economies have been mired in slow growth. Commodity prices have been unrewardingly low for the past several years. Trade blocs may restrict access by African (and Asian) countries to markets in Europe and North America. Investors are more attracted to other developing regions, Asia and Eastern Europe in particular, than to Africa. And Africa's nearest market, itself, generates little effective demand and is segmented by trade barriers.

These difficulties are sobering, but they are not completely discouraging. The industrial economies will eventually step up their growth and new opportunities will appear in markets in Asia, Latin America, and Eastern Europe. The recently completed Uruguay Round of the GATT has extended the fifty-year trend toward more open world markets. Trends since the 1920s suggest that commodity prices will recover. There is much that Africa can accomplish even within the constraints of sluggish world markets in the 1990s.

Poor policies, especially toward primary exports, have cost Africa market shares in many of its major exports over the past twenty years. Correcting those policies should help regain some market share, which would boost economies even at low world prices. Greater competitiveness in traditional and new export lines is also necessary for Africa to capture its share of market expansion when the industrial economies break out of the doldrums. Africa's share of manufactured export markets is so small that competitiveness is the only problem: any conceivable expansion should be absorbed without difficulty.

Despite regionalization of trade in Europe and North America, the recent GATT agreement provides hope that world markets will remain open to goods from Africa and other developing countries. Exploitation of markets in Europe, Asia, and North America will be essential to a growth-oriented strategy. Within Africa, some gains could be made if trade barriers were reduced, but this approach can be fully effective only in the context of Africa's greater openness to world trade. Africa has two potential growth poles of its own: if Nigeria and South Africa were to become dynamic export economies, with their own borders open to African neighbors, the effects would radiate across the continent.

We reject the pessimism that surrounds so much discussion of African prospects, even though the obstacles are formidable. The continuing successes in Asia provide both hope and guidance. It is important to remember that Asia's achievements were neither automatic nor inevitable. Each country had to overcome major barriers to growth, including war, revolution, political instability, ethnic competition, corrupt regimes, and grinding poverty. The policy agenda, although ambitious, has been proven under conditions in Southeast Asia that have important similarities to those in Africa. Most of what could be accomplished in Southeast Asia beginning thirty years ago can be accomplished by several African countries today.

NOTES

1. The normal approach is to use $g(Y) = \sigma_L g(L) + \sigma_K g(K) + \tau$, where σ is the share of labor (L) or capital (K); $g()$ is the growth rate of GDP (Y), labor, or capital; and τ is the unexplained residual, taken to be a measure of the growth of total factor productivity. In this rough approximation, however, we employ an alternative formulation: $g(Y) = \sigma_L g(P) + r(I/Y) + \tau$, where $g(P)$ is the population growth rate, r is the marginal product of capital, and I/Y is the share of investment in GDP. We further assume that, for all countries, $\sigma_L = 60\%$ and $r = 12\%$. See Perkins and Syrquin (1989, 1737).

2. Unpublished World Bank calculations, prepared for *The East Asian Miracle*

(World Bank 1993), give estimates of the residual net of increases in human capital. These are all in the range of 1.1 percent to 3.6 percent a year for the Asian countries listed in Table 1.1 and in the range of −2.8 percent to 1.3 percent for the African countries in the table.

3. This consensus is represented by Frank, Kim, and Westphal (1975), Balassa (1980), Bhagwati (1978), Krueger (1978), and World Bank (1987).

4. Especially Jones and Sakong (1980), Luedde-Neurath (1986), Westphal (1987), and Amsden (1989) on Korea; Wade (1990) on Taiwan; and the World Bank (1993) on the entire region.

5. The use of East Asia as a model for Africa is suggested in the well-known 1981 World Bank study, *Accelerated Development in Sub-Saharan Africa*.

6. The Association of Southeast Asian Nations includes these three plus Brunei, Philippines, and Singapore. For convenience, we treat Singapore as part of the East Asian newly industrialized countries (NICs); Brunei has more in common with the Persian Gulf emirates than with its ASEAN partners; and the Philippines, although much like Indonesia, Malaysia, and Thailand in terms of endowments, has not matched their policies or economic performance.

7. For the remainder of this chapter, we draw substantially on material from the chapters that follow and do not repeat the citations of sources from those chapters.

8. The measure used is effective rate of subsidy, which combines the effects of tariffs, other taxes, subsidies, and interest rates; see Roemer (Chapter 7).

9. The World Bank (1993, 337) estimates a regression equation covering 51 countries from 1960 to 1989 with total factor productivity growth as the dependent variable. To represent outward orientation, the Bank used an index developed by Dollar (1992) that compares domestic and world prices. The more an economy is open to world market influences through trade, investment, and migration, the closer its domestic prices to world prices. Because openness depends crucially on government policies, the Dollar index is also an indicator of the outward orientation of government policies. Dollar's measure of outward policy orientation contributes to the explanation of productivity growth at the 1 percent level of significance.

BIBLIOGRAPHY

Amsden, Alice. 1989. *Asia's Next Giant: South Korea and Late Industrialization*. New York: Oxford University Press.

Balassa, Bela. 1980. "The Process of Industrial Development and Alternative Development Strategies," *Essays in International Finance* No. 141. Princeton, N.J.: Princeton University, Department of Economics.

Bhagwati, Jagdish. 1978. *Foreign Exchange Regimes and Economic Development: Anatomy and Consequences of Exchange Control Regimes*. Cambridge, Mass.: Ballinger.

Dollar, David. 1992. "Outward-Oriented Developing Economies Really Do Grow More Rapidly: Evidence from 95 LDCs, 1976–1985." *Economic Development and Cultural Change* 40(3): 523–44.

Fields, Gary S. 1991. "Growth and Income Distribution." In *Essays on Poverty, Equity and Growth,* ed. George Psacharopoulos, 1–52. New York: Pergamon Press.

Frank, Charles R., Kwang Suk Kim, and Larry E. Westphal. 1975. *Foreign Trade Regimes and Economic Development: South Korea.* New York: Columbia University Press.

International Monetary Fund. 1992. *International Financial Statistics Yearbook.* Washington, D.C.

Johansen, Frida. 1993. "Poverty Reduction in East Asia: The Silent Revolution." World Bank Discussion Paper 203. Washington, D.C.

Jones, Leroy P., and Il Sakong. 1980. *Government, Business, and Entrepreneurship in Economic Development: The Korean Case.* Cambridge, Mass.: Harvard University Council on East Asian Studies.

Krueger, Anne O. 1978. *Foreign Trade Regimes and Economic Development: Liberalization Attempts and Consequences.* Cambridge, Mass.: Ballinger.

Leith, J. Clark, and Michael F. Lofchie. 1993. "The Political Economy of Structural Adjustment in Ghana." In *Political and Economic Interactions in Economic Policy Reform Programs: Evidence from Eight Countries,* ed. Robert H. Bates and Anne O. Krueger. London: Basil Blackwell.

Luedde-Neurath, R. 1986. *Import Controls and Export-Oriented Development: A Reassessment of the South Korean Case.* Boulder, Colo.: Westview Press.

Perkins, Dwight H., and Moshe Syrquin. 1989. "Large Countries: The Influence of Size." In *Handbook of Development Economics,* Volume 2, ed. Hollis Chenery and T. N. Srinivasan. Amsterdam: North-Holland, 1691–1753.

Wade, Robert. 1990. *Governing the Market: Economic Theory and the Role of Government in East Asian Industrialization.* Princeton, N.J.: Princeton University Press.

World Bank. 1981. *Accelerated Development in Sub-Saharan Africa: An Agenda for Action.* Washington, D.C.

———. 1987. *World Development Report 1987.* Washington, D.C.

———. 1990. *World Development Report 1990.* Washington, D.C.

———. 1992a. *World Development Report 1992.* Washington, D.C.

———. 1992b. *World Tables 1992.* Washington, D.C.

———. 1993. *The East Asian Miracle: Economic Growth and Public Policy.* Washington, D.C.

CHAPTER 2

Differing Endowments and Historical Legacies

Dwight H. Perkins and Michael Roemer

Most of the essays in this volume look at various economic policies that were tried in Asia and Sub-Saharan Africa. Conclusions are drawn about which policies worked best in Asia and what Africa can learn from Asia's experience with these policies. But a policy that works well in Asia will not necessarily do so in Africa, and vice versa. Successful policies must be rooted in the underlying structures and characteristics of particular countries or societies, and the underlying structures and characteristics of Asia and Africa differ in marked ways.

This essay discusses three fundamental features of Asian and Sub-Saharan societies: their natural resource endowments, their human resource endowments, and the nature of their systems of politics and government. These three features are picked in part because they are central to the development process in all nations, but also because the differences between Africa and Asia in these underlying endowments are pronounced, and the resulting impact on policy choices is profound.

The differences between Africa and *East* Asia—Japan, Korea, China, Taiwan, Hong Kong, and Singapore—are so pronounced that relatively few policy lessons from East Asia can be readily applied to Africa. The differences in endowments between *Southeast* Asia (Indonesia, Thailand, Malaysia, and the Philippines) and Africa are less pronounced. Although hardly identical, the natural and human resource endowments of Southeast Asia a few decades ago and Sub-Saharan Africa today have enough in common to make the comparisons meaningful. The same can be said of some features of the inherited political systems of Africa and Southeast Asia.

There are also large differences in the underlying endowments within Sub-Saharan Africa and Asia. There is an enormous gulf in the level of education and modern sector management experience between Ghana and Chad, just as in Asia there is a gulf between Singapore and Indonesia. But for all the differences within the two continents, the generalizations made in this essay about Asia and Africa hold for a surprisingly large share of the individual countries within each continent.

Natural Resources

Arable Land

East and Southeast Asia include some of the most densely populated areas on the globe, whereas on average Sub-Saharan Africa is among the least densely populated. In 1987 Asian countries as a group, including South Asia, had 1.0 hectare of agricultural land per agricultural worker; Africa had 5.5 hectares per worker. If pasture land is excluded, the difference shrinks: 1.1 hectares in Africa and 0.5 hectares in Asia. There is also considerable overlap among countries: Kenya and Tanzania have less cropland per worker than Indonesia, Malaysia, or Thailand (See Chapter 5, Table 5.1).

Underlying these people–land ratios was an agricultural development experience in Asia that contrasted markedly with that in Africa. In Asia the people–land ratio and yields per hectare have been rising steadily for several centuries. Farmers in East Asia and in the more densely settled parts of Southeast Asia, notably Java, built elaborate irrigation systems, developed their use of fertilizer, and employed other techniques to increase yields. Well before World War II, Japan introduced modern scientific methods for raising crop yields into its home islands and its colonies in Taiwan and Korea. After the war, research on new high-yielding plant varieties spread to other countries in the region, reinforced by the founding of the international crop research institutes, such as the International Rice Research Institute in the Philippines. Throughout East Asia, little new land was brought under cultivation, but food output managed to stay well ahead of population growth through yield increases. This was made easier by the fall in population growth to well under 2 percent per year. By the 1970s food imports did begin to rise rapidly, but this was due to sustained increases in per capita income.

In Sub-Saharan Africa, food supply also kept ahead of population growth in the 1950s and 1960s, but virtually all of this increase was achieved by expanding sown acreage. Yields per hectare stagnated. With large amounts of arable land potentially available, this did not matter much at first. But Africa's population growth rate continued rising from 2.7 percent per year in 1965–1980 to 3.1 percent per year in 1980–1990 (World Bank 1992, 268–69). Because of rising population pressure, parts of Africa, such as Kenya and Malawi, ran out of land onto which new settlers could expand. The domestic supply of food could not keep up and food imports began rising rapidly, eating into limited foreign exchange earnings.

Africa's population is forecast to rise from about 500 million persons in 1990 to 1.2 billion in the year 2025 (World Bank 1992a, 268–69), by which time person–land ratios will be approaching those in Asia thirty or forty years ago. Even if incomes remain stagnant, Africa must begin achieving yield increases in food crops of 2 or 3 percent per year or suffer severe consequences, including starvation, malnutrition, or, at best, heavier dependence on food imports. Scarce food would also lead to higher real wages, penalizing Africa's ability to produce competitive exports. And by devoting more of its limited foreign exchange earnings to food imports, Africa would jeopardize the supply of imports to modern industry and cripple its development, as happened during the 1980s.

In most of Africa, such yield increases will have to be achieved primarily by smallholder farmers. In this, Africa resembles Asia, which has demonstrated that small farms can become as productive as large farms in North America. But Asia had centuries to build the critical infrastructure and accumulate the learning needed to achieve high yields. Africa will have to move much faster than did Asia and must operate under more difficult ecological conditions. The Asian experience demonstrates the need for rapid growth of food production and the possibility of achieving it on smallholdings, but it does not provide clear examples of how this might be done in Africa.

An alternative use for arable land is export crops. In this respect, there are strong similarities between African countries such as Cameroon, Côte d'Ivoire, Ethiopia, Ghana, Kenya, Nigeria, Tanzania, and Uganda, and the Southeast Asian countries of Indonesia, Malaysia, Philippines, and Thailand. All have exploited a share of their richest agricultural land to grow export crops such as coffee, tea, cocoa, rice, cassava, palm oil, rubber, spices, and tropical hardwoods.

Here there are clear lessons from both Africa and Southeast Asia, which are explored in Chapter 5 of this volume. The most successful agricultural exporters, especially those in Southeast Asia, have invested heavily in research, extension, and infrastructure to increase yields and reduce the costs of growing exportable crops; they also have maintained exchange rates that offer attractive rewards to exporters over long periods. Their reward has been growing earnings of foreign exchange, which have helped the Asian exporters to avoid the foreign exchange shortages that paralyzed many African economies. The rapid industrialization of Indonesia, Malaysia, and Thailand was supported by the savings and foreign exchange generated by the growth of primary exports, including cash crops and minerals.

Some African countries have also enjoyed periods of reasonable growth partly as a result of investment in exportable crops, such as Côte d'Ivoire in cocoa and coffee; Kenya in coffee, tea, and other crops; and much of West Africa in a variety of crops during the colonial period. Similar opportunities may be available to several African countries today (in horticulturals, for example).

Minerals

Parts of Africa are rich in minerals, which, along with cash crops, are the main source of foreign exchange earnings for the region. In contrast, South Korea, Taiwan, and Japan never had much in the way of minerals (other than coal), and Hong Kong and Singapore are city-states with no hinterland of any kind. China has many minerals within its borders, but like most large countries that have experienced several decades of industrial growth, most of these minerals are consumed at home.[1] In the four ASEAN countries— Indonesia, Malaysia, Thailand, and the Philippines—minerals and cash crops accounted for 40 to 60 percent of export earnings in 1990; during the 1960s the share was over 90 percent in all cases (World Bank 1992a, 248– 49). Indonesia and Malaysia export oil, natural gas, tin, copper, and other metals. Although the primary share of export earnings is declining in both countries, there is much that other mineral-rich nations can learn from Indonesia's and Malaysia's experience since the 1960s.

Africa's mineral surplus is a product of its rich endowment, the small population of most of Africa's nations, and its low incomes. A nation of a few million people in possession of a large copper mine, such as Zambia, is bound to vent its huge surplus of copper. Several of Africa's mineral exporters are small, notably Botswana, Gabon, Congo, Zambia, Togo, and Niger, but several others are among Africa's larger countries, notably Nigeria and

Zaire. These latter countries continue to export minerals because their poverty limits domestic demand. Nigeria, with a per capita income of $290 in 1990, has limited use for its petroleum resources other than for export, despite having about 100 million people. If Nigeria follows Indonesia's consumption pattern, when its per capita income doubles it will consume twice the oil per capita that it does today and, with a growing population, export much less of its production.[2] Exports will also fall, of course, if new petroleum and other mineral deposits prove difficult to find or expensive to exploit and existing deposits are depleted.

Three characteristics of mineral exports place large demands on government to convert mineral wealth into sustained development. *First,* because minerals yield few benefits to the economy other than the high rents that accrue to the government, government bears the burden of converting these benefits into productive investment for the rest of the economy. Although Indonesia and Malaysia wasted some of their resource rents on unproductive projects, for the most part they used their mineral wealth to raise investment in education, health, infrastructure, irrigation, agricultural research and extension, and subsidized farm inputs, which contributed directly to enhanced growth and poverty reduction. With the important exception of Botswana, the mineral-rich countries of Africa have failed to invest their resource rents so productively.

Second, when mining and petroleum industries generate substantial foreign exchange relative to the size of the economy, the real exchange rate appreciates, rendering nonmineral export and import substitution industries less competitive on world markets. This is one symptom of the familiar Dutch disease. Avoiding it requires strong macroeconomic countermeasures, which were utilized by Indonesia during the oil boom but not by Nigeria, for example.

Third, the prices of both minerals and cash crops fluctuate widely. Indonesia's ability to manage these fluctuations has been a hallmark of its development; Indonesia used fiscal, monetary, and exchange rate management to dampen the impacts of shifts in the terms of trade (Lewis and McPherson, Chapter 4).

It should be noted that many African nations are not at all rich in mineral resources or even in a climate and soil suited for export crops. The nations of the Sahel, for the most part, have no natural resource surpluses and relatively little good arable land. The implication of this modest natural resource endowment is that most of Africa, unlike parts of the Middle East, is not likely to be able to pursue a development strategy centered on natural resource exploitation alone.

Natural resources have been called both a blessing and a curse. Southeast Asian countries have seemed adept at realizing the blessing, while several African countries, especially Nigeria, Zaire, and Zambia, have not managed their wealth productively. Could these primary product-exporting nations in Africa become more like Malaysia, Thailand, and Indonesia of two decades ago with the appropriate mix of policies? Botswana has been remarkably proficient at converting mineral wealth into sustained development, so African countries have a model of their own. There is enough of a natural resource base in many African countries to follow along the path blazed by Botswana and Southeast Asia.

Human Resource Endowments

The contrast between the human resource endowments of Africa and Asia, both today and over the past century, is as great as the differences in natural resource endowments. There was, and is, considerable variation within Asia as well, but there are guides for Africa in how the least well-endowed Asian nations worked to overcome this disadvantage.

Formal Education

There are two elements to a nation's human resource endowment: formal education and experience; the latter is sometimes referred to as learning by doing. In terms of formal education, Japan, Korea, and the Chinese-populated areas of Asia, which include Singapore, Bangkok, and sizable minorities elsewhere, were well ahead of much of the developing world at the time when each entered into a period of sustained economic growth. Fifty percent of the males were literate in Japan, China, and probably Korea in the middle of the nineteenth century.[3] Hundreds of thousands of individuals had received fifteen or twenty years of formal education, albeit in the classics. Modern universities on the Western model were established first in Japan, but they started in China at the beginning of the twentieth century and existed in Taiwan and Korea during the Japanese colonial period. Modern primary and secondary schools were also common throughout the region in the 1920s and 1930s, although a great majority of youth, particularly in the rural areas, had no access to those schools. The Koreans speak of having only a few hundred university graduates at the time independence was regained in

1945, but the number graduated from universities in Japan as well as Korea was probably much higher.

Whatever the precise situation prior to World War II, from the late 1940s on the entire East Asian region experienced a rapid expansion in education at all levels. Universal primary education was achieved in most parts of the region by the early 1960s and secondary education had expanded rapidly. In South Korea and Taiwan there was also a rapid expansion in university graduates, but growth at the tertiary level was more moderate in China, Hong Kong, and Singapore. Tens of thousands of students from South Korea, Taiwan, Hong Kong, and Singapore also went abroad, particularly to the United States. Initially most of the students who trained abroad stayed there, but the flow back grew from a trickle to a flood in the 1970s.

Formal education is as much a question of quality as of quantity. Measures of quality are hard to establish, but there is little doubt that East Asian education has markedly improved since 1945. Graduates of the universities in Korea, Taiwan, China, Hong Kong, and Singapore compete easily with the best students anywhere.

In the 1950s and 1960s much of East Asia enjoyed a large stock of reasonably well-trained primary and secondary school teachers. University teachers took longer to develop, and it was not until American and European Ph.D.'s began to return from abroad in substantial numbers in the 1970s and 1980s that the universities in South Korea and Taiwan began to match developed country standards. The University of Malaya, now the National University of Singapore, was a high-quality university much earlier, but it then used a predominantly foreign teaching staff.

Most of Southeast Asia began the postwar era in a much less favorable position than East Asia. Indonesia, with a population approaching 100 million at the time of independence in 1948, had around 200 university graduates. Conditions in primary and secondary education were poor. Dutch colonial policy had been to keep the Indonesian population isolated from the modern sector, and few schools of any kind were built for Indonesians. Indigenous education, where it existed, was in Koranic schools that stressed rote learning. But after independence, except for a few years during the Sukarno era, expansion of primary education was rapid. Near-universal primary education was achieved by the mid-1980s, but at that time only 3 or 4 percent of any age cohort made it all the way through secondary school (Government of Indonesia 1989, 117). A high proportion of those who did get through secondary school went on to university or other postsecondary training. As a result, Indonesian universities expanded rapidly but faced a desperate shortage of qualified teachers. Except for three or four elite universities, the quality of tertiary education was low.

Malaysia and Thailand achieved independence in a stronger educational position than Indonesia, but much of Malaysia's advantage resulted from the heavy emphasis placed on education by its large Chinese minority. By the 1960s primary education was becoming available to most of the relevant age cohort, but only 30 percent of those who completed primary school went on to secondary school (Government of Malaysia 1969, 102–6). As secondary school students graduated, pressure built up to expand the university system rapidly. Standards were maintained in some cases, but political influence often overcame quality considerations. Malays from poor rural backgrounds, many of whose parents were illiterate, frequently could not compete with the better-educated urban Chinese. Special programs in subjects such as Malay studies were created; these programs could have been culturally enriching for all Malaysians, but in practice the programs often ended up being vehicles for circumventing more rigorous curricula. Ethnic considerations also played a central role in the hiring and promotion of teachers.

In Asia, as this brief discussion indicates, there was enormous pressure to expand the education system at all levels. In many cases private demand outstripped the government's ability to respond, and schools such as those in South Korea drew increasingly on private funding (McGinn et al. 1980). In East Asia this expansion began with a core of able teachers and at least a few high-quality schools at each level. The quality of education steadily improved as the quality of teachers was gradually upgraded. Southeast Asia experienced much the same expansion in demand for education but with a much weaker supply of teachers. Occasionally quality could be maintained and strengthened by isolating a few elite schools from these expansionary pressures. Thailand's top universities, for example, maintained high standards and limited enrollments, while the rising demand for tertiary education was met through a separate open university system with minimal standards.[4] This defense of quality was more the exception than the rule. At the primary level quality undoubtedly improved as teachers with only minimal schooling were gradually replaced with teachers who had spent years in secondary school. As one went up the educational hierarchy, however, this upgrading became more difficult to accomplish.

Africa's experience with the expansion of its education system is more like that of Indonesia than anywhere else in Asia. In Sub-Saharan Africa around 1900 there were handfuls of highly educated Africans, but illiteracy was the norm. Coastal Ghana, the Dakar area, Freetown, and Monrovia had tiny literate elites even before the nineteenth century, and there were a few African Ph.D.'s as early as 1910, but these were the exceptions. Before 1939, colonial Africa had fewer than ten real secondary schools. The only real university entrance courses offered in French Africa were at the Ecole William Ponty near Dakar. In British Africa, education was encouraged only in the West African colonies, Uganda, and Sudan. The Belgians did little to promote education in Africa, and the Portuguese actively discouraged it.[5]

After World War II the colonial government began to make more of an effort to formally educate Africans. By 1960, 36 percent of the relevant age cohort in all of Sub-Saharan Africa was in primary school but only 3 percent was in secondary school (World Bank 1981, 181). By 1960 university students constituted a minute fraction of their age cohort, perhaps a few thousand students overall in school in Britain or France or in the handful of universities that then existed in Africa.

Enrollment expanded rapidly after independence in the mid-1960s, with most of the growth coming before the fiscally stringent 1980s. The percentage of the primary age cohort in school rose to 69 percent by 1989, the secondary school percentage multiplied sixfold to 18 percent, and the percentage of the age cohort in universities reached 2 percent (see Table 2.1). This last figure may not seem large, but it indicates that tertiary enrollment by 1989 was around one million students, up from a few thousand a quarter of a century earlier.

Any expansion of this magnitude was bound to leave a host of quality problems in its wake. The weakness of much of the political leadership, described below, made it difficult for governments to deal effectively with the problem of quality, but the most enlightened leadership would have faced a formidable task. Even by Indonesian standards, Africa was starting from a weak position. By 1965 Indonesia had 72 percent of its age cohort in primary school and 12 percent of the secondary school age cohort as compared to 41 percent and 4 percent in Africa in that year (if the figures for these earlier years can be believed and are measured in a comparable way).

The problem of educational quality stands in the way of any short-term solution to Africa's shortage of well-educated personnel. Universal education at the primary level plus 40 percent enrollment at the secondary level would put 70 to 80 million children in school, perhaps twice the number that are there now. Depending on class size, the number of teachers would have to expand by 1 to 2 million. Paying for these teachers is a problem, but it would not be beyond the economic capacities of many African nations to devise a

TABLE 2.1
Human Capital Indicators—Asia and Africa

	Education: Enrollment as % of age group						Government expenditure % on education		Adult illiteracy	
	Primary		Secondary		Tertiary					
	1965	1989	1965	1989	1965	1989	1972	1990	1960	1990
East and Southeast Asia										
Korea	101	108	35	86	6	38	15.8	19.6	29	4
Taiwan	—	—	—	—	—	—	17.3[a]	19.8[a]	—	—
Hong Kong	103	105	29	73	5	—	—	—	30	—
Singapore	105	110	45	69	10	—	15.7	18.1	—	—
China	89	135	24	44	1	—	7.4	8.4	57	23
Indonesia	72	118	12	47	1	—	7.4	8.4	61	23
Malaysia	90	96	28	59	2	7	—	—	47	22
Philippines	113	111	41	73	19	28	16.3	16.9	28	10
Thailand	78	86	14	28	2	16	19.9	20.1	32	7
East Asia and Pacific	88	129	—	46	1	5	—	—	—	24
Sub-Saharan Africa										
Botswana	65	111	3	37	—	3	10.0	20.2	—	26
Cameroon	94	101	5	26	0	3	—	12.0	81	46
Chad	34	57	1	7	—	1	14.8	—	94	70
Côte D'Ivoire	60	—	6	20	0	—	—	—	95	46

Ghana	69	75	13	39	1	2	20.1	25.7	73	40
Kenya	54	94	4	23	0	2	21.9	19.8	80	31
Mali	24	23	4	6	0	—	—	9.0	98	68
Mauritius	101	103	26	53	3	2	13.5	14.4	—	—
Tanzania	32	63	2	4	0	0	4.5	—	90	—
Nigeria	32	70	5	19	0	3	—	—	85	49
Senegal	40	58	7	16	1	3	17.3	—	94	62
Zaire	70	78	5	24	0	2	15.1	1.4	69	—
Zambia	53	95	7	20	—	2	19.0	8.6	71	27
Zimbabwe	110	125	6	52	0	6	—	23.4	61	33
Sub-Saharan Africa	41	69	4	18	0	2	—	—	—	50

NOTE: Dash = not available.

a. Includes science and culture.

SOURCES: From Republic of China, *Taiwan Statistical Data Book, 1990* (Taipei), 157; The World Bank, *World Development Report 1992* (New York: Oxford University Press, 1992); The World Bank, *World Development Report 1985* (New York: Oxford University Press, 1985).

universal education program that would raise the salaries of teachers to attract able people and provide them with well-built classrooms and quality training materials. Six percent of Africa's current GNP plus a third of its foreign aid would provide a total of about $100 per pupil.[6] Some countries—Botswana, Côte d'Ivoire, Senegal, and Zimbabwe—spent more than this in 1983, but for most African countries, $100 per pupil would more than double public expenditures on primary and secondary education in 1983 (World Bank 1988, 141). The barrier to meeting this 6 percent target is more political than economic. These political barriers to raising the share of educational expenditures, however, are often formidable.

Indonesia has attempted what is being suggested here. In the 1970s and 1980s Indonesia used a portion of its oil revenues to expand education, particularly in the rural areas. By the 1980s it was spending 3.2 percent of GNP on education at all levels, around $60 to $70 per pupil (Boediono et al. 1992). The Indonesians argued convincingly that this sum would not be sufficient if they wanted to begin to catch up to the educational levels of East Asia, but their achievements in the education field to date suggest that much can be accomplished even if a country cannot allocate as much as 6 percent of GNP to education.[7]

Does Africa have the capacity to attract its ablest people into teaching and mount an educational effort of either the Indonesian or 6 percent of GNP magnitude? Or would the money be frittered away by weak ministries of education? Several countries probably could manage such an all-out effort. Zimbabwe spends over 9 percent of its GDP on education. Botswana and Kenya each spend at least 6 percent, a higher share than in most East and Southeast Asian countries in 1990 or even 1965 (see Table 2.1). But even if a broad initiative of this kind is started, the results will come slowly. Indonesia began its big educational push over two decades ago, and as indicated above, its educational system still suffers from severe quality problems at all levels. Even with tens of thousands of Indonesians trained abroad, it may be another generation before the system catches up to levels achieved today in much of East Asia. Africa today is behind Indonesia in the early 1970s. An optimistic projection would have Africa matching Indonesian 1990 levels of educational development two decades from now and those of East Asia some decades thereafter. If African nations do not begin a major educational effort soon, educational levels such as those of Indonesia in 1990 will take even longer to achieve.

In the appendix to this chapter, we report some statistical tests of the proposition that Africa in 1990 is behind Asia at the beginning of its rapid growth in the mid-1960s. On the basis of economic structure, there is no statistical difference between Asia then and Africa today. In human capital endowments, however, there are statistically significant differences: Asia had enrolled twice the eligible population in secondary education; had half the adult illiteracy; had reduced infant mortality to 70 percent of Africa's 1990 level; and enjoyed five to seven years' longer life expectancy. There is, however, substantial overlap, even in human capital. The more advanced African countries today are comparable to those of Asia thirty years ago; and Indonesia in 1965 would be behind many African countries today.

Moreover, all of these differences between samples except adult illiteracy can be explained by the differences in income per capita. In purchasing power parity prices of 1985, Asian average income in 1965 was twice that of Africa in 1990. The regressions reported in the appendix suggest that Africa might be on a growth path similar to East and Southeast Asia, although it starts much farther behind most of those economies. Africa's significantly higher adult illiteracy raises a caution, however. Literacy is crucial to rapid transformation, which requires upgrading the labor force.

Learning by Doing

Much of what a person requires to be effective in a modern economy is learned on the job, not in school. Here East Asia had enormous historic advantages over both Southeast Asia and Africa. Japan never lost its political independence, so Japanese, not foreign colonials, gained experience in running the government. Japanese also owned and ran their own firms. China was closer in this respect to Japan than to Southeast Asia. China's government was run by Chinese, and commerce and banking were largely in Chinese hands. There was a thin veneer of foreigners on the Chinese coast, but they sat atop organizations staffed and mostly managed by Chinese. Even farmers were familiar with written contracts, commerce, and credit. Taiwan and Korea under Japanese colonialism fared less well because Japanese held many of the top posts, but there were large numbers of Taiwanese and Koreans at all levels of the system except the top. And millions more lived for long periods in Japan, where they gained experience with urban life and the organizations of a modern economy.

Indonesia is an extreme example of a pattern found in much of Southeast Asia; the pattern contrasts sharply with that in East Asia and has much to do with why Indonesia's experience is more relevant to the countries of Africa. The colonial service of the Dutch East Indies was staffed almost entirely by

Dutch. A few traditional Indonesian rulers were retained but they played little role in the management of the colony. Commerce and other businesses of any size were also run by Dutch. Smaller-scale commerce was largely in the hands of Chinese immigrants, who brought knowledge of commerce and credit with them from China and had little trouble outcompeting local people as commerce expanded under the Dutch. Native Indonesians were effectively cut off from any experience other than farming and fishing.

The experience was similar in Malaysia, only the number of British co-lonials was a smaller proportion of the total population and the number of Chinese and Indians was much larger, constituting over 40 percent of the total population. Although Thailand was never colonized, the commerce of Bangkok was largely in Chinese hands.

Once independence was regained, in 1949 in Indonesia and 1957 in Malaysia, government service at least became localized, but commerce re-mained in foreign and Chinese hands for the most part. Then independent governments in much of Southeast Asia faced the question of how to bring indigenous majorities into ownership, management, and employment in the modern sector. Three different strategies could have been used to achieve this goal. One was to integrate fully the ethnic minority into the mainstream of society. Integration could be accomplished both by incentives, such as full privileges of citizenship for those who accepted them, and by sanctions, such as discriminatory legislation against those who retained their foreign citizen-ship and ethnic identity. This strategy was followed in Thailand with suc-cess, and Thais and Chinese lost most of their separate identities. Much of Bangkok's business world is still controlled by individuals of Chinese de-scent, but this is neither a political issue nor a significant barrier for those of Thai descent rising within the system.

A second strategy was to throw the ethnic minority out of the country. Burma carried this policy to its logical extreme, expelling its entire Indian community and all foreigners, including the international aid agencies. Much of the three decades of stagnation in the Burmese economy can be attributed to the xenophobia reflected in this act. Indonesia under Sukarno (until 1965) also threw out most of the foreigners, notably the Dutch, and there were major tensions between Indonesians and Chinese; this tension contributed to the slaughter of many thousands of Chinese during the political turmoil in 1965. Anti-Chinese feeling in Vietnam helps to explain why so many members of the Chinese minority became boat people in the 1980s.

This second strategy did open up positions for the indigenous people, but to what purpose? To gain useful experience on the job, individuals must work within efficiently functioning organizations. Expelling all of the experienced managerial personnel ensured that most of these businesses would collapse or at best would operate inefficiently, often with heavy dependence on government subsidies. The new indigenous managers learned the wrong lessons, inimical to sustained development. Certainly the two countries that followed this strategy, Burma and Sukarno's Indonesia, had disastrous economic performances. The consequences of Vietnam's policies have been fewer partly because those policies have been abandoned.

The third, middle strategy was followed with variations by Malaysia and Suharto's Indonesia after 1965. The Chinese business community was retained and, in many ways, encouraged in its entrepreneurial and even managerial roles in commerce and industry. Foreign investment was also encouraged, especially in export industries. To this extent, entrepreneurial and managerial experience for the ethnic majority was deemed subordinate to economic growth that promised higher incomes for all citizens, including the ethnic majority. But in Malaysia after 1970 under the New Economic Policy (NEP), government took major initiatives to promote ownership and management by Malays, as well as their increased employment in the modern sector. Malaysia applied targets for increased Malay ownership. In both Indonesia and Malaysia, although both remained resolutely capitalist, state ownership of production, through nationalization or expansion, became an important means of exerting control over the economy on behalf of the ethnic majority.

The results of Malaysia's experiment were pronounced. The Malay majority's ownership of firms rose dramatically, from 2 percent in 1970 at the beginning of the NEP to 20 percent in 1990. This was far short of the goal of 30 percent; furthermore, 8 of the 20 percent Malay ownership share was in the hands of state agencies, not individuals. But it was a substantial change nonetheless. Outright Chinese ownership did not decline; it rose from 34 percent to over 45 percent, while foreign ownership fell precipitously (Government of Malaysia 1991, 48–49). Government eventually took countermeasures to encourage foreign investors.

Malays also made large gains in their share of modern sector employment: by 1990 they represented 48 percent of employment in manufacturing. Moreover, the NEP had a dramatic impact on the incidence of poverty in Peninsular Malaysia, which fell from 49 percent in 1970 to 15 percent in 1984; among Malays the decline was from 65 percent to 21 percent (Government of Malaysia 1991, 46). This decline was due partly to the employment impact of the NEP and partly to investments made in small-scale farming and rural development. Indonesia, which did not employ as aggressive a policy toward the Chinese majority as Malaysia, also invested heavily in rural areas and had an even more dramatic decline in poverty, the incidence of which fell from about 60 percent of the population in 1970 to 17 percent by 1987 (World Bank 1990, 7–10).

As in Southeast Asia, Africa has its own local ethnic minorities that dominate commerce and industry: Indians in East Africa, Lebanese in parts of West Africa, and Europeans and others scattered throughout the continent. Moreover, some commercially oriented indigenous ethnic groups, like the Ibo in Nigeria and Kikuyu in Kenya, have been under economic and political pressure from other groups. How should African governments deal with these ethnic minorities? Uganda demonstrated that throwing out foreigners works no better in Africa than in Burma. The Thai solution, fully integrating the principal minority groups with the dominant ethnic group, is probably not feasible in the near future, as the ethnic and cultural differences are too great. It is clear from Europe and Africa that tribal conflict can only destroy a country's economic potential for years or generations.

For Africa, as for Asia, some middle path, one that employs the strengths of the foreign minority groups but uses them in part as vehicles for training Africans, is the only solution consistent with rising living standards. But the experience of Malaysia, which made a determined effort to improve the participation of the ethnic majority, gives pause. Malaysia was most successful in reaching its employment goals and in reducing poverty. But in African countries the wealthy minority is much smaller than in Malaysia and does not present much of a barrier to African employment. And the reduction of poverty is best attacked by investment in rural activities, especially small-scale farming, as in Malaysia and Indonesia, and also in Kenya and Zimbabwe. Managerial advancement for the Malay majority came mostly through government employment and state-owned firms, not so much through the private sector. But state-owned enterprises have performed poorly in all parts of the world and Malaysia itself is in the midst of a major privatization effort.

The Asian experience, then, suggests a clear trade-off for Africa. Aggressive solutions to majority management and ownership are likely to be frustrated or, if successful, to result in substantial inefficiencies and the inevitable reduction in income growth. Real progress in reducing poverty and increasing majority employment, on the other hand, is quite consistent with—and indeed may depend upon—encouraging the entrepreneurial minority to continue investing, while government enforces policies of gradual change toward majority employment, management, and eventually ownership.

Political Conditions

At times, discussions of government failure and market-led development seem to suggest a withering away of government's development role toward laissez faire. Properly framed, however, the debate on government's role is not about lesser or greater intervention, but about the kind of state intervention that promotes private activity and rising productivity. Sustained development is inconceivable without an effective government devoted to development. Infrastructure in most nations is provided through government investment. Macroeconomic policy can only be managed by government. Law and order is a government function and is essential if private agents are to be productive. The recent literature on Korea and Taiwan suggests that promarket government intervention in resource allocations may be very helpful to development (Amsden 1989; Wade 1990).

As with learning by doing, the current effectiveness of government derives in part from the colonial experience or lack of it. Several East and Southeast Asian countries—Japan, Thailand, and China—never completely lost their independence. Many of the others—Vietnam, Korea, Cambodia, and Burma—had been independent for centuries prior to the advent of brief colonial rule that lasted less than a century. In contrast to Africa, many of these nations were ethnically and linguistically homogeneous, with centuries-old boundaries based on these ethnic and linguistic groupings. When outside powers did create artificial boundaries, such as the demilitarized zone in Korea or the seventeenth parallel in Vietnam, political and military pressures to obliterate such boundaries were immediate and powerful.

The major exceptions to this picture are Indonesia, Malaysia, and Singapore. Singapore exists as a country partly to help diffuse Malay–Chinese ethnic tensions. Although a similar ethnic split exists in East and West Africa, nowhere in Africa is the Asian or Lebanese community as strong a political force as are Chinese in Southeast Asia.

The Indonesian experience is closer to that of Africa, but with important differences. The current boundaries of Indonesia are a product of Dutch colonialism, not of some inherent unity of the region. However, that colonial regime lasted centuries, not decades as in Africa. Opposition to Javanese control led the outer islands to attempt secession in 1958, and a brief civil war ensued. By the 1980s, however, most Indonesians thought of themselves as one nation, not as a collection of Javanese, Sundanese, Sumatrans, Balinese, and other ethnic groups. The common fight for independence from the Dutch brought the core leadership of the country together under Sukarno. The decision to pick a national language, Bahasa Indonesia, which was spoken by only a small minority, rather than ethnically based Javanese, which was the language of the dominant majority, helped to solidify the country. Sukarno's charisma and even his posturing on the international scene helped people to think of themselves as being part of one country.

In addition to national unity, most Asian nations were ruled for decades at a time by one individual or by one group within the society without effective challenge. In some cases there were the trappings of multiparty democracy, as in Singapore, or even genuine democracy, as in Malaysia and Japan, but there was no shift in power to the opposition. In most cases the system was openly authoritarian, based on a large modern combat army, as in South Korea before 1987 and in Indonesia after 1965, or based on a Communist party, as in China, Vietnam, and North Korea. In several Asian states Confucian beliefs, with their hierarchical emphasis on obedience of son to father, father to official, and official to emperor, provided cultural support for authoritarianism and discipline. Governments did not have to rely on guns alone to stay in power.

Many of Asia's leaders in the decades immediately after World War II were just as preoccupied with international activities and utopian visions for society as the early postindependence leaders in Africa. One only needs to mention the names of Mao Zedong, Sukarno, and Sihanouk to make the point. Others concentrated on trying to restore unity over their historical territory: Ho Chi Minh in Vietnam, Syngman Rhee and Kim Il Song in Korea, and Chiang Kai-Shek in Taiwan.

In the 1960s, however, a number of Asian leaders came to the fore who dedicated themselves to achieving sustained economic development in their countries. The motive in many cases was survival, both for themselves as political leaders and for their country. In the face of strong external threats, failure to achieve economic growth could well have doomed South Korea, Taiwan, Hong Kong, and Singapore as states in control of their own destinies. Rapid growth and a relatively fair distribution of its benefits, thanks in part to land reform, provided a measure of popular support to regimes otherwise considered illegitimate because of the way in which they came to power.

The leaders of South Korea and Taiwan were well situated to learn from the successful development experience of Japan, which was becoming more and more obvious by the 1960s. Hong Kong and Singapore could build on their already formidable commercial and financial structure. The success of the four tigers then became a model for Southeast Asian nations in the 1970s and 1980s. Prime Minister Mahathir in Malaysia was explicit about the need for Malaysia to become more like South Korea. Indonesia, Thailand, and, sporadically, the Philippines also looked to East Asian examples in building strategies of sustained growth through manufactured exports. Most dramatically, the People's Republic of China shifted over to an export- and market-oriented development strategy with reforms beginning in 1979, thereby abandoning three decades of Soviet-style emphasis on central planning and autarky. Vietnam followed suit in 1986.

Though they have very different political structures, Indonesia and Thailand tell a remarkably similar story about the interaction of military regimes and economic development policy. Thailand is a constitutional monarchy under a highly revered king. Since World War II, however, the country has been ruled by a self-enriching military that rotates the prime ministership and has, until recently, kept itself in power principally to retain its lucrative control of timber and mining concessions and of the boards of state enterprises. Indonesia is ruled by Suharto, a general whose principal support has expanded from the military to include businessmen and Islamic organizations. Both regimes maintain clientelistic relationships in which rents are created through concessions, state-enforced monopolies, trade protection, and other devices and are then distributed to allies of the regime (the clients) in return for their active support.

Rent-seeking and clientelism are common features of government in developing (and many industrial) countries. The four tigers seem to have avoided the worst manifestations of these features, which seems to have been essential to the ability of governments in Korea, Taiwan, and Singapore to intervene actively in the market to promote development. In Southeast Asia clientelism is more prevalent. It has played havoc with development in the Philippines, where Marcos's rapacious clientelism outran the capacity of the economy to support it. Yet both Thailand and Indonesia have so far kept rent-seeking within bounds. The leaders of both countries appear to recognize, as do many other Asian leaders, that the legitimacy and stability of their regimes depend on a well-managed, growing economy. In Indonesia, as in Malaysia, legitimacy of the regime is also perceived to depend on improving the welfare of the majority of the population, particularly those in rural areas. These regimes also recognize, tacitly or explicitly, that rent-seeking has limits that can only be expanded by economic growth.

Thus the governments of the ASEAN three have all bestowed a high priority on sound macroeconomic management and measures for long-term development. Macroeconomic and development policies are under the control of skillful technocrats whose counsel is respected and followed by the leadership. In Thailand the National Economic and Social Development Board, the Ministry of Finance, and the Central Bank were shielded from political control and left to manage the macroeconomy. In Indonesia, a coterie of senior economic managers controlled the ministries of finance and planning and the central bank for twenty-five years. Although the president has the final word on economic policy, he has usually listened to his technical advisers whenever the economy has required difficult measures.

Asian politics, as this brief overview has indicated, are rooted in Asia's own culture and history. Africa's political history is radically different. The boundaries of African nations were drawn by colonial powers with no regard for the traditional political and economic structures that existed before the late nineteenth-century European scramble for colonies. Ethnic, religious, and political affiliations evolved within ecological zones, such as the fertile coastal belt, the rain forest, the savannah, and the desert, which strongly influence the way people live their lives. But colonial influence and boundaries were based on different considerations, such as the competition among powers for good harbors and the favorable trading routes that emanated upcountry from these ports. Thus the African countries that emerged from colonialism contain many different ethnic groups, and many ethnic groups are divided between countries. During the six or seven decades of colonial rule, European colonists kept these ethnic groups divided to avoid a challenge to their rule.

Few Africans played any role in governance of the colonies until well after World War II. When independence was granted in the late 1950s and 1960s, European-style parliamentary democratic systems were created. In most cases Africans were thrown into this system with no preparation. Francophone countries had been a part of Metropolitan France, at least in theory, so a tiny group had participated in French elections, but this system disappeared with independence.[8] In Europe an effective parliamentary system depends on a widely educated population and a large middle class. Neither existed in most of Africa.

Three different patterns emerged from this chaotic approach to nation building. The worst was civil war. There have been prolonged civil wars along the Islamic-Christian fault line in Nigeria and Sudan; between ethnic groups within Liberia, Chad, Ethiopia, Somalia, Angola, Mozambique,

Rwanda, Uganda, and Zaire; and between whites and blacks in Zimbabwe, Kenya, and Namibia before independence. Some of these clashes were prolonged and highly destructive.

A second common pattern was for the leader at independence to rule for two decades or more using increasingly authoritarian instruments of control. Many of these independence leaders, like revolutionary leaders elsewhere in the world, were more interested in international affairs or in new utopian visions for their societies. Kaunda in Zambia, Sekou Toure in Guinea, Nkrumah in Ghana, and Nyerere in Tanzania are the prime examples. Others did concentrate on economic development to a large degree, notably Kenyatta in Kenya, Mugabe in Zimbabwe, Houphouët-Boigny in Côte d'Ivoire, and Banda in Malawi. The development strategies chosen in these latter cases can be criticized on a number of grounds, but these states did have a nonutopian strategy of some kind; this could not be said about the majority of states in Africa.

The third and most common pattern was a military government brought to power through a coup. Often one coup was followed by another a few years later. Altogether there were sixty-one military coups in Africa from independence to 1985 (Decalo 1990, 2). With the exception of a few nations in the middle of civil wars, such as Angola, Ethiopia, and Nigeria, these armed forces have been small, numbering a few tens of thousands in most cases. Most of these forces have been poorly educated and trained. A few may come to power with genuine modernizing goals, but most appear to seize control because it is there for the taking if one possesses a few heavy weapons. Zaire under Mobutu is the most extreme and corrupt version of this model, but more than a few others have nothing that could be called a development vision, let alone the will or the skill to carry it out.

What has this contrast between Asian and African politics meant for development policies in the two regions? The most important difference is that many Asian nations had coherent development strategies that were sustained over several decades. After survival of the state, economic growth was the primary goal of these governments. The specific policies varied from country to country, and the choice of policies did affect performance, particularly when they were inward looking as in China before 1978 and Vietnam before 1986. But even inward-looking policies pursued consistently and vigorously did better than the shifting or indifferently executed policies of many African countries.

Few African governments, other than those headed by independence leaders, have had much legitimacy in the eyes of their people. The nations themselves are not entirely legitimate among people whose first loyalties are often to their ethnic group. Power, once gained, is less an opportunity for designing a coherent development policy than a chance to take care of one's supporters and oneself.

Most African governments are deeply clientelistic, and their power is rooted in the creation and distribution of rents. This trait is compounded by an ethic that holds family and local loyalties on a higher plane than loyalties to the nation, in what Hyden (1983) called the "economy of affection." Asian experience has two lessons for such governments. One is from East Asia: it takes a highly nationalistic, Confucian, or puritanical government to accelerate development. This would be a counsel of despair, as few if any African (or most other Asian) governments are likely to reform themselves so drastically in one generation. Tanzania's gallant try was crippled by its devotion to a socialism that undercut economic growth.

The second lesson is from Southeast Asia: even clientelistic, rent-seeking governments can promote development if they give priority to, and insulate from political interference, the functions of macroeconomic management and most long-term development strategy. This lesson seems more transferable from Asia to Africa. Leith and Lofchie (1993) have heuristically modeled rent-seeking potential as a common property resource. If managed by a cohesive state, as in Southeast Asia, exploitation of rents can be consistent with a healthy economy. If, however, rent-seeking is unregulated, as Leith and Lofchie observe in Ghana, its external costs reduce the economy's productive potential and thus reduce the realization of rents. Some African governments, such as those in Côte d'Ivoire and Kenya, once appeared to understand this model, but most do not.

Even if clientelism is likely to remain, political conditions can change. Much of Asia from the 1920s through the 1950s was not fruitful territory for the pursuit of economic development. But politics in most Asian nations changed fundamentally in the 1960s and 1970s. Africa's political systems are also evolving and will look very different a decade or two from now.

Before the 1990s, for example, only a handful of countries, such as Botswana and The Gambia, maintained the multiparty democracies with which they embarked on independence. But changes in Eastern Europe, among other things, brought renewed pressures to reinstitute genuine democratic procedures in nations from Zambia and Kenya to Côte d'Ivoire. If democracy takes hold in many parts of the region, it may elect governments devoted to broad-based economic growth in order to develop coalitions for electoral support. Or it may lead to a continuation of rent-seeking and payoffs to the coalitions that put the leaders in power. Africa's brief experiences with democracy over the past two decades fit more often into the latter category than the former. Political changes, however, if they are to be perceived as legitimate by the people being ruled, must come largely from within the country. Only rarely will external pressures affect a favorable outcome when internal support is missing.

Conclusion

As this essay has argued, there are large differences between the human and natural resource endowments of Africa and East Asia. There are also differences between Africa and the nations of Southeast Asia, but they are less pronounced than in the case of East Asia and Africa, which is why Southeast Asia provides more potential lessons for Africa. The political systems of Southeast Asia are also more like those of Africa than are the culturally homogeneous states of East Asia with their hundreds of years of self-rule within established borders.

Are there specific lessons, even at this very general level, that can be applied to Africa from this Asian experience? Do the differences in endowments themselves dictate certain outcomes over others?

One important lesson derives from the interaction of the political system with the human resource endowment. When a nation with low levels of literacy and limited experience managing complex organizations is also a nation where politics is dominated by clientelism and ethnic rivalry, some version of the neoclassical prescription of an economy dominated by market forces is the only viable option. The highly interventionist model of development of South Korea or Japan, let alone that of the centrally planned economies of China or North Korea, simply will not work.

The basic neoclassical prescription is primarily that prices, including the prices of capital, labor, and foreign exchange, should be left mainly to the market. Specific state interventions with the price mechanism, such as infant industry tariff protection, should be kept to a minimum. The trained and experienced human resources needed to staff an interventionist government probably do not yet exist in much of Africa. The weaknesses of these technically diverse and clientelistic states ensure that even well-trained people will be under great pressure to pursue short-term rent-seeking at the expense of long-term development. The Philippines demonstrates that the development program of even a human resource-rich country can be undone by rampant clientelism.

Although the neoclassical approach eschews discretionary government interventions for particular sectors or firms, there is still a large role for government. Among other things, macroeconomic policy must be well managed in a way that avoids excessive inflation, an overvalued exchange rate, and much else. Good macroeconomic policy, however, requires a few well-trained economists and the government's willingness to insulate those economists, at least to some degree, from political pressures that would undermine development-oriented fiscal, monetary, and balance of payments policies. As Indonesia and Thailand have demonstrated, sound macroeconomic policy is possible even when the number of well-trained economists available is small and the government is elsewhere buffeted by the demands of clientelism.

A weak base of education and experienced personnel also suggests that, in the first phases of a development program, the major emphasis of that effort should be on agriculture and rural development. The people of Africa are already experienced farmers. They need more infrastructure and better technology, but they do know the basic principles of how to raise crops and animals. The improvements required are at the margin. With large-scale industry, in contrast, most Africans are starting from scratch and know little about either industrial technology or industrial enterprise management. Improvements involve major discontinuous leaps, not marginal improvements. Some investment in industry is required so that the learning-by-doing process can begin. But the rate of return to investment in agriculture is likely to be much higher for the next decade or two precisely because large discontinuous leaps in knowledge will not be required.

This emphasis on agriculture also suggests that there will be a payoff from successful efforts to reduce the rate of growth of population. East and Southeast Asia have demonstrated that it is possible to raise crop yields as the density of the population on the land rises, but the process is a slow one. The same yields can be achieved, for the most part, in the absence of a rise in population density. Africa's 3+ percent rate of population growth virtually ensures that increased food production will have to accelerate simply to keep farm incomes and consumption where they are. A lower growth rate in population would make increases in farm output per capita more likely.

For a nation with low literacy and limited experience with modern organizations and technologies, there obviously must be a major effort to expand and improve education at all levels, and the learning-by-doing process must also begin in earnest. Expanding the education system is straightforward in principle but difficult to manage in practice. The greatest challenge is to expand the quantity of trained people while simultaneously raising the quality of that training. Providing the necessary learning-by-doing raises even more complex issues. The way to learn to build and manage a large factory is to build and manage one, but such learning can be prohibitively costly if the rate of return on infant industries is as low as frequently observed in both Asia and Africa. (This issue is explored further in Chapter 7.)

Finally, the nature of the political system matters a great deal for development. Governments capable of focusing the nation's efforts on development goals will do better than governments whose policies are driven by ethnic rivalries and rent-seeking goals. Because so many governments in Africa fit this latter description, there is every reason to believe that a dramatic shift of focus or more basic political change will have to precede economic development. That too is a lesson that can be seen in the Asian experience. Divided clientelistic governments can change into governments unified around government goals. The rent-seeking government of Syngman Rhee in Korea became the growth-oriented government of Park Chung Hee in the 1970s. More relevant to Africa, over a period of three decades the fragmented ethnic groups of the many islands of Indonesia were turned into the unified and development-oriented nation that emerged over the 1970s and 1980s. Malaysia responded to bloody race riots in 1969 by instituting a two-decade development program that has integrated Malays into the modern economy and substantially reduced poverty.

African states will need to make similar transformations to those that occurred in Asia if sustained economic progress is to be realized. But there is no cookbook approach to achieve this change. Politics is deeply rooted in culture, and there is great variation in culture within the many nations of Africa and between Africa and Asia. Solutions ranging from multiparty democracy to military dictatorship may work in one place and fail in another. They are especially likely to fail if the form chosen is imposed by outside powers, however noble the intentions of outsiders might be.

It is not difficult to define what political change must achieve if development is to succeed. Governments must be created that are capable of providing a stable and supportive environment for efficient investment, both public and private. Creating governments that can accomplish this goal is another matter. Scholars of Africa may be able to increase our understanding of this political transformation in particular countries, but only the people of those countries are capable of making that transformation a reality.

APPENDIX TO CHAPTER 2

Comparing Africa Today with Asia Twenty-Five Years Ago

From the perspective of 1990, after a quarter-century of rapid growth, the countries of East and Southeast Asia may seem to pose daunting conditions for accelerated growth in Africa. But what if we view Asia from the perspective of 1965? Were those countries, a quarter-century ago, so very different from Africa today? If not, Africa may have better hopes of following Asia's growth path, assuming that world markets are as accommodating to Africa in the 1990s as they were to Asia in the 1960s and 1970s.

Two kinds of comparisons are relevant to a judgment about Africa's similarity to Asia. First, did Asian economies then have economic structures similar to those found in Africa now? Within the limits of readily available data, the two groups can be compared along dimensions such as incomes per capita; the shares of agriculture, manufacturing, saving, investment, and exports in GDP; and the share of the population living in urban areas.

Second, is Africa today as well endowed with human and physical capital as Asia in 1965? Indicators for the provision of infrastructure, such as the density of the road network, the population per telephone, and the availability of water supplies, are unfortunately not available for the countries and years needed. As proxies for human capital, three indicators are used: the share of primary- and secondary-aged children attending school (measures of inputs) and the rate of adult illiteracy (a measure of educational output and quality). As measures of health, two indicators of health outcomes are infant mortality and life expectancy, and an indicator of health inputs is the average population per doctor.

The sample consists of twenty-nine African and seven Asian countries (Hong Kong, Indonesia, Korea, Malaysia, Philippines, Singapore, and Thailand). A list of countries and the available data are given in Table 2.2.

The null hypothesis is that African countries today are statistically indistinct from Asian countries in 1965. A simple test of this hypothesis is the differences in means between the two groups of countries for each of the indicators. Table 2.3 gives the results of these tests. In each case, the test is run using all thirty-six countries first (outcomes labeled *a*) and then repeated for all except the three outliers, Hong Kong, Singapore, and Botswana, whose incomes per capita are substantially higher than others in their respective groups (outcomes labeled *b*). Given their very different physical

TABLE 2.2
Data for Comparison: Asia 1960s versus Africa 1990

	Income per capita	Agriculture/ GDP (%)	Manufacturing/ GDP (%)	Savings/ GDP (%)	Investment/ GDP (%)	Exports G&NFS[a]/ GDP (%)	Urban population % of total	Primary enrollment % of age cohort	Secondary enrollment % of age cohort	Adult Illiteracy % adult population	Population per doctor (thousands)	IMR per 1000 births	Life expectancy
Botswana	2741	3	6	—	—	64	28	111	37	29	6900	38	67
Cameroon	1041	27	13	19	17	21	41	101	26	46	—	88	57
Chad	279	38	14	6	12	26	30	57	7	70	38390	125	47
Côte d'Ivoire	902	47	—	14	10	37	40	—	20	46	—	95	55
Ghana	441	48	9	8	18	21	33	75	39	40	20390	85	55
Kenya	753	28	11	18	24	25	24	94	23	31	10050	67	59
Mali	475	46	8	10	26	18	19	23	6	68	25390	166	48
Nigeria	762	36	7	29	15	40	35	70	19	49	—	98	52
Senegal	850	21	13	9	13	26	38	58	16	62	—	81	47
Tanzania	430	59	10	-6	25	18	33	63	4	—	24970	115	48
Zaire	218	30	13	—	11	25	40	78	24	28	13540	94	52
Zambia	637	17	43	17	14	32	50	95	20	27	7150	82	50
Zimbabwe	1073	13	26	21	21	28	28	125	52	33	6700	49	61
Hong Kong	2704	2	24	29	36	75	89	103	29	23	2520	27	68
Indonesia	461	51	8	8	8	13	16	72	12	43	31700	128	44
Korea	797	38	18	8	15	10	32	101	35	12	2680	62	57
Malaysia	1309	28	9	24	20	41	26	90	28	42	6200	55	58
Philippines	972	26	20	21	21	18	32	113	41	17	—	72	56
Singapore	1753	3	15	10	22	123	100	105	45	31	1900	62	66
Thailand	833	32	14	19	20	19	13	78	14	21	7160	88	56

NOTE: Dash = not available.

TABLE 2.3

Africa in 1990 versus Asia in 1965: Differences in Means of Economic and Social Indicators

Characteristic		Mean value for		Value of t-statistic	Level of significance
		Asia 1965	Africa 1990		
GDP per capita	1.	1261	658	1.87	.05−
(US$, ICP)	2.	874	583	1.79	.1−
Agriculture share GDP	1.	25.7	35.3	1.22	.1+
(%)	2.	35.0	36.4	0.25	Accept
Manufacturing share GDP	1.	15.4	11.5	1.40	.1−
(%)	2.	11.7	11.7	0.01	Accept
Saving share GDP	1.	17.0	8.7	1.88	.05+
(%)	2.	16.0	8.7	1.56	.1−
Investment share GDP	1.	20.3	18.1	0.54	Accept
(%)	2.	16.8	18.1	−0.36	Accept
Export (gnfs)[a] share	1.	42.8	23.5	1.11	.1+
GDP (%)	2.	21.6	22.0	−0.07	Accept
Urban population share	1.	44.0	27.9	1.10	.1+
(%)	2.	23.8	27.9	−0.80	Accept
Primary education	1.	94.6	71.4	2.83	.005−
(% of eligible population)	2.	90.8	69.8	2.11	.025−
Secondary education	1.	29.1	17.6	2.00	.025
(% of eligible population)	2.	30.3	16.8	1.65	.05
Adult illiteracy	1.	27.0	53.0	4.17	.0005−
(% of adult population)	2.	27.0	54.0	3.29	.005−
Population (1000)	1.	8.7	20.6	1.74	.05−
per doctor	2.	10.9	21.3	1.34	.1+
Infant mortality	1.	70.6	106.9	2.59	.01−
per 1000	2.	75.7	109.4	2.18	.025−
Life expectancy	1.	57.6	50.7	2.07	.025
(years)	2.	55.1	50.0	1.69	.05

NOTES:

1. All countries.
2. Without Hong Kong, Singapore, Botswana.

Significance levels:

$n−$ means that the t-statistic is significant at the probability n or less.

$n+$ means the t-statistic is significant at a slightly higher probability than n.

Accept means the hypothesis of no difference in means cannot be rejected.

a. Goods and nonfactor services.

endowments and economic structures, Hong Kong and Singapore are at best only marginally relevant to this comparison.

In one fundamental respect, Asia in 1965 was already well ahead of Africa in 1990. Asian *income per capita,* measured in purchasing power parity prices of 1985,[9] was twice as high as Africa's today if all the countries are included and 50 percent higher for the reduced sample. These differences are statistically significant at the 10 percent level or better. Because we know that indicators of structure and human capital change with average income, this finding weakens any further results that show Africa behind Asia but strengthens results that show no statistically significant difference between the two groups.

For most of the indicators of *economic structure*—the GDP shares of agriculture, manufacturing, investment, and exports, and the urban share of the population—Africa in 1990 looks similar to Asia in 1965, particularly when Hong Kong and Singapore are eliminated, as they should be. The only exception is the share of *saving,* which was almost twice as high in Asia then as in Africa now (16.0 percent compared with 8.7 percent). As Africa's investment share is actually higher than Asia's for the reduced sample, this suggests that Africa's saving deficiency has been compensated by foreign capital, almost certainly dominated by foreign aid.

Human capital endowments give a different picture. In all cases, the education and health indicators show Asia in 1965 to have been significantly ahead of Africa in 1990 at probabilities mostly in the range of 0.5 percent to 5 percent, whether the full or reduced sample of countries is used. Asia had enrolled twice the eligible population in secondary education, had half the adult illiteracy, had reduced infant mortality to 70 percent of Africa's 1990 level, and enjoyed five to seven years' longer life expectancy.

Could these differences in human capital be explained by the difference in average income? Indeed, could 1990 Africa have been ahead of 1965 Asia in economic structure, with income held constant? These propositions can be tested by assuming that structure or endowment are determined by only two independent variables: income per capita and location in Asia or Africa. The equations take the following form:

$$X = a_0 + a_1 D + b_0 Y + b_1 DY + c_0 Y^2 + c_1 DY^2$$

where X is the dependent variable, D is the dummy (0 for Africa, 1 for Asia), and Y is ICP income per capita. The second-order terms in Y permit curvature in the regression line.

TABLE 2.4
Regression Results Comparing Africa in 1990 with Asia in 1965 (T-ratios in parentheses; **boldface** if level of significance is 10% or less)

Dependent variable[a]		Constant	Dummy, D	Income per capita, Y	DY	Y_2	DY_2	R_2
Agriculture	1.	54.82	19.97	**−35.78**	−21.51	6.02	5.11	.570
			(0.95)	**(2.50)**	(0.65)	(1.20)	(0.49)	
	2.	52.69	7.00	**−27.87**	−0.36			
			(0.40)	**(3.63)**	(0.02)			
Manufacturing	1.	6.38	6.57	12.56	−13.40	**−4.68**	6.37	.142
			(0.46)	(1.25)	(0.59)	**(1.33)**	(0.90)	
	2.	No significant coefficients						.115
Saving		No significant coefficients						≤.120
Investment	1.	9.76	−2.53	**14.24**	−3.89			.210
			(0.28)	**(2.08)**	(0.45)			
	2.	9.76	−5.91	**14.25**	0.20			.144
			(0.35)	**(2.01)**	(0.01)			
Exports	1.	10.32	**−78.64**	20.27	**117.14**	−0.27	**−29.59**	.681
			(3.07)	(1.17)	**(2.90)**	(0.04)	**(2.34)**	
	2.	10.31	**−19.23**	**20.11**	13.27			.358
			(1.38)	**(3.28)**	(0.84)			
Urban population[b]	1.	15.72	**−41.47**	**26.55**	45.35	−8.04	−2.01	.570
			(1.60)	**(1.52)**	(1.12)	(1.30)	(0.16)	
	2.	19.25	−6.57	**14.75**	−2.03			.132
			(0.36)	**(1.86)**	(0.10)			
Primary education[c]	1.	25.30	33.05	**96.05**	−47.43	**−23.38**	11.35	.489
			(0.84)	**(3.14)**	(0.75)	**(2.25)**	(0.57)	
	2.	32.91	36.25	**67.10**	−42.35			.425
			(1.10)	**(3.80)**	(1.11)			
Secondary education[c]	1.	−1.76	−7.18	**39.28**	16.11	**−9.05**	−6.21	.510
			(0.37)	**(2.63)**	(0.52)	**(1.78)**	(0.64)	
	2.	17.81	−51.49	−30.88	**154.50**	43.69	−101.3	.458
			(1.18)	(0.60)	**(1.42)**	(1.17)	(1.56)	
Adult illiteracy[c]	1.	62.95	**−34.68**	**−14.86**	13.86			.391
			(2.44)	**(2.21)**	(1.23)			
	2.	67.36	**−41.14**	**−22.90**	23.80			.339
			(1.49)	**(1.76)**	(0.76)			
		67.78	64.54	−24.29	**−238.4**	0.941	**147.1**	.407
			(0.88)	(0.38)	**(1.35)**	(0.02)	**(1.46)**	
Medical services[d]	1.	48.22	−6.29	**−57.94**	12.13	**15.76**	−3.99	.355
			(0.20)	**(2.15)**	(0.24)	**(1.74)**	(0.25)	

Continued on next page

Dependent variable[a]		Constant	Dummy, D	Income per capita, Y	DY	Y_2	DY_2	R_2
	2.	68.70	31.94 (0.41)	**−133.2** **(1.51)**	−59.03 (0.30)	73.55 (1.14)	18.26 (0.16)	.341
Infant mortality[e]	1.	142.2	7.58 (0.18)	**62.36** **(2.12)**	−30.56 (0.45)	9.23 (0.89)	9.03 (0.42)	.584
	2.	166.4	62.08 (0.64)	**145.2** **(1.72)**	−126.7 (0.54)	66.93 (1.20)	40.54 (0.30)	.455
Life expectancy	1.	43.78	−8.36 (1.21)	**11.57** **(2.38)**	**15.00** **(1.37)**	−1.08 (0.64)	**−4.36** **(1.27)**	.742
	2.	44.26	−3.42 (0.58)	**9.98** **(3.75)**	5.03 (0.75)			.476
		43.89	**−24.52** **(1.54)**	11.19 (0.79)	**57.13** **(1.49)**	−0.81 (0.09)	**−29.14** **(1.33)**	.521

NOTES:
1. All countries.
2. Excludes Hong Kong, Singapore, and Botswana.
a. Share of gross domestic product except where noted.
b. Share of total population.
c. Share of relevant age group.
d. Population (in 1000s) per doctor.
e. Deaths per 1000 infants, age 0 to 1 year.

If a dummy coefficient is significantly different from zero, it implies that Asian countries are different from the sample as a whole and are therefore different from African countries. If, for example, a_1 is negative and b_1 is positive, then Asian countries start from a lower level than African countries at similarly low incomes but progress more rapidly as cross-section incomes rise. This result is observed in some regressions.

The regression results are contained in Table 2.4.[10] None of the dummy coefficients is significantly different from zero in the *economic structure* regressions for agriculture, manufacturing, saving, or investment shares of GDP, or for the urban population share. This confirms the results of the differences-in-means tests: in structural economic terms, Africa today resembles Asia in the 1960s. Africa in 1990 does have a higher intercept for export share than 1965 Asia in the reduced sample (significant at the 1 percent level), but exports grow more slowly with cross-section income.

The *human capital* regressions show mixed results, however. Regressions for primary education, medical services, and infant mortality contain no significant dummy coefficients. In the reduced sample for *secondary education,* Asian countries might actually start from a lower base (the intercept dummy is not quite significant at the 10 percent level) but appear to broaden access to secondary schools more rapidly than Africa in higher-income countries (the slope dummy is significant).

In the linear regressions, Asian countries appear to start with less *adult illiteracy* (negative intercept dummy). In the second-order equation, however, the difference comes in the slope dummy: Asian illiteracy falls more rapidly with income than that in Africa. Curiously, in the reduced sample, second-order regression, Asian *life expectancy* is significantly lower at lower incomes (negative intercept dummy), but rises more rapidly (positive slope dummy). Neither difference is significant in the linear equation.

It is worth noting that, even where there are statistically significant differences between Asia then and Africa now, there is substantial overlap. In adult literacy and life expectancy, for example, Botswana, Kenya, and Zimbabwe today are comparable to Asia in 1965, and Indonesia in 1965 would be behind several African countries today.

Summary

The similarity in economic structure between Asian countries in 1965 and African countries in 1990 seems robust. The disparities in human capital, observed in differences-of-means tests, can to some extent be explained by differences in per capita incomes. Africa starts with a clear disadvantage in adult literacy, however. This may be a crucial shortcoming because literacy is so important to upgrading workforce productivity in both agriculture and industry. In the other two cases where the regressions show significant differences, secondary education and life expectancy, the poorest Asian countries may actually have started behind comparable African countries. However, by 1965 the higher-income Asian countries had already progressed well beyond African countries with comparable incomes today. Although not conclusive, this analysis cannot dispel the impression that Africa has some catching up to do in the provision of human capital before it can enter a development path resembling that in East and Southeast Asia over the past quarter-century.

NOTES

1. The limited role of natural resource exports in large countries is analyzed in Perkins and Syrquin (1989, 1691–1753).

2. This prediction is based on data from the World Bank (1992, 218–19, 226–27). Based on data from Malaysia, with per capita income almost eight times that in Nigeria, energy consumption per capita will rise almost proportionately to income per capita for the indefinite future in Nigeria.

3. For a discussion of premodern education and literacy in the region, see Dore (1965), Rawski (1979), and Mason et al. (1980, Chapter 3).

4. Private communication from Dr. Charles Myers.

5. This paragraph is based on Rotberg (1965, 326–28).

6. The "Education for All" initiative, using somewhat more sophisticated calculations, arrives at similar figures (UNICEF 1990, 158–60).

7. Boediono et al. (1992, 10) imply that a figure of $130 per student at the primary, secondary, and tertiary levels in 1998 and $190 in 2003 would be required.

8. Political parties were formed in Francophone Africa right after World War II, and by 1952 these parties had taken on an ethnic orientation. At independence, all Francophone countries had multiparty parliamentary, democratic regimes. See Manning (1988, Chapter 6).

9. As given by Summers and Heston (1989) in the International Comparison Project (ICP). They give data for 1965 for Asia and for 1985 for Asia and Africa. To convert Africa to 1990 incomes, we projected from 1985 using the real growth rate as measured from IMF 1992 information.

10. Although the table reports regressions for both the complete and the reduced samples, it is inappropriate to compare Africa to Hong Kong and Singapore. Regressions with second-order terms in Y are reported if they yield significant coefficients and a higher R^2. Where the second-order results differ from those of linear equations, both are reported.

BIBLIOGRAPHY

Amsden, Alice. 1989. *Asia's Next Giant: South Korea and Late Industrialization.* New York: Oxford University Press.

Boediono, Walter, W. McMahon, and Don Adams, eds. 1992. *Education, Economic and Social Development: Second 25-Year Development Plan and Sixth 5-Year Development Plan Background Papers and Goals.* Jakarta: Ministry of Education and Culture.

Bruton, Henry, et al. 1992. *The Political Economy of Poverty, Equity, and Growth: Sri Lanka and Malaysia.* New York: Oxford University Press for the World Bank.

Decalo, Samuel. 1990. *Coups and Military Role in Africa.* New Haven, Conn.: Yale University Press.

Dore, Ronald. 1965. *Education in Tokugawa Japan.* Berkeley: University of California Press.

Hyden, Goran. 1983. *No Shortcuts to Progress: African Development Management in Perspective.* Berkeley: University of California Press.

Government of Indonesia (Central Bureau of Statistics). 1989. *Statistik Indonesia 1988.* Jakarta.

Government of Malaysia. 1969. *Mid-term Review of the First Malaysia Plan, 1966–1970.* Kuala Lumpur.

————. 1991. *The Second Outline Perspective Plan, 1991–2000.* Kuala Lumpur.

Jesudason, James V. 1989. *Ethnicity and the Economy: The State, Chinese Business, and Multinationals in Malaysia.* Singapore: Oxford University Press.

Leith, J. Clark, and Michael F. Lofchie. 1993. "The Political Economy of Structural Adjustment in Ghana." In *Political and Economic Interactions in Economic Policy Reform Programs: Evidence from Eight Countries,* ed. Robert H. Bates and Anne O. Krueger. Cambridge, Mass.: Basil Blackwell.

Manning, Patrick. 1988. *Francophone Sub-Saharan Africa 1980–85.* New York: Cambridge University Press.

Mason, Edward S., M. J. Kim, D. H. Perkins, K. S. Kim, and D. C. Cole. 1980. *The Economic and Social Modernization of the Republic of Korea.* Cambridge, Mass.: Council on East Asian Studies.

McGinn, Noel, Donald Snodgrass, Yung Bong Kim, Shin-Bok Kim, and Quee-Young Kim. 1980. *Education and Development in Korea.* Seoul: Council on East Asian Studies.

Perkins, Dwight H., and Moshe Syrquin. 1989. "Large Countries: The Influence of Size." In *Handbook of Development Economics,* Volume 2, ed. Hollis Chenery and T. N. Srinivasan. Amsterdam: North-Holland.

Rawski, Evelyn S. 1979. *Education and Popular Literacy in Ch'ing China.* Ann Arbor: University of Michigan Press.

Rotberg, Robert. 1965. *A Political History of Tropical Africa.* New York: Harcourt Brace.

United Nations Children's Fund (UNICEF). 1990. *Children and Development in the 1990s: A UNICEF Source Book.* New York: United Nations.

Wade, Robert. 1990. *Governing the Market: Economic Theory and the Role of Government in East Asian Industrialization.* Princeton, N.J.: Princeton University Press.

World Bank. 1981. *Accelerated Development in Sub-Saharan Africa: An Agenda for Action.* Washington, D.C.

————. 1988. *Education in Sub-Saharan Africa.* Washington, D.C.

————. 1990. *World Development Report 1990.* Washington, D.C.

————. 1992. *World Development Report 1992.* Washington, D.C.

CHAPTER 3

Reform Bargains:
The Politics of Change

Jennifer A. Widner

In Chapter 2, Perkins and Roemer note that the sharpest distinction between Southeast Asia and Africa lies in the effectiveness of government. They suggest that the higher rates of growth and development in the economies of Thailand, Malaysia, and Indonesia, compared with most countries of Sub-Saharan Africa, reflect differences in politics even more than differences in resource endowments; and they observe that even clientelistic, rent-seeking governments can promote development if they give priority to, and insulate from political interference, the functions of macroeconomic management and most long-term development strategy. Southeast Asian governments have by and large succeeded in doing so, whereas most African governments have not.

This chapter proposes an explanation for the difference in the character of governance between the countries of Southeast Asia and Africa and among the countries in the two regions. As does other recent writing on the political economy of development, it tries to understand the patterns observed by focusing on the "autonomy of the state" from fluctuating, short-term economic interests of elites and interest groups. The chapter begins by operationalizing this concept in a way that is slightly different from much of the political science literature. It introduces the notion of a "reform bargain." Liberalizing economic reform is understood as the consequence of more or less explicit "deals" negotiated between leaders, technocrats, and the heads of the networks or groups that structure political life. These compromises insulate policy in the short and medium term.

The governments that have succeeded in improving macroeconomic management[1] and in shifting to an export-oriented strategy of development have sought to counter the resistance and demands of the "barons" who previously were the most influential and powerful supporters of the regime. Governments circumvented the barons by cultivating the growth of economic interest groups, ad hoc coalitions, or diffuse bodies of public opinion, and by providing fledgling institutions that could support bargaining and compromise with these new actors. Faced with "aristocratic" rent-seeking and demands for resources that threatened to undermine the economic viability of the country, some rulers perceived that they could pit the growing power of new economic interests against the "nobles" of the clientelist order.

There are three key conditions for reform bargains. *First,* bargains may occur when some kinds of *horizontal associations* are able to organize and can be drawn into reform negotiations through informal consultation, corporatist structures, national dialogues, or other mechanisms. These new groups may be economic interests too new to have entered into rent-seeking themselves. Where the interests of key rent-seekers diverge, bargains may also result from efforts by a leader to set the demands of one clientelist network against another to force a reduction in the demands made by both.

Second, compromises or reform bargains require some level of *trust* among parties. Governments without long experience of working together or widespread belief that impersonal rules will guide relationships must devise ways to instill confidence that they will live up to their agreements in order to succeed in negotiating reform bargains.

Third, where reform bargains occur, the leaders, including the senior ministers or officials responsible for macroeconomic management, have *incentives to propose reform* and to invest in the politically costly effort to negotiate terms. These incentives may derive from personal belief, the electoral system, donor conditionality, the desire of senior technocrats to maintain international professional status, or a number of other sources.

In short, where governments have successfully shifted to export-oriented strategies of development from import substitution, leaders or ministers of finance have usually acted as *technopols,* economists who involve themselves in political life in order to create constituencies for outward-oriented policies (Dominguez 1993, 4). These men and women are especially visible in Latin America and Asia, but they exist in African countries as well.

The chapter first offers a brief survey of the explanations scholars have constructed for patterns of economic policy in Southeast Asia and Africa. The chapter then develops the explanation outlined here with regard to several important cases from the two regions. The conclusion relates the explanation and findings to other social science research and to policy.

Ways of Thinking about the Politics of Reform

The literature on the politics of economic policy in Southeast Asia and Africa remains fairly limited in volume and motivated until recently by questions other than the ones posed in this chapter. In thinking about the differences between Southeast Asia and Africa, several explanatory variables inevitably surface: ethnic or cultural homogeneity, political "culture," the character of colonial rule, the "autonomy of the state" from societal pressures, and the pro-reform demands of interest groups themselves. This section outlines these approaches briefly and indicates their strengths and weaknesses.[2]

Ethnic or Cultural Homogeneity

Ethnic or cultural differences within a population can make economic policy difficult to formulate and implement in two respects. They can lower levels of trust, making negotiations among policy clienteles a longer, costlier, and in some cases inconclusive process. Alternatively, where the burdens and benefits of policies are distributed to some groups and not others, cultural heterogeneity can trigger ethnic claims against the state and promote instability.

Complicated transactions and transactions across time, including political compromises, require trust among parties that each will adhere to the terms originally agreed to or modify these only in accordance with procedures accepted in advance. Where language differences or variations in attitudes and habits impede effective communication, levels of social trust are likely to be lower.

The relationship between cultural heterogeneity and levels of social trust is by no means straightforward, however. Cultural heterogeneity may be rejected as an explanation for economic reform on three grounds.

First, where individuals have multiple group affiliations that create "cross-cutting cleavages"—for example, memberships in economic associations that include people of diverse backgrounds—the tendency of people from different cultural communities to come into conflict with one another is reduced. The relevant independent variable is not ethnic fragmentation (heterogeneity) or the number of communities, but the way the members of these different groups come into contact with each other in economic and social institutions, or the degree to which ethnic group interests and economic interests overlap.

Second, some numbers are more stable than others. That is, the evidence of the past thirty years in Africa suggests that countries whose members belong to two or three ethnic groups are more likely to experience disruption and competing ethnic claims against the state than those with many more cultural communities. In Africa, ethnic identities have less political importance in Côte d'Ivoire and Tanzania—both countries with large numbers of communities, many of roughly equal size—than they do in Rwanda, Burundi, or even Kenya, where there are fewer groups.

Third, there is abundant evidence that cultural identities are not fixed, and that where differences do not exist, people often create them. For example, the phenomenon of converting to Islam for economic or political advantage is common in large parts of both Africa and Southeast Asia. As a result, there is no permanent relationship between ethnic or religious heterogeneity and levels of trust or conflict.

Where cultural boundaries and economic status or occupational groupings correspond, differences reinforce one another and can provide a basis for conflict that disrupts the economy and increases the risk surrounding investment calculations. Postindependence Nigeria is a case in point. Again, however, the Nigeria case illustrates the need to consider political institutions as critical intervening variables. Various Nigerian governments have sought to use redistricting and modifications in electoral rules to attenuate the influence of ethnic communities and ethnic claims in politics. The returns from the 1983 elections suggested that they had achieved some measure of success, as have the results of the recent presidential election. Although communal divisions continue to be important in Nigerian politics, there are other sources of instability as well, and these often overshadow ethnic divisions in importance. The example suggests that even when ethnic group boundaries and economic situations coincide, the effect of these on economic policy and political stability depends on the pattern of incentives and disincentives created by political institutions.

In Malaysia, where ethnic group boundaries and economic status have long coincided, ethnic heterogeneity is an explanatory variable in the sense that, as Bowie (1991, 9) wrote, policy reflects the nature of the "communal settlement that has prevailed in Malaysia since 1957." Policy change within Malaysia has taken place as the content of the contract between social groups has altered. The groups that count most are not economic actors but communal groups. Bowie (1991, 154) writes that "Malay, Chinese, and Indian communities are linked at the top in Malaysia in a coalition that embodies a political settlement of differences—a *quid pro quo* acknowledging spheres of political and economic influence. . . . Changes in the scope of this settlement in successive decades have altered the extent to which the (Malay-dominated) state has felt constrained from using its psychological power to advance the economic interests of the Malay community." This form of explanation is fundamentally different from other theories that consider ethnicity or communal identities important in that it recognizes the explicit use of communal organizations by leaders to control the behavior of clientelistic networks.

Political Culture

An alternative view is that political cultures shape the content of policy and the process of reform. Confucianism first appeared as a way of explaining economic outcomes in the work of Max Weber, who argued that the doctrine fostered backwardness in China. More recently, scholars have used the same approach to account for rapid development in East and Southeast Asia. But they have often chosen cases selectively: Vietnam's slow industrialization correlated with the deep infusion of Confucian ideas in local culture (McVey 1992, 9–10).

Nor is it possible to explain change on the basis of cultural continuity. Unless some aspect of political culture has altered in the period before policy change, it is not logically possible to use culture per se as a variable to explain policy shifts or modifications in the behavior of economic decision makers.

The Character of Colonial Rule

As Perkins and Roemer point out, there are differences in the character of colonial rule between Southeast Asia and Africa. Some of the countries of Southeast Asia had existed as cohesive political units before the advent of colonial rule, unlike their African counterparts. Further, Japanese colonial policy and investment patterns in these areas may have had different long-term developmental consequences than British or Dutch control. Although the relationships between colonial policies and current development patterns are underspecified in this account, there does appear to be an association between the character of economic management and two aspects of colonial rule: the degree to which the colonial power invested in agriculture and infrastructure and the extent to which it trained local people and incorporated them into economic and political institutions.

Differences in patterns of colonial rule within Africa may also have had repercussions for patterns of economic and political development. Most countries that were formerly settler colonies display relatively lower levels of "urban bias" against agricultural production. (Zambia, with its mining base, is a former settler colony that later discriminated against agriculture.) The policies pursued in most of the former Belgian and Portuguese areas, where colonial rulers prohibited association and invested little in either people or infrastructure, generated high levels of political fragmentation and political instability in countries. British and French rule left different "institutional legacies" that bequeathed varying degrees of preference for centralization in public administration, forms of parallel association, monetary systems, and attitudes or policies toward circulation of information.

These forms of explanation have compelling aspects. However, they are of little use in explaining why a country such as Indonesia, subject to a highly repressive Dutch rule that invested little in the country, should eventually see high levels of economic growth, whereas the overwhelming majority of African countries, including those in which imperial powers invested more extensively, should continue to experience comparatively low rates of growth. Further, like political culture explanations, colonial policies that shaped subsequent patterns of development may be useful for understanding some kinds of events and outcomes and not others. They may help us understand broad patterns of interest group formation, for example, but they provide little leverage for explaining why some leaders have incentive to negotiate with these groups and associations, while others have not, outside of periods of crisis.

State-Centered Approaches

Research by political scientists has tended to define states in both regions as "patrimonial": the relationship between leaders and people is mediated not by institutions, but instead by shifting personal relations between patrons and clients. Theories that invoke the state and stop there merely reify "the state." If all states have this same defining character, then the problem is to explain the variety of economic policies and performances observed. Most efforts to do so explain differences in policy choices, especially degree of reliance on the market, as a function of the "autonomy of the state" from strong societal interests. These analyses take several forms.

Autonomous elites In his study of Indonesia, Liddle (1991) writes, "In Indonesia . . . patrimonial rule does not seem to have been a significant obstacle to the adoption of market-oriented growth policies. The reason, in my view, is Soeharto's [Suharto's] discovery that some of the golden eggs produced by growth can be distributed to patrimonial clients without starving the capitalist goose" (Liddle 1991, 5). He explains the empowerment of this view within government as the consequence of the rise of decision makers who had both American training in economic analysis (and therefore had the analytic tools to answer politicians' questions as well as a promarket orientation) and backgrounds in the nationalist movement. Because of the mix of heritages, these men secured acceptance from many quarters and were able to secure support for their ideas—or buy time for experimentation (Liddle 1991, 408).

This analytic strategy is of considerable interest. Liddle comments elsewhere that these economists "were also nationalists, Western-educated but not Westernized, trained in a foreign science but brought up in colonial Netherlands India and revolutionary Indonesia" (Liddle 1992). By contrast, their counterparts in most parts of Sub-Saharan Africa are younger, born after the nationalist movements of the 1940s and 1950s. Independence came when they were children. Comparatively fewer attended American universities. Those who urge economic reform and pursuit of market-conforming policies today are young and often performed their "internships" with the World Bank or the International Monetary Fund and may therefore lack legitimacy in the eyes of many fellow citizens. For example, the Ivoirien opposition press, not generally given to extreme statements, routinely characterizes Alassane Ouattara, prime minister of Côte d'Ivoire, as a representative of an international, technocratic elite who will simply flee the country when the policies he implements cause hardship.

Even if some technocrats are more politically acceptable than others, whether they are allowed to manage the economy insulated from the pressures of short-term interests depends heavily on whether they have the backing of leaders who have responsibility for maintaining order. Ultimately, says Liddle (1992, 800–1), Suharto was also able "to construct a set of political arrangements—legitimating principles, a base of support, and means of coercion—compatible with [the economists' solutions] . . . if Soeharto had not seen how liberal economic policies could be made to fit into a supportive political structure, it is highly unlikely that he would have adopted them." Why these ideas could be "made acceptable" in some countries and not in others has elicited much speculation.

Decision makers with stakes in enterprise A second way of understanding "state autonomy" has rested on analysis of alliances between politicians and businessmen. Some types of links between civil servants and businessmen may be more conducive to reform than others. Scholars have pursued a number of avenues of inquiry. For example, McVey (1992, 23) has posited that those who secured political power in Southeast Asia "were not businessmen, but they were for the great part political entrepreneurs, men who had made their way up by finding footholds on the crumbling face of a decaying power system. . . . Men like these were glad to make business arrangements which provided a slice of the profits in return for protection and preference, but where real money was concerned they were unlikely to leave it at that. Who could know if his portion was fair if he did not really understand how the business was being run?" For that reason, she suggests, coupled with nervousness about the "vulnerability of riches based on office holding," many government decision makers invested in enterprise. By so doing they could protect themselves against the economic consequences of dismissal from office, ensure an income stream after retirement, and build equity to pass on to heirs. "In capitalist Southeast Asia," McVey writes, "access to office-holding could not effectively be restricted by aristocratic, caste, or nomenklatura systems. What was available instead was investment in business enterprise."

Office holding in many parts of Africa is similarly unstable, although until recently governments have been reluctant to dismiss any but their most senior officials. According to this analysis, one would thus expect a similar outcome in Africa as well. By and large, however, African office holders have invested the combined proceeds of salaries and rent-seeking not in productive businesses in competitive sectors but in protected enterprises, or they have shifted their capital abroad. The perception that tenure in office is unstable does not automatically lead to attempts to build manufacturing enterprises or invest in agriculture as a way of diversifying risk to the family sources of livelihood. Indeed, the greater the uncertainty, the more intense is the effort to extract rents from official positions. As Achebe (1987, 22) paraphrases a Nigerian proverb, "[The] giant iroko . . . is not scaled every day, so I must get all the firewood it can yield me now while I am atop." Researchers have suggested that where there is a threat of losing office, the "political discount factor" is very high and encourages adoption of policies that actually diminish the future worth of a government's political assets (Leith and Lofchie 1993, 257).

McVey (1992, 30) is attentive to this problem and notes that "had it not been for the East Asian capitalist boom, the connections of Southeast Asian businessmen around the Pacific Rim, and the desire by more industrialized countries to invest in a region with low environmental protection and cheap labor, it would have been much less easy for the region's political leaders to see the virtues of encouraging rather than bleeding domestic enterprise." In short, whether public officials invest the rents they collect in productive enterprise and develop a stake in the welfare of agriculture and manufacturing sectors depends on the incentives to invest provided by macroeconomic conditions. In its general form, this approach gives researchers little way to explain the differences that exist among Southeast Asian countries. Thailand, Malaysia, Indonesia, and the Philippines all responded very differently to the opportunities that investment in the Pacific Rim by other countries has created.

Further, although it is certainly important to understand the conditions under which business and political groups work together, this approach cannot explain why investment of bureaucrats and politicians in business produced not monopolists but competitive enterprises (it has not in some cases) or why these relationships supported a shift toward export orientation. Social scientists have invested too little effort in deciphering these patterns.

The locus of rent-seeking Among Southeast Asia specialists there has recently developed a debate about whether the locus of rent-seeking activity critically influences the ability of governments to redirect their policies and pursue new strategies for promoting growth. One argument tries to explain low rates of growth in the Philippines, compared with other Southeast Asian economies, as the consequence of rent-seeking activities by entrepreneurs outside the state instead of within it. "Patrimonial rule" in Thailand and the Philippines varies in character. In the case of Thailand, "a bureaucratic elite extracted privilege from a historically weak business class," whereas in the other, "a powerful oligarchic business class extracts privilege from a largely incoherent bureaucracy" (Hutchcroft 1991, 449). Writes Hutchcroft (1993, 9), "Where rents are most commonly grabbed by a bureaucratic elite based inside the state (as in the former 'bureaucratic polity' of Thailand and Indonesia), we can speak of 'bureaucratic capitalism': where they are generally grabbed by groups with an economic base outside the state . . . we can speak of booty capitalism." The consequence of this division for economic policy and macroeconomic management remains somewhat unclear in these accounts. The contention is that "booty capitalism" is "more resistant to fundamental transformation" than other forms of rent-seeking based in the state because the entrepreneurs who seek such rents are in a position outside government to monitor and repress the emergence of new business and interest groups. In these systems, the power of technocrats is sharply circumscribed.

This view might be considered a political economy approach that does not take the autonomy of the state as its focus. As posed, however, the argument appears to suggest that the most serious effect of rent-seeking outside the state is the elimination of the social forces that can vie for power with the barons of a clientelist system and thereby free decision makers from dependence on their cronies. For that reason, it appears here as a variant of the state-centered approaches that have the autonomy of the state as their principal concern.

To date, the research to establish this hypothesis has concentrated on a single case, the Philippines. More comparative investigation is needed, with some way of assessing the magnitude of rent-seeking outside the state. It is also not clear that rent-seeking within the state leads to different behavior on the part of state elites, who could certainly close down independent associations, given their privileged access to means of repression, if they believed their opportunities threatened. The difference between the two loci of rent-seeking, if there is one, may lie in the greater willingness of nonstate rent-seekers to "run down" or exhaust the rents available through government because of their greater independence from the revenues these activities provide over the long run.[3]

The African cases also raise a challenge to this analysis. Although the outcomes resemble those in the Philippines more than those of other Southeast Asian countries, these countries tend to have very small numbers of citizens with significant businesses. The locus of rent-seeking is predominantly *within* the state, not outside of it.

Whether the autonomy of the state is an appropriate focus for research at all is an important question. Doner (1991, 833) has pointed out that all approaches focusing on the state misunderstand the problems governments face. "An autonomous state may not always be best suited for development tasks. Autonomously developed preferences may lead to predatory behavior by state officials." Doner suggests that governments of Southeast Asian countries have little independence from powerful groups, in any event, yet they continue to grow. He points to the need to study nonstate institutions and their role in solving some of the problems that confronted business in earlier periods. These include business groups, which try to overcome market failure "by internalizing transactions within a firm or group of firms"; networks, which perform functions similar to those of business groups, but involve "regularized linkages between or among independent firms"; business interest associations; and informal consultative mechanisms.

Interest Group Explanations

In an earlier period, political scientists often understood policies as the result of interest group competition or a struggle between conflicting, organized "horizontal" associations including people of common economic position but often dissimilar community origins. If there is one thing upon which most contemporary observers agree, however, it is that economic policy reform does not result from interest group pressure in any straightforward fashion. In the many case studies from all parts of the world, it is hard to find examples of potential beneficiaries organizing to bring pressure to bear *for* reform. Proreform interest groups are very hard to organize. The benefits these policy packages generate are diffuse and unfurl over a long period. It is difficult to rally people to lobby for such policies anywhere in the world (Bates and Krueger 1993, 456–57), but nowhere is that task more challenging than in countries where there is an expectation of political instability that leads people to discount the future heavily.

This is not to say that interest groups play no role in the reform process. Reform policies often create clear short-run losers, and these individuals and groups can mobilize against proposals offered by technocrats or reform-minded politicians. The variation in patterns of structural adjustment is explained by the way formal and informal institutions shape the bargaining strength of various actors. Specifically, some studies suggest, politicians can adjust or augment these institutions to create new constituencies, diminish the bargaining power of opponents, or alter the views of others. For example, in their review of reform in several developing countries, Bates and Krueger (1993, 461) suggest that

> efforts at economic reform led to attempts to restructure the pattern of interest group representation. Scattered evidence suggests that reform-minded elites attempted to create corporatist political structures and, in at least one case, to underpin these with government programs that could forestall protectionist reactions against liberalizing policy changes.

An Alternative Explanation

An alternative explanation is that where governments have adopted liberalizing reforms, leaders have appealed to these horizontal groups or to even more diffuse public opinion against the clientelistic barons in order to reassert control over key customs and institutions such as important public enterprises. They have tried to develop mechanisms or institutions for procuring compromise, a form of autonomy from any single interest. In short, they have created reform bargains by accepting and sometimes encouraging the mobilization of new groups and using these to counter the political leverage of those who developed vested interests in a protected economy.

African countries differ as a group from their Southeast Asian counterparts, but they also vary among themselves, in the level of organization of interest groups and civic associations and the degree to which technocrats have appealed to these and to public opinion in forging support for reform. Authoritarian rule in Africa was long hostile to economic interest groups and many forms of less formal, horizontal association and the governments stamped them out when they were able to do so. Governments in Southeast Asia did so to varying degrees, but even those most hostile to political life outside the inner circles of government tolerated the formation and consolidation of business groups during the 1970s. Further, in Africa high levels of instability favored membership in vertical associations instead of horizontal groups. Prolonged periods of political instability have blocked the formation of cohesive horizontal associations or interest groups and forced the use of vertical networks and identities—ethnic and religious affiliations, for the most part, or patron–client ties (Callaghy 1990, 263). Although the early 1990s have spawned political opening and new forms of social mobilization in many parts of Africa, these are new and fragile developments compared with their Southeast Asian counterparts.

More serious for leaders who seek to curtail the power of clientelist barons is the absence of vehicles for interest intermediation. Opposition parties in some Southeast Asian countries are extremely weak and constitute poor vehicles for representing interests and exerting influence. The same is true of the emerging African opposition parties, which have few ties to unions or other interest groups and, in many cases, no platforms. In both Southeast Asia and many parts of Africa, national assemblies lack the constitutional authority to initiate legislation or simply choose not to do so. Interest groups have few contacts with representatives seated in the assemblies.

In Southeast Asia, informal consultation that includes members of different interest groups, especially multiple business factions, is more common as part of policy making than in Africa. The few forums available in Africa, such as Félix Houphouët-Boigny's "Days of Dialogue," are occasions for taking "soundings" of public opinion, not for facilitating resolution of conflict or negotiating compromises among groups. Only in Botswana, the country with the highest growth rates in Africa, is consultation institutionalized. In Southeast Asia, the country closest to the African cases with respect to both criteria is the Philippines, the country whose economic situation has not followed the pattern of its neighbors.

This chapter takes a first step toward a different conceptualization of state autonomy and introduces three necessary conditions, no single one of which is sufficient to explain the patterns Perkins and Roemer observe, but which taken together account for the variations within and between regions.

At the center of this analysis is a definition of state autonomy that centers on the notion of a *reform bargain*. When policy makers speak about the need for autonomy from special interests, they do not mean that governments should be insulated from the demands of social groups. Rather, the compromises governments facilitate among these groups create "political space": they enable policy makers to act according to impersonal rules and indeed to take steps that abrogate the short-term interests of some groups without provoking street demonstrations or other forms of participation that lead to instability. "Autonomy" refers not to isolation from social pressures but to the short-term and medium-term capacity to pursue policy agendas that comes from more or less explicit deals or negotiations with the leaders of the networks or groups that structure political life.

Interest Group Formation

Countries that have successfully insulated macroeconomic management and promoted export-oriented policies are different from others in three key respects. First, and most important, these governments have tolerated or even promoted formation of some economic interest groups or new forms of communal identity (as in Bowie's analysis of Malaysia) alongside personal networks, and they have created formal or informal forums for what political scientists call "interest intermediation." In this respect Western industrial democracies are historically no different. At some point, all sought to contain rent-seeking behavior on the part of aristocrats. Indeed, all societies have to periodically re-create new groups and structures in order to contain the kinds of rent extraction in which clientelist networks, communal groups, and interest groups variously engage.

In all of the countries of Africa and Southeast Asia, rulers long secured order through manipulation of clientelist systems, and all continue to use these to varying degrees. The governments that have succeeded in improving macroeconomic management and in shifting to an export-oriented strategy of development, however, are those that sought to counter the resistance and demands of the "barons" who were the past pillars of order by cultivating the growth of "horizontal" associations—usually economic interest groups. In most cases, this means that there must first be sufficient diversity in forms of economic life to provide the basis for competing economic identities, and that governments have tolerated the organization of at least some of these new identities. Authoritarian governments vary greatly in the degree to which they do so.

Further, the governments that have succeeded in reorienting economic policies and insulating macroeconomic management have put in place institutions that can support bargaining and compromise among these different actors. To do so, they not only had to give these new interest groups greater latitude for public activity, but also had to provide formal or informal opportunities for consultation and thus for compromise. Where they did not or could not do so because horizontal interest groups had long been repressed, reform proved difficult to implement and rent-seeking proliferated.

There are various forms of interest intermediation; some are commonly associated with democracies, and others are not. Political parties are one way of organizing interests, and elections are means of organizing compromises among them. These are the institutions to which Huntington (1968) assigned priority in his study of the bases of political order in changing societies. In most developing countries in Southeast Asia and Africa, however, political parties have few strong ties to the interest groups or communities that can mobilize street demonstrations, strikes, and other forms of activity to confront government policies. They are often poor vehicles for aggregating and expressing interests.

Securing a bargain (an acceptable package of trade-offs) can take place in other ways, through some forms of informal consultation, national dialogues, or formal incorporation of centralized association into government decision making.

Trust among Parties

Second, reform bargains require some level of trust among parties. Reforms that succeed in insulating macroeconomic management and pursuing export-oriented strategies pursue at least one of the following approaches to making their commitments credible.

- In some cases, rulers have coupled proposals for economic reform with shifts to more competitive political systems, securing agreement on the former by ensuring that the population will have the opportunity to throw them out of office through defeat at the ballot box if they fail to adhere to the terms of the deal. In 1985, for example, Nigeria's President Ibrahim Babangida tried to win acceptance of a reform package modeled after IMF proposals but without IMF financial support by simultaneously announcing a phased transition to a Third Republic. In Côte d'Ivoire, Félix Houphouët-Boigny did much the same in the aftermath of a series of strikes that protested sharply higher tax rates on urbanites by coupling revised proposals to limit public sector spending with legalization of opposition parties and announcement of competitive elections. Asian examples of this tactic are less common. Where parties have alternated in power before through multiparty elections, this pledge may carry more weight than in countries where the rulers had long circumscribed political participation.

- In the generally undemocratic systems of the two regions, rulers can offer noninstitutional tests of trustworthiness. They can agree to act first on other concrete concerns of key actors as an indication of intention to adhere to the main terms of a reform bargain. In Indonesia, for example, Suharto sent a clear message of his intentions to members of the political elite when he drastically restructured Pertamina, the state oil company, at the expense of a close political ally.

- Some kinds of institutions, practicable under either democratic or authoritarian systems, can also lend confidence to potential coalition partners. For example, the East Asian NICs made extensive use of joint public-private export committees to publicize export goals. The World Bank (1991, 22) has suggested that these may increase confidence in three ways: by lending credibility to claims that the government will adhere to the terms of its bargain over the medium term, by conveying information about export bottlenecks, and by developing vested interests in promoting exports, which is a source of political pressure on governments that try to back away from outward-oriented policies.

- Governments can arrest or suspend high-level officials or political elites engaged in corruption in an effort to secure concessions or acceptance of the terms of reform from groups suspicious that such high officials intended to renege on the government's arrangements.

Most governments that have succeeded in securing reform bargains have pursued one or more of these strategies for signaling credibility.

Motivation to Negotiate

Third, in those systems where reform bargains occur, the leaders, senior ministers, or officials responsible for economic management must have incentives not only to propose reform but also to invest in the politically costly effort to negotiate terms. One possible motivation is that the family incomes of decision makers arise disproportionately from enterprises hurt by the political economy of import substitution, and these men or women have few opportunities to invest their assets abroad. With no exit available, they try to change the circumstances they face at home. A second motivation centers on preserving reputation; decision makers consider that their future job prospects lie in multinational enterprise or abroad in multilateral aid agencies such as the World Bank or International Monetary Fund, and they act so as to maintain their credentials. Alternatively, the head of state may cultivate an *esprit de corps* among reform-minded technocrats, making clear their value by meeting with them, taking the time to become conversant in the main tenets of the programs they advocate, and defending them when other politicians seek to frustrate their efforts. Uganda's president, Yoweri Museveni, is a good example of a leader who has sought to foster such a spirit among technical staff, taking the time to listen to his advisers, bolster his own knowledge of economics, and occasionally remove "barons" on the take. None of these sets of conditions is both necessary and sufficient, however. In all instances, the technocrats must have adequate training and openness of mind, or critical analytic skills, to learn from mistakes, acquire information from the experiences of others, and develop alternatives tailored to local circumstances. It is training in combination with one or the other of these three sets of conditions that makes the difference.

Summary: The "Technopols"

In sum, the governments that succeed in insulating their macroeconomic policies from the day-to-day pressures of special interests and in reorienting development strategies toward an export orientation are those that manufacture political space or autonomy for themselves. There are three components of that effort:

1. These leaders tolerate some level of association among economic interest organizations, civic associations, or ad hoc groupings and provide institutions for facilitating compromise among these groups, the government, and the barons of the old order.
2. They engage in one or more measures to win the trust of these new groups.
3. They give prominence to technocrats who either derive part of their

personal income from export manufacturing, believe their future job prospects lie in multilateral organizations where free market or market-conforming policies are promoted, or simply share developmentalist perceptions and goals.

This explanation is similar to that offered in other recent comparative studies of the ways technocrats translate their ideas into policy (Williamson 1994). This new literature observes that successful technocrats are often "technopols," people who not only have technical expertise but are also "1) at or near the top of their country's government and political life, who 2) go beyond their specialized experience to draw on various different streams of information and who 3) vigorously participate in the nation's political life, 4) for the purpose of affecting policies well beyond the economic realm and who may, at times, be associated with an effort to 're-make' their country's politics, economics, and society" (Dominguez 1993, 4).

Technopols gained influence in Chile, Brazil, Argentina, and Mexico when four conditions converged. First, each of these countries suddenly found itself amid economic crisis. Second, the crisis discredited the authoritarian regimes in power. Third, technocrats and technopols occupied positions of power in these authoritarian governments and faced challenges to their style of governing. Fourth, the political process became more competitive, for various reasons, in each country (Dominguez 1993, 11–12).

This essential political role of the technocrat is one of building political space or medium-term autonomy from fluctuating, short-term interests through compromise. The words of a successful Latin American technopol highlight this perspective. Asked how he would define his role as finance minister in Chile, Alejandro Foxley replied in part,

> To do a good technical job in managing the economy you have to be a politician. If you do not have the capacity to articulate your vision, to persuade antagonists, to bring people around on some unpopular measures, then you are going to be a total failure. . . . Economists must not only know their economic models, but also understand politics, interests, conflicts, passions— the essence of collective life. For a brief period of time you could make most changes by decree; but to let them persist, you have to build coalitions and bring people around. You have to be a politician. (Dominguez 1993, 50)

This essay suggests that it need not be the technocrats themselves who do the work of compromise, but they must at the least have senior political allies who are able to do so. Accomplishing that end presupposes that there are individuals or groups whose interests run counter to those of the rentiers; that there are institutions, formal or informal, in which these differences of opinion can be negotiated; and that the key brokers have personal incentives to assume the costs of bargaining. This finding is echoed in recent research on the implementation of radical economic reform in Mexico, New Zealand, Poland, Portugal, South Korea, Spain, and Turkey (Williamson 1994).

Evidence

This chapter makes no attempt to test this explanation systematically. For the time being, the absence of comparable data about the countries in the two regions means that it is possible only to make illustrative use of cases. To that end, this section examines the utility of these variables in helping us understand one paired case (the different receptivity of Côte d'Ivoire and Thailand to structural adjustment reforms) and makes brief reference to two other significant cases, Ghana and Indonesia.

The choice of Côte d'Ivoire and Thailand for comparison is based on several considerations. First, because the adoption of policies to promote export orientation was part of the structural adjustment packages of the two countries, patterns in the implementation of structural adjustment policies constitute "what is to be explained" in the comparison. Second, to prevent bias, comparative analysis requires that at least some of the cases chosen for study vary with respect to the dependent variable. In this pair of cases, Côte d'Ivoire and Thailand both seek to implement structural adjustment reforms. To date, Côte d'Ivoire has implemented very few of the items that are part of the program, whereas Thailand has implemented several. In this case, then, there are different outcomes or values of the dependent variable. Third, to establish possible cause, the key independent variables should differ among the cases. In this comparison, Côte d'Ivoire and Thailand differ primarily in whether their governments sought to incorporate key interest groups in a reform bargain that struck at the privileged positions of clientelist leaders.

Côte d'Ivoire

Once one of Africa's success stories, Côte d'Ivoire has recently slid from the category of "middle income countries" in the World Bank's classification system to "lower income countries." Although the country has some off-shore oil fields, its gross domestic product and its foreign exchange revenues come largely from production of primary agricultural commodities, including coffee, cocoa, cotton, rubber, bananas, and pineapples. In the first years of the post-independence period, the government created a number of barriers to open market competition, including a stabilization fund to buffer farmers from fluctuations in world prices; tariff and nontariff barriers to insulate domestic infant industries from competition of imports; tax exemptions, tax holidays, and preferential interest rates for priority sectors; laws to prevent hiring, firing, or salary reductions for workers; and government equity participation in a wide variety of enterprises. These policies resulted in widespread inefficiencies and steadily declining international competitiveness (Poulin 1993).

By the mid-1970s, the signs of strain were already apparent. Economic growth slowed through the 1970s and 1980s. The effectiveness of government declined. For example, Côte d'Ivoire has spent and continues to spend more on health and education per capita than any other country in West Africa, but key social indicators lag behind those for many African countries with lower GDPs, and they continue to decline (Poulin 1993, 9). Some studies suggest, too, that corruption is rampant. In a study of transportation costs, exaction of "tolls" by police and military officials along the roadways and rail systems in Côte d'Ivoire was found to exceed levels in other West African countries studied, including Nigeria (Holtzman and Kulibaba 1992). Although the government engaged the services of a Swiss firm to oversee its administration, customs remains the site of considerable rent-seeking activity.

By the end of 1987, the government of Côte d'Ivoire and the country's principal donors, including the World Bank, had settled on a plan for medium-term structural adjustment. The plan included five main components: liberalization of agricultural export pricing and marketing; balancing the budget, mainly through reductions in the public wage bill and improved public sector management; elimination of nontariff barriers and associated internal price controls, reducing the level and range of tariffs; liberalizing the labor market; restructuring and privatizing public enterprises; and reforming the financial system. A special medium-term program to liberalize agricultural marketing and improve its management was developed in tandem with these proposals (Lewis 1993).

The government moved very slowly on the program, first seeking to reduce or eliminate nontariff barriers in 1987 and then backing off of that reform and most others until the 1990s.[4] By mid-1993, except for limited financial sector restructuring and privatization of a few public enterprises, the government had undertaken few of the negotiated changes, and when it did so it did not always adhere to the criteria or forms envisioned in the agreements.

The interests of senior decision makers   The president of Côte d'Ivoire, Félix Houphouët-Boigny, led the country's nationalist movement and has held power since independence. At the time of this writing, he was about ninety years old. The degree to which he backed the effort to reorient Ivoirien economic policy is unclear. In 1990 he created the post of prime minister, to which he appointed Alassane Ouattara, an Ivoirien with roots in Burkina Faso who holds an American economics Ph.D. and who worked for the IMF and the Banque Centrale de l'Afrique de l'Ouest, one of the key institutions of the franc zone, until accepting the president's offer. At the same time, he indicated that his "designated successor" as leader of the Parti Démocratique de Côte d'Ivoire and as interim president in the event of his death would be Henri Konan Bédié, a central figure in the country's clientelist networks over the previous decades. A minister at the time of the infamous investment in sugar refineries in the northern part of the country (in which many millions of dollars went astray), Bédié was a beneficiary of the country's import licensing system and president of the National Assembly.

Ouattara's office became the nerve center of the reform effort but it remained poorly staffed, with a handful of talented young advisers—most paid with the assistance of international foundations and donors in an effort to compensate them at international rates and remove them from the temptations of rent-seeking—and an admixture of representatives from the clientelist networks. Although the office met with business groups and other, emerging associations, it was unable to keep up with the demands on its time or to curtail the rent-seeking practices of the "old regime" that had helped manufacture the economic crisis.

Ouattara could most certainly have returned to positions in the multilateral development organizations at the end of his tenure. Many in Côte d'Ivoire assumed that he was appointed prime minister precisely because he was a man whose skills were transferable and allowed him to leave the country if his reforms did not work or generated political discontent. His Burkinabé origins meant that in the eyes of many he would always remain a stranger, incapable of mounting a bid for political power. Possibly because he sought a greater mandate or base of support for structural adjustment reforms, however, or because he had ambitions no one anticipated, Ouattara quickly appeared to step out of the role of the technocrat and to throw his hat in the ring as a contender for the presidency. Subsequently, Houphouët encouraged the new prime minister to construct a lavish house, divorce his Jamaican wife, who remained in the United States, and marry the president's real estate broker, a French woman. Houphouët's motive may have been to compromise Ouattara's image or to give him greater stature among the clientelist politicians.

Ouattara sought to counter this image and build support for his program by taking his case to "the people." In October 1992 he convened a televised four-hour press conference on the American model, responding to questions from newspaper reporters and citizens from every part of the country's political spectrum. The newspapers carried extensive portions of the discussion, along with commentary, in the days that followed. Bédié and Laurent Gbagbo, the main opposition candidate, followed with their own performances over succeeding weeks, attempting to counter Ouattara's claims. Although the press conferences generated interest and helped educate the elite public, they did little in the short run to help build support for the reform program.

In sum, the motivation for reform among the president and senior elites in the country was limited at best. The country had only one Ivoirien industrialist, Philippe Bambara, the chief officer of Cosmivoire, an agro-processing firm. Other manufacturing enterprises were in the hands of French and Lebanese owners, who dominated the country's business organizations. The members of the country's clientelist networks were invested most heavily in the export of agricultural products from the country (not in their production, in most cases) or in import enterprises. The president himself had diversified his assets and sent considerable capital overseas. Absent individual incentives to improve the economic environment for export-oriented manufacturing, the motive for reform rested in the hands of a very small group of technocrats whose presidential backing remained uncertain. Moreover, their own long-term interests evidently lay as much at home as in the international arena.

Clientelist networks, interest groups, and interest intermediation The major opponents of reform are the "barons" of the Houphouët-Boigny government, or, in local terms, *les pouvoirs en place*. In the clientelist political system of the period 1960–1990, the economic policies the country pursued reflected the preponderant influence of individual political or business figures, who mobilized support for their personal interests through political machines. The president encouraged this behavior, extending legal recognition to "horizontal" associations or interest groups only to the degree that these could be attached to or subsumed under the wing of the sole political party, the Parti Démocratique de Côte d'Ivoire (PDCI), which was itself primarily organized through ethnic committees and cells at the local level. Many members of the elite benefited financially from privileged access to rent-seeking opportunities. Mme. Therese Houphouët-Boigny has long exacted a charge for each bag of rice imported into the country, by way of her access to the Caisse de Pérequation, and she is suspected of engaging in similar skimming in the wheat trade.[5] In the early 1980s, such personal politics subverted privatization of public enterprises in Côte d'Ivoire. In 1987, protests from the well-connected, largely foreign-owned textile industry prevented elimination of nontariff barriers. Several prominent individuals currently benefit from policy distortions and are likely to mobilize their clients in the National Assembly or in institutions such as the customs service to block reform.

The character of the political system is changing, however. In 1990 the government extended legal recognition to opposition parties and sponsored the country's first multiparty elections in what was generally considered a preemptive move. Since that time, multipartyism has become "multi-syndicalisme." Unions and associations have proliferated, and economic interest groups are beginning to mobilize. Instead of a highly centralized, corporatist union structure in which the government maintained control over the activities of associations, in part through the PDCI and in part through the official labor federation, the Union Genéral des Travailleurs de Côte d'Ivoire (UGTCI), there are now multiple unions in most sectors, some autonomous from political parties and others not. The most powerful of the autonomous unions have banded together in the Féderation des Syndicats Autonomes de Côte d'Ivoire (FESACI), a group that encompasses public sector doctors, radio and television reporters, many energy sector engineers and workers, the most vocal of the university teachers, computer programmers and specialists, the bus drivers who work within Abidjan, and others. Business has formed multiple syndicates, too, most of which are grouped together either in the Union Patronal de Côte d'Ivoire (UPACI), the Mouvement des Petits et Moyennes Entreprises (MPME), or the Club des Hommes d'Affaires Franco-Ivoiriens. Personal politics and interest group politics now compete for influence in Côte d'Ivoire, creating new kinds of opportunities and new kinds of obstacles for the reform of the economy.

None of these groups is monolithically opposed to structural adjustment reforms. Although some parts of the program have greater and broader support than others, it is simply not the case that the pressures of "mass demands" or "popular demands" are the source of the government's hesitance to act on the reforms.

In the industrial democracies, the demands of interest groups are mediated through national assemblies and institutions designed to facilitate compromises and long-term negotiations among government, business, and labor. Like many countries in Africa, Côte d'Ivoire has a new union movement but none of the institutions for interest intermediation. This institutional lacuna has made securing acceptance of reform more difficult here than in the many other regions of the world.

Ironically, although opposition political parties are now legal, most have little or no contact with important interest groups, several of which participated in street demonstrations in early 1990 and helped force the move to a multiparty system. This seeming paradox has its root in a lack of any perceived imperative to consult with these groups, instilled by a long history of clientelist rule and by the reluctance of the unions themselves, many of whose leaders and members do not consider the parties credible agents for channeling, articulating, or aggregating interests. Because of this (and also because it still operates under tight restrictions and under the surveillance of clientelist politicians), the national assembly also cannot be counted as an institution for interest intermediation.

Further, only the Prime Minister's office, with its small staff of twenty-five, plays a significant role in trying to mediate conflicting demands in the policy process, and it does not encourage contact between groups in different sectors. Currently, there is no real forum in which interest group leaders can make their views known to one another and negotiate over demands. The occasional "Days of Dialogue" the president convenes are an occasion for controlled airing of grievances in the style of the French *cahiers de doléances,* but they provide no opportunity for groups to negotiate the terms of reform.

Most interest groups, newly formed and with relatively little access to information or to contact with each other, have not had to evaluate the opportunity costs associated with the demands they make. The government long controlled access to information tightly, sanctioning only government-produced newspapers, radio, and television. When single-party rule gave way to multiparty rule in 1990, alternative newspapers appeared on the city streets, but like the new political parties few have thought to feature and communicate the views of interest associations. Although there are three labor federations now active in the country, along with several, somewhat older business lobbies, most syndicats frame their objectives and programs with little or no information about the economic effects of different alternatives or the concerns of other Ivoirien citizens.

As a result of the deficit of information and forums for negotiation, the programs of some of the syndicats, new and old, reflect little consideration of the costs and benefits associated with different courses of action when the behavior of other groups is taken into account. Lack of information and absence of a forum in which demands can be measured and bartered against those of other groups creates a rigidity in the positions pursued that does not accurately capture the attitudes and ideas of either the members or the leaders.

The problem of trust In common with many other African countries, Côte d'Ivoire is caught in a crisis of confidence in the public sector, too. Although urban interest groups are generally agreed on the need for some reforms, especially those designed to improve the quality of public sector management, few currently have enough faith in government leaders to accept short-term sacrifices for longer-term gain. Lack of confidence of the governed in the intentions and abilities of the governors is perhaps the major obstacle to reform. This skepticism about the ability of the governors to implement reforms efficiently and fairly does not yet amount to rejection of all current political leaders or of a role for government in the economy. At the time, officers of most of the urban interest groups indicated that one or more of the senior officials with whom they regularly had contact took their concerns seriously.

This lack of trust has three main components. First, there is a deep, shared fear that a few of the most powerful politicians continue to pursue their individual interests at the expense of other Ivoiriens. The absence of transparency surrounding some of the sales of public companies fueled this perception. Second, the absence of information that would allow groups to monitor government behavior in their sectors and to follow changes in the economy was also an important source of insecurity. All of the interest groups the author interviewed in Côte d'Ivoire during this period placed a high priority on the creation of a *banque des données,* to which all members of the public could have access. Third, several interest group leaders believed that the level of malfeasance among lower-level civil servants had risen to such levels that even if senior officials chose to implement well-conceived reforms, they would lack the capacity to do so. Customs officials came in for particular criticism from producers' groups in this regard.

In sum, in the Ivoirien case, although "horizontal" interest associations and less organized civic groups had emerged in the country and could potentially be tapped to counter the power of the older clientelist networks, there were few officials with an interest in constructing a reform bargain, few institutions for interest intermediation, and very little public confidence that the government could or would bargain in good faith, although some members of the prime minister's office were considered reliable. Without these elements, a serious reform effort could not occur.

Ghana

If Côte d'Ivoire is a case in which reform is imperiled, Ghana is an example of reform enacted—although not always with the consequences anticipated. In Ghana, as elsewhere, economic crisis brought the question of reform to the fore, as it had several times in the country's history. By 1982–1983, official mismanagement and corruption had so reduced the pool of rents available for division that it was no longer possible to use patronage and spoils to hold the state and society together. Leith and Lofchie (1993, 226) have suggested that "the extreme to which the Ghanaian policy-induced atrophy took the economy, beyond any kind of political optimum, was the outcome of a set of political institutions which permitted a 'tragedy of the commons' to emerge. In the end, the economy and the state hit bottom."

Leith and Lofchie (1993, 260–61) ascribe the about-face that followed the 1983 Rawlings coup to several factors. First, there were multiple problems that intensified the crisis in which Ghanaians found themselves. These included food shortages that stemmed from the collapse of transport, forest fires in some of the cocoa areas, the murders of a series of high court judges, the expulsion of large numbers of migrant Ghanaians from Nigeria, and two failed coup attempts against Ghanaian governments. Second, the rents were exhausted. The economy was in such a state of decline that no one could afford to pay off public officials and the government could no longer afford to dole out patronage positions. Third, the second Rawlings coup had wide popular support for its effort to supplant an ineffectual civilian regime.

Throughout Africa, the relationship between "crisis" and adoption of reform is weak, however. There are other conditions present in Ghana but not in the Côte d'Ivoire that may explain the differences in reform politics.

First, the group of people who would lose from adjustment in the short run in Côte d'Ivoire was larger than it was in Ghana. As one of the country's earlier "success stories," Côte d'Ivoire had a large nascent, urban middle class that would see prices of imported consumer goods rise with devaluation and see disposable incomes fall through layoffs, possible wage reductions, or increased taxation. Although most of the groups whose members belonged to this class saw a need for reform, they were alarmed by the government's exclusion of their views from the design of a program. Although not democratic, the institutions set up by Rawlings, by contrast, did provide for substantial interest representation. Rawlings made widespread use of the device of the Presidential Commission, and these committees, when constituted, moved about the country to hold hearings on critical issues. Members of parliament were able to ask pointed questions of government representatives and availed themselves of this opportunity frequently. A tripartite National Employment Manpower and Incomes Council provided a forum for negotiating incomes policies. District Assemblies were created to air views at the local level. Moreover, Rawlings showed much greater respect than his predecessors for the office of the chieftancy and consulted at the local level through this network as well.[6]

Second, in Ghana, both Rawlings and some senior technocrats had strong incentives to see the reforms implemented. Rawlings owed much of his political support to rural Ghanaians, who stood to benefit from the reforms. Indeed, when the country held elections, Rawlings won heavily in rural parts of the country. Second, there was a technopol motivated to maintain his ties with the international development community. Joe Abbey, a key designer of the Economic Recovery Program, had long maintained good relations with the International Monetary Fund and the World Bank and could certainly look to employment there in the future if he left Ghana with his professional credentials as an economist intact.

Thailand

Recent analyses of the success of structural adjustment reforms in Thailand suggest important contrasts with the Ivoirien case. This discussion draws heavily on the excellent research by Doner and Laothamatas (1992). Although they did not intend to profile the three independent variables, the evidence available in their careful analysis of Thai economic reform suggests that the basis of a reform bargain existed in the Thai case, and key elements of the structural adjustment package were implemented.

As in Côte d'Ivoire, agricultural occupations in Thailand account for a relatively high share of overall employment. Movement of labor out of agriculture in Thailand has been relatively slow compared with countries like

Korea and Taiwan, dropping from 78.9 percent in 1971 to 67.1 percent in 1986 (World Bank 1991, 16). Given the share of agriculture in GDP, Thailand employs proportionately more people in agriculture than Indonesia or Thailand. Côte d'Ivoire and Thailand produce many of the same agricultural export commodities, and there are high levels of rent-seeking by officials in both places. One of the main differences between the two countries is that Côte d'Ivoire is a member of the franc zone and thus has no ability to devalue its currency, whereas Thailand is under no such restriction. Thailand undertook reforms in the early 1980s in response to a growing economic crisis and continued these through most of the decade. In a manner quite different from that of Côte d'Ivoire, the Thai reforms were accompanied by compensatory measures" (Doner 1991, 26–27). Manipulation of the fears that the military and political parties had of each other also supported the reform effort.

The interests of senior decision makers In the mid-1980s, the Thai prime minister, Prem Tinasulanond, was under considerable external pressure to address the problems of the Thai economy. Indeed, further assistance depended on action.

Prem was an outsider acceptable to the military and the major parties, which feared military intervention. He had substantial backing from the king and the palace. Thus, unlike Alassane Ouattara a few years later, he had a political base at the time of economic reform.

In contrast to Côte d'Ivoire, the Thai reform program had fairly unequivocal backing from the top. Further, a much larger cadre of often Western-trained economists was available to monitor the reform process and conduct the implementation of the reforms than was the case in Côte d'Ivoire. The technocrats maintained their authority under successive prime ministers and actually implemented many of the reforms initiated under Prem in 1988, when Chartchai Choonavan was elected.

Prem created several new organizations to facilitate formulation of policy and implementation of reform measures. One of these was charged with monitoring the reform process. The most important body was the "economic cabinet" or "council of economic ministers," headed by Prem. This group could make decisions that bound members of the full cabinet (Doner and Laothamatas 1992, 43–44). Doner and Laothamatas report that the economists on this council acted very much as the technopols Dominguez has identified in Latin America. "The reform was . . . led by what may be best understood as technocratic-oriented political leadership," they note.

"The non-party members reportedly went to great lengths to persuade and, if necessary, compromise with party-based cabinet members. . . . Compromise was further facilitated by the lack of an entrenched ISI force in the private sector and in the cabinet."

The reforms had several components. The government devalued the baht twice in 1981 and again in 1984, after which it tied the baht to a basket of currencies instead of to the U.S. dollar, depreciating the currency in this way by over 20 percent between 1985 and the end of 1987. The government undertook limited privatization of public enterprise, although it failed to act on many of the parastatals slated for sale. The reformers also made some progress in reducing use of nontariff barriers, although it failed to implement significant trade liberalization because of its heavy dependence on import taxes for government revenue (Doner and Laothamatas 1992, 20). The government also engaged in liberalization in marketing of agricultural exports, measures to increase the efficiency of key industrial sectors, and banking sector reform.

Clientelist networks, interest groups, and interest intermediation Like many of its Southeast Asian counterparts, the character of Thai politics was a mix of clientelism and interest group competition. Thailand had long had a reputation for "patrimonial rule." Clientelist networks were important in structuring political life. Noncompetitive rent-seeking was often extensive. At the same time, Thai politics had undergone some important changes. In 1973, the countryside mobilized in new forms of organization, new political parties emerged, and the House of Representatives acquired the power to call a no-confidence vote. Although some of these new rules and institutions disappeared at the time of the 1976 military coup, the basis for participation in politics through horizontal associations endured. Relatively new trade associations and representatives of the government began to meet through Joint Public and Private Sector Consultative Committees (JPPCCs) (Laothamatas 1992).

When the structural adjustment reforms were introduced, they met with considerable opposition. Doner (1991) remarks that the political parties came out against "sectoral liberalization," while segments of the military and business communities opposed the 1987 devaluation. There were coup attempts in 1981 and 1985, and elections occurred in 1983, 1986, and 1988.

Doner and Laothamatas (1992, 33) write that both manipulation of perceptions and compensation tactics enabled different parties to agree on a medium-term compromise. "By playing off the [military and political parties] . . . against each other, by utilizing their fear of each other, and by capitalizing on the desire of each force to have him lead the regime, Prem was able to protect his pro-adjustment cabinet ministers and senior technocrats from those hurt by adjustment."

The "bargain" the Prem government struck with constituents had several key components. Doner and Laothamatas (1992, 26–27) write that "one type of compensation involved transfers to those adversely affected by reform measures, especially devaluation. . . . A second type of compensation, most apparent after the mid-1986 election, involved modest, general spending to weaken political pressures for stimulation." They included, further, the maintenance of funds for rural development. They were carefully sequenced to have specific distributional effects. Finally, "the general combination of sequencing and positive incentives for trade reform operated as an indirect but highly effective form of compensation." The government sidestepped elimination of protection. Although the reforms left some of the sector-specific problems unattended, such as protection of particular industries, it succeeded in building a political base for remedying macroeconomic problems. In short, by tolerating the formation of "horizontal" associations and seeking to address or preempt their concerns, as well as by creating institutions in the government that forced technocrats and party representatives to negotiate, the Prem government was able to constitute a "reform bargain."

Prem was able to negotiate this deal in part because economic groups were already mobilized, but even more significantly because institutions for limited interest intermediation already existed. As in Côte d'Ivoire, the political parties were largely clientelist organizations with few ties to economic interest groups, including business and labor, and no clear policy positions. Prem expanded the number of ministerial posts in some of the ministries that provided opportunities for pork barrel politics (mainly Commerce, Agriculture, and Industry) and gave positions in these to members of the different parties, purchasing their support. In return, the parties surrendered their voice over fiscal and monetary policy and had to accept reforms that hurt their constituents. Neither of the two houses of the legislature could initiate money bills or approve projects (Doner and Laothamatas 1992, 31).

The economic interest groups best positioned to block reform were the business factions. Some favored an export-oriented strategy and supported the government on that ground. Others feared military rule and were brought warily into a broad coalition. The major peak associations included representatives of both import-substitution industries and export-oriented manufacturing and therefore developed no cohesive position on the government's reform proposals. Prem reached out to consult all of these groups, but he also played on their internal divisions.

Although labor did take to the streets to protest some of the reforms, the compensatory measures in the "bargain" defused severe conflict. Doner and Laothamatas (1992, 26–27) note particularly the government's modest increase in the minimum wage and monitoring of price increases after devaluation. Further, a substantial proportion of Thai labor secured opportunities for work overseas in this period. Foreign labor demand created a safety valve in Thai society that most African countries do not share.

The problem of trust Prem built trust in his leadership in a number of different ways. He played up his role as a defender and promoter of democracy, which bought him the support of the parties and those segments of society that feared the consequences of a military takeover. He did so by giving the parties more cabinet positions than they had received before, by opposing the efforts of the military in 1983 to revise the constitution in a manner that curtailed participation, and simply by persisting in office despite multiple coup attempts.

Indonesia

If there is some evidence that the explanation of reform articulated here works in Thailand, does it account for the other Southeast Asian successes? Lack of systematic evidence stands in the way of strong conclusions. In the community of development economists and aid agencies, it is the case of Indonesia that appears discordant. Unlike the Philippines and many African countries, Indonesia has experienced significant rates of economic growth. Its government is widely considered less tolerant of divergent views within the ranks of elites and of association among its citizens. The prevailing view is that Indonesia was able to enact reforms in the early and mid-1980s because the military listened to the country's technocrats, believed that rents would decline if the country continued to have a high-cost economy, and acted on that basis. A review of the evidence suggests a number of other alternative hypotheses, too, but the evidence currently available leaves standing the notion that adoption of reform required a bargain with opponents and new kinds of allies.

The early 1980s were a period of crisis. In 1977 voters in Jakarta had dealt a defeat to the GOLKAR government. Although the loss in the capital was inconsequential in one sense, given the party's massive victory in other areas,

it did signal a weakening of the government's hold over the popular imag-
ination. Throughout the campaign in 1977 and again in the electoral contest
of 1982, popular dissatisfaction with elite corruption was a topic for frequent
public discussion. In May 1980 fifty prominent community figures had
petitioned Parliament to review some of Suharto's speeches, referring to his
statements about socialism and nationalism as values of a past era and
inappropriate for contemporary Indonesia (Cribb 1984, 657). This action
developed during the 1980s into an upsurge of political debate, termed
keterbukaan, or "openness" (MacIntyre 1989). With the collapse of oil prices
and reduction in OPEC members' production quotas at the beginning of the
1980s and in the context described, the government moved in 1984 to
devalue the currency by 15 percent, reschedule major investment projects,
liberalize banking sector policy, simplify investment and export procedures,
reform the tax structure, and revise customs.

The reigning explanation among students of Indonesia is that technocrats
gain power during crises. Booth (1992, 2) has reported senior Indonesian
officials as saying "that the end of the oil boom was a 'blessing in disguise'
for the Indonesian economy in that it created a political climate which
allowed them to implement broad-ranging economic reforms." Many others
share this view (Robison 1987). Yet regimes in the Philippines and many
governments in Africa have found themselves in similar circumstances without the inclination or capacity to shift course. Crisis may be a necessary
condition for reform in the context of rent-seeking, but it is not sufficient.

There are a number of alternative understandings, some of which have
been discussed but not explored through research and writing. One possibility is that the technocrats secured acceptance for their ideas at least in part
because they had nationalist credentials. It is also possible that Indonesia's
military and the technocrats who advised them had longer time horizons
than counterparts in African contexts. That difference in time horizon may
well have made the benefit streams generated by reform appear to exceed the
short-term costs to the men at the helm in Jakarta. There are African leaders
who have long held power, however, and yet reform has proven difficult in
their countries. Côte d'Ivoire, where Houphouët-Boigny has held power
since independence, is a case in point. Moreover, for much of his time in
power, Ferdinand Marcos led a government few would have called highly
unstable. The length of the time horizon does make a difference for whether
reform takes place, but perceptions of time can be manipulated by shrewd
politicians; those perceptions need not derive from a long history of stability.

The growth of conglomerates may also contribute to making reform possible. Owners of conglomerates derive their earnings from a portfolio of subsidiaries in different sectors and thus have diverse interests, as do those who work in individual companies. That means that they are more concerned about the overall health of the economy than they might be otherwise. Not only did such conglomerates develop in Indonesia at about the time of some of the reform efforts, but also some of these conglomerates were very close to the president.

An alternative view is that there were no "tough cases" in Indonesia. When the first reforms occurred they did not drive anyone out of business. They did not remove protection; instead, they insulated exporters from costs of protection by giving access to imports at world market prices. Where it looked as though they might drive some to bankruptcy, the reforms did not take place and reform bargains were unnecessary. The example of the benefits that flowed from the earlier reform of Pertamina, the state oil company, provided reassurance that although reform was not painless, it could provide medium- and long-term benefits, too.

Although some of the proposals were relatively costless, while others that did injure key constituents never made it onto the agenda, some steps were bound to create resentment, and there is limited evidence of bargains struck in those cases.

One example is the effort to clean up customs facilities. In 1984 Finance Minister Radius Prawiro took charge of the warehouses; kept customs officials in their jobs but banned them from the port; and installed the Société Générale de Surveillance (SGS), the same Swiss firm the Ivoirian government later employed, to take over the customs inspection and tariff assessment.

There were several reasons for the agreement to reform customs. Military and the technocrats had interests in common. The military thought that corruption at customs would reduce growth and therefore diminish the amount that other forms of rent-seeking would yield. Customs was the site of extensive corruption, which rendered imports more expensive than they would be otherwise and made non-oil exports less competitive. With the collapse of oil prices in the early 1980s, it became extremely important for Indonesia to promote its non-oil exports. The value of customs agents as political clients diminished relative to the value of making these exports more competitive. The contribution of Suharto was to convince the military that its interests lay in cleaning up the activities from which at least some of its officers benefited. Thus there was a reform bargain, but it took place between Suharto and the military against the customs officials.

There were at least two other reasons why the cleanup of customs occurred, despite some political cost (Robison 1987, 33). Customs was highly
visible to the country's aid donors, who encountered the corruption at the
port facility directly because they moved their own supplies through this
system. Moreover, the president's family had started to become involved in
business at this stage, and members received an object lesson in the costs the
system imposed. By contrast, in Côte d'Ivoire, where the port facilities are
also the locus of considerable nonproductive rent-seeking, donors encounter
the same kinds of problems, but government will was lacking. That may be
because the country has fewer exports currently that could compete successfully in the international marketplace. Further, senior politicians benefit
from the elaborate system of import licenses and the rent-seeking opportunities they create; they do not encounter the same difficulties of which other
businesses complain.

One way in which the government has sought to build reform bargains in
opposition to the interests of a few senior politicians or members of the
military is to cultivate general acceptance of the changes through the press,
so that the beneficiaries of protection or special privilege risk appearing
unpatriotic if they object or sabotage the outcome. In this case, the government sought to create public and civil service support for reform by producing buttons, shirts, and bumper stickers sporting the slogan, "I love
taxpayers."

Liddle (1987, 209) has suggested that the ability of technocrats inside
government to find a technical audience outside government may have
provided the beginnings of a coalition for reform in 1986–1987. He points
to the way in which the term "high-cost economy"—a euphemism for
protectionism, bureaucratic red tape, and corruption—began to diffuse into
everyday conversation as a result of the technocrats' lobbying efforts and
efforts to generate public exposure for their views. The diffusion of these
ideas helped forge a consensus among economists in and outside government
that the proliferation of import licenses and quotas was the main source of
Indonesia's economic ills.

Robison (1992, 67) has remarked that "the transition from ISI [in In-
donesia] has also been accompanied by changes in the political relations
between state and capital and away from those characterized by networks of
patronage linking particular firms with particular political factions and leaders, towards relationships which increasingly institutionalized the general
interests of capital and its various factions." He adds, "Just as the LDP in
Japan has long been a brokering house for the various and often competing

elements of Japanese capital in their attempts to influence state policy, so too have the capitalist classes of Taiwan, South Korea, and Thailand begun to focus their energies on state policy, often through political parties." Indonesia is beginning this process too, he remarks. The evidence presented above, although anecdotal, suggests that it is not "interest associations" and mediation of their demands through various forums for negotiation that explain outcomes in Indonesia at this point, but that the Suharto government has used more informal groupings and even the divergent interests of different rent-seeking elites to negotiate political space for the technocrats and their policies.

Conclusions

This chapter argues that reform bargains are essential to the reorientation of economic policy toward export-oriented manufacturing and to sound macroeconomic management, both of which require compromises that endure over time among key social groups. Without such a bargain, a renegotiated "social contract," reform is unlikely to occur, even in societies where governments are in a position to repress dissent outside their ranks.

Reforms and bargains are supported by three conditions. First, the countries' chief decision makers must either have a long-term personal stake in improving the economic environment for export-oriented manufacturing or include technocrats with transferable skills who can afford to be oblivious to the way their actions alienate key elements of their own societies. That is, there must be motivation to engage in reform. Second, horizontal associations must have evolved and a country must possess formal or informal institutions for interest intermediation. That is, a reform bargain pits clientelist networks and broad economic interests against one another. It requires a forum in which compromises can be effected among these different groups. Third, to negotiate effectively senior decision makers must either be perceived to be trustworthy or they must create mechanisms for assuring others of their credibility.

Where one or more of these conditions is missing, the prospects for reform are dim. The chapter argues that whereas Southeast Asian governments have succeeded in meeting these conditions, albeit often in a minimal, sporadic, and halting fashion, most of their African counterparts have not, with the major exception of Botswana and the possible exception of post-1983 Ghana.

The chapter represents only a first step in developing a better understanding of the differences in economic policy choices within Southeast Asia and Africa and between the two regions, however. A real test of the explanation offered requires data collection from a broader set of countries, with an effort to secure information about each of the three main explanatory variables.

NOTES

The author would like to thank Glenn Jenkins, Clark Leith, David Lindauer, Michael Roemer, Peter Timmer, Thomas Tomich, and Louis Wells for the helpful comments and challenges they provided and their collective effort to think about the Indonesian case. Errors of interpretation are those of the author alone.

1. Although sound macroeconomic management is not technically a reform in most cases, its insulation from popular and elite pressures results from the same kind of bargaining in process.

2. For alternative ways of organizing the theoretical debates within this field, see Bowie (1991) and Doner (1991).

3. Leith and Lofchie (1993, 257) suggest that the "political discount rate" attached to rent-seeking might increase when the future seems to portend political instability, but also when the locus of rent-seeking lies with people who have alternative sources of income in the long term. In conditions of relative political stability, then, when the locus of rent-seeking is within the state, rent protection is a more likely outcome than when rent-seeking is outside the state.

4. The textile industry blocked the changes. Côte d'Ivoire has a number of firms in which the government or Ivoirien interests hold equity, along with French and other foreign investors. These firms have received protection for extended periods and are unable to compete effectively with Asian-produced textiles.

5. Côte d'Ivoire purchases both of these crops at about $250 per ton. The mills that process them pay $500 per ton after off-loading from freighters. The 100 percent markup in price in part reflects rent-seeking by important figures of the PDCI and of Houphouët-Boigny's inner circle.

6. I owe these observations and others on Ghana to Clark Leith, personal communication, March 1, 1993.

BIBLIOGRAPHY

Anderson, Benedict. 1983. "Old State, New Society: Indonesia's New Order in Comparative Historical Perspective." *Journal of Asian Studies* 43: 477–96.

Anderson, Benedict, and A. Kahir, eds. 1982. *Interpreting Indonesian Politics: Thirteen Contributions to the Debate.* Ithaca, N.Y.: Cornell Indonesia Project.

Barraclough, Simon. 1984. "Political Participation and Its Regulation in Malaysia: Opposition to the Societies (Amendment) Act of 1981." *Pacific Affairs* 57: 450–61.

Bates, Robert, and Anne Krueger. 1993. "Generalizations Arising from the Country Studies." In *Political and Economic Interactions in Economic Policy Reform,* ed. Robert Bates and Anne Krueger, 444–71. Cambridge, Mass.: Blackwell.

Booth, Anne. 1988. *Agricultural Development in Indonesia.* Sydney: Asian Studies Association of Australia with Allen and Unwin.

Booth, Anne, ed. 1992. *The Oil Boom and After: Indonesian Economic Policy and Performance in the Soeharto Era.* Oxford: Oxford University Press.

Bourchier, David. 1984. *Dynamics of Dissent in Indonesia.* Ithaca, N.Y.: Cornell Modern Indonesia Project.

Bowie, Alisadair. 1991. *Crossing the Industrial Divide: State, Society, and the Politics of Economic Transformation in Malaysia.* New York: Columbia University Press.

Callaghy, Thomas. 1990. "Lost Between State and Market: The Politics of Economic Adjustment in Ghana, Zambia, and Nigeria." In *The Politics of Economic Adjustment in the Third World,* ed. Joan Nelson, 257–320. Princeton, N.J.: Princeton University Press.

Chan, Heng Chee. 1975. "Politics in an Administrative State: Where Has the Politics Gone?" In *Trends in Singapore,* ed. Chee Meow Seah, 51–60. Singapore: Institute of Southeast Asia Studies.

Cribb, Robert. 1984. "Elections in Indonesia." *Asian Survey* 24(6): 655–64.

Crone, Donald K. 1988. "State, Social Elites, and Government Capacity in Southeast Asia." *World Politics* 15: 252–68.

Crouch, Harold. 1985. *Economic Change, Social Structure and the Political System in Southeast Asia: Philippine Development Compared With the Other ASEAN Countries.* Singapore: Institute of Southeast Asian Studies.

———. 1979. "Patrimonialism and Military Rule in Indonesia." *World Politics* 31: 571–87.

Dominguez, Jorge. 1993. "Technopols: Ideas, Leaders, and Their Impact on Freeing Politics and Freeing Markets in Major Latin American Countries in the 1980s and 1990s." Paper prepared for the Harvard University Workshop on Technopols in Latin America, April 16.

Doner, Richard F. 1991. "Approaches to the Politics of Economic Growth in Southeast Asia." *Journal of Southeast Asian Studies* 50(4): 818–49.

Doner, Richard F., and Anek Laothamatas. 1992. "The Political Economy of Structural Adjustment in Thailand." Draft Paper prepared for the World Bank Project on the Political Economy of Structural Adjustment in New Democracies.

Feeney, David. 1982. *The Political Economy of Productivity: Thai Agricultural Development 1880–1975.* Vancouver: University of British Columbia Press.

Gereffi, Gary, and Donald L. Wyman. 1990. *Manufacturing Miracles: Paths of Industrialization in Latin America and East Asia.* Princeton: Princeton University Press.

Gray, Cheryl W. 1991. "Legal Process and Economic Development: A Case Study of Indonesia." *World Development* 19(7): 763–78.

Hewison, Kevin. 1987. "National Interests and Economic Downturn: Thailand." In *Southeast Asia in the 1980s: The Politics of Economic Crisis,* ed. Richard Robison, Kevin Hewison, and Richard Higgott, 52–79. Boston: Allen and Unwin.

Holtzman, John S., and Nicolas P. Kulibaba. 1992. *Livestock Marketing and Trade in the Central Corridor of West Africa.* Report prepared for the United States Agency for International Development, Sahel West Africa Office, Africa Bureau. Washington, D.C.: Abt Associates.

Huntington, Samuel. 1968. *Political Order in Changing Societies.* New Haven: Yale University Press.

Hutchcroft, Paul D. 1993. "Booty Capitalism: An Analysis of Government-Business Relations in the Philippines." Manuscript.

———. 1991. "Oligarchs and Cronies in the Philippine State: The Politics of Patrimonial Plunder." *World Politics* 43(3): 414–50.

Jomo, K.S. 1990–91. "Whither Malaysia's New Economic Policy?" *Pacific Affairs* 63(4): 469–99.

Laothamatas, Anek. 1992. *Business Associations and the New Political Economy of Thailand: From Bureaucratic Polity to Liberal Corporatism.* Boulder, Colo.: Westview Press and the Institute of Southeast Asian Studies.

Leith, J. Clark, and Michael F. Lofchie. 1993. "The Political Economy of Structural Adjustment in Ghana." In *Political and Economic Interactions in Economic Policy Reform Programs: Evidence from Eight Countries,* ed. Robert Bates and Anne Krueger. Cambridge, Mass.: Basil Blackwell.

Lewis, Barbara. 1993. "Is There a Rural Constituency for Structural Adjustment in Côte d'Ivoire?" In *Interest Groups and Medium-Term Structural Adjustment in Côte d'Ivoire,* ed. Jennifer A. Widner, Roger J. Poulin, and Barbara C. Lewis. Report prepared for the United States Agency for International Development. Abidjan: REDSO.

Liddle, R. William. 1985. "Suharto's Indonesia: Personal Rule and Political Institutions." *Pacific Affairs* 58: 68–90.

———. 1991. "The Relative Autonomy of the Third World Politician: Soeharto and Indonesian Economic Development in Comparative Perspective." *International Studies Quarterly* 35(4): 403–27.

———. 1987. "The Politics of Shared Growth: Some Indonesian Cases." *Comparative Politics* 19(2): 127–46.

———. 1992. "The Politics of Development Policy." *World Development* 20(6): 793–807.

Lindenberg, Marc, and Shantayanan Devarajan. 1993. "Prescribing Strong Economic Medicine: Revisiting the Myths About Structural Adjustment, Democracy, and Economic Performance in Developing Countries." *Comparative Politics* 25(2): 169–82.

Macintyre, Andrew. 1990. *Business and Politics in Indonesia.* Sydney: Asian Studies Association of Australia with Allen and Unwin.

———. 1989. "Political Control and Political Change under the New Order." Discussion paper prepared for "Conference on Indonesia's New Order: Past, Present, and Future," Australian National University, December 4–9.

Mackie, J.A.C. 1988. "Economic Growth in the ASEAN Region: The Political Underpinnings." In *Achieving Industrialization in East Asia,* ed. Helen Hughes, 283–327. Cambridge: Cambridge University Press.

McVey, Ruth. 1992. "The Materialization of the Southeast Asian Entrepreneur." In *Southeast Asian Capitalists,* ed. Ruth McVey, 7–34. Ithaca, N.Y.: Cornell University.

Moon, Chung-In. 1988. "The Demise of a Developmentalist State? The Politics of Stabilization and Structural Adjustment." *Journal of Development Studies* 4: 67–84.

Perkins, Dwight H., and Michael Roemer. 1993. "What is Asia's Legacy for Africa?" In *Lessons for Africa from Asian Development,* ed. Dwight H. Perkins and Michael Roemer. Draft, February.

Pharr, Susan J. 1990. *Losing Face: Status Politics in Japan.* Berkeley: University of California Press.

Pletcher, James. 1990. "Public Interventions in Agricultural Markets in Malaysia: Rice and Palm Oil." *Modern Asian Studies* 24(2): 323–40.

Poulin, Roger J. 1993. "An Overview of the Côte d'Ivoire Structural Adjustment Program." In *Interest Groups and Medium-Term Structural Adjustment in Côte d'Ivoire,* ed. Jennifer A. Widner, Roger J. Poulin, and Barbara C. Lewis. Report prepared for the United States Agency for International Development, January 28. Abidjan: REDSO.

Prizzia, Ross. 1985. *Thailand in Transition: The Role of Oppositional Forces.* Honolulu: University of Hawaii Press.

Radelet, Steven. 1992. "Reform without Revolt: The Political Economy of Economic Reform in The Gambia." *World Development* 20(8): 1087–99.

Robison, Richard. 1986. *Indonesia: The Rise of Capital.* Sydney: Allen and Unwin.

———. 1990. *Power and Economy in Suharto's Indonesia.* Manila: Journal of Contemporary Asia Publishers.

———. 1987. "After the Gold Rush: The Politics of Economic Restructuring in Indonesia in the 1980s." In *Southeast Asia in the 1980s: The Politics of Economic Crisis,* ed. Richard Robison, Kevin Hewison, and Richard Higgott, 16–51. Boston: Allen and Unwin.

———. 1992. "Industrialization and the Economic and Political Development of Capital: The Case of Indonesia." In *Southeast Asian Capitalists,* ed. Ruth McVey. Ithaca, N.Y.: Cornell University.

Scalapino, Robert, Seizaburo Sato, and Jusuf Wanandi. 1990. *Power and Economy in Suharto's Indonesia.* Manila: Journal of Contemporary Asia Publishers.

Suehiro, Akira. 1992. "Capitalist Development in Postwar Thailand: Commercial Bankers, Industrial Elite, and Agribusiness Groups." In *Southeast Asian Capitalists,* ed. Ruth McVey, 35–64. Ithaca, N.Y.: Cornell University.

Wade, Robert. 1990. *Governing the Market: Economic Theory and the Role of Government in East Asian Industrialization.* Princeton, N.J.: Princeton University Press.

———. 1993. "Managing Trade: Taiwan and South Korea as Challenges to Economics and Political Science." *Comparative Politics* 25(2): 147–68.

Widner, Jennifer. 1993. "Interest Groups and the Politics of Structural Adjustment in Côte d'Ivoire." In *Interest Groups and Medium-Term Structural Adjustment in Côte d'Ivoire,* ed. Jennifer A. Widner, Roger J. Poulin, and Barbara C. Lewis. Report prepared for the United States Agency for International Development. Abidjan: REDSO, January 28.

Williamson, John, ed. 1994. *The Political Economy of Policy Reform.* Washington, D.C.: Institute for International Economics.

World Bank. 1991. *Decision and Change in Thailand: Three Studies in Support of the Seventh Plan.* Asia Country Department 2. Washington, D.C.

CHAPTER 4

Macroeconomic Management:
To Finance or Adjust?

Jeffrey D. Lewis and Malcolm F. McPherson

The importance of sound macroeconomic management in fostering strong and sustained economic growth is widely acknowledged. The 1980s were characterized by economic shocks, including sharp swings in oil prices and in interest and exchange rates, and severe drought in Africa. In many countries of Africa and Latin America, these shocks and their consequences, especially the debt crisis and IMF stabilization programs, brought economic growth to a halt. Countries in East and Southeast Asia, however, not only weathered the storms but maintained and even accelerated their economic growth. For the most part during the 1980s, countries that sustained high growth rates had sounder macroeconomic policies than countries that lost their growth momentum.

Many comparisons can be made between macroeconomic management of Asian countries and the countries of Sub-Saharan Africa (SSA). At one extreme, it could be argued that macroeconomic management in any meaningful sense has been absent in SSA. How, for example, could any responsible government allow its external debt situation to deteriorate as dramatically as has occurred in SSA, where it is relatively common for the stock of debt to reach twice the size of GDP? In comparison, Asia's successful economies have rarely let ratios of debt to GDP exceed one-half, and several (such as Korea) have acted forcefully to reduce debt when the servicing burden has become too large.

At the other extreme, apologists for SSA performance argue that African governments have had to cope with a seemingly endless stream of difficulties. From this perspective, terms of trade shocks, droughts, dramatic changes in the international setting, and the weakness of basic institutions in these countries have imposed major (and perhaps insurmountable) challenges to effective economic management in Africa. Implicitly, this line of argument suggests that Asian countries have been luckier or perhaps just better equipped to deal with the adverse external shocks and domestic short-comings.

In support of each of these views there has developed a body of oft-cited "stylized facts." For example, some observers assert that African countries borrowed too much, maintained overvalued exchange rates, financed fiscal deficits through resort to the printing press, and were riddled with corruption and cronyism, whereas Asia borrowed more prudently, maintained an "appropriate" (or even undervalued) exchange rate, pursued conservative fiscal policies, and avoided the worst excesses of a rent-seeking society.

When one turns from rhetoric to reality, it is rapidly apparent that neither of these stylized polar positions provides a satisfactory framework for ana-lyzing the similarities and differences between the two regions. Instead of the absolute standards of the caricatures, one is confronted instead by a continuum of performance. While most African countries failed to grow, Botswana did quite well, as did Mauritius. While exchange rate policy in most African economies was characterized by inconsistency and ad hoc trade and capital controls, for thirty-five years the dozen countries in the two franc zones have remained committed until recently to an exchange rate policy of fixed parity with the French franc and minimal controls on capital flows. While several Asian countries avoided or reined in the worst excesses of rent-seeking associated with trade and industrial policies, both Indonesia and Thailand provide evidence that rent-seeking and growth are not always mutually exclusive. Each regional stylization has exceptions, both positive and negative.

Further muddying the comparison between regions are the variations in development strategy that occurred in most, if not all, of these countries since the mid-1960s. To some extent, these shifts can be attributed to swings in the "prevailing wisdom" of development policy. For example, the evo-lution of trade and industrial policies mirrored the debate over import substitution and export-led expansion that occurred during the period. Al-ternatively, exchange rate regimes in developing countries were affected by the breakdown of the Bretton Woods system of fixed exchange rates char-acteristic of the immediate post-war period. But the shifts of policy within each country were also influenced by country-specific factors. These factors include both the effectiveness of so-called "agencies of restraint," as Collier (1991) has referred to the factors that impose limits on government behavior, as well as the persistence and consistency with which specific policies were pursued.

This chapter examines macroeconomic management and performance in Asia and Africa and attempts to identify ways in which the two regions differ. In doing so, we steer away from the tendency to draw strong lines between the regions. Instead, we argue that the major distinction in economic management in the two regions involves the approach taken to dealing with the internal and external imbalances that emerge in any economy. Policy makers differ in their willingness to *adjust* rather than just *finance* such difficulties. This distinction is illustrated through consideration of four different areas of policy concern: exchange rates, external debt, the budget, and the financial system.

The remainder of this chapter is organized as follows. The second section outlines the basic features of macroeconomic balance and describes how appropriate policies can be used to create those features. The third section presents some economic data on the relative economic performances of countries in the two groups. The fourth section highlights the major differences in policy that were pursued. The fifth section contains concluding observations.

Macroeconomic Objectives and Policies

Central to any program of long-term growth and development is a set of economic policies that achieves *and* maintains internal balance (a sustainable fiscal deficit and savings–investment balance)[1] and external balance (a sustainable current account). In this regard, the historical lessons are explicit. No country has been able to sustain large budget or balance of payments deficits and continue to grow and develop. Although the limits of tolerance have differed across countries, difficulties have always emerged whenever governments attempted to sustain budget deficits that exceeded the growth of national income or committed themselves to future patterns of debt service that increased at rates faster than the sustainable growth of exports. The principal limit, in both cases, has been the debt capacity of the respective governments. That, in turn, is not a fixed quantity but varies according to creditors' perceptions of the sustainability of the government's economic policies and its ability to manage the economy in ways that still promote growth and development.

A virtuous circle does exist. When governments adopt a set of economic policies and pursue management strategies that promote growth and development, they effectively embark on a program that can help achieve and maintain external and internal balance. This approach *simultaneously* expands the country's debt capacity. By contrast, policies and management strategies directed toward objectives other than growth and development eventually generate internal or external imbalances (or both), which in turn lead to a reduction in debt capacity. To remedy the situation, the country has to take measures to transform the economy fundamentally.

No government is so well organized and no country so well endowed that imbalances of some sort do not emerge. From an economic management perspective, the important factor is not the imbalances themselves, or their source, but the government's response. Because resources are limited, all governments face the same choices: they can ignore underlying structural problems and finance the imbalance, or they can adjust their economies. Countries with larger debt capacities have the initial option of relying more heavily on finance than adjustment, whereas countries with smaller debt capacities have fewer degrees of freedom.

Governments in well-managed economies are predisposed toward the removal of imbalances through adjustment; governments in poorly managed economies are predisposed to finance the imbalances. Because the financing option is dynamically unsustainable, the countries that have tended to adjust have regularly outperformed those that have not. In this sense, the commitment by a government to policies that achieve and maintain internal and external balance is both *diagnostic* and *prescriptive*. Countries with those policies grow and develop; countries without them do not.

How does this come about? Consider a situation in which the exchange rate is fixed and the country is holding a "normal" level of foreign exchange reserves. Suppose a government decides to increase its spending. Unless its revenue (from taxes or grants or dividends) rises by an equivalent amount, a deficit emerges. This has to be financed, either by borrowing abroad or by local borrowing. External borrowing directly raises the future debt servicing requirements. Local borrowing expands the monetary base, which, through the normal process of deposit expansion, leads to an expansion of domestic demand. At a fixed exchange rate, the higher level of domestic absorption spills over to imports. Foreign reserves will be drawn down.

If continued, the internal deficit will be reflected in a continued decline in foreign reserves or a buildup in external debt. Over time, the country either exhausts its reserves or begins to encounter difficulties obtaining external loans. At this point, financing is no longer a viable option, and adjustment (whether systematic or ad hoc) is inevitable.

Similar scenarios can be worked through with different combinations of exchange rate regimes (fixed, floating, or managed) and sources of imbalance (emanating from changes in domestic policies or external conditions). Moreover, the failure to adjust can generate a wide variety of consequences—accelerating inflation, emergence of parallel foreign exchange markets, arrears on external debt, capital flight, and, ultimately, declining per capita incomes.

In dynamic terms, the key relationships involved are the growth of government revenue and expenditure (as reflected in the trajectory of the budget deficit), the ratio of domestic savings to domestic investment (as reflected in the trajectory of absorption), and the ratio of exports to imports (as reflected in the trajectory of the current account balance). Recent work on three-gap models provides a formal framework for linking together and analyzing these three imbalances. For our purposes, the issue is not so much how each imbalance emerges or spills over into other areas of the economy, but rather how the imbalance is dealt with once it has emerged. This is the essence of economic management.

Relative Economic Performance: Africa and Asia

In virtually any dimension of macroeconomic performance, Africa is perceived as lagging behind Asia. The data presented in Chapter 1 by Lindauer and Roemer summarize just how substantial this gap has been. Per capita GDP growth over the twenty-five years from 1965 to 1990 has averaged 5.3 percent per year in their sample of nine East and Southeast Asian economies, while it averaged only 0.2 percent in the thirteen Sub-Saharan Africa countries reported. In virtually every other dimension of performance or structure, SSA is substantially behind the Asian group. Moreover, there is little overlap in most dimensions of comparison: for example, the 7.2 percent annual growth in exports of the Philippines places it last among the Asian nations, but ahead of the export growth in all but two of the SSA group (the exceptions are Botswana and Nigeria).

Although such summary statistics present a convincing picture on the divergence in performance between the two regions, they fail to shed any light on the question of when the divergence began and whether it happened

FIGURE 4.1

Changes in Real Per Capita GDP Growth

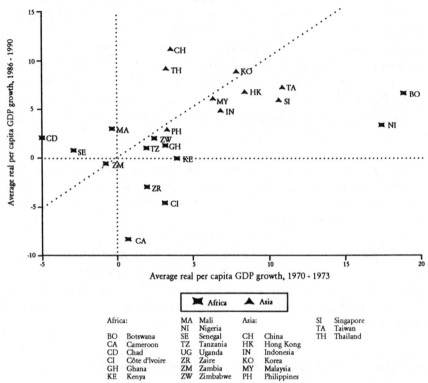

NOTE: In all figures covering a range of years, not all data cover all years shown, but all available data within the time period were used.

at the same time in all countries in the sample. Figure 4.1 provides evidence on GDP growth for two different periods: 1970–1973 (before the oil-related price shocks) and 1986–1990 (the latest period for which complete data are available). The dotted diagonal line corresponds to equal growth rates in the two periods. The picture presented is striking: all of the Asian economies experienced strong positive growth in both subperiods, with Singapore the major "decelerator" (from 10 to 6 percent) and Thailand and China the big "accelerators." Botswana and Nigeria experienced rapid GDP growth fueled by resource-based booms in the 1970–1973 period. Their performance has dropped off substantially during the 1986–1990 period, even though they are still the top performers in Africa. Most of the other African economies have experienced decelerations in growth (they lie below the 45-degree line);

FIGURE 4.2

Changes in Growth Rate of Exports, 1970–1973 to 1986–1990

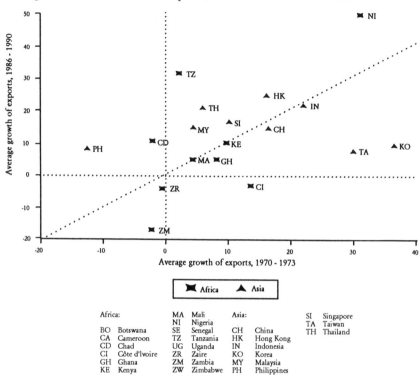

only those with negative growth rates in the first period (Chad and Senegal) were doing much better in relative terms in 1986–1990 than in 1970–1973.

Figure 4.2 displays merchandise export performance (in dollar terms) for the same two subperiods.[2] Although the evidence is a little more varied than with GDP alone, Asian performance is generally superior to that of Africa. In Asia, all economies except the Philippines grew in both periods, and Malaysia, Thailand, and Hong Kong had accelerations in export growth. Most SSA economies had export growth in the 0 to 10 percent range during 1970–1973; by 1986–1990 the performance had scattered to a range from −20 to +50 percent.

One possible explanation for the poor performance of the African economies is that they were simply the victims of "bad luck," or more precisely, that they were more vulnerable to and affected by the adverse external shocks and changing international conditions that characterized much of the 1970s and 1980s. In many ways it is difficult to quantify or even catalogue all of the aspects of the external environment that have changed in the last several decades, but one dimension in particular has received a great deal of attention. Movements in the international terms of trade provide a rough measure of a country's position relative to the rest of the world by providing an index of how export prices have changed relative to import prices. If the empirical evidence were to support the hypothesis that SSA had been more adversely affected, and that this in turn might provide some basis for the poorer economic performance, then to some degree the search for what "went wrong" *within* Africa would be less compelling.

However, there is little support for this hypothesis of strongly differentiated terms of trade. The external shocks on the import side, including the oil price increases of 1973 and 1980, hit all the oil-importing countries in both regions quite hard. There is ample variation in the individual country export price trends, depending on the commodities important to each, but with no strong evidence of a much greater overall impact in SSA compared with Asia.

Figure 4.3 portrays the terms of trade for selected country groupings in Asia and Africa.[3] The major oil exporters in these regions (Indonesia and Nigeria) during the period are omitted from the figure; other smaller oil exporters (Cameroon, Malaysia) are left in. In Asia, we distinguish between the East Asian NICs (Korea, Hong Kong, and Singapore; Taiwan data are not available from the same source) and the other (non-oil) economies (Malaysia, Philippines, Thailand, and China). Africa is grouped by income level: middle income (Botswana, Cameroon, Côte d'Ivoire, Senegal, and Zimbabwe) and low income (Ghana, Kenya, Mali, Tanzania, Uganda, Zaire, and Zambia).

There are some clear regional differences. The Asian NICs have been affected less by terms of trade movements since 1970, a reflection of their low degree of dependence on primary commodities; the major adverse movement for these four countries can be identified primarily with the effect of the oil price increases during the 1970s. During 1970–1974 and 1980–1988, little movement in their terms of trade is apparent. The shocks to the other regions show up quite sharply, particularly in the early 1970s. The low-income SSA economies were most adversely affected, with a 40 percent decline in their terms of trade between 1970 and 1975, reflecting the rise in oil prices and steep decline in commodity prices. The terms of trade

FIGURE 4.3
Terms of Trade

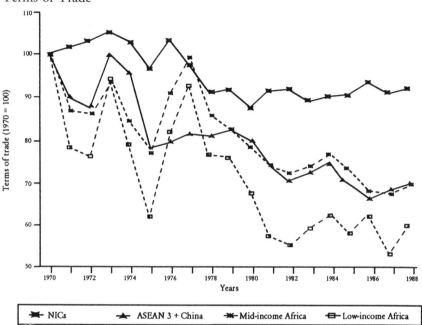

recovered substantially during 1975–1977 before plunging again with the second round of oil price increases. Since 1981, there has been little apparent trend for this low-income group, although the terms of trade have yet to recover to a level anywhere near that characteristic of the pre-oil shock era.[4] The middle-income SSA economies exhibit the same pattern as the low-income SSA economies in the 1970s, although the magnitude of the decline was somewhat less; in the 1980s, this middle-income group and the ASEAN plus China group followed similar patterns.

Overall, low-income Africa clearly suffered from more volatile terms of trade over the period, as well as larger overall decline, although the difference between the three non-NIC groupings by 1988 was relatively small. The fact that the middle-income African economies and the ASEAN plus China grouping experienced similar terms of trade movements suggests that differences in the "adversity" of the external environment (at least as reflected in the terms of trade) fail to explain their substantially divergent

FIGURE 4.4
Changes in Merchandise Exports/GDP

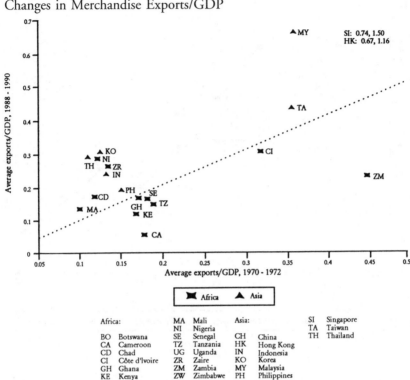

growth trajectories. Faced with similar terms of trade movements, Asian economies expanded their links to the rest of the world and grew; African economies cut themselves off and contracted.

The importance of terms of trade movements to an individual economy will of course depend on its openness. As one measure of openness, Figure 4.4 shows the evolution of the merchandise export/GDP ratio for the individual countries in the two regions by graphing the average ratio in the period 1970–1972 against the average ratio in the period 1988–1990. The dotted line corresponds to equal shares in the two subperiods, so that any country lying near or on this line has had little or no change in its export/GDP ratio.

If SSA economies had larger-than-average export/GDP shares, particularly during the 1970s, we might expect that they would be more adversely affected than Asian economies by the seesawing terms of trade shown in

Figure 4.3 for this period. But all the African economies except Côte d'Ivoire and Zambia had initial export shares lower than 20 percent, which does not support this hypothesis. Note that Botswana, Chad, Uganda, and Zimbabwe are omitted for lack of comparable data. The dramatic fall in Zambia's export share is no doubt related to the collapse of copper prices in the 1970s, but its 1988–1990 share of around 21 percent places it among the averages of other African economies at this time. All of the countries that witnessed a decline in average export shares (those below the dotted line) are African, with Zambia and Cameroon the biggest losers. Correspondingly, all of the Asian economies experienced sizeable increases in export shares, except the Philippines, where the increase was only from 15 to 19 percent. The rest of the ASEAN countries did quite well, with Indonesia's share up from 14 to 24 percent, Thailand's from 11 to 28 percent, and Malaysia's from 36 to 65 percent. Two of the Asian NICs are off the charts, with Singapore's share up from 75 to 150 percent and Hong Kong's from 67 to 116 percent.

From the evidence presented here, there is little basis for attributing Africa's difficulties to the adverse impact of terms of trade movements, which are simply not different enough to explain the radical divergence in GDP and export growth since the 1970s. Instead, the problem appears to be more related to an inability to capitalize on the export growth that did occur by converting such growth into GDP gains and a lack of commitment to continued export expansion. In no SSA economy in our sample except Botswana has the government been committed to an expansion of exports as a means of encouraging the whole economy to grow. Exports in SSA have been viewed as a necessary but unfortunate consequence of not being self-sufficient; some exports were needed in order to allow the economy to become *more* self-sufficient. Manifestations of this attitude are not hard to find, ranging from extreme examples such as the Tanzanian "bootstrap" approach to industrialization or Zambian efforts to seal itself off from the outside world following (then) Rhodesia's declaration of independence, to the more standard approach of combining high external tariffs with domestic monopolies to provide protection from both internal and external competition.

To some extent, the contrast between the performance of the African and Asian country groups is more pointed than the numbers presented here would suggest. Asian economies faced many of the same shocks as African economies, as we have noted; moreover, most of them initially chose to finance rather than adjust. But the key difference was that difficulties in Asia were confronted within an overall strategy oriented toward growth and expansion, whereas in Africa the policy environment resulted in contraction. Thus the context within which policy analysis and economic management were undertaken was *fundamentally* different. Growth allows a lot of mistakes to be covered, as it continually opens new options and opportunities; contraction compounds the mistakes that are made and closes off many options.

For example, by international standards, Korea went deeply into debt during the 1970s. But Korean policy makers recognized the costs associated with the burgeoning debt burden and were able to reassert control over macroeconomic policy, drastically reduce borrowing, and restore growth. The resulting expansion in GDP and exports in turn helped address the internal and external imbalances that had precipitated the difficulties. African countries also stopped borrowing, but largely because lenders stopped lending. But rather than correcting the problem, this cutoff only exacerbated it, since the resulting reduction in essential imports led to a further slowdown in GDP growth, lower exports and debt service capacity, and stagnation.

Approaches to Macroeconomic Policy Making

In this section we concentrate on economic policies that relate to whether an economy responds to internal and external imbalances by financing or adjustment, examining four areas of macroeconomic management. *Exchange rates* provide powerful leverage for inducing adjustment, because exchange rate changes directly affect the incentives to export, import, or produce domestically. Increased *external debt* and *fiscal deficits* involve efforts to finance an imbalance: governments can try to obtain finance externally, through increased foreign borrowing, aid, or running down reserves; or domestically, by running a larger fiscal deficit, and thereby borrowing from the public. *Financial and monetary policy* is also linked to the choice between finance and adjustment, because governments manipulate interest rates to finance imbalances with cheap domestic credits; monetary growth, which leads to domestic inflation, is also used to finance deficits and postpone or avoid adjustment.

Exchange Rates

There is nearly universal agreement that one of the most potent instruments in the government's arsenal is its control over the exchange rate. Inappropriate exchange rate policies have a much wider and more immediate negative impact than almost any other policies. Attention devoted to the exchange rate has increased over the last decade or so, as the importance of economic *openness* in the development of the successful Asian economies has led to the emphasis on *outward orientation* as a central pillar of the stabilization and structural adjustment policies urged on dozens of developing countries by the IMF, World Bank, and others. In its simplest form, this approach argues that Asian management of exchange rates has been dominated by their export orientation.

In this section, we compare exchange rate management in Asian and African economies primarily through an examination of exchange rate *movements*. But to consider such movements in a cross-country framework, it is necessary to adjust for differences in individual country conditions. In particular, the exchange rate is a nominal price, and therefore it is influenced by the overall level of inflation in an economy and the rest of the world.[5] In order to compare exchange rates and their movement among countries, it is necessary to correct for the influence of different price levels (and inflation rates) in the various countries.

The standard method for such comparisons is to focus on measures of the *real exchange rate,* defined in the theoretical literature as the relative price of tradables to nontradables. But price indexes corresponding to tradables and nontradables are difficult if not impossible to find, so that for empirical purposes, the approach adopted is nearly always the same: identify *tradable* prices with prices in the other countries, and identify *nontradable* prices with domestic prices, even though these include prices of some tradables. Thus, starting with the observed *nominal* exchange rate series for a country, efforts are made to eliminate the impact of inflation on these rates by removing the influence of foreign inflation (from tradable prices in the numerator) and domestic inflation (from nontradable prices in the denominator).[6] The resulting relationship can be thought of as

$$\hat{R}^r = \hat{R} - (\hat{P}^d - \hat{R}^w)$$

where R^r and R are the real and nominal exchange rates, P^d and P^w are the domestic and world price levels, and a hat ($\char`\^$) over a variable means it is a percentage change. Thus, the change in the real exchange rate equals the change in the nominal exchange rate *minus* the difference between domestic and world inflation. This means that nominal devaluations cause the real rate to devalue only if the nominal adjustment is bigger than the difference between domestic and world inflation.[7]

The real exchange rate index that results from these calculations can be used to analyze *changes* in competitiveness for each country over time. Increases in the index imply depreciations in the real exchange rate; volatility in the index implies variability in the incentives facing exporters and import-competing producers. This is valuable information, and it will be the focus of our analysis. But the limitations of this approach must be recognized.

Movements in the real exchange rate index say nothing at all about how the *equilibrium* real exchange rate is moving. The equilibrium value, which is unobserved, is the rate that would bring about both internal balance (in the market for nontradable goods) and external balance (a sustainable current account), given appropriate monetary and fiscal policies. This dual (internal and external) role is largely responsible for the prominent role that exchange rate policy can play in the adjustment strategies of economies facing serious difficulties: the exchange rate is more effective than any other instrument in simultaneously addressing both the internal and external imbalances, although it generally cannot do the job alone.

The equilibrium rate depends on a variety of "fundamentals," including terms of trade, capital inflows, domestic supply conditions, technological progress, and the fiscal and monetary policy stance. Changes in these fundamentals lead to changes in the equilibrium real exchange rate; in countries pursuing active exchange rate management, there should be corresponding changes in the nominal exchange rate (and therefore the real exchange rate index). The point for our analysis is that *stability* in the real exchange rate is an important objective only if there are no changes in the underlying equilibrium rate.

In countries where exchange rate misalignment prevails for an extended period, *parallel market rates* for foreign exchange can provide alternative market-based signals of the extent of overvaluation in the economy. If the official exchange rate remains overvalued, powerful incentives encourage the emergence of channels of foreign exchange purchase and sales that are outside the control of the authorities. The rates that prevail in these parallel markets may provide a more realistic guide to the underlying value of a currency because the exchange rate is set through supply and demand, not by the government. It is sometimes argued that movements in the parallel real rate are more likely to reflect movements in the underlying equilibrium rate because of the greater role played by market forces.

However, because parallel rates are determined in illegal or fringe markets, their interpretation as "market-clearing" rates is not necessarily justified. Parallel rates will change not only with market fundamentals, but also according to government actions taken to encourage or eliminate them. Because such markets typically apply only to a fairly small portion of total foreign exchange, they can be quite volatile. There is no guarantee that the parallel market rate is the same as the "equilibrium" rate that would prevail if the government removed all regulations and the official and parallel rates were unified.

Armed with this long list of reservations, we now turn to an analysis of exchange rate patterns in Asia and Africa. If it were necessary to choose one indicator to highlight the difference in exchange rate management between Asian and African countries, the first column of Table 4.1 would be a leading candidate. It shows the average ratio between the parallel market exchange rate and the official exchange rate during 1986–1991. Any ratio over one implies that those able to sell dollars outside official markets receive a premium, which further implies that traders believe the currency is overvalued and that it will be or should be depreciated. An overvalued currency puts both exporters and import-competing producers at a competitive disadvantage in world markets, inviting unfinanceable current account deficits and leaving the economy vulnerable to foreign exchange shortages that stifle growth.

In 1986–1991 and for most of the period since 1965 most Asian countries had official exchange rates quite close to the parallel market rates. China was the only significant exception, with an average premium of 27 percent; Korea, Taiwan, Indonesia, and the Philippines had premiums of around 5–8 percent, while the other Asian economies exhibited no significant overvaluation. In contrast, six of the fourteen African countries in the sample had moderately overvalued rates, with ratios from 1.10 for Kenya to 1.53 for Nigeria, while three others were severely overvalued, with ratios greater than two (implying average overvaluation greater than 100 percent). The remaining five countries are all in the franc zone: with currencies tied to the French franc and backed by grants from the French government, ratios close to 1.00 are expected and say little about export competitiveness.[8] This evidence for 1986–1991 provides some confirmation of the hypothesis that African governments faced with internal and external imbalances have avoided adjustment through active management of the exchange rate, relying instead on financing through, in part, an overvalued exchange rate and controls over the allocation of foreign exchange.

Looking at movements in the *real exchange rate* (RER), we can analyze changes in a country's competitiveness over time. The pattern of change in the RER suggests a great deal about the evolution of a country's macroeconomic policy and trade strategy. If governments respond aggressively to macro imbalances, then the expected pattern of movement in the RER would be (1) a sharp rise (devaluation) of the real rate during a period of economic reform in which a nominal devaluation is validated by tight monetary and fiscal policies; (2) an extended period of relatively constant RER for many years, giving farmers and firms a steady incentive and the confidence to

TABLE 4.1

Parallel Exchange Market Premia and Real Exchange Rate Variability

	Ratio of parallel to official exchange rate, 1986–1991	RER coefficient of variation	
		Using official rate, 1970–1990	Using parallel rate, 1970–1990
East/Southeast Asia			
Korea	1.07	12.8%	13.9%
Taiwan	1.06	na	na
Hong Kong	1.00	12.1	12.2
Singapore	1.02	11.8	12.4
China	1.27	na	na
Indonesia	1.08	38.7	41.3
Malaysia	1.01	21.2	21.4
Philippines	1.05	15.4	44.8
Thailand	1.02	13.0	14.4
Sub-Saharan Africa			
Botswana	1.35	20.4	33.3
Cameroon	1.03	13.0	12.9
Chad	1.03	na	na
Côte d'Ivoire	1.03	14.0	13.8
Ghana	1.38	60.8	34.0
Kenya	1.10	16.5	15.9
Mali	1.03	na	na
Nigeria	1.53	56.7	52.3
Senegal	1.03	12.0	13.0
Tanzania	2.13	54.6	39.8
Uganda	3.35	51.2	43.8
Zaire	1.16	59.5	31.3
Zambia	3.87	60.6	108.3
Zimbabwe	1.48	33.0	25.6

NOTE: na = not available.
SOURCES: Official exchange rates and price indexes from International Monetary Fund, *International Financial Statistics* (Washington, D.C., 1992). Parallel market exchange rates are from *International Currency Yearbook* (various years) (Brooklyn, N.Y.: International Currency Analysis, Inc.). RER calculations are by the authors.

FIGURE 4.5

Changes in Official SDR RER, 1979–1981 = 100

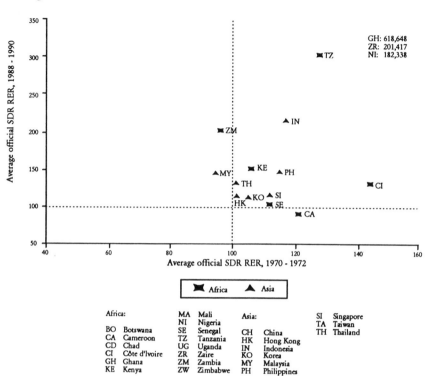

invest in new and expanded exportable products; and (3) perhaps a fall (appreciation) of the real rate as export growth eventually moves the balance of payments into surplus.

Figure 4.5 provides a scatter graph of the real official exchange rate in 1970–1972 (using a simple arithmetic average of the three years) against the real exchange rate in 1988–1990 for our sample of countries.[9] The real exchange rate index uses 1979–1981 as a base, so that the quadrants created by the intersection of the dotted lines (corresponding to 1970–1972 = 100 and 1988–1990 = 100) provide an indication of how the real exchange rate has changed across three subperiods in each country. For example, countries appearing in the upper left (NW) quadrant (such as Malaysia and Thailand) have had ongoing *depreciation* of the exchange rate—the 1970–1972 average was lower than the 1979–1981 value (of 100), and the 1988–1990 value was higher than that in 1979–1981. Countries in the lower right (SE) quadrant

(Cameroon) had a steady *appreciation* of the real exchange rate over the period. Countries in the upper right (NE) quadrant (Kenya, Indonesia) had an initial appreciation followed by depreciation. The closer a country lies to the intersection of the dotted lines in the center of the graph, the greater has been the stability in the real exchange rate, at least for the three subperiods in question.

Most of the Asian economies cluster quite closely around the origin, indicating relatively little movement in the RER over time, although in all Asian economies the 1988–1990 RER had depreciated relative to the 1979–1981 value. In Africa, the franc zone countries (Senegal, Cameroon, and Côte d'Ivoire) had appreciating RERs from 1970 to 1980; from 1980 to 1990, the RER in Cameroon appreciated further (reflecting oil inflows) while Senegal's RER exhibited little trend and Cote d'Ivoire depreciated. These franc zone differences reflect the role of domestic inflation in RER movements. Indonesia, Kenya, the Philippines, and Tanzania all appreciated around 20–30 percent from 1970 to 1980 and then underwent major depreciations of 50–200 percent from 1980 to 1990. Finally, there are three countries whose data points did not fit on the graph, lying far beyond the upper right corner: Ghana, Zaire, and Nigeria. In all three cases, the 1979–1981 midpoint was greatly appreciated relative to either endpoint.

As a summary measure of the RER movements for each country, we consider the overall degree of RER volatility for each country. The last two columns of Table 4.1 display the *coefficient of variation* (COV) for the RER using the official exchange rate as well as the parallel market rate.[10] Based on the official RER figures, three different patterns of RER movement can be identified, which are shown in Figures 4.6 to 4.8 using representative countries from each group.[11]

The first pattern (Figure 4.6) shows quite low variation in the official RER (COV between 11 and 21 percent), which remains steady or depreciates gently for most of the twenty-year period. This group includes Korea, Hong Kong, Philippines, Singapore, Thailand, Malaysia, and Kenya. All Asian countries in this group except the Philippines experienced rapid growth during the period, and Kenya, the only SSA country in this group, was one of the few African countries sustaining moderate growth since 1965. Korea's pattern is one of early depreciation followed by a steady RER. For the other countries except Singapore, the pattern is reversed, with the depreciation coming mostly in the late 1980s. A second pattern (Figure 4.7) is shown by the three franc zone countries for which data are available. In

FIGURE 4.6
Low Volatility RER, Steady Depreciation

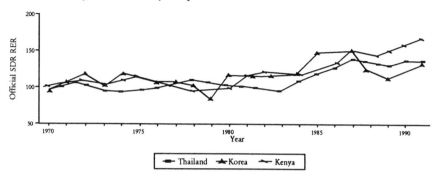

FIGURE 4.7
Low Volatility RER, No Trend

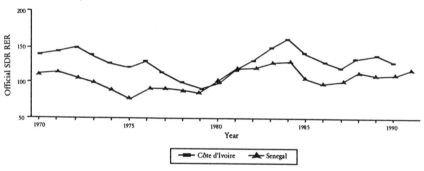

Cameroon, Côte d'Ivoire, and Senegal, the variation is also low (COV between 12 and 14 percent), but with little appreciable trend over time rather than depreciation. Cameroon had moderate economic growth, but Côte d'Ivoire and Senegal suffered declines in per capita income. In the franc zone, however, the real exchange rate may be a less significant indicator than elsewhere, since the strong links created by the fixed exchange rate regime also mean that domestic price levels in these countries are closely tied to conditions in France. Thus most of the variability in the RER for the franc zone countries involves movements relative to other currencies represented in the SDR; in other words, the movement of the French franc against other

FIGURE 4.8
High Volatility RER

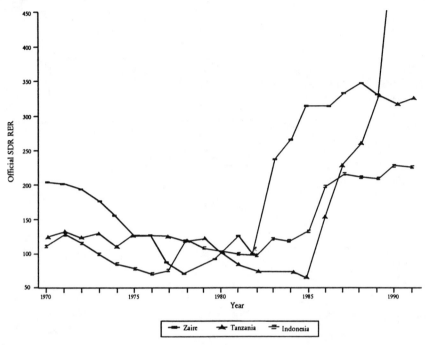

major currencies causes the variation. The stability of the CFA franc during the 1980s is thus driven primarily by the French policy of stabilizing the franc against the deutsche mark.

The third pattern (Figure 4.8) is of much wider fluctuations in the RER, with the COV varying from around 20 percent in Botswana to over 60 percent in Ghana and Zambia. Other countries in this group include Indonesia, Nigeria, Tanzania, Uganda, Zaire, and Zimbabwe. For many of these economies, changing external conditions, and volatile commodity prices in particular, forced periodic major devaluations, resulting in sharp RER movements and relatively high variance. For Indonesia and Nigeria, oil price fluctuations were responsible for the major pressures, whereas in other economies it was various agricultural commodities.

The COV figures using the parallel market rates provide a somewhat different perspective on RER performance during the period. For countries with small parallel market premia (reflected in ratios of less than 1.10 in the first column of Table 4.1), there is little difference between the official and parallel exchange rate COVs. But for those economies with more significant parallel market premia, the picture is more mixed. For some countries, such as Botswana and Zambia, the parallel rate COV is substantially higher than the official rate COV. But for most others, including Ghana, Tanzania, Uganda, Zaire, and Zimbabwe, the parallel rate COV is lower than the official rate COV, implying that the unofficial market rates are *less* volatile than the official ones. This might appear surprising at first, but it makes sense if one considers the function that these parallel markets provide. In most of these economies, policy makers have generally failed to undertake *timely* adjustments in the official exchange rate in response to shocks and imbalances. As a result, the exchange rate becomes increasingly overvalued, until the resulting balance of payments crisis requires one or more very large devaluations, thereby creating sizeable "spikes" in the RER series. But while the official rate remains fixed and largely unaffected by market fundamentals, the parallel rate is responding quite rapidly to changing conditions, with the result that the RER using the parallel rate never gets as far out of line and therefore does not have the large jumps to drive up the COV. Of course, other factors, such as changing exchange controls or stricter enforcement of currency restrictions, can generate fairly high short-run variations in the parallel market rates as well.

Two additional points are of interest. First, both Indonesia and Nigeria were major oil exporters during the period and therefore were strongly influenced by the Dutch disease effects associated with booming oil prices during the 1970s.[12] Figures 4.9 and 4.10 portray movements in the RER and terms of trade for these two countries. For each country, the terms of trade spikes associated with the 1973 and 1979–1980 oil price increases are easy to identify. But the RER rate performance is quite different. In 1978, for example, Indonesia devalued substantially, even though export earnings were rising sharply. This was driven by concerns over what the RER appreciation of the previous half-dozen years had done to the competitiveness of the non-oil sector. By *actively* adjusting rather than passively waiting, Indonesia was able to avoid the near destruction of its agricultural and non-oil export sectors. When oil prices fell after 1983, total export earnings did not drop off as precipitously as in Nigeria, and discrete further devaluations in 1983 and 1986 were sufficient to encourage a substantial non-oil export boom. In Nigeria, policy makers rode the oil boom up to its peak but then lost control, as export earnings fell by 75 percent, a series of foreign exchange difficulties led to crisis-driven devaluations in 1985 and 1987, and the parallel market rate moved erratically.[13] In large measure, the differential

FIGURE 4.9
RER and TOT Movements in Indonesia

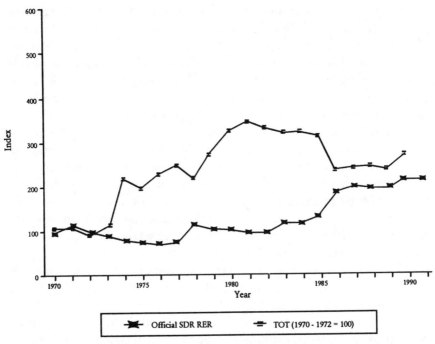

performance can be linked to our earlier point about the *willingness to adjust:* Indonesian policy makers responded to imbalances with positive steps to bring about adjustment, while in Nigeria nothing was done until the situation had already deteriorated beyond easy repair. Indonesia had an explicit exchange rate policy based on some notion of an appropriate real rate. Nigeria did not, and it simply fixed its nominal rate and maintained it as long as foreign reserves held out.

The second point concerns the intriguing possibility, not explicitly considered above, that a *convertible currency,* including an open capital account, can enforce beneficial macroeconomic discipline on a government that promotes sustained growth. In Asia, Hong Kong, Singapore, Indonesia, Malaysia, and Thailand have maintained fully or nearly convertible currencies and totally or nearly unrestricted capital flows for many years. This has two major effects on growth. First, convertibility gives investors confidence that they can get their money out at will, reducing their risk and thus lowering the return they require to invest. Second, convertibility forces a government

FIGURE 4.10

RER and TOT Movements in Nigeria

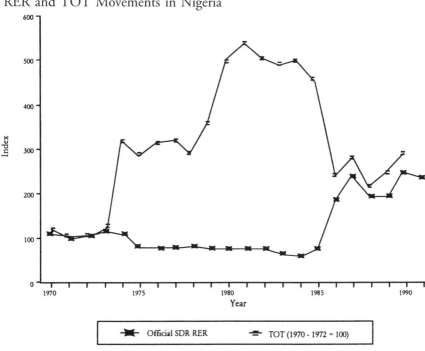

to be much more prudent in its fiscal and monetary policies, because without exchange controls these are the only tools left to protect reserves, avoid sharp devaluations of the exchange rate, and maintain economic stability. Convertibility is not an ironclad guarantee of sound macroeconomic management: a government unwilling to live within the disciplines of convertibility has the option of imposing restrictions if it wants to run deficits and an inflationary monetary policy. Once a country has established convertibility, however, the costs of reversing course become more obvious and place a restraint on government. Thus, Asian experience indicates that convertibility adds a layer of credibility to stabilizing policies.

One reason that Kenya has not attracted foreign investment despite its well-managed exchange rate has been its insistence on retaining exchange controls, which the government has recently begun to dismantle. The Gambia has no such controls and, despite its small size, is viewed favorably by investors. Ghana also appears to be moving toward convertibility. The franc zone countries have, of course, had convertibility with the French franc since their independence. The consequence of French backing, however, is that value of the CFA franc is largely unrelated to economic scarcities and conditions in franc zone countries. Exports become tied to French (and related) markets, and the exchange rate ceases to be an instrument of export promotion or diversification. Apparently, for convertibility to promote investment and growth, it should be combined with flexible exchange rate management.[14]

What lessons can we draw from these patterns? A steady or gradually depreciating real exchange rate is associated with rapid export and income growth, especially in Asia. Widely varying real rates, especially those marked by spikes of appreciation, are associated with slow growth or decline in exports and incomes. Where appreciation is caused by export booms, as in Indonesia and Nigeria, policies can reverse the real exchange rate and channel resources into industries otherwise injured by Dutch disease.

It seems clear that East and Southeast Asian countries managed their exchange rates with better results than did most African countries. Exports grew faster and export shares in GDP rose in all of the Asian economies, while in more than half of the SSA economies export shares actually fell. As has been argued above, policy making in an environment of expansion is very different from that in a context of contraction. The foreign exchange shortages that have paralyzed African economies from time to time are virtually unknown in East and Southeast Asia. The palpable dynamism of Asian economies draws much of its energy from export growth, which builds up a virtuous circle of investment leading to increased productivity and competitiveness, feeding back to continued export growth. Nothing like this dynamic has been evident in Africa, except perhaps in Botswana.[15] Of course, management of all aspects of the economy, from the budget deficit to reductions in poverty, is far easier when one large sector provides growing resources over a long period.

External Debt and Reserve Management

The accumulation of foreign debt and management of foreign exchange reserves provides a direct measure of the attitude of governments toward adjustment. Prudent external borrowing provides an opportunity for governments to "smooth over" short-term variations in the current account balance, as well as take advantage of high-return domestic investment opportunities that otherwise would not be undertaken because of low domestic savings rates. Similarly, sensible foreign exchange reserve management im-

FIGURE 4.11
Changes in Debt/GDP

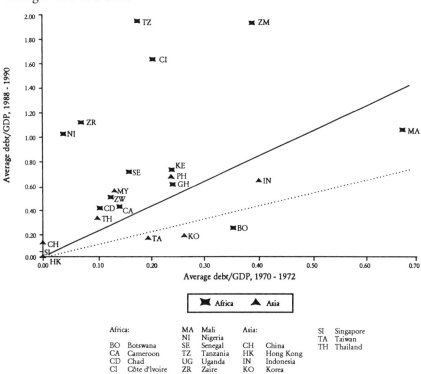

plies that governments recognize the disruptions and costs associated with "running out" of reserves, and take exchange rate and other policy actions as needed to ensure that adequate reserves are maintained.

Figure 4.11 summarizes the evolution of total external debt in the sample of Asian and African economies. On the horizontal axis is the average debt/GDP ratio during 1970–1972; the vertical axis contains the average debt/GDP ratio for the 1988–1990 period. The dotted line from the origin corresponds to the case where the debt/GDP ratio remains unchanged over the twenty-year period $(y = x)$; the solid line above it corresponds to a 1988–1990 ratio two times the 1970–1972 level $(y = 2x)$.

The graph confirms that increases in total debt/GDP were a nearly universal feature of the two decades under examination.[16] Only Korea, Botswana, and Taiwan fall below the dotted line, indicating that their ratios had fallen over the period. For Korea, this represents a policy decision to pay back much of its external indebtedness during the mid-1980s; in 1980–1982, Korea's debt/GDP ratio had risen to 48 percent, which would have placed it well above the solid line. Adding countries whose debt/GDP ratios rose less than 100 percent introduces only two more countries, Indonesia and Mali. For Indonesia, this reflects the high initial debt/GDP ratio and a well-controlled program of external borrowing in the late 1980s undertaken to compensate for the adverse oil price movements; it also reflects the revaluation of Indonesia's nondollar debt (measured in dollars) that occurred because of the substantial depreciation of the dollar. For Mali, with a debt/GDP ratio of almost 70 percent in 1970–1972, it is clear that there was little justification for increased borrowing; presumably whatever external support they have received has come in the form of grants.

On the higher end of the scale, the five countries with debt/GDP ratios larger than 100 percent in 1988–1990 are all in Africa. Nigeria's debt/GDP ratio increased twentyfold, in contrast to Asia's oil exporter, Indonesia, which had higher initial debt but much more restrained growth in external borrowing. Zambia, Zaire, Tanzania, and Côte d'Ivoire fill out the high-debt group and to a large extent identify the worst economic performers of SSA: of the four, only Tanzania avoided falling per capita GDP from 1965 to 1990, and its growth was only 0.3 percent. It is interesting that in the intermediate range of countries, the Asian and African samples are difficult to separate. Kenya and Ghana look like the Philippines (which admittedly had Asia's worst record of external debt management); Zimbabwe and Cameroon look like Malaysia; and Thailand looks like Chad (although the latter is probably another that has received little lending because of its dismal performance and prospects).

Although the total debt/GDP ratio does provide a good indication of the overall debt service burden in the economy, it includes components (such as private sector borrowing) that lie beyond the direct control of the government, and others (such as state enterprise borrowing) that are partially autonomous from central government control in most countries.[17] Focusing on the borrowing that the central government itself undertakes allows us to evaluate how well or poorly the government has managed its borrowing; comparing these results to the pattern of total borrowing allows consideration of whether or not the government has acted as a force of restraint in borrowing.

Figure 4.12 compares the central government debt/GDP ratios for the two subperiods (eliminating private, public enterprise, and financial institution debt from the data used in Figure 4.11). The picture changes somewhat from

FIGURE 4.12

Changes in Central Government Debt/GDP

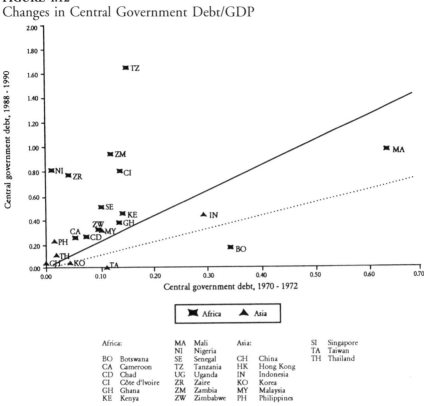

Africa:

				Asia:			
		MA	Mali			SI	Singapore
		NI	Nigeria			TA	Taiwan
BO	Botswana	SE	Senegal	CH	China	TH	Thailand
CA	Cameroon	TZ	Tanzania	HK	Hong Kong		
CD	Chad	UG	Uganda	IN	Indonesia		
CI	Côte d'Ivoire	ZR	Zaire	KO	Korea		
GH	Ghana	ZM	Zambia	MY	Malaysia		
KE	Kenya	ZW	Zimbabwe	PH	Philippines		

the earlier results. The initial distribution of debt ratios is compressed substantially, with only Indonesia, Botswana, and Mali above 20 percent. The Asian NICs are very closely grouped: Korea has an initial debt ratio lower than 5 percent and a final ratio less than 10 percent; Taiwan started at 10 percent but paid off its government debt by 1988–1990. China also has low ratios, while three of the ASEAN four (Philippines, Malaysia, and Indonesia) have ratios in the same range as the more prudent African countries.

The numbers presented here seem to support the idea that policy makers in Asia and Africa generally have placed different emphasis on the use of external resources to finance imbalances. The low borrowers (that is, low relative to the size of the economy) are Asian and include the East Asian NICs, China (which is low for a variety of historical reasons), and Thailand (where government has acted to limit official borrowing but where private external borrowing and investment have been substantial). Similarly, the high borrowers are all in SSA, with five countries experiencing fourfold to eightfold increases in official debt/GDP ratios from 1970 to 1990. But the dichotomy is not a clean one: there is a broad intermediate range containing a group of Asian and African economies that had significant but not extreme increases in debt, for whom foreign borrowing policies alone fail to provide much of an explanation for why some grew and others did not.

On a broader level, there is no example of any African economy showing recognition of the costs associated with excessive reliance on external financing, and subsequently taking systematic actions to reduce its borrowing and adjust. As noted earlier, Korean debt was quite high, reaching almost 50 percent of GDP in 1980; by 1990, as a result of very deliberate government policies, this had been reduced to below 15 percent. Over the same period (1980–1990), Nigerian debt/GDP ratios rose from only 10 percent to 110 percent, and in Kenya, once considered one of the better-managed African economies, the debt/GDP ratio rose from around 50 percent to over 80 percent. Since SSA economies also receive more aid per capita than Asian economies, the distinction between Asian and African reliance on total external financing (borrowing plus aid) is probably even greater than the borrowing figures suggest.

A second perspective on foreign exchange management comes from an examination of patterns of foreign reserve levels in our sample of countries. Foreign exchange reserves provide an important "shock absorber" role in a country's external payments system by providing some cushion to alleviate short-run pressures caused by transitory export earnings declines or import expenditure increases. The difficulty for policy makers in developing countries is how to distinguish between transitory movements, for which reserve drawdown is a legitimate response, and more serious shocks, which call for a more active policy response. The danger is that failure to respond promptly to these large shocks can result in rapid depletion of the country's foreign exchange reserves, leading to a disruption in patterns of trade and a foreign exchange crisis, and the inevitability of a fairly sizable exchange rate adjustment to restore external equilibrium and allow for the accumulation of lost reserves.

One standard indicator for foreign exchange reserves is to measure total reserves in terms of the number of months of imports it can finance. This presumably reflects the role of reserves as a financing cushion.[18] Although there is no optimal level of reserves from a theoretical point of view, and very little agreement regarding the operational targets for reserve levels, many

FIGURE 4.13
Reserves as Months of Imports

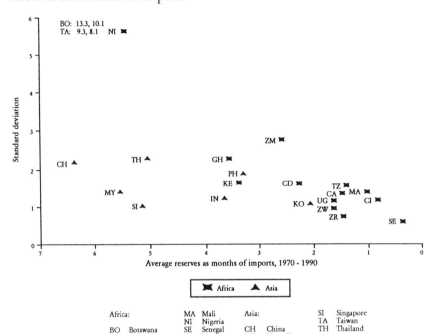

analysts would accept that desired reserves should be equivalent to around three to six months of imports. Less than three months makes the cushion excessively fragile; more than six months and one might legitimately question whether there are alternative investments of these resources that would have a higher return to the economy than their use as reserves.

Figure 4.13 shows the reserve levels for our sample of countries. On the horizontal axis is the average level of reserves (measured in terms of months of imports) and on the vertical axis is the standard deviation of this average reserve measure. Note that the scale on the horizontal axis has been reversed, so that *higher* levels of reserves are closer to the origin in the lower left, while *lower* reserve levels appear toward the right hand side of the graph. Thus, from the lower left corner of the graph, movements to the right imply lower average reserves (a smaller cushion) and movements up imply a higher standard deviation (greater volatility) in reserve levels. Good reserve management takes a country *toward* the origin, although not all of the way, since reserves can be too high.

Nearly all the sample of countries had average reserve levels of less than six months of imports. Botswana and Taiwan are off the graph, with average reserves equivalent to nine to thirteen months of imports. There is also a fairly clear division between Asian and African performance. All of the Asian economies except Korea had average reserve levels greater than three months of imports and none had standard deviations much over two months. Nearly all of the SSA economies had reserve levels less than three months, often with standard deviations as large as their average. The implication is that African economies have spent much of this period in chronic risk of running out of reserves, with little or no cushion. Even Nigeria, with an average of over five months' worth of reserves, had a standard deviation nearly as large, suggesting that even with extensive oil earnings, it was unable to provide any sustained cushion against adverse external movements.[19]

Budgetary Control and Fiscal Deficits

Recent experience with economic adjustment in both Africa and Asia has demonstrated conclusively that very little progress toward the twin objectives of "stabilization" and "structural adjustment" can be made without fundamental changes in the system of government budgetary control.[20] Efforts to assert macroeconomic control are difficult if not impossible in the context of large and growing deficits because of the strain that the financing of these deficits places on all segments of the economy. Deficits inevitably lead to aggregate demand pressures, expansionary monetary policies, inflation, and the undermining of efforts to restore confidence in the domestic environment. Although apologists might argue that the external shocks of the last decade or so (such as commodity price slumps and droughts) have created enormous budgetary pressures that were beyond the governments' control, many aspects of expenditure, such as wages and subsidies, remained at the discretion of these governments, as did the option of concentrating efforts on increased revenue performance. In this section, we evaluate the fiscal performance of Asian and African countries through an examination of government deficit and revenue performances.

Government budgetary deficits have three consequences for macroeconomic policy and economic growth, depending on how they are financed. If financed through overseas borrowing, deficits add to external debt. As long as foreign debt service grows no faster than exports, this should cause no problems. But if external borrowing by government causes debt service to rise faster than exports, eventually a debt crisis is likely to disrupt growth by requiring a reduction in aggregate demand through higher taxes, reduced government expenditures (including investment), or both. If the deficit is financed through domestic borrowing, it will compete with and "crowd out" private (and public enterprise) investment. If the deficit is financed by borrowing from the central bank, it is equivalent to printing money and contributes to higher rates of inflation, with all of its attendant consequences for maintaining external balance.

All three consequences argue for a restrained government deficit. Moreover, there is a strong consensus among economists that any stabilization program—whether to reduce external deficits, cut inflation, or both—requires a reduction in the budget deficit. Not only does this reduce aggregate demand in the economy, but it also signals to the private sector that government is serious about achieving macroeconomic balance. Without reduced deficits, adjustment programs have little credibility.

There is no a priori level of budget deficit that is right for every economy, or even for a single economy in different circumstances. The Asian economies listed in Table 4.2 show a range of budget outcomes for the 1980s, from an average surplus of 3 percent of GDP for Singapore to an average deficit of almost 11 percent of GDP for Malaysia. Most Asian countries ran small deficits, from 0.3 percent for China to under 4 percent for Thailand. Yet in all these countries except the Philippines, the economy grew briskly.

Given the importance we place on sound macroeconomic management in achieving rapid growth, the extreme outcome for Malaysia appears to be an anomaly. During the 1980s, Malaysia saved a third of its GDP, one of the highest savings rates in the world. In that context, a large government deficit is unlikely to be inflationary and could still be consistent with rapid economic growth even if the deficit-financed resources were not invested efficiently.[21]

African deficits appear generally to have been higher than those in Asia, but not dramatically so. Nigeria ran a small surplus on average during the 1980s, while four other countries ran average deficits well under 5 percent of GDP. Even Tanzania, Zambia, and Zimbabwe, which had the highest deficits in our sample, were not so different in this respect from Malaysia. However, the African countries in our sample have savings rates well below those in Asia: all but two countries saved 20 percent of GDP or less during the 1980s, seven of them saved less than 15 percent, and five of them—

TABLE 4.2
Government Expenditures, Deficits, and Finance (percentage of GDP)

	Government expenditure, 1986–1990	Budget balance, 1980–1990
East/Southeast Asia		
Korea	18.3	−1.0
Taiwan	na	0.0
Hong Kong	na	na
Singapore	27.7	3.0[d]
China	na	−1.0[e]
Indonesia	22.9	−1.8[d]
Malaysia	32.7[a]	−10.7[d]
Philippines	15.1	−2.9
Thailand	17.4	−2.3
Sub-Saharan Africa		
Botswana	44.1	na
Cameroon	21.9	na
Chad	na	na
Côte d'Ivoire	31.2[b]	na
Ghana	14.0	−2.4[e]
Kenya	28.1	−5.6[d]
Mali	31.1	−3.4[e]
Nigeria	27.8[c]	0.3
Senegal	na	−4.6[f]
Tanzania	22.4[b]	−7.2[g]
Zaire	15.7	na
Zambia	29.2	−14.2
Zimbabwe	39.1	−8.0

NOTE: na = not available.
a. Except 1989.
b. 1986 only.
c. 1987–89.
d. To 1989.
e. To 1988.
f. To 1987.
g. To 1985.
SOURCES: International Monetary Fund, *International Financial Statistics Yearbook* (Washington, D.C., 1992); Asian Development Bank, *Key Indicators of Asian and Pacific Countries* (London: Oxford University Press, for the Asian Development Bank, 1992).

FIGURE 4.14
Changes in Deficit/GDP

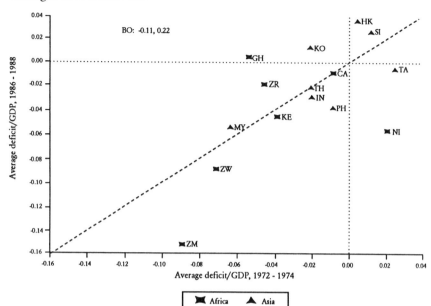

Chad, Ghana, Mali, Senegal, and Tanzania—saved less than 7 percent of GDP. Thus African governments have less room to run deficits without stimulating inflation or crowding out private investment and reducing growth rates.[22]

Deficits provide a measure of the net impact of government on the financial system, since they must be financed through either domestic or external borrowing, or by resort to the printing press. Large and growing deficits imply an ever increasing drain on available resources and indicate an unwillingness to confront imbalances with positive policies to promote adjustment. Volatility in deficits suggests a budget process over which the government exercises little direct control, instead letting expenditures evolve according to whatever political pressures exist and allowing revenues to drift.

Figure 4.14 summarizes the evolution of deficits in our sample of countries by portraying the average deficit/GDP ratios for the sample countries for the 1972–1974 and 1986–1988 periods.[23] Countries lying on or near the diagonal dotted line had little change in the average deficit/GDP ratio in the two subperiods; those above the diagonal had a *decreasing* deficit, while those below had an *increasing* deficit. It is interesting that for most countries, there was relatively little change in the size of the deficit over the fifteen-year period; Ghana and Korea had decreasing deficits, Nigeria and Zambia quite substantial increases in deficits, and Zimbabwe and the Philippines more moderate rises. At the extreme, Botswana (which lies off the graph) went from an 11 percent deficit in 1972–1974 to a 22 percent surplus in 1986–1988. The Asian economies lie, for the most part, to the northeast of the African economies, which implies that they had *lower* average deficits during both the beginning and final subperiods.

Figure 4.15 looks at the volatility of government deficits, as measured by the standard deviation of the deficit/GDP ratio. Three of the four NICs and Botswana averaged budget surpluses throughout the period (Botswana's 3.6 percent average surplus and a standard deviation of over 13 percent is not shown). The fiscal restraint of the other Asian economies shows up quite clearly in the bunching of average deficit/GDP ratios at −2 percent or less for Philippines, Indonesia, Korea, and Thailand. Nearly all of the African countries averaged more than −2 percent, with substantially higher variability as well; average deficits exceeded −5 percent for seven of the African countries.

The evidence thus appears to suggest that African policy makers were less successful at curtailing the level, as well as the variability, of the fiscal deficit, which in turn generated significant destabilizing pressures in these economies. Moreover, deficits of 5 percent or more in a broader context of economic contraction signal major difficulties. A downward spiral can easily be set off, in which higher deficits lead to reduced savings and investment, which lowers growth and further exacerbates the deficit. The Asian examples, including the outlier example of Malaysia for which domestic savings was exceptionally high, demonstrate the importance of keeping the deficit small enough relative to savings, investment, and overall economic growth.

Large and varying deficits may of course be attributable to poor revenue performance, inability to control expenditures, or both. Figure 4.16 provides information on how revenue/GDP shares have changed over time. Again, the diagonal line corresponds to equal shares in 1972–1974 and 1986–1988. Zambia, Taiwan, and China all experienced declining revenue/GDP shares. For Zambia, this was due primarily to the fall in copper prices, although,

FIGURE 4.15
Variability of Deficit/GDP

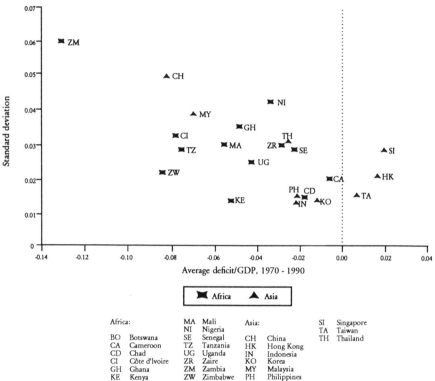

because its 27 percent share in 1972–1974 was the highest except for Botswana and China at around 30 percent, the decline is not so remarkable. Revenue shares in the remaining countries follow no clear regional pattern; Malaysia and Singapore had high shares, but Zimbabwe had higher (all three are middle-income countries); the remaining countries are all quite closely grouped.

Figure 4.17 shows the variability in revenue for our sample, measured by the standard deviation in the revenue/GDP share. The African economies appear to have far greater variability in the revenue share in GDP, perhaps reflecting the large and continuing importance of commodity exports for this group. Combined with the deficit data, these revenue results suggest that the fiscal problem for Africa was not related to revenue performance, since Asian and African shares and trends are quite similar, but attributable instead to an inability to manage expenditure growth.

FIGURE 4.16
Changes in Revenue/GDP

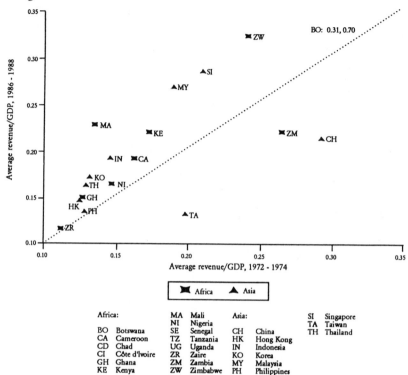

In a broader sense, the difference between Asian and African economies in the fiscal arena revolves around their use and mastery of stabilization techniques. In Asia, governments have consistently acted to ensure that the government's own actions would not generate instability. In Africa, this was not the case; African policy makers tended to view the role of government as one of promoting development irrespective of the impact of its borrowing and spending on overall macroeconomic fluctuations. For example, in Indonesia, the decline in oil revenues led directly to efforts to reduce government spending and investment and increase non-oil revenue performance; in Nigeria, the oil revenue decline was viewed as something for which government should compensate by higher spending, rather than something to which it needed to adjust. These two options have drastically different implications for macroeconomic stability.

FIGURE 4.17
Variability of Revenue/GDP

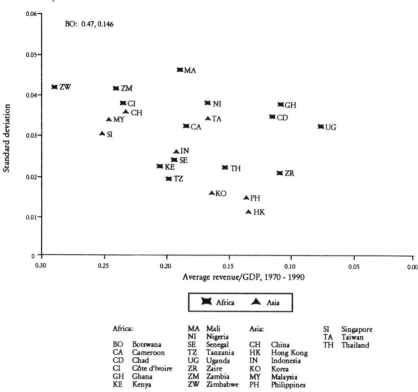

Financial Development and Monetary Policy

Both Asian and African countries have had rigidly controlled financial systems, based on a belief in the efficacy of centralized direct control of finance, including controlled interest rates, direct allocations of subsidized credit to favored borrowers, and the like. Postcolonial governments in both regions sought "financial independence" by establishing their own central banks. The prevalent development doctrine of the time was that governments and their central banks could encourage (or "lead") financial development by the creation of the appropriate institutions. This doctrine proved erroneous mainly because the policies adopted did not address the need to increase the demand for financial assets. Further restrictions emerged through the pervasiveness of state intervention. Much of the credit was directed to public enterprises. In recent years, financial liberalization programs have been promulgated throughout these regions as part of a more general move toward financial market development and more indirect government regulation of and intervention in financial markets.

The path of such reform efforts, and the trend of financial development in general, has been an erratic one. It is difficult to draw any definitive conclusions, either as to the outcome of the process or to the contribution of financial development to other aspects of economic performance such as growth. But in general, monetary authorities have a dual role to play in development. First, they need to promote *financial development,* the increasing availability and efficiency of financial services in response to the demands of developing economies. Second, in achieving this rise in the use of financial services, monetary authorities need to avoid accelerated *inflation* by limiting increases in the supply of money to match the rise in demand for money.

Improved financial services may increase domestic saving and thus increase investible resources. Its greater impact, however, is likely to be a more efficient channeling of saving into investment, thus raising the productivity of capital and contributing to the growth of total factor productivity. One partial indicator of financial development is the ratio of money to GDP. Table 4.3 shows that most of the Asian countries in our sample had far higher ratios in the latter half of the 1980s than did most of the African countries. Taiwan, Singapore, China, Malaysia, and Thailand had ratios of more than 66 percent. The most monetized African countries in the sample, Botswana, Côte d'Ivoire, Kenya, Tanzania, Zambia, and Zimbabwe, had ratios of 29 to 36 percent. In terms of financial development, these countries were more like Indonesia and the Philippines in the 1980s, though Indonesia has recently embarked on a determined effort to expand its financial system.

The conclusion that Asia and Africa exhibit different degrees of financial development is difficult to interpret, since by the late 1980s the two regions were at substantially different levels of per capita income and development. There are many theoretical reasons to expect the ratio of M2/GDP to rise as per capita income rises, as one component of the "financial deepening" that accompanies income growth. In Figures 4.18 and 4.19, we graph the M2/GDP ratio against per capita GDP (in log terms) for both 1970–1972 and 1986–1988.[24] Both graphs show the impact of rising incomes on financial development, as measured by M2/GDP ratios. In 1970–1972, there is a fairly clear upward trend with rising incomes, although financial development in Asia would appear somewhat more advanced even then, since the Asian economies tend to be above the African economies at the same income

TABLE 4.3

Financial Development, Monetary Policy, and Inflation, 1980–1990 (percentage)

	Money (M2) as share of GDP, 1986–1990	Average annual real interest rate on loans, 1986–1990	Average annual inflation in CPI, 1980–1990
East/Southeast Asia			
Korea	38.2	4.6	6.3
Taiwan	138.1	na	4.5
Hong Kong	na	na	8.1
Singapore	88.4	5.2	2.3
China	87.2	4.9	7.3
Indonesia	32.3	13.2	8.6
Malaysia	69.6	6.2	3.2
Philippines	29.8	9.5	14.0
Thailand	66.4	11.7[a]	4.4
Sub-Saharan Africa			
Botswana	30.6	−1.2	10.6
Cameroon	18.8	5.5[b]	9.1
Chad	25.4	11.7[a]	na
Côte d'Ivoire	28.6	3.0	5.3
Ghana	14.6	−6.1[b]	43.0
Kenya	29.2	8.1[b]	10.5
Mali	23.2	na	na
Nigeria	25.3	−1.5[c]	21.6
Senegal	na	8.0[b]	5.9
Tanzania	29.1[b]	−2.7[b]	28.9
Zaire	9.1[b]	−27.0[b]	60.9
Zambia	36.1[b]	−19.2[b]	23.5
Zimbabwe	31.0[a]	2.7[b]	13.9

NOTE: na = not available.
a. To 1989.
b. To 1988.
c. To 1987.
SOURCE: International Monetary Fund, *International Financial Statistics Yearbook* (Washington, D.C., 1992).

FIGURE 4.18

Money Supply vs. GDP Per Capita, 1972

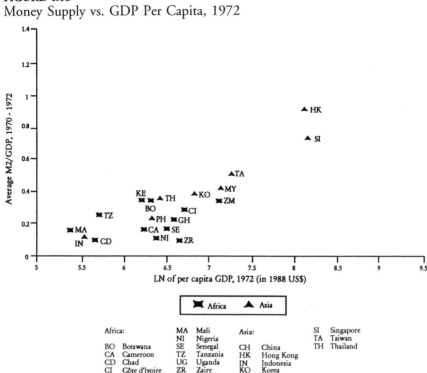

Africa: MA Mali   Asia: SI Singapore
                 NI Nigeria   TA Taiwan
BO Botswana   SE Senegal   CH China   TH Thailand
CA Cameroon   TZ Tanzania   HK Hong Kong
CD Chad   UG Uganda   IN Indonesia
CI Côte d'Ivoire ZR Zaire   KO Korea
GH Ghana   ZM Zambia   MY Malaysia
KE Kenya   ZW Zimbabwe   PH Philippines

levels. By 1986–1988, the regular upward trend is far less apparent, primarily due to the tremendous variation for the Asian economies. For example, Malaysia's M2/GDP ratio has nearly tripled, even though its per capita GDP grew by half; Thailand's M2/GDP ratio doubled as its per capita GDP grew by two-thirds; but Korea's M2/GDP ratio grew by only a quarter while its per capita GDP more than tripled. Among the African countries, there seems to be less upward trend as well.

Full exploration of the measures needed to encourage financial development is a task beyond the scope of this chapter.[25] One requirement is that governments give up some direct control and permit financial markets to determine interest rates and allocate credit.[26] When markets rule, the real interest rate on deposits and bank loans will be positive; a negative real rate means that government has intervened to repress financial development. Among the Asian countries in Table 4.3, all had positive real interest rates

FIGURE 4.19
Money Supply vs. GDP Per Capita, 1988

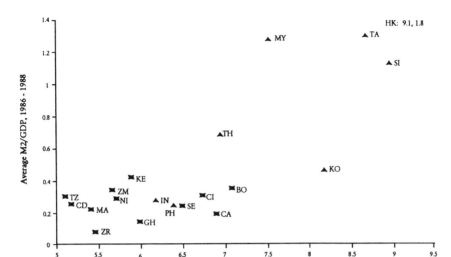

on bank loans during the latter half of the 1980s. Among the African countries, six had negative real rates, and three of these—Ghana, Zaire, and Zambia—had large negative rates, suggesting severe financial repression.

Uncontrolled financial markets, it must be said, have not been a prerequisite for rapid development in Asia. Hong Kong and Singapore have long had market-based financial systems. In Japan, Korea, and Taiwan, however, government-controlled banks allocated subsidized credit to favored firms and industries. This approach was consistent with rapid growth for two reasons: cheap credit was often earmarked for new and growing export industries; and, in Korea and Taiwan, a parallel credit market, with much higher, market-determined interest rates, was permitted to handle the credit needs of firms denied access to government-controlled funds.

Southeast Asian countries also used subsidized credit to preferred borrowers, but the favored borrowers were not so much exporters as clients of the political system. In these countries, domestic financial systems have been supplemented by financial services from Singapore and Hong Kong, which have helped meet the needs of the more dynamic firms. Overseas financial services, sound macroeconomic policies, and generous resource endowments have been able to compensate for the deficiencies of domestic financial systems.

In recent years, however, financial reform and development have accelerated in Southeast Asia. Indonesia freed up interest rates in 1983, cleared the way for more domestic and foreign banks to enter the market in 1988, and has been gradually phasing out subsidized credit. This trend has also affected Africa, where Kenya and Ghana have begun to remove controls over the banking system and to allow interest rates to find their market levels. Financial reform may be more essential to accelerated growth in Africa than it was in Asia for three reasons: African governments are not capable of widespread, disciplined financial interventions on the scale practiced in Korea; they have neither efficient parallel financial markets, as in Korea and Taiwan, nor access to overseas financial centers like Singapore and Hong Kong; and they have not been as adroit as Indonesia, Malaysia, and Thailand in using macroeconomic policies to convert resources from primary export growth into export diversification and sustained income growth.

The other side of monetary and financial policy is the control of inflation. There is no "correct" level of inflation for all countries, nor is there any evidence that zero or any other particular rate of inflation is more consistent with rapid growth. Rates that are too high undermine confidence. Some economies adjust well to rates of inflation that would disrupt other economies. Much has to do with history and custom. Germany and China, with histories of destructive hyperinflation, try to maintain very low rates of inflation, as do Japan, Singapore and Malaysia, which are all countries with rapid income growth. Korea, however, managed growth of over 6 percent a year in per capita income from 1965 to 1980 despite inflation of 15 percent a year, while Taiwan grew by over 7 percent a year with inflation of over 8 percent a year.

Figure 4.20 correlates GDP growth with inflation during the 1980s. The picture is quite striking: no country with average inflation greater than 10 percent sustained real GDP growth higher than 3 percent annually. All of the rapidly growing Asian economies (with GDP growth greater than 5 percent) had inflation rates below 10 percent.

Of course, the link between inflation and growth is complex and it is not

FIGURE 4.20
Growth and Inflation, 1980–1990

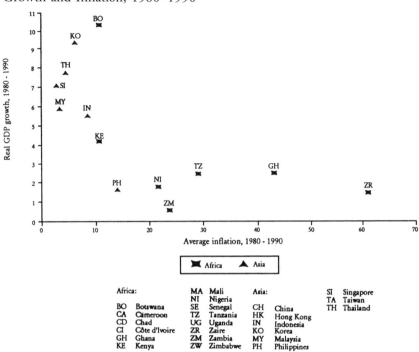

possible to identify a single channel through which the effects are felt. But one factor that can lead to a disruption in investment and growth is an *acceleration* of inflation. Higher-than-customary inflation, or the fear of it, has three deleterious effects on development: (1) it distorts relative price signals, compromising the ability of markets to allocate resources efficiently; (2) it increases the uncertainty faced by investors, who anticipate either changing price signals or a deflationary stabilization, thus raising the required return and reducing the amount invested in productive real assets; and (3) it diverts entrepreneurial and managerial energies from productivity-enhancing activities to financial management.

Figure 4.21 portrays the inflation experience for African and Asian economies during the last two decades by graphing the average inflation rate for 1970–1980 against the average inflation rate for 1980–1990.[27] Points lying above the diagonal line imply an increase in average inflation from one decade to the next, and points below the diagonal imply a decrease. During

FIGURE 4.21
Inflation, 1970s vs. 1980s

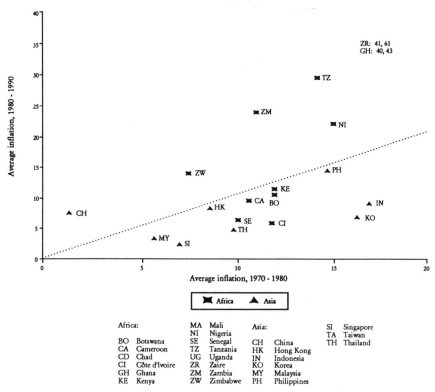

the 1980s, all of the seven rapidly growing economies in Asia had inflation averaging 8.5 percent a year or less (as shown in Table 4.3), and in all cases except China, the rate was lower than over the previous ten years. Of the African countries, only three managed inflation in the range of the Asian economies. In Ghana, Nigeria, Tanzania, Zaire, Zambia, and Zimbabwe, inflation was not only high during the 1980s, but markedly higher than during the previous decade.[28] These inflations were severe enough to disrupt investment and growth: in all six cases, investment was a much lower share of GDP during the 1980s than during the previous fifteen years.

For governments that respond to imbalances by financing rather than adjusting, high inflation provides an additional means to mobilize domestic resources through the involuntary "inflation tax" that is levied on domestic currency holders. The revenue accrues to government because of its control

FIGURE 4.22
Seignorage, 1970s vs. 1980s

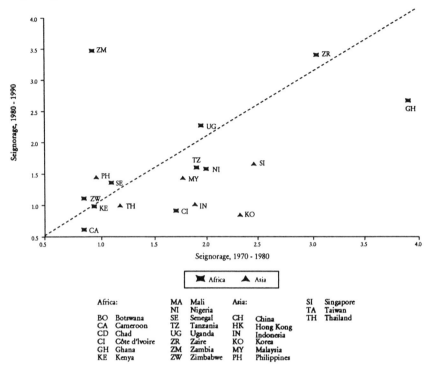

over the creation of money. One standard measure of this *seignorage* is the annual change in the money base divided by base year GDP. It thus measures the percentage of GDP that governments extract from the economy through the process of money creation. Countries that finance their imbalances are likely to rely on this channel of resource mobilization more often than countries that adjust.

Figure 4.22 shows how reliance on seignorage has changed by presenting data on the average seignorage share (expressed relative to GDP) for the 1970s and 1980s for selected Asian and African countries. The dotted line corresponds to equal seignorage shares in the two decades; points below the line imply a falling seignorage share. During the 1970s the Asian and African economies seemed fairly mixed in their reliance on seignorage, as the array of points along the horizontal axis suggests. Except for the Philippines, however, Asian economies have relied less on seignorage during the 1980s than during the 1970s, whereas for many African economies, the role of seignorage has increased. This provides further support of the hypothesis that Asian economies have avoided excessive reliance on financing imbalances, choosing instead to confront the difficulties through more direct measures that address the underlying causes.

Conclusions

Over time, imbalances will emerge in all economies, no matter how well run. Economic management in different countries can be distinguished by the approach taken to imbalances and whether governments choose to finance rather than adjust. Governments in well-managed economies are predisposed toward the removal of imbalances through adjustment; governments in poorly managed economies are predisposed to finance the imbalances. Countries that adjust grow and develop; countries that finance do not.

Most Asian countries, though they financed fiscal and foreign deficits to absorb some of the shocks they faced, generally moved quickly to adjust. Exchange rates were kept close to parallel market rates, except for China. Foreign borrowing was generally less in Asian than African countries, though with some overlap. All Asian countries except Malaysia ran budget deficits below 4 percent of GDP. Asian countries used money creation sparingly to finance deficits, kept inflation below 10 percent during the 1980s, and maintained positive real interest rates.

Although African performance varied widely across countries, for the most part governments chose to finance rather than adjust. Outside the franc zone countries, exchange rates were overvalued by anywhere from 10 percent to well over 100 percent and real rates were more volatile than in Asia. All the high-borrowing countries in our sample are African and five of them experienced fourfold to eightfold increases in debt-to-GDP ratios. Budget deficits were generally over 5 percent of GDP during the 1980s. Money creation, though not excessive, rose during the 1980s, inflation accelerated in six of the thirteen countries in our sample, and five of these (plus one other) had negative real interest rates.

The divergence between African and Asian performance can be linked to the importance of macroeconomic management (or alternatively, adjustment rather than financing) as an objective in its own right. In Asia macroeconomic policy making was more frequently left in the hands of a technocratic bureaucracy, which often remained remarkably stable for two decades or more and permitted a long-run view of policy choice. Political stability more often than not provided the framework within which the policy making technocracy was able to move slowly forward in a number of areas, secure in the knowledge that if reform initiatives faltered one year, there would be another chance. Even in countries such as Thailand and Indonesia, where political uncertainties and rent-seeking are common, the major components of macro management were left largely outside the political sphere, in the hands of well-respected, influential technocrats who were partially insulated from political pressures and rent-seeking. In Africa, this separation rarely, if ever, occurred, and all aspects of decision making in the economy were considered fair game in the political give and take characteristic of these settings. Even strong, long-lived governments, such as those in Côte d'Ivoire, Kenya, Malawi, Tanzania, Zaire, and Zambia, did not manage macro policy with a long-term perspective. In Asia, even the rent-seekers recognized that growing economies underlie sustainable generation of rents. Few regimes in Africa appear to have recognized this truth.

Finally, presenting each of the four components of policy making in isolation obscures one key point: effective macroeconomic policy making requires a broad, unified perspective, together with a commitment to act, rather than avoid adjustment. Policy makers must exhibit a willingness (if not necessarily an enthusiasm) to confront rather than avoid internal and external imbalances before they overwhelm the existing range of policy instruments. Devoting attention to an exchange rate misalignment this month and a budget deficit next month is not sufficient. All of the spheres of macroeconomic policy are interconnected; efforts to choose the "correct" exchange rate policy without addressing the budget deficit (as has happened in countless African stabilization and structural adjustment programs) are not likely to succeed. Only when these linkages become the basis for macro policy can the macroeconomic environment be expected to contribute to growth in Sub-Saharan Africa rather than prevent it.

NOTES

We are grateful to David Lindauer and Michael Roemer for extensive and constructive comments on various drafts, and to workshop participants for their suggestions.

Dan Gilligan assisted enthusiastically and capably with the data compilation and analysis, and he and Alison Barrows prepared the graphs. We accept responsibility for any remaining errors.

1. This defines internal balance in Keynesian terms. In the Salter–Swan tradables-nontradables model often used to analyze these relationships, internal balance is defined as equilibrium in the domestic market for nontradable goods.

2. Some countries appearing in Figure 4.1 are not in Figure 4.2 because of a lack of data. Other figures have omissions for the same reason.

3. Data are derived from the World Bank's *World Tables* files on disk using the dollar-based terms of trade series for individual countries. All indexes end in 1988 because this is the last year for which data are available for all the sample of countries. The 1992 *World Tables* data are the primary source, supplemented in some instances by data contained in the 1991 tables but not in 1992. The individual country series in *World Tables* have 1987 as the base year. To calculate the regional series presented in the figure, we converted each country series to a 1970 base and then calculated a simple average of the individual country series.

4. Of course, the debate over whether there are identifiable long-term trends in the commodity terms of trade is both longstanding and contentious. In Chapter 5, Tomich et al. conclude from a survey of existing studies that there is no significant trend in the commodity terms of trade from 1921 to 1988.

5. All exchange rates presented in this chapter are defined in terms of local currency per dollar. An increase in the exchange rate (that is, a bigger number) thus means it takes more local currency to buy a dollar and therefore amounts to a *depreciation* of the local currency.

6. See Devarajan, Lewis, and Robinson (1993) for a more thorough discussion of these issues.

7. In fact, the calculations become more complicated, since frequently efforts are made to correct not just for general "world" inflation or inflation in a single foreign country, but rather for "average" world inflation in a group of countries. Debates rage over the appropriate composition of the country group (and hence the weights used in the calculation), with import weights, export weights, SDR weights, and others all having their proponents among analysts of real exchange rates. In the RER estimates presented in this paper, we have chosen to use SDR weights.

8. Overvaluation of the CFA franc will not result in the emergence of a parallel currency market, because convertibility of the CFA franc means traders can always buy French francs at the official rate. Rather, adjustment to overvaluation will take place through transfer payments from France to the governments of the franc zone countries.

9. The RER is calculated using the official rate and, in countries where significant parallel markets operate, again using the prevailing parallel rates. Each RER is calculated using an SDR basket of currencies in order to facilitate comparisons across countries. In other words, the relationship for each country h is $RER_h =$

$(E_h/P_h)/(\Sigma_i w_i E_i/P_i)$ where RER_h is the real exchange rate of the home country in any year, w_i is the share of each foreign currency in the SDR basket (yen, francs, pounds, dollars, etc.), E_i and E_h are the nominal exchange rates for each currency (in local currency per dollar), and P_i and P_h are consumer price indexes for each country. In calculating the parallel market RER, E_h is replaced by the parallel rate. Note that the use of SDR weights means that the denominator of the RER expression is the same for all countries.

10. The coefficient of variation is defined as the standard deviation divided by the mean. Assuming a normal distribution, a coefficient of variation of 1.00 means that 32 percent of the annual index values differ from the mean by at least 100 percent; a value of 0.5 means that 32 percent differ from the mean by at least 50 percent.

11. For a more detailed discussion of real exchange rates in Asia, see Intal (1992); Sahn (1990) analyzes real exchange rate trends in Africa in the context of their impact on income distribution.

12. Dutch disease refers to the tendency for export "booms" (such as that created by the OPEC-led oil price increases) to lead to real exchange rate overvaluation (as domestic prices rise faster than the nominal exchange rate) and the resulting shift of resources away from tradable to nontradable sectors. See Gelb and Associates (1988).

13. Gelb and Associates (1988) argue that Nigeria's growth rate would have been higher without oil revenue. It certainly would have been higher with oil revenue had it avoided the severe real appreciation from 1974 to 1984.

14. Another argument for convertibility is that capital controls do not keep capital from being transferred. Moreover, they send the wrong signals to potential foreign investors. For a review of the issues on opening up capital accounts, see Mathieson and Rojas-Suarez (1992).

15. Botswana and Nigeria have enjoyed rapid growth of export revenues since 1965. In Botswana's case this was due to growth of both diamonds and other exports. There was also a high investment ratio and rapid productivity growth, suggesting a possible virtuous circle. In Nigeria, however, export growth was due entirely to oil; other export industries were destroyed by Dutch disease.

16. Hong Kong and Singapore have no external debt to speak of, reflecting the long history of balance of payments surpluses on these economies and, for Hong Kong, certain colonial restrictions on its ability to borrow.

17. Of course, autonomy has different implications in different circumstances. Many parastatals in Africa, while nominally autonomous from the central government, have frequently been used as a separate channel for official government borrowing.

18. The idea that reserves sit around in the vaults of the central bank (or in vaults in London or New York) to cushion short-term trade flow fluctuations is an admittedly crude characterization of the reserve management objectives of developing

country policy makers. A more appropriate stylization would be to consider the problem as akin to the cash management problem of a bank or firm: cash (or foreign reserves) is but one instrument with which to meet the broader objective of maintaining sufficient liquidity at minimum cost. Other instruments in the portfolio include standby lines of credit with banks or special financing facilities from the IMF and other international agencies.

19. A further difficulty in using reserve levels as an indicator of the economy's cushion occurs when the accumulation of arrears is left out of the picture. For example, Zambia is approximately $3 billion in arrears to all creditors, yet it always seems to have a month or so of import coverage in gross reserves. Under such circumstances, the level of reserves ceases to be an instrument over which governments can exercise much control; reserve management becomes a continual task of reconciling conflicting demands. For example, any reserve accumulation over "essential" levels is likely to lead to pressures to reduce outstanding arrears and bring reserves back down again.

20. Where public enterprises constitute a large component of GNP the focus has to expand to include the broader public sector budget.

21. All the Asian countries in our sample saved at least 21 percent of their GDP and all but two of them saved more than 30 percent.

22. For those African countries with severe external debt difficulties, the deficit figures shown here underestimate the problem, since they are calculated on a cash rather than a commitment basis (that is, on what was actually paid rather than what was owed) and thus omit important items such as the accumulation of arrears.

23. Note that the period is shorter than for the exchange rate graphs, and the sample of countries is smaller, reflecting less complete coverage in available statistical sources.

24. The per capita income figures are from *World Tables* data in current dollars; the 1972 data were converted to 1988 prices by the scalar 2.828, which is the change in the U.S. CPI for 1972–1988.

25. The sequencing and extent of financial reform in Africa and Asia is covered extensively in Chapter 9 by Cole and Duesenberry. For an extensive treatment of issues of monetary management and the evolution of financial institutions in Sub-Saharan Africa, see Duesenberry and McPherson (1991).

26. This does not suggest laissez faire in financial markets. Prudential regulation by government over banks and other financial institutions is essential to reduce the risks to savers and make markets work more efficiently.

27. The 1980–1990 figures are the same as those presented in Table 4.3.

28. Moreover, in many SSA countries, the widespread reliance on controlled prices means that official inflation figures are probably too low. This factor also helps explain the very low Chinese inflation during 1970–1980.

BIBLIOGRAPHY

Asian Development Bank. 1992. *Key Indicators of Asian and Pacific Countries.* London: Oxford University Press, for the Asian Development Bank.

Collier, Paul. 1991. "Africa's External Economic Relations: 1960–90." In *Africa 30 Years On,* ed. D. Rimmer. London: Royal Africa Society in association with James Currey.

Devarajan, Shantayanan, Jeffrey D. Lewis, and Sherman Robinson. 1993. "External Shocks, Purchasing Power Parity, and the Equilibrium Real Exchange Rate." *World Bank Economic Review* 7 (1): 45–63.

Duesenberry, James S., and Malcolm F. McPherson. 1991. "Monetary Management in Sub-Saharan Africa." Development Discussion Paper No. 395 EPS. Harvard Institute for International Development, Harvard University (September).

Easterly, William, and Klaus Schmidt-Hebbel. 1991. "The Macroeconomics of Public Sector Deficits: A Synthesis." Working Paper WPS 775. World Bank, Washington, D.C.

Gelb, Alan, et al. 1988. *Oil Windfalls: Blessing or Curse?* New York: Oxford University Press.

Intal, Ponciano S., Jr. 1992. "Real Exchange Rates, Price Competitiveness and Structural Adjustment in Asian and Pacific Economies." *Asian Development Review* 10 (2): 86–123.

International Monetary Fund. 1992. *International Financial Statistics.* Washington, D.C. (on disk).

Mathieson, Donald J., and Liliana Rojas-Suarez. 1992. "Liberalization of the Capital Account: Experiences and Issues." International Monetary Fund Working Paper WP/92/46.

Sahn, David E. 1990. *Fiscal and Exchange Rate Reforms in Africa: Considering the Impact Upon the Poor.* Monograph No. 4, Cornell Food and Nutrition Policy Program, Cornell University (August).

World Bank. 1992. *World Tables 1992.* Washington, D.C. (on disk).

CHAPTER 5

Development from a Primary Export Base

Thomas Tomich, Michael Roemer, and Jeffrey Vincent

Pessimism about primary exports is one of the strongest strands in the intellectual history of development. Prebisch's (United Nations, 1950) and Singer's (1950) seminal observations of declining terms of trade for primary exporters, supported by Nurkse's (1961) structural arguments that markets for primary commodities must shrink over time, have survived forty years of counterargument to influence development strategists in the 1990s, nowhere more than in Africa. The success of the four Asian tigers lends credibility to the case that industrialization can proceed without support from primary exports. After all, Korea, Hong Kong, and Singapore are among the most resource-poor countries in the world.

This chapter argues, to the contrary, that primary exports can play a pivotal role in development generally, and specifically in support of industrialization. Silk exports, all but forgotten now, constituted nearly 46 percent of the value of Japan's merchandise exports between 1925 and 1930 (Hemmi 1969). Although Taiwan has not been a major primary exporter for a quarter-century, crude and processed agricultural products accounted for over 85 percent of its exports at the beginning of its industrialization drive in the 1950s (Etherington and Forster 1992). The focus of this chapter, however, is the more recent experience of the Southeast Asian countries. Three of them, Indonesia, Malaysia, and Thailand, were and continue to be aggressive primary exporters even as they focus on industrialization; a fourth, the Philippines, let its primary export base deteriorate and was also a less successful industrializer. The proposition draws support from Africa itself, where the countries that were able to maintain some development momentum, such as Botswana, Kenya, Malawi, and Mauritius, also sustained a growing primary export base.

The next two sections make a case for primary exports from the perspectives of supply, with data on country outcomes for Asian and African primary exporters, and demand, considering commodity market trends. We follow with a discussion of the linkages through which primary exports can contribute to economic development and then explore factor endowments to determine whether African countries are comparable to those in Southeast Asia. The balance of the chapter reviews strategic lessons from Asia and Africa regarding investments in primary exports, focusing on land-augmenting investments, including agricultural research priorities, and the economics of smallholder production.

Supply: Primary Export Performance in Africa and Southeast Asia

Indonesia, Malaysia, and Thailand have entered the ranks of the rapidly industrializing countries. Exports of manufactures from these countries rose at rates from 19 percent per year in Malaysia to 30 percent per year in Indonesia between 1970 and 1990. Yet all three countries continued to be major exporters of primary commodities. Table 5.1 shows that in Indonesia and Thailand the primary export share of gross domestic product increased from 1970 to 1990, while in Malaysia it was maintained at nearly 40 percent of GDP. Indonesia's and Malaysia's performances were helped substantially by oil discoveries and world price increases. In both countries the share of nonfuel primary exports declined significantly, although in Malaysia this ratio was still very high (28 percent) in 1990.

These results were not entirely strokes of fortune. In all three countries, government directed efforts at sustaining comparative advantage in primary exports. Malaysia decided during the 1950s not to abandon rubber exports, despite declining prices and intensifying competition from synthetics. Instead, it invested in research, extension, and planting to drive production costs down and remain competitive in world markets. Malaysia's share of

TABLE 5.1

Export Shares of Gross Domestic Product, 1965–1990

Country	Primary exports		Exports of goods plus nonfactor services	
	Share (%) in 1990	Change in share (%) since 1965	Share (%) in 1990	Change in share (%) since 1965
Southeast Asia				
Indonesia	16.1	+ 102	26.9	+ 118
(Nonfuel)	(5.1)	(− 36)		
Malaysia	38.2	+ 3	77.8	+ 86
(Nonfuel)	(27.9)	(− 18)		
Philippines	7.6	− 48	26.1	+ 33
Thailand	10.2	+ 15	36.7	+ 138
Africa				
Burkina Faso	8.5	+ 46	11.1	+ 32
Cameroon	14.3	− 17	21.1	− 11
Congo	46.0	+ 205	50.4	+ 72
Côte d'Ivoire	24.0	− 25	36.6	− 4
Ethiopia	5.8	− 13	11.0	+ 10
Gabon	46.2	− 6	52.0	−18
Ghana	14.0	− 26	15.5	− 27
Kenya	9.2	− 32	25.3	− 12
Liberia	33.2[a]	− 35	37.6	− 29
Madagascar	9.9	− 19	15.3	− 12
Malawi	21.8	+ 11	24.7	+ 2
Mauritius	33.1	+ 3	68.4	+ 59
Nigeria	38.2	+ 298	39.5	+ 275
(Nonfuel)	(0.8)	(− 80)		
Rwanda	16.8	+ 43	16.8	+ 43
Senegal	10.2	− 29	25.2	− 9
Sierra Leone	10.4	+ 13	23.4	− 16
Somalia	13.3	+ 43	17.5	+ 31
Tanzania	15.2	+ 1	22.7	− 4
Togo	22.4	− 12	34.6	+ 16
Uganda	6.3	− 68	7.7	− 60
Zaire	25.8	+ 66	30.5	+ 18
Zambia	27.0[b]	− 48	33.8[b]	− 37

a. 1987.
b. 1989.
SOURCES: International Monetary Fund, *International Financial Statistics Yearbook 1992* (Washington, D.C., 1992); World Bank, *World Tables 1992* (Washington, D.C., 1992); World Bank, *World Development Report 1992* (Washington, D.C., 1992).

world rubber exports increased by more than a quarter, to 34 percent between 1970 and 1987. The country made similar investments in palm oil and almost quadrupled its share, gaining half of the tropical vegetable oil market by 1987.

Even where good fortune did strike, in the form of rising petroleum prices in the 1970s, it took shrewd management to avoid a decline in other primary exports. Rising oil revenues tended to cause real exchange rate appreciation that reduced incentives for non-oil exports.[1] Indonesia maintained close macroeconomic balance throughout the oil boom and devalued its exchange rate in 1978, despite a strong balance of payments, specifically to protect the incomes of farmers. The government established macroeconomic conditions that encouraged private non-oil producers to expand. Malaysia and Thailand also avoided exchange rate appreciation and continued expansion of export agriculture.

In contrast to the three Southeast Asian countries, many African countries allowed their primary export bases to shrink. Table 5.1 shows that, of the twenty-two African countries for which data are available, eleven saw the primary export share of GDP fall by at least 10 percent from 1970 to 1990. In three of these cases (Côte d'Ivoire, Ethiopia, and Togo) enough export diversification was taking place to maintain or increase the ratio of all exports to GDP, but in the other eight countries the export ratio also fell. Another three of the twenty-two countries approximately maintained the primary export share of GDP, while eight countries had significant increases in the share. Primary export growth is not a sufficient condition for income growth, however: about half the countries with growing primary shares had stagnant or declining per capita incomes. But it is notable that only two of the countries with declining primary export shares had any growth in income per capita.

One implication of export pessimism is that all primary exporters should expect earnings to decline, either absolutely or certainly as a share of GDP. In this view, African countries can be considered victims of their initial endowments and the colonially enforced dependence on minerals and cash crops. The trouble with this argument is that, by and large, African exporters failed even to maintain their world market shares in the commodities in which they had comparative advantage. Table 5.2 shows that African countries lost world market share in thirty-one of forty-three cases.[2] For minerals, export volumes could have more to do with depleting endowments than with policies. For cash crops (including wood products), however, the tally is similar: in twenty-two of thirty cases African market share declined. By

TABLE 5.2
Changes in World Market Shares of Primary Exports, 1970–1990

Countries in	Whose market shares	All exports	Crops + wood	Minerals
Africa	Rose	12	8	4
	Fell	31	22	9
Southeast Asia	Rose	16	12	4
	Fell	7	5	2

SOURCE: World Bank, *Commodity Trade Statistics.*

contrast, Southeast Asian countries increased market shares in sixteen of the twenty-three cases overall and in four of the six mineral markets.

Some of the specific market outcomes are even more telling. Southeast Asian countries have been gaining export shares in the same markets previously dominated by Africa and Latin America. Indonesia and Malaysia have entered the cocoa market at the expense of Ghana and Cameroon, although the major gainer has been Côte d'Ivoire. All four African entrants lost market share in coffee while Indonesia gained. Nigeria lost ground in rubber exports while all three Southeast Asian exporters gained markedly. Indonesia continues to dominate several spice markets while Tanzania has nearly gone out of the business. Nigeria and Zaire, along with Malaysia, have lower shares of the tin market while Indonesia's share expanded. Malaysia's expansion in tropical vegetable oils came at the expense of several West African countries as well as the Philippines.

In the face of such direct competition, it seems almost certain that different government policies or effectiveness played a role, along with natural conditions such as drought. Malaysia's decisions on rubber and palm oil contrast with those of Ghana, which in the 1960s put resources into industrialization at the expense of cocoa and mineral production. Indonesia's macroeconomic policies to counter Dutch disease encouraged diversified agricultural growth, in contrast to Nigeria where Dutch disease destroyed the non-oil primary export base.

Not all African governments turned away from primary exports: Côte d'Ivoire invested aggressively in cocoa and other export crops; Kenya was innovative in moving coffee and especially tea production from estates to smallholdings, doubling its world market share in tea; and Liberia encouraged foreign investment in rubber and iron ore. Nor did all Southeast Asian countries invest productively: in the Philippines, policies did not encourage exports and the country lost market share in all but copper.

Demand: Changes in World Market Conditions

Prebisch (1950) and Singer (1950) based their case against primary exports on the persistence of declining terms of trade for primary exporters. Although their data and argument are fatally flawed (Kindleberger 1973, 74–77), recent, more careful investigations continue to show a decline in the terms of trade for nonfuel primary commodities from 1900 to the mid-1980s.[3] But the period of analysis turns out to be crucial. Cuddington and Urzúa (1989) reach a striking conclusion: all of the observed decline in the primary terms of trade from 1900 to 1986 can be explained by the precipitous fall in prices over 1920–1921. Taking the period since 1921, they find plenty of fluctuation but no trend in the terms of trade for primary commodities. The kinds of investment and policy decisions made by Malaysia in the 1950s and made subsequently by Indonesia, Thailand, Botswana, Côte d'Ivoire, and Kenya in the 1960s and 1970s may be equally valid for African countries today, insofar as the terms of trade are a consideration.

Nurkse's (1961) contribution to export pessimism was to identify several factors that might continue to reduce the demand for primary commodities relative to supply: Engel's law that food's share of total expenditures diminishes with rising incomes; technological change that reduces the use of raw materials per unit of output and creates synthetic substitutes; a shift toward non-commodity-using services as income grows in the industrial countries; and growth rates in the industrial country markets that are slower than potential increases in supply of some primary commodities.

Although export prices may not be declining secularly, it appears that, as Nurkse predicted, the growth of demand for primary exports in world markets is slowing. World Bank data show that the share of nonfuel raw material and food imports in the total imports of industrial countries has fallen from 39 percent in 1965 to 17 percent in 1990 (World Bank 1992). With imports to industrial countries growing at 4.5 percent per year, imports of nonfuel primary commodities, valued at constant prices, appear to have grown by only 1.1 percent per year from 1965 to 1990.

But this broad trend is not the whole story of export demand. The tale of the early twentieth century was that innovation and rising incomes led to entirely new export markets, including those for petroleum, rubber, copper, aluminum, newsprint, plywood, and vegetable oils. Even since 1960, export growth has been 5 percent per year or more over at least twenty years for sorghum, wheat, fish, soybeans, vegetable oils, oilseed cake and meal, alumina and aluminum, nickel, timber, and phosphates. Fresh fruits and vegetables and shrimp farming are new growth industries. Ecological concerns may boost exports of natural gas. Tourism is another growth industry with high income elasticity; although not a primary commodity, it is a service export based on two natural endowments: climate and nature.

World demand is not the only side of the balance for an exporting country to consider. Its own demand depends on supply conditions in other countries as well. Rising incomes and urbanization have raised the costs of labor and land and have reduced the productive capacity of many traditional exporters. In other cases poor policies or natural disasters affected production. Kenya's and Indonesia's incursion into the tea market took advantage of growing incomes and expanding domestic demand in India and counterproductive policies toward plantations in Sri Lanka. Malaysia and Côte d'Ivoire picked up cocoa exports as Ghana did nothing to reduce its costs of production. Moreover, even granted slowing market growth for many commodities, it may still be economically profitable for a country to invest sufficiently in primary commodities to reduce costs and maintain or increase market share, as some Southeast Asian and African countries have done.

Linkages: Primary Exports and Economic Development

Primary products can promote income growth and structural change through at least four mechanisms.

First, the most obvious mechanism is the *supply of foreign exchange* to finance imports or intermediate and capital goods, especially in the early stages of structural transformation when manufacturing is a small share of economic activity. Foreign exchange shortages have starved new industries of capital and intermediate goods in many African countries, a constraint that does not afflict Indonesia, Malaysia, or Thailand. But a surge of foreign exchange earnings can be a mixed blessing.

When mining and petroleum industries generate substantial foreign exchange relative to the size of the economy, there is a strong tendency for nominal exchange rates to appreciate. This can also happen during price booms in agricultural exports, such as coffee and tea. Even if the central bank prevents appreciation through exchange rate management, the accumulation of reserves raises the money supply, which boosts the demand for home-produced goods and stimulates inflation. Either way, the real exchange rate appreciates, rendering nonmineral export and import-substitution industries less competitive on world markets; this phenomenon is called *Dutch disease*.[4] Avoiding Dutch disease requires strong macroeconomic countermeasures—such as exchange rate devaluation, sterilizing foreign exchange earnings by reducing domestic credit pari passu, and redirecting mineral rents to investment in other tradable industries (Roemer 1985). Indonesia has been skilled at counteracting Dutch disease during the oil boom, but Nigeria suffered a full-blown case that slowed its development (Gelb et al. 1988). Among African countries, Botswana has been the most successful in avoiding real appreciation and other symptoms of Dutch disease.

Second, primary exports can enable a country to *utilize its factor endowments* more completely. Adam Smith and Hla Myint used the term "vent for surplus" to describe the export of commodities that have little value at home because demand is so small relative to potential supply, but much greater value abroad. The concept remains valid for many mineral and timber exports, especially from poorer and smaller countries rich in such resources. But it is increasingly of only historical interest for agricultural commodities, as population pressure makes land relatively less abundant.

Third, primary exports can *expand endowments of labor and capital.* In Malaysia, the labor needs of the tin mining and rubber industries were met by immigrants from China and India, respectively. Migrant workers, now from Indonesia and the Philippines, remain important today in the timber industry of sparsely populated Sabah and Sarawak and in the plantations of peninsular Malaysia, as rapid industrialization has driven up rural wage rates. Ghana in the early twentieth century and Côte d'Ivoire since its independence have also attracted migrant farmers to grow cocoa and other crops. In Southeast Asia, Africa, and most of the world, however, migrant workers are considered a mixed blessing by the indigenous population. Primary products also attract capital, plus the management and technology that often come bundled with it. Foreign capital played a major role in developing plantation and mining industries in both Southeast Asia and Africa since colonial times and raised investment levels well beyond what they otherwise would have been.

Fourth, growth in primary exports stimulates development through economic linkages with the rest of the economy. This is the domain of *staple theory* and its lessons will occupy much of this chapter. The linkages are of four types: (1) *consumption linkages* that stimulate growth through the pattern of domestic demand, (2) *forward linkages* through expansion of transport and other marketing services as well as primary product processing, (3) *backward linkages* to input suppliers, and (4) *rent linkages,* the domestic savings funded from natural resource rents; when these rents accrue to government, the rent linkage is called a *fiscal linkage.*

Consumption Linkages

The magnitude of consumption linkages depends on the amount of employment generated through export expansion, the workers' earnings, and their expenditure patterns. Petroleum, mining, and forestry are capital intensive. Wages tend to be relatively high, but few jobs are generated in any of these activities, except perhaps in small-scale mining of diamonds and gold. Large-scale plantations are far more labor intensive than mines and logging operations, but few plantation workers receive more than the prevailing rural wage, which limits their effective demand.

Capital–labor ratios are no higher in smallholder[5] than in estate agriculture, so that expansion of smallholder agriculture offers at least as much (and often more) employment than large-scale plantations. But smallholders also earn land rents (unless they are tenants), returns to management, and any economic rents from innovation, better management, and superior location. With higher incomes than the estate labor force, smallholders create greater demand linkages to farming, to manufacturing (of goods such as clothing, footwear, and bicycles), and to rural services.

The growing literature on smallholder growth linkages demonstrates that they are substantial and that consumption linkages account for half or more of the multiplier effect from agricultural growth.[6] Most of these results are from studies of foodgrains. One study that compares smallholder export crops and foodcrops found equally strong growth linkages for rice, coffee, vanilla, and cloves in Madagascar (Dorosh and Haggblade 1992). Because consumption linkages account for 80 percent of the multiplier effects from agricultural growth in Madagascar, any increase in income, whether from food or export crops, has similar linkage effects.

Forward Linkages

Primary exports generate two kinds of forward linkage: (1) activities necessary for export and (2) optional downstream industries that may increase the value added from a commodity export. Necessary forward linkages include transport infrastructure and services, telecommunications, marketing services, and some processing.

Transportation and marketing services established for export crops help a country's traders and entrepreneurs gain experience and market connections that can be useful in developing other export industries. Evolution of marketing skills can begin when some of the more enterprising members of a country's trading community establish reputations as reliable sources of higher-quality traditional exports, such as coffee, cocoa, natural rubber, or spices. As infrastructure improves, trading contacts in overseas markets become a basis for diversification into higher-value, "nontraditional" exports. In Indonesia, for example, a former coffee exporter has switched to production and export of frogs' legs to France, and a major exporter of cocoa also is a leader in exports of cut flowers to a number of European markets.

These "nontraditional" exports often are perishable commodities that depend on reliable, rapid communication and transport for exporters to deliver top-quality products that fit specific tastes in importing countries at the right time to secure peak seasonal prices. Horticultural exports from Kenya and Zimbabwe could only take off when government restrictions on foreign air service were relaxed enough to allow sufficient freight capacity into European markets. Expansion of horticultural exports, at least in Zimbabwe, also led to downstream investment in dehydration, canning, juicing, and freezing plants as well as custom packaging and labeling for European supermarket chains (Rusinga 1993). Domestic capacity to ascertain and serve specific needs of customers in importing countries is just as important in, say, the manufacture of high-fashion garments and trendy athletic shoes as it is in exporting flowers or snow peas. Although industrial production may require entrepreneurial skills not found in the primary sector, marketing skills learned in primary exporting may be transferable to industries in which African countries could compete in world markets.

Road networks established for smallholder agriculture reduce costs for all rural economic activity, as is evident in places such as Java and central Kenya. The same cannot always be said for the infrastructure and services developed for mineral and timber exports. When mines, oil fields, or forests are in remote areas, as is true in much of Southeast Asia and parts of Africa, roads and railroads dedicated to them cannot reduce costs for industries that gravitate toward populous areas. Marketing of minerals, more often than not, is carried out by government or multinational companies, with little learning that is useful in other sectors.

Governments are generally keen to promote the second kind of forward linkage: *downstream processing* or *resource-based industrialization* (RBI). Some downstream processing is necessary for export and belongs in the first category: tea leaves, sugarcane, oil palm, other crops, and several ores need to be treated, reduced, or refined to make export profitable or even possible. Many governments wish to go beyond these relatively simple processing industries, however, with the aims of adding value, generating employment, reducing dependence, diversifying exports, or otherwise spurring development by performing at home some processes that previously were done abroad. Common examples include more complete processing of edible oils by Malaysia and Indonesia; the promotion of plywood and other wood industries through bans or taxes on log exports by Malaysia, Indonesia, and Ghana; the establishment of refineries in many petroleum-exporting countries; the development of new steel technology to process ores in Mexico and Venezuela; and building an aluminum industry to process bauxite in Venezuela.

Attractive as resource-based industries may appear, their economic rationale is often questionable (Roemer 1979). Much downstream processing or manufacturing takes place abroad because importing countries have a comparative advantage in these industries. For example, cocoa producers lack the milk required to produce chocolate; end-users often prefer to process edible oils themselves to accommodate their own specifications; the reduction of bauxite creates by-products that can only be used in industrial markets; and the further refining to aluminum requires abundant, cheap electric power.

Even if a primary exporter could compete in processing for export, the opportunity costs of moving investment and labor from other potential industries may be too high. Vincent (1992a) estimates that Malaysia's restrictions on log exports did increase output and employment in sawmilling by about 25 percent from 1973–1989. But each sawmill job, which paid an average $2,200 per year, cost Malaysia $6,100 in lost value added and $16,600 in forgone export earnings as log exports fell. When log exports are banned, not only is the volume of timber exports reduced, but the domestic price of logs falls, encouraging inefficient processing into products with reduced value added in world prices. Similar calculations apply to Indonesia's log ban, which nevertheless promoted a booming plywood industry. These processing industries, like many others, fail on basic tests of economic efficiency; some even consume resources of greater value than the product they export.

Not only do downstream industries often fail to deliver higher value added than would obtain with unprocessed exports; they generally fail to satisfy other development goals as well. Agricultural and timber processing can be labor intensive, but mineral processing creates relatively few jobs. RBI does not diversify an economy or reduce its dependence. Downstream industries only commit more capital and labor to the same markets, with much the same risk factors, concentrating earnings and making a country even more dependent on a few commodities. The same resources invested in other industries are likely to create more employment, diversify the economy, and reduce its dependence.

The basic lesson on RBI derives from experience throughout the developing world. Downstream industries should be encouraged only if they pass basic tests of economic advantage. No particular benefit is gained by favoring an industry related to one's primary exports over an unrelated industry with a higher economic profit.

Backward Linkages

Primary sectors have relatively weak backward linkages. Petroleum and most types of mining tend to be enclaves. Of the few inputs required by timber companies and plantations, many are imported (such as heavy equipment for logging or land clearing). Backward linkages are small even in smallholder treecrops. For agriculture as a whole, the most important backward linkage by far is chemical fertilizer, followed by farm equipment. With rare exceptions (Indonesia is one), fertilizer imports are far cheaper than promotion of domestic fertilizer production (Tomich, Kilby, and Johnston 1995). In any event, compared with foodcrop producers, smallholder treecrop producers in developing countries often make little use of either chemical fertilizer or farm equipment.

Rent Linkages

The most important growth linkages for forestry, petroleum, and mining derive from economic rents, the difference between the world price of exports and the costs of production, including normal returns on capital. Estimating the magnitude of such rents is notoriously difficult. One study estimated that resource rents from timber and minerals (including petroleum and natural gas) were equivalent to 37 percent of gross capital formation in Malaysia during the 1980s (WWF Malaysia 1992). Rents captured by both the public and private sectors have provided funds for investment in industry, which now is the greatest source of economic growth and new jobs in

Malaysia.[7] In similar fashion, yield increases and land-augmenting investments such as roads and irrigation systems raise the economic rent on land. Higher resource rents accruing to landowners, especially when these are smallholders, contribute to the consumption linkage, but a significant portion of these higher economic rents also is invested.

Governments have gained increasing shares of resource rents over time. Taxes and royalties on petroleum and natural gas constituted over a quarter of Malaysian federal government revenue in 1990 (Ministry of Finance, Malaysia 1991, 68) and close to 40 percent of Indonesian government revenues in the early 1990s. These governments have been adept at extracting resource rents without discouraging investment, especially in petroleum and other minerals. For the rent linkage to work, however, it is essential that governments invest their revenues in projects that contribute to development goals. Indonesia and Malaysia, like most resource-rich countries, have dissipated a share of their revenues in poor projects. But they also directed a substantial share into strategic investments, especially in agriculture, education, and health facilities, that contributed to rapid economic growth and dramatic reductions in poverty.

African countries with similar resource endowments have been less successful in converting rents into rapid, broadly-based economic growth. Because of its oil revenues, Nigeria has grown more rapidly than most African countries. But Gelb et al. (1988) argue that growth was slower than it would have been without the oil boom and investment, because Nigeria suffered an untreated case of Dutch disease and dissipated its oil rents on wasteful projects. Botswana has parlayed diamond and other primary exports into one of the fastest growing economies in the world. But other well-endowed countries such as Ghana before the mid-1980s, Zaire, and Zambia have, through poor policies or wanton use of revenues, squandered their natural advantages and experienced declining incomes over a twenty-five-year period. It can be argued that booms in resource rents, by relaxing budgetary constraints, contribute to lax fiscal discipline and poor investment decisions (Roemer 1985). But experience in Southeast Asia and Sub-Saharan Africa suggests that some governments manage resource rents productively. The reasons for successes and failures lie in both political and economic considerations.

Governments can extract a share of natural resource rents through agricultural *export taxes*. Malaysia's Rubber Research Institute and the Palm Oil Research Institute have been funded primarily by cesses (earmarked taxes) on rubber and palm oil exports. Cesses have also been levied with the intention of funding replanting with high-yielding varieties in Malaysia, Thailand, and Indonesia. Even in Malaysia, total taxes paid by treecrop producers exceeded the value of the services they received in return (Barlow and Jayasuriya 1986) (indeed, Malaysia's various cesses were only a small part of taxes imposed on rubber). In Indonesia, smallholders received only a small fraction of the funds collected at various times through cesses and "rehabilitation funds" for rubber, coconut, and cloves. Indonesia's problems of weak financial control are common in Africa. When it is easy for bureaucrats and politicians to divert the funds, it is neither administratively feasible nor economically desirable to attempt to use agricultural export taxes to finance government projects.

As a rule, export *marketing boards* simply create implicit taxes for agricultural producers. Especially in Africa, but also in Indonesia and the Philippines, it has been common for the public sector (or officially designated private firms) to appropriate sole authority for marketing certain export crops and for other essentially commercial activities that are difficult for bureaucratic organizations to manage effectively. A study of Tanzania "shows that a large share of potential surpluses was diverted to marketing boards where it was used essentially to pay inflated civil service costs" (Ellis, quoted in Maxwell and Fernando 1989, 1682). Rent linkages were dissipated as a result.

Of course, there are cases (such as diamonds and petroleum) where export taxes or quotas can create economic benefits for exporting nations. But as a practical matter, the *optimal export tax* argument rarely applies in agriculture. International commodity agreements are unwieldy and there are few agricultural commodities where single countries have sufficient market power (see Appendix 5.1). No country in Africa or Southeast Asia had even 4 percent of world coffee exports, and only Kenya had a significant share (12 percent) of tea exports in 1987. Among major agricultural commodities, cocoa is (perhaps) the most plausible case for an optimal export tax for certain African producers. But by any economic measure, the cocoa export taxes of 40 to 70 percent imposed in the early 1980s by Ghana, Nigeria, and Cameroon were several times the optimum (Imran and Duncan 1988, 21). These policies raised world prices but also undermined domestic investment in cocoa and increased incentives for the dramatic expansion of cocoa production by Malaysia and Indonesia.

Many agricultural commodities face competition from natural and synthetic substitutes, so even a large share of exports does not guarantee market power for the producing country. For example, Malaysia produced a third of the world's exports of natural rubber and almost half of exports of tropical oils in 1987. After accounting for competition from synthetic rubber and other edible oils (and including production in consuming countries that is not exported), Malaysia's share of world supply falls to 11 percent and 9 percent, respectively. While Madagascar accounted for 70 percent of natural vanilla exports in 1987, 90 percent of the U.S. market was supplied by synthetic vanilla.

Even in cases where there is a valid optimal export tax argument, there should be concern about its incidence. If the crop in question is a perennial, the elasticity of supply is likely to be small, at least in the short run. As a result, the export tax not only will extract monopoly rent from foreign consumers but will also fall (probably even more heavily) on the country's own producers. In many cases, it is possible that these resource rents could be invested better by individual producers than by government.

Endowments

Southeast Asian and some African countries have exploited their natural resource base to sustain primary export growth and promote development partly through the linkages emanating from farming, forestry, and mining. The extent to which more African countries can follow this path depends on the similarity of their resource endowments to those in Asia, the topic of this section.

Minerals and Petroleum

Indonesia and Malaysia have been particularly favored by mineral endowments. Both have large oil reserves and substantial deposits of metal ores, including tin in Malaysia and copper and others in Indonesia. Relative to its population, Malaysia is probably wealthier in minerals than any country in either Asia or Africa. Nevertheless, several African countries can be considered resource rich, as Table 5.3 shows. Nigeria has greater oil reserves than Indonesia and, with a smaller population, is more generously endowed. Zaire, with 3.6 percent of world metal reserves,[8] has more than Malaysia and Indonesia combined, and Botswana, Guinea, and Zambia are also rich in deposits relative to their populations. Thus a number of African countries, with a large share of Africa's population, have as great a natural potential as Malaysia and Indonesia to turn mineral wealth into development.

TABLE 5.3
Minerals and Forestry

	Crude oil reserves (million MT), 1987	Metal reserve index[a] (%), 1990	Forest and woodland (000 ha), 1990	Forest share of total land (%), 1990	Roundwood production (000 m³), average 1987–89	Roundwood net trade (X−M) (000 m³), average 1987–89
ASEAN Four						
Indonesia	1,142	1.54	113,433	63	173,580	1,099
Malaysia	434	1.32	19,330	59	47,691	21,482
Philippines	2	0.30	10,350	35	38,158	198
Thailand	13	0.47	14,100	28	38,239	−423
Total	1,591	3.63	157,213	53	297,668	22,356
Sub-Saharan Africa						
Angola	156	0.00	52,000	42	5,262	0
Benin		0.00	3,470	31	4,845	0
Botswana		0.60	10,910	19	1,276	0
Burkina Faso		0.00	6,600	24	8,300	0
Burundi		0.00	66	3	3,969	0
Cameroon	71	0.21	24,540	53	12,615	479
Central African Republic		0.00	35,800	57	3,449	32
Chad		0.00	12,730	10	3,837	0
Congo	98	0.00	21,160	62	3,119	803
Côte d'Ivoire	16	0.00	7,380	23	12,799	572
Equatorial Guinea		0.00	1,295	46	607	120
Ethiopia		0.00	27,100	25	38,859	0
Gabon	130	0.43	20,000	78	3,618	1,018
Gambia, The		0.00	156	16	912	0
Ghana		0.15	8,070	35	17,006	286
Guinea		1.73	14,580	59	4,560	8
Guinea-Bissau		0.00	1,070	38	565	0
Kenya		0.00	2,340	4	34,206	0
Lesotho		0.00	0	0	579	−33
Liberia		0.05	1,740	18	5,825	544
Madagascar		0.03	15,530	27	7,637	2
Malawi		0.00	3,630	39	7,366	0
Mali		0.00	6,950	6	5,359	0
Mauritania		0.02	4,430	4	12	0

Continued on next page

	Crude oil reserves (million MT), 1987	Metal reserve index[a] (%), 1990	Forest and woodland (000 ha), 1990	Forest share of total land (%), 1990	Roundwood production (000 m³), average 1987–89	Roundwood net trade (X−M) (000 m³), average 1987–89
Mozambique		0.05	14,260	18	16,001	3
Namibia		0.14	18,120	22	na	0
Niger		0.01	2,000	2	4,287	0
Nigeria	2,200	0.02	11,900	13	104,926	15
Rwanda		0.00	554	22	5,842	0
Senegal		0.00	10,550	55	31,966	0
Sierra Leone		0.11	2,060	29	2,941	0
Somalia		0.00	9,060	14	6,757	0
Sudan	41	0.01	44,840	19	21,584	0
Swaziland		0.00	104	6	2,223	198
Tanzania		0.00	40,940	46	34,206	0
Togo		0.00	1,600	29	840	0
Uganda		0.01	5,560	28	13,880	0
Zaire	15	3.55	174,310	77	34,255	135
Zambia		1.00	28,850	39	12,030	0
Zimbabwe		0.82	19,130	49	7,755	9
Total		8.94	665,385	30	456,155	4,166
World	122,848	100.00	4,027,569	31	3,425,613	0

NOTES: na = not available Cape Verde, Comoros, Djibouti, Mauritius, and South Africa are not included.
a. "Metal reserve index" is the average of the country's global shares of fifteen metals: copper, lead, tin, zinc, iron and seven ferro alloys, bauxite, titanium, and lithium.
SOURCES: Crude oil reserves: United Nations, *Energy Statistics Yearbook 1992*. Metal reserves index: World Resources Institute, *World Resources 1992–93* (New York, Oxford: Oxford University Press, 1992). Land: Food and Agriculture Organization of the United Nations, *FAO Production Yearbook* (Rome: FAO, 1991). Roundwood production and net trade: World Resources Institute, *World Resources 1992–93* (New York, Oxford: Oxford University Press, 1992).

Forests

Over half the area of the ASEAN four (Indonesia, Malaysia, the Philippines, and Thailand) was classed as "forest and woodland" in 1990 by the FAO (see Table 5.3). The main timber-producing areas of Southeast Asia are Peninsular Malaysia, Borneo, and Sumatra.[9] Africa's forests are not nearly as rich in timber as Southeast Asia's dipterocarp forests. Sub-Saharan Africa's total forest area in 1990 and average roundwood production for 1987–1989 were much greater than that of the ASEAN four. But while Gabon, the Congo, Côte d'Ivoire, Liberia, and Cameroon accounted for over 80 percent of Africa's roundwood exports, Africa's top five combined exported less than 16 percent of Malaysia's roundwood exports. There has been much less forest surplus to "vent" in Africa than in Southeast Asia because of the lower quality of the basic timber stocks combined with mounting domestic consumption of fuelwood.

Agricultural Land and Labor

The ratio of agricultural land (arable land plus area under permanent crops and pasture) to the number of agricultural workers is the most basic indicator of resource endowments in the sector. Sub-Saharan Africa in 1990 had 6.3 hectares of agricultural land per agricultural worker, compared to about one hectare per worker in the ASEAN four (see Table 5.4). This sixfold average difference masks huge variations within Africa: from Rwanda, Burundi, and The Gambia, with less agricultural land per worker than Indonesia or the Philippines, to Botswana and Namibia, with among the highest land/labor ratios in the world. Soil quality, water availability, and length of growing season affect the suitability of land for specific agricultural activities, however. When these characteristics are taken into account, the land endowment in much of Africa looks much more like that in Southeast Asia.

Virtually all of Southeast Asia lies in the humid tropics with average annual rainfall in excess of 2,000 mm and a growing season longer than 180 days per year. On the other hand, soils are relatively poor in much of Peninsular Malaysia, Borneo, and Sumatra, the heartland of Asian export crop production. In contrast, a large area of the African continent has no inherent soil constraints, but the bulk of this land is in arid regions where rainfall is inadequate for most crops (World Resources Institute 1992). There are great differences in water availability and growing season both within countries and across regions in Sub-Saharan Africa. At least fifteen "humid" African countries have endowments that resemble the ASEAN four in water availability, land quality, and growing season. Another fifteen countries are in a "mixed" category, including countries that encompass significant dry areas (average rainfall below 400 mm per year) not found in Southeast Asia and humid lowlands comparable to land found in Malaysia or Indonesia. Finally, there are ten countries in Africa that are predominantly dry.[10]

Sub-Saharan Africa's apparent advantage in agricultural land per worker stems entirely from a much greater area of permanent pasture. Over 80 percent of Sub-Saharan Africa's agricultural land is pasture, compared with only 20 percent in the ASEAN four. However, poor range quality, climate,

TABLE 5.4
Agricultural Land and Labor, 1990

	Agricultural land, 000 ha	Agricultural labor, 000 workers	Agricultural land/ agricultural labor, ha/worker	Permanent pasture/ agricultural land, %	Livestock pasture average 1988–90, no./ha	Cropland, 000 ha	Cropland/ agricultural labor, ha/worker
ASEAN Four	70,857	67,517	1.05	20	5.17	56,990	0.84
Indonesia	33,800	35,769	0.94	35	3.16	22,000	0.62
Malaysia	4,907	2,255	2.18	1	137.33	4,880	2.16
Philippines	9,230	10,503	0.88	14	11.75	7,970	0.76
Thailand	22,920	18,990	1.21	3	20.34	22,140	1.17
Sub-Saharan Africa	886,691	140,356	6.32	84	0.64	141,824	1.01
Humid Sub-Saharan Africa	187,904	57,082	3.29	68	0.63	60,850	1.07
Congo	10,168	506	20.09	98	0.05	168	0.33
Zaire	22,860	8,683	2.63	66	0.42	7,860	0.91
Gabon	5,157	351	14.69	91	0.09	457	1.30
Central African Republic	5,006	884	5.66	60	1.41	2,006	2.27
Nigeria	72,300	26,577	2.72	55	1.13	32,300	1.22
Angola	32,400	2,851	11.36	90	0.17	3,400	1.19
Rwanda	1,617	3,216	0.50	29	4.71	1,155	0.36
Burundi	2,252	2,594	0.87	41	1.89	1,338	0.52
Uganda	8,510	6,569	1.30	21	4.83	6,710	1.02
Côte d'Ivoire	16,690	2,545	6.56	78	0.26	3,690	1.45
Sierra Leone	2,854	891	3.20	77	0.40	650	0.73
Liberia	6,073	666	9.12	94	0.12	373	0.56
Gambia, The	268	316	0.85	34	8.71	178	0.56
Guinea-Bissau	1,415	353	4.01	76	0.97	335	0.95
Equatorial Guinea	334	80	4.18	31	0.51	230	2.88
Mixed Sub-Saharan Africa	310,660	63,450	4.90	83	0.79	51,997	0.82
Senegal	5,450	2,466	2.21	57	2.87	2,350	0.95
Tanzania	38,367	10,315	3.72	91	0.76	3,367	0.33
Kenya	40,530	7,645	5.30	94	0.74	2,430	0.32
Guinea	6,878	1,835	3.75	89	0.46	728	0.40
Madagascar	37,102	3,953	9.39	92	0.40	3,102	0.78
Mozambique	47,130	6,666	7.07	93	0.05	3,130	0.47

Continued on next page

TABLE 5.4 (Continued)

	Agricultural land, 000 ha	Agricultural labor, 000 workers	Agricultural land/ agricultural labor, ha/worker	Permanent pasture/ agricultural land, %	Livestock pasture average 1988–90, no./ha	Cropland, 000 ha	Cropland/ agricultural labor, ha/worker
Zambia	35,268	1,872	18.84	85	0.12	5,268	2.81
Cameroon	15,308	2,656	5.76	54	1.49	7,008	2.64
Malawi	4,259	2,690	1.58	43	1.28	2,419	0.90
Ghana	7,720	2,751	2.81	65	1.26	2,720	0.99
Ethiopia	58,830	15,461	3.81	76	1.76	13,930	0.90
Zimbabwe	7,668	2,600	2.95	63	2.01	2,812	1.08
Togo	2,459	995	2.47	73	1.82	669	0.67
Benin	2,302	1,338	1.72	19	7.93	1,860	1.39
Swaziland	1,389	207	6.71	85	0.89	204	0.99
Dry Sub-Saharan Africa	388,127	19,824	19.58	93	0.53	28,977	1.46
Lesotho	2,320	653	3.55	86	1.68	320	0.49
Botswana	34,380	271	126.86	96	0.15	1,380	5.09
Namibia	38,662	184	210.12	98	0.30	662	3.60
Mali	32,093	2,371	13.54	93	0.57	2,093	0.88
Mauritania	39,455	417	94.62	99	0.25	205	0.49
Burkina Faso	13,563	4,004	3.39	74	1.23	3,563	0.89
Sudan	122,900	4,923	24.96	90	0.53	12,900	2.62
Somalia	44,039	2,108	20.89	98	1.08	1,039	0.49
Chad	48,205	1,472	32.75	93	0.22	3,205	2.18
Niger	12,510	3,421	3.66	71	1.79	3,610	1.06
World	4,846,294	1,101,503	4.40	70	1.21	1,444,217	1.31

NOTE: Cape Verde, Comoros, Djibouti, Mauritius, and South Africa are not included.
SOURCES: Land and labor in 1990: Food and Agricultural Organization of the United Nations, *FAO Production Yearbook* (Rome: FAO, 1991). Livestock (includes cattle, buffaloes, camels, horses, mules, donkeys, domestic sheep, goats, and pigs): World Resources Institute, *World Resources 1992–93* (New York, Oxford: Oxford University Press, 1992).

and the prevalence of pests and diseases severely constrain livestock populations in large parts of Sub-Saharan Africa. On average, there is more than one hectare of pasture per animal in Sub-Saharan Africa, and for dry countries 2 to 4 hectares per animal is common. Neither pasture endowment nor livestock production in Sub-Saharan Africa bears much resemblance to Southeast Asia.[11]

Differences in land/labor ratios disappear when comparisons between Sub-Saharan Africa and the ASEAN four are restricted to cropland.[12] The fifteen "humid" African countries had only 30 percent more cropland per agricultural worker than the ASEAN four in 1990 (see Table 5.4). For the fifteen African countries classed as "mixed," the endowments of cropland and agricultural labor were virtually identical to the ASEAN four. Moreover, Binswanger and Pingali (1988) reckon that population pressures in Kenya, Nigeria, Niger, Ethiopia, Mali, and Tanzania—indeed, most countries of Sub-Saharan Africa—will drive cropland-per-worker ratios below those in the Philippines by the year 2000. There is little scope for expanding cropland in many of these countries, and certainly not at a rate to match the pace of labor force growth.

Thus, for many countries in Africa, cropland endowments look quite similar to those of Southeast Asia, especially when allowance is made for continuing population growth. Neither Africa nor Asia has much surplus land to "vent" as primary exports. This fact suggests that Africa, to reinvigorate its comparative advantage in primary exports, would do well to emulate Southeast Asia by investing in such land-augmenting investments as rural infrastructure, treecrops, and research on export crops, and by continuing to focus efforts on its most efficient form of production, smallholder agriculture. The next three sections deal with these policy issues.

Land-Augmenting Investments

The effective supply of agricultural land can be increased through innovations that raise yields and through investments in transport infrastructure, irrigation works, and trees and other perennial crops. As population pressure mounts in Africa and Asia, land-augmenting investments and research to produce higher-yielding varieties will become more profitable.

Transport and Marketing Infrastructure

In their review of the available estimates of agricultural growth linkages, Haggblade, Hazell, and Brown (1989, 1192–93) found that estimates for Africa tend to be lower than for Asia. If this is indeed the case, one plausible reason is Africa's poorer stock of transport infrastructure. Investments to improve and extend roads and other transport infrastructure will become more feasible as African population densities increase. Because Africa's economic decline and fiscal stringency caused roads to deteriorate in many areas, road rehabilitation may already be an urgent need and a profitable investment for most economies.

Irrigation

The extent of irrigation investment provides a major contrast between Asia and Africa. Merely 4 percent of cropland in Sub-Saharan Africa was irrigated in 1990. Only five countries have irrigated as much as 10 percent of their cropland; Madagascar and Swaziland had the largest share, 30 percent (see Table 5.5). Most of the rest have extended irrigation to 5 percent of cropland or less: 2 percent in Kenya, 3 percent in Nigeria, and 4 percent in Tanzania. In Southeast Asia, however, the range is from only 7 percent in Malaysia to about 20 percent in Thailand and the Philippines, and 35 percent in Indonesia.

Irrigation projects have been more productive in Asia than in Africa. When economic linkages were taken into account along with direct benefits, Bell, Hazell, and Slade (1982, 216) estimated that the real social rate of return to the Muda irrigation project in Malaysia exceeded 20 percent. But in Sub-Saharan Africa, large-scale projects are expensive and net social benefits have been low or negative (Binswanger and Pingali 1988; Pearson, Stryker, and Humphreys 1981). Africa is not as well endowed with rivers as East and Southeast Asia, and its groundwater tends to be deeper than in South Asia. For most of Sub-Saharan Africa, rainfed crop production will continue to be the rule.

Treecrops

With limited opportunities for expanding irrigation, treecrops appear to hold the most promise for enhancing land productivity in the "humid" and "mixed" countries of Sub-Saharan Africa. Treecrops do better under rainfed conditions than most annuals, including foodgrains (Ruthenberg 1980, 320). Furthermore, large areas of Southeast Asia and the "humid" and "mixed" countries in Africa are better suited to farming systems based on treecrops than intensive production of annual crops because their fragile soils are susceptible to erosion.[13] For example, what Malaysia lacks in irrigation investment it makes up in permanent crops: almost 80 percent of Malaysia's

TABLE 5.5
Irrigation and Permanent Crops, 1990

	Irrigated land, 000 ha	Irrigated land/ cropland, %	Permanent crops, 000 ha	Permanent crops/ cropland, %
ASEAN Four	13,802	24	16,400	29
Indonesia	7,600	35	6,000	27
Malaysia	342	7	3,840	79
Philippines	1,560	20	3,420	43
Thailand	4,300	19	3,140	14
Sub-Saharan Africa	5,383	4	14,104	10
Humid Sub-Saharan Africa	1,081	2	7,940	13
Congo	4	2	24	14
Zaire	10	0	610	8
Gabon	na	na	162	35
Central African Republic	na	na	86	4
Nigeria	870	3	2,535	8
Angola	na	na	500	15
Rwanda	4	0	305	26
Burundi	72	5	218	16
Uganda	9	0	1,710	25
Côte d'Ivoire	64	2	1,260	34
Sierra Leone	34	5	150	23
Liberia	2	1	245	66
Gambia, The	12	7	na	na
Guinea-Bissau	na	na	35	10
Equatorial Guinea	na	na	100	43
Mixed Sub-Saharan Africa	1,991	4	6,051	12
Senegal	180	8	15	1
Tanzania	150	4	636	19
Kenya	54	2	500	21
Guinea	25	3	118	16
Madagascar	920	30	522	17
Mozambique	115	4	230	7
Zambia	32	1	8	0
Cameroon	30	0	1,068	15

Continued on next page

TABLE 5.5 (Continued)

	Irrigated land, 000 ha	Irrigated land/ cropland, %	Permanent crops, 000 ha	Permanent crops/ cropland, %
Mixed Sub-Saharan Africa				
Malawi	20	1	29	1
Ghana	8	0	1,580	58
Ethiopia	162	1	730	5
Zimbabwe	220	8	92	3
Togo	7	1	69	10
Benin	6	0	450	24
Swaziland	62	30	4	2
Dry Sub-Saharan Africa	2,311	8	113	0
Lesotho	na	na	na	na
Botswana	2	0	na	na
Namibia	4	1	2	0
Mali	205	10	3	0
Mauritania	12	6	3	1
Burkina Faso	20	1	13	0
Sudan	1,900	15	70	1
Somalia	118	11	17	2
Chad	10	0	5	0
Niger	40	1	0	0
World	237,421	16	94,194	7

NOTE: na = not available. Cape Verde, Comoros, Djibouti, Mauritius, and South Africa are not included.
SOURCE: Food and Agricultural Organization of the United Nations, *FAO Production Yearbook* (Rome: FAO, 1991).

cropland was planted with permanent crops in 1990. Indonesia is broadly representative of the ASEAN four with just over a quarter of cropland in permanent crops.

The gap between Africa and Asia is substantial. The 16 million hectares of permanent crops in the four Southeast Asian countries surpasses the total for Sub-Saharan Africa. Seven African countries have more than 25 percent of their cropland planted with permanent crops, but only Ghana (58 percent) and Liberia (66 percent) come close to the proportion in Malaysia. No African country has as many hectares planted to permanent crops as Thailand, the smallest of the ASEAN four. The Southeast Asian countries have also continued to expand their treecrop production and exports, while Africa has lagged behind (see Table 5.2).

Yet the fifteen "humid" countries of Sub-Saharan Africa include much of the lowlands within 10 degrees latitude of the equator, the optimal range for cocoa, oil palm, and rubber. Rainfall, even in this equatorial zone of Africa, is less than in Southeast Asia, but the World Resources Institute (1992) reckons that these fifteen countries have over 28 million hectares of land with no soil constraints, almost twice as much as the ASEAN four. The fifteen "mixed" countries in Africa also have a substantial area of good land with long growing seasons. This category includes areas of humid lowlands as well as equatorial highlands that are suited to tea and coffee. According to the World Resources Institute (1992), Ethiopia has more good land in regions with long growing seasons than Indonesia, the best endowed among the ASEAN four.

Can Africa compete with treecrop producers in Southeast Asia? Berg and Berlin (1993, 13) cite one study by Hirsh and Benhamou of three palm oil plantations in Southeast Asia and two in French West Africa, which concluded that production costs in Côte d'Ivoire and Cameroon were double the costs of production on two Malaysian plantations and four to five times those of an Indonesian plantation; another study by Hirsh of eleven rubber plantations found production costs on plantations in Côte d'Ivoire and Cameroon were more than double the costs on a sample of Indonesian plantations. Berg and Berlin rightly point to the overvalued CFA franc as a major culprit in West Africa's competitive disadvantage, but these problems extend beyond the franc zone. Indonesia's high cocoa yields, low costs, and large cropland base in Borneo and Sulawesi have enabled it to edge ahead of Nigeria. Now Malaysia and Indonesia seem set to challenge Ghana's number two position in cocoa.

Malaysia's decision in the mid-1950s to invest to retain its share of the rubber market contains lessons for African treecrop producers as they face mounting competition from Southeast Asia.[14] In 1954, almost half the area of estates and two-thirds of the smallholdings were planted with trees over thirty years old (Barlow 1978, 81), with falling yields. Meanwhile, industrial countries were investing in production of synthetic rubber. Malaysia acted to regain its competitive position. According to Barlow (1978, 82),

The active rural development from the mid-1950s transformed the situation of most smallholdings, and much enhanced the position of estates. The infrastructure of roads, irrigation, drainage systems, supplies of water and electricity, health services and schools, was greatly improved in most areas of rubber growing. The majority of old trees were replanted and an ambitious programme of new land development was implemented. Institutions to assist processing and marketing were set up, and comprehensive advisory services for smallholders were established.

Over 90 percent of the area of Malaysia's estates and two-thirds of its smallholdings had been replanted with higher-yielding rubber trees developed by the Rubber Research Institute of Malaysia, "the largest research organization of its kind in the tropics" (Barlow 1978, 86, 91–92). Despite the onslaught from synthetics (and rising rural wages), Malaysian natural rubber output increased 157 percent from 1955 to 1988.

Africa has made similar investments in the three decades after World War II: Côte d'Ivoire in cocoa and coffee, Kenya in smallholder coffee and tea, and Tanzania in cashews, for example. In recent years, however, it has been more common for Africa's export base in perennial crops to be neglected, so costs rise and market shares are lost. Several African countries should be capable of mounting similar efforts again, and the Southeast Asian experience suggests that they should do so.

Timber plantations

Many countries—such as the United States, Scandinavian countries, New Zealand, and Chile—base their export-oriented timber industries to a significant degree on timber plantations. The economics of sustainable management is straightforward: if forests are privately owned (or the public forestry agency behaves like a private owner) and timber markets are efficient, then forest resource rents will rise in response to increasing timber scarcity as deforestation proceeds and timber stocks in remaining forests are depleted. This sends a signal that timber consumption, and therefore harvests, should decrease (timber is more expensive) and that investments in forest management should increase (they are increasingly profitable). These adjustments tend to move the forest sector toward sustained yield, in which harvests equal growth (Vincent and Binkley 1992; Vincent 1992b).

Nonsustainable logging—deforestation, rapid harvests, and low investment in forest management—makes economic sense where little logging has occurred and forest resource rents are low. The forest is exploited much like a mine as it is converted to agriculture and other higher-yielding uses. Mining of the forest remains the dominant mode of production in Southeast Asia.

Malaysia emerged as the world's leading exporter of tropical hardwood after World War II. Despite its impressive performance, however, future prospects for the forest sector are uncertain, largely because of policy failures. The eleven states that own the forests in Peninsular Malaysia captured only about a fifth of the resource rents from forests harvested during 1966–1985 (Vincent 1990). Because they undervalue the forest resource, states have not established incentives and collected revenues for sustainable forest management. Concessionaires have also failed to act as forest owners because their contracts tend to be much shorter than harvest cycles and because concessions, which are based on political patronage, are insecure. Indonesia's extensive tropical forests are also being mined, and Thailand's tropical forests are virtually gone.

The prospects for sustainable logging are equally dim in Africa. Macroeconomic instability in West Africa undermined investment in the timber industry and policy failures in the forestry sector depressed resource rents and promoted depletion of West Africa's forests. Ghana's timber harvests, for example, declined by about 50 percent during the last three decades. "Ghanaianization" led to higher logging costs because Ghanaian logging companies tended to be too small to take advantage of increasing returns to scale. Page, Pearson, and Leland (1976) found that logging costs for very small Ghanaian firms were more than twice those of large foreign firms. Improved policies, beginning with a devaluation in 1983, helped spur a modest increase in exports and harvests in the 1980s.

Agricultural Research

Strategic thinking—not merely riches found in nature—enabled diversification and intensification of Malaysia's primary export base. The development of Malaysia's internationally competitive agricultural sector has been based on judicious crop selection and one of the premier agricultural research programs in the tropics. Research conducted by the Rubber Research Institute and Palm Oil Research Institute of Malaysia has raised the yields of rubber trees and oil palms and enabled diversification from rubber to oil palm. Substantial research expenditures also were made in support of Malaysia's move into cocoa in the 1980s.

Sub-Saharan Africa can have little hope for agricultural development without a similar transition to science-based productivity growth, but it may face especially difficult challenges. Indeed, national research systems in Africa are viewed as less effective than their Asian counterparts despite comparable (if not higher) relative expenditures on agricultural research in general and export crops in particular (Judd, Boyce, and Evenson 1991). There have been successes, however, such as the research on oil palm undertaken in the Congo, Nigeria, and French West Africa near the end of the colonial era that produced high-yielding crosses between Asian and African strains (Anthony et al. 1979, 252–53).

The task of creating effective national research programs is complicated by the small size of many of the countries of Sub-Saharan Africa. The supply of trained personnel is grossly inadequate, especially in view of the wide variation in agroclimatic conditions and fragmented farming systems. Moreover, small national programs may be inadequate to achieve a critical mass of research activity even if research expenditure ratios are high. Malaysia's experience shows, however, that it is possible for a small country to create an effective agricultural research system.

Differences in endowments, especially the limited opportunities for irrigation and the consequent reliance on rainfed cropping, mean that the task of increasing agricultural productivity in Africa differs fundamentally from the opportunities presented by the "Green Revolution" in Asia. The dominance of relatively homogenous irrigated agriculture in Asian "rice economies" gives them a significant advantage in generating technological innovations that can be adopted widely. Nevertheless, Malaysia's research programs in rubber, oil palm, and cocoa show that it is possible to foster increases in productivity even with fragile soils under rainfed conditions and to maintain competitiveness in traditional export crops despite stagnant or declining prices.

National capacity for adaptive research to address location-specific production problems is especially important for smallholders operating in rainfed agriculture. Much work remains to be done to devise cost-effective methods of increasing the relevance of research to smallholders. Techniques to exploit the complementarities between formal experiment station research and the local knowledge of farmers deserve particular emphasis (Biggs 1989; Chambers, Pacey, and Thrupp 1989; Tomich 1992).

Smallholders versus Estates

Smallholder production may generate more employment and greater consumption linkages than estates, but are strategies aimed at smallholders the best way to expand agricultural exports? Faith in economies of scale in export crop production was entrenched under colonialism; it was reinforced by the Stalinist model of agricultural development that was especially influential when Indonesia, Malaysia, and many African countries were gaining independence; and it persisted for some time as the conventional wisdom of Western advisers. To this day, a misplaced skepticism about the productive potential of smallholders remains among policy makers and intellectuals in Sub-Saharan Africa. The view also is influential in Asia and among officials in international organizations (Tomich 1991).

Yet the myth of scale economies in production of export crops has been exploded in case after case:

- The expansion of treecrops by Malaysia's estates early this century led to a spontaneous response by smallholders who recognized the opportunities demonstrated by large-scale planters.

- Smallholders have lower production costs than rubber estates in Indonesia (Barlow, Jayasuriya, and Tan, 1994), which probably makes Indonesian smallholders the lowest-cost producers of natural rubber in the world.

- Hayami, Quisumbing, and Adriano (1990) found no evidence of scale economies in production of coconuts, bananas, or pineapples in the Philippines.

- For sugarcane, Hayami, Quisumbing, and Adriano (1990, 119) found evidence that yields on farms over 50 hectares are higher than for farms under 10 hectares, but production costs also are higher on the larger farms. Moreover, they attribute higher yields to larger farms' preferential access to subsidized credit. It is likely that the Philippines' small-scale sugarcane growers are socially more efficient because they make greater use of abundant labor and economize on scarce capital.

- For coffee in Kenya and tobacco in Malawi, yields are higher on large estates than on smallholdings. Nevertheless, Lele and Agarwal (1989) found that, because higher production costs largely offset the estates' higher yields, Kenyan coffee smallholders and Malawian tobacco smallholders are more efficient than estates.

Although they can often be grown at lower unit cost on smallholdings than estates, crops such as sugarcane, tea, palm oil, bananas, and pineapples are perishable, so their harvest must be closely coordinated with processing or marketing, both of which are subject to economies of scale. Innovative organizations have been devised in several countries, however, to marry efficient smallholder production with large-scale processing or marketing.

- In Taiwan, independent small-scale producers supplied the bulk of the sugarcane for its mills.
- A similar approach appears feasible for palm oil in Malaysia (Barlow 1986). Small-scale oil palm production appeared on independent plots of 5 to 20 hectares in Sumatra, Indonesia, in the late 1980s and has always been the norm in Nigeria. Success of oil palm smallholders in Malaysia and Indonesia relies, in part, on the presence of large-scale processing facilities. But these examples demonstrate the feasibility of coordinating production by smallholders with processing that achieves economies of scale.
- The Kenya Tea Development Authority (KTDA) provides an organizational model that efficiently meshes tea production on 140,000 smallholdings with timely, large-scale processing. The KTDA restricts itself to activities in which economies of scale are important: dissemination of new varieties and growing methods, collection and processing of tea leaves (in factories owned by growers), and investments in "tea roads."[15]
- Large-scale growers of pineapples and bananas may have a competitive edge in producing large quantities of uniform fruit. Vertically integrated multinationals appear to have given the Philippines a competitive advantage over Taiwan in both commodities, at least partly because of their marketing advantages (Ranis and Stewart 1987). Thailand, however, has surpassed the Philippines in canned pineapple, even though much of its output is grown by small-scale growers under contract (Hayami, Quisumbing, and Adriano 1990, 142–43).

Recognizing the competitiveness of small growers, how can governments encourage them? Malaysia's smallholder development strategy included processing schemes, projects to promote replanting with higher-yielding rubber varieties, and resettlement of smallholders on new land. These smallholder projects have been more successful in meeting social goals than they have as economic investments. In a benefit/cost analysis of twenty rubber schemes in Peninsular Malaysia, for example, only three had a real rate of return of 10 percent or better (Lim 1972, 245). Economic returns generally have been higher for Malaysia's oil palm schemes, with estimates for the best (the FELDA schemes) in the range of 15 to 18 percent per year (World Bank estimates reported in Malek and Barlow 1988, 27–32). Malaysia was able to promote smallholder development in parallel with rapid expansion of estates because of its abundant land and because much of the capital, management, and technical expertise needed in the early stages of plantation development came from abroad.

Indonesia took a similar approach to smallholder development in the 1970s and 1980s, opting to transfer production techniques from large-scale rubber plantations to treecrop smallholdings. After more than a decade, this strategy had failed to generate widespread increases in rubber productivity. Although land was available and the scheme was well funded, the techno-logical package was inappropriate and the large projects stretched the man-agement capacity of Indonesia's public agencies. It would have taken more than sixty years for those schemes to cover even the existing population of rubber producers. Much broader coverage probably could have been achieved in Indonesia through private nurseries or through the distribution of planting materials and agronomic information to smallholders by public agencies, leaving smallholders to manage their own investments (Barlow and Jayasuriya 1984; Barlow, Shearing, and Dereinda 1991; Tomich 1991).

Smallholder development projects require time, money, and skilled per-sonnel. So does building agricultural research capacity that meets smallhold-ers' needs. Experience with treecrops indicates that, although no planting project can succeed without appropriate technology, smallholders have am-ply demonstrated willingness to plant on their own if it is profitable (Bauer 1948; Hill 1963; Lewis 1970; Tomich 1991; Tomich, Hastuti, and Bennett 1993). Faced with a choice between research and planting projects, African countries should concentrate their efforts on building capacity for effective agricultural research, which is itself a difficult task, and leave the rest to smallholders and the market.

A substantial literature, especially on Africa, argues that smallholder de-velopment based on export crops jeopardizes food security and nutrition (reviewed in von Braun and Kennedy 1986 and Maxwell and Fernando 1989). Timmer (1992, 28) goes so far as to assert that "concentration on export agriculture misses much of the potential for agricultural development to alleviate poverty by providing direct access to food." But Malaysia fol-lowed its comparative advantage and emphasized treecrops, which provided ample foreign exchange for food imports. Successful pursuit of rice self-sufficiency has been a central feature of Indonesia's agricultural development and accorded with comparative advantage on Java's irrigated land. Other regions of Indonesia, however, have emphasized agricultural exports in line with their factor endowments. In Thailand rice is a major export crop. The debate on cash crops *versus* food security has played little or no role in these three primary exporters. Research in Kenya (Kennedy and Cogill 1987; Kennedy 1989) and The Gambia (von Braun, Puetz, and Webb 1989) suggests that concerns about adverse nutritional effects of cash cropping are overstated for Africa, too.[16]

Conclusions

Countries in Southeast Asia have continued to invest in their primary export base of treecrops and other perennials. Consequently, they have made inroads into world markets previously dominated by African and Latin American countries. Growing earnings from primary exports have provided a strong foundation for rapid industrialization in Indonesia, Malaysia, and Thailand. In export agriculture, the main investments have been in infrastructure, especially rural transportation; research, of which Malaysia's work on rubber and palm oil has been outstanding; and planting programs on both plantations and smallholdings. Ample evidence suggests that smallholders can produce export crops at least as efficiently as plantations.

Many countries in Africa have land endowments similar to those in Southeast Asia and export similar crops. Countries such as Kenya and Côte d'Ivoire have made major efforts to expand production of coffee, tea, cocoa, horticulturals, and other crops, grown increasingly on smallholdings. In other countries, however, political and economic instability and a preference for industrial investments have contributed to a neglect of export agriculture and a loss of world market share. Experience in both Southeast Asia and parts of Africa suggests that, for many countries in Africa, export crops grown by smallholders have substantial potential for future growth. Government efforts should be focused on research. Although public institutions played an important role in Kenya, private agents may be able to substitute for government effort in disseminating new varieties and organizing marketing.

A few countries in Africa are, like Indonesia and Malaysia, relatively rich in natural resources. These African countries, with the notable exception of Botswana, have failed to channel resource rents into productive investments in agriculture, education, and public health, as was done in Southeast Asia.

But the policy tools for doing so, including sound macroeconomic management, are well known and should be within reach for governments determined to use them.

APPENDIX 5.1

World Market Share in Primary Exports, 1970 and 1987

Commodity	Country	World market share (%) in 1987	Change in share (%) from 1970 to 1987
Cocoa	Cameroon	3.0	− 52
	Côte d'Ivoire	23.0	+ 122
	Ghana[g]	14.3	− 48
	Nigeria	5.1	− 73
	Indonesia[g]	1.4	+ ∞
	Malaysia[g]	4.8	+ ∞
Coffee	Cameroon	1.7	− 41
	Côte d'Ivoire	3.5	− 32
	Kenya	1.8	− 8
	Tanzania	0.8	− 44
	Indonesia	3.5[a]	+ 68
Copper[g]	Zaire	7.5	− 30
	Zambia	11.9	+ 260
	Philippines	3.6	+ 24
Cotton	Cameroon	5.4	− 35
	Mali	2.1	+ 501
	Tanzania	8.7	− 47
Groundnuts[g]	The Gambia	2.6	+ 13
	Nigeria	0.0	− 100[b]
	Senegal	1.3	− 71
	Sudan	4.8	− 23

Continued on next page

Appendix 5.1 (Continued)

Commodity	Country	World market share (%) in 1987	Change in share (%) from 1970 to 1987
Groundnut oil[g]	The Gambia	2.5	− 34
	Nigeria	0.0	− 100[c]
	Senegal	31.6	− 15
	Sudan	3.4	+ ∞
Iron ore[g]	Liberia	4.1	− 31
Maize	Thailand	2.4	− 55
Manganese ore[g]	Gabon	28.7	+ 51
	Ghana	1.5	− 75
	Zaire	0.1	− 95
Natural gas	Indonesia	13.3	+ ∞
Nuts (dry)	Tanzania	0.1	− 85
Petroleum (crude)	Nigeria	5.7	+ 20
	Indonesia	4.1	− 72
	Malaysia	2.2	+ ∞
Phosphate rock[g]	Senegal	3.0	− 17
	Togo	5.1	+ 13
Rice	Philippines	0.0	− 100[d]
	Thailand	29.8	+ 128
Rubber (crude)	Liberia[g]	2.3	+ 10
	Nigeria[g]	0.8	− 50
	Indonesia	18.1	+ 54
	Malaysia	33.6	+ 26
	Thailand	18.0	+ 153
Spices	Tanzania	0.3	− 94
Tea	Kenya	12.2	+ 102
	Malawi[g]	2.6	+ 30
	Tanzania[g]	1.0	− 10
	Indonesia[g]	6.7	+ 252

Continued on next page

Commodity	Country	World market share (%) in 1987	Change in share (%) from 1970 to 1987
Tin[g]	Nigeria	0.9	− 84
	Zaire	0.7	− 76
	Indonesia	15.1	+ 132
	Malaysia	28.7	− 29
Vegetables, fresh	Thailand	7.8	+ 58
Vegetable fiber	Tanzania	1.2	− 92
Tropical oils	Senegal	1.3	− 76
	Malaysia	48.9	+ 178
	Philippines	11.3	− 33
Veneer, plywood	Indonesia	32.9	+ ∞
Wood (rough)	Cameroon	1.2	+ 15
	Côte d'Ivoire	1.5	− 73
	Indonesia	0.0[e]	− 100
	Malaysia	22.0	+ 54
	Philippines	0.0	− 100[f]
Zinc[g]	Zaire	1.8	− 36
	Zambia	1.1	− 58

NOTE: +∞ Country share was too small to be listed in 1970.
a. 1989.
b. 39.6% in 1971.
c. 19.7% in 1971.
d. 5.8% share in 1970.
e. Exports banned 1980; 17.5% share in 1970.
f. 16.1% share in 1970.
g. Data are from 1971 and 1982–84.
SOURCES: United Nations, *International Trade Statistics Yearbook,* (New York, 1991), vols. I and II. World Bank, *Commodity Trade and Price Trends* (Washington, D.C., 1972, 1987–88).

APPENDIX 5.2

Land Quality

Data on soil and water deficiency factors were compiled for agroecological zones by Buringh, Van Heemst, and Staring (1979) and converted to national weighted averages by Seckler and LaBore (1988). These measures are supplemented with FAO data compiled by the World Resources Institute (1990, 1992) on soil constraints and the extent of area with different growing seasons.

Indonesia, Malaysia, the Philippines, and Thailand (the ASEAN four) all fall within the same category by these broad measures, although there are important differences within the region and even within countries (between Java and Sumatra, for example). These countries all are "humid," which means production potential is constrained more by soil than water availability. In all cases growing seasons exceed 180 days per year—indeed, the growing season approaches 365 days in Indonesia. (Although the growing season concept applies strictly to annual crops, a long growing season also is crucial for tropical perennials such as rubber and oil palm that require uniform distribution of rainfall through the year.)

Three broad categories can be distinguished within Sub-Saharan Africa by sorting countries by water deficiency factor, soil deficiency factor, and share of area with long growing season. The first group comprises fifteen humid African countries where land quality is most comparable to the ASEAN four. These are all "humid" in the sense that they are constrained more by soil deficiency than water deficiency. With but three exceptions (Angola at 87 percent, Nigeria at 92 percent, and Uganda at 95 percent of total area), all land in this category has a growing season in excess of 180 days. The constraining soil deficiency factors are comparable to the ASEAN four. The fifteen "mixed" countries either are intermediate between "humid" and "dry" or have substantial regions of each. Water is the constraining factor in this group. Indeed, to the extent the averages are meaningful, the soils in this group are equal to or better than the soils of the humid tropics of Africa or of Malaysia and Indonesia.

These measures put Senegal at the end of the "humid" list and Namibia last on the "mixed" list. These borderline cases were moved to "mixed" and "dry," respectively, to conform better with conventional classifications and cropping patterns. Surprisingly, Swaziland, Lesotho, and Botswana all sorted on the "humid" list. Swaziland was moved to the "mixed" group, while the other two were moved to head the list of dry countries. These anomalies arise because pasture was not considered when soil and water deficiency factors were assigned.

NOTES

We are grateful to David Lindauer, Colin Barlow, and Donald Snodgrass for their constructive comments.

1. This phenomenon is Dutch disease, now well known but little appreciated then. Dutch disease is discussed more fully later in this chapter.

2. A case is a country position in each commodity. Appendix 5.1 contains world market shares for twenty-four commodities or commodity groups. It includes the market shares for the four Southeast Asian countries and those in Africa whose market shares were at least 1 percent in either 1970 or 1987.

3. Grilli and Yang (1988), for example, show statistically significant declines averaging between 0.3 and 0.8 percent per year for all primary commodity groups, with the notable exception of tropical beverages, whose terms of trade rose by 0.7 percent per year.

4. The name comes from the Dutch exploitation of gas deposits in the North Sea in the 1960s, which caused a real appreciation of the guilder and forced many formerly competitive Dutch industries out of business.

5. The term "smallholder" is used to refer to the majority of rural households, which spans a range of farm sizes. In much of Sub-Saharan Africa, farms up to fifteen hectares typically have more in common with small farms than they do with the technology or economics of large ones.

6. See, for example, Mellor (1976), Hazell and Röell (1983), and Haggblade, Hazell, and Brown (1989).

7. According to Huff (1992, 765), Singapore also benefited from the investment of resource rents derived from Malaya (now Malaysia): "During the interwar years most of the Chinese who emerged as major industrialists and bankers in town had as a base for these activities their involvement in estate agriculture in Johore. They reinvested profits from agriculture in domestic manufacturing and, as business leaders, were instrumental in the growth of local Chinese deposit banks, now a major component of Singapore's role as an international financial center."

8. This figure is actually an index that averages shares of world reserves for fifteen metals.

9. Peninsular Malaysia accounts for eleven of the thirteen states of Malaysia. The island of Borneo comprises the Malaysian states of Sabah and Sarawak, the Sultanate of Brunei, and the Indonesian provinces of Kalimantan. Sumatra lies entirely within Indonesia.

10. See Appendix 5.2 for explanation of classifications.

11. In densely populated Asia, fodder is raised on arable land; gleaned as crop by-products; gathered along roads, canals, and from common property; or purchased and brought to animals.

12. Cropland is arable land plus land under permanent crops, excluding permanent pasture.

13. Complex intercropping characterizes many smallholder farming systems, especially in Africa. A variety of cash-crop-based smallholder systems also involve production of food, fodder, fiber, and fuel as joint products. The cash-versus-food

debate, taken up in the final section, rests too often on misleading oversimplification of smallholders' options.

14. This discussion draws heavily on Barlow (1978, 76–96).

15. The move in Kenya during the 1980s toward personalized bureaucratic politics and patronage appointments have weakened the KTDA through slower payments to smallholders, deterioration of tea roads, and delays in collection of tea leaf for factories.

16. Nevertheless, it is clear that export crops are no panacea for rural poverty: increases in income had only a small effect on calorie intake in the Kenyan studies and, because of high morbidity, this translated into little or no positive effect on children's nutritional status. Similar patterns were found in a study in Mindanao in the Philippines, where insecure land tenure and biased agricultural research priorities proved detrimental to smallholders when sugar production expanded (Bouis and Haddad 1990).

BIBLIOGRAPHY

Abdullah bin Sepien, and Dan M. Etherington. 1980. "Economic Efficiency with Traditional and New Inputs on Smallholder Rubber Holdings in Malaysia." *Oxford Agrarian Studies* 9:63–88.

Anthony, K. R. M., B. F. Johnston, W. O. Jones, V. C. Uchendu. 1979. *Agricultural Change in Tropical Africa.* Ithaca: Cornell University Press.

Barlow, Colin. 1978. *The Natural Rubber Industry: Its Development, Technology, and Economy in Malaysia.* New York: Oxford University Press.

———. 1986. "Oil Palm as a Smallholder Crop." Palm Oil Research Institute of Malaysia (PORIM) Occasional Paper No. 21 (August).

Barlow, Colin, and S. K. Jayasuriya. 1984. *Bias towards the Large Farm Subsector in Agricultural Research: The Case of Malaysian Rubber.* Canberra: Australian National University.

———. 1986. "Stages of Development in Smallholder Tree Crop Agriculture." *Development and Change* 17: 635–658.

Barlow, Colin, S. K. Jayasuriya, and C. S. Tan. 1994. *The World Rubber Industry.* London: Routledge.

Barlow, Colin, Colin Shearing, and Ridwan Dereinda. 1991. "Alternative Approaches to Smallholder Rubber Development." HIID Development Discussion Paper No. 368 (January). Harvard Institute for International Development, Cambridge, Mass.

Bauer, P. T. 1948. *The Rubber Industry: A Study in Competition and Monopoly.* Cambridge, Mass.: Harvard University Press.

Bell, Clive J., Peter Hazell, and Roger Slade. 1982. *Project Evaluation in a Regional Perspective: A Study of an Irrigation Project in Northwestern Malaysia.* Baltimore, Md.: Johns Hopkins University Press.

Berg, Elliot, and Phillip Berlin. 1993. "Exchange Rate Issues in the Franc Zone." Background note prepared for seminar on the CFA franc. U.S. Agency for International Development, Washington, D.C.

Biggs, Stephen D. 1989. "Resource-Poor Farmer Participation in Research: A Synthesis from Nine National Agricultural Research Systems." International Service for National Agricultural Research (ISNAR), The Hague.

Binswanger, Hans P., and Prabhu Pingali. 1988. "Technological Priorities for Farming in Sub-Saharan Africa." *World Bank Research Observer* 3 (1): 81–98.

Bouis, Howarth E., and L. J. Haddad. 1990. "Effects of Agricultural Commercialization on Land Tenure, Household Resource Allocation, and Nutrition in the Philippines." Research Report 79. International Food Policy Research Institute, Washington, D.C.

Buringh, P., H. D. J. Van Heemst, and G. J. Staring. 1979. "Potential World Food Production." In *MOIRA: Model of International Relations in Agriculture: Report of the Project Group "Food for a Doubling World Population,"* ed. Tinbergen, Jorgenson, and Waelbroeck. Amsterdam, New York, Oxford: North-Holland.

Chambers, Robert, Arnold Pacey, and Lori Ann Thrupp. 1989. *Farmer First: Farmer Innovation and Agricultural Research.* London: Intermediate Technology Publications.

Cuddington, John, and Carlos M. Urzúa. 1989. "Trends and Cycles in the Net Barter Terms of Trade: A New Approach." *The Economic Journal* 99 (June): 426–42.

Deaton, Angus. 1992. "Commodity Prices, Stabilization, and Growth in Africa." Discussion Paper #166. Research Program in Development Studies, Center of International Studies, Princeton University, with the Institute for Policy Reform.

Dorosh, Paul, and Steven Haggblade. 1992. "Agriculture-Led Growth: Foodgrains versus Export Crops in Madagascar." In *Agricultural Economics.* Revised typescript forthcoming.

Etherington, Dan, and Keith Forster. 1992. "The Structural Transformation of Taiwan's Tea Industry." *World Development* 20 (3): 401–422.

Food and Agriculture Organization of the United Nations. 1976–1992. *FAO Production Yearbook.* Vols. 29–45. Rome: FAO.

Gelb, Alan, et al. 1988. *Oil Windfalls: Blessing or Curse.* New York: Oxford University Press for the World Bank.

Gillis, Malcolm, Dwight H. Perkins, Michael Roemer, and Donald R. Snodgrass. 1992. *Economics of Development* (3rd edition). New York: W. W. Norton & Company.

Grilli, E. R., and M. C. Yang. 1988. "Primary Commodity Prices, Manufactured Goods Prices, and Terms of Trade in Developing Countries: What the Long Run Shows." *World Bank Economic Review* 2–1: 1–48.

Haggeblade, S., J. Hammer, and P. Hazell. 1991. "Modeling Agricultural Growth Multipliers." *American Journal of Agricultural Economics* (May).

Haggeblade, S., P. Hazell, and J. Brown. 1989. "Farm–Nonfarm Linkages in Rural Sub-Saharan Africa." *World Development* 17 (8): 1173–1201.

Hayami, Yujiro, Ma. Agnes R. Quisumbing, and Lourdes S. Adriano. 1990. *Toward an Alternative Land Reform Paradigm.* Manila: Ateneo de Manila University Press.

Hazell, Peter B. R., and Ailsa Röell. 1983. "Rural Growth Linkages: Household Expenditure Patterns in Malaysia and Nigeria." IFPRI Research Report 41 (September).

Hemmi, Kenzo. 1969. "Primary Product Exports and Economic Development: The Case of Silk." In *Agriculture and Economic Growth: Japan's Experience,* ed. Kazushi Ohkawa, Bruce F. Johnston, and Hiromitsu Kaneda.

Hill, Polly. 1963. *The Migrant Cocoa-Farmers of Southern Ghana: A Study in Rural Capitalism.* Cambridge: Cambridge University Press.

Huff, W. G. 1992. "Sharecroppers, Risk, Management, and Chinese Estate Rubber Development in Interwar British Malaya." *Economic Development and Cultural Change* 40 (4): 743–773.

Imran, Mudassar, and Ron Duncan. 1988. "Optimal Export Taxes for Exporters of Perennial Crops." Policy, Planning, and Research Working Papers, WPS 10. The World Bank, International Economics Department, Washington, D.C.

International Monetary Fund. 1993. *International Financial Statistics Yearbook 1992,* Vol. 45. Washington, D.C.: International Monetary Fund.

Judd, M. Ann, James K. Boyce, and Robert E. Evenson. 1991. "Investment in Agricultural Research and Extension Programs: A Quantitative Assessment." Chapter 1 in *Research and Productivity in Asian Agriculture,* ed. Robert E. Evenson, Carl Pray, and others. Ithaca, N.Y.: Cornell University Press.

Kennedy, Eileen T. 1989. "The Effects of Sugarcane Production on Food Security, Health, and Nutrition in Kenya: A Longitudinal Analysis." Research Report 78. International Food Policy Research Institute, Washington, D.C.

Kennedy, Eileen T., and Bruce Cogill. 1987. "Income and Nutritional Effects of the Commercialization of Agriculture in Southwestern Kenya." Research Report 63. International Food Policy Research Institute, Washington, D.C.

Kindleberger, Charles P. 1973. *International Economics* (5th edition). Homewood, Ill.: Richard D. Irwin.

Lele, Uma, and Manmohan Agarwal. 1989. "Smallholder and Large-Scale Agriculture in Africa: Are There Tradeoffs between Growth and Equity?" MADIA Discussion Paper No. 6. World Bank, Washington, D.C.

Lewis, W. Arthur, ed. 1970. *Tropical Development 1880–1913.* London: Allen and Unwin.

Lim Sow Ching. 1972. "Land Development Schemes in West Malaysia: A Study of Benefits and Costs." Thesis submitted for the Degree of Doctor of Philosophy at the Australian National University, Canberra, July 1972.

Malek bin Mansoor and Colin Barlow. 1988. "The Production Structure of the Malaysian Oil Palm Industry with Special Reference to the Smallholder Subsector." Palm Oil Research Institute of Malaysia, Occasional Paper No. 24 (March).

Maxwell, Simon, and Adrian Fernando. 1989. "Cash Crops in Developing Countries: The Issues, the Facts, the Policies." *World Development* 17 (11): 1677–1708.

Mellor, John W. 1976. *The New Economics of Growth: A Strategy for India and the Developing World.* Ithaca, N.Y.: Cornell University Press.

Ministry of Finance, Malaysia. 1991. *Economic Report 1990/91.* Kuala Lumpur.

Nurkse, Ragnar. 1961. *Equilibrium Growth in the World Economy.* Cambridge, Mass.: Harvard University Press.

Page, J. M., Jr., S. R. Pearson, and H. E. Leland. 1976. "Capturing Economic Rent from Ghanaian Timber." *Food Research Institute Studies* 15 (1): 25–51.

Pearson, Scott R., J. Dirck Stryker, and Charles P. Humphreys. 1981. *Rice in West Africa: Policy and Economics.* Stanford, Calif.: Stanford University Press.

Prebisch, Raul. 1950. *The Economic Development of Latin America and Its Principal Problems.* Lake Success, N.Y.: United Nations.

Ranis, Gustav, and Frances Stewart. 1987. "Rural Linkages in the Philippines and Taiwan." In *Macro-Policies for Appropriate Technology in Developing Countries,* ed. Frances Stewart. Boulder, Colo.: Westview Press.

Roemer, Michael. 1979. "Resource-Based Industrialization: A Survey." *Journal of Development Economics* 6 (June): 163–202.

———. 1985. "Dutch Disease in Developing Countries: Swallowing Bitter Medicine." In *The Primary Sector in Economic Development,* ed. Matts Lundahl. London: Croom-Helms.

Rusinga, Andrew. 1993. "Zimbabwe Expands Horticulture." *African Business* (January): 38.

Ruthenberg, Hans. 1980. *Farming Systems in the Tropics.* Oxford: Clarendon Press.

Seckler, David, and John LaBore. 1988. "Agroclimatic Indices for Asia and Africa." Mimeographed draft manuscript. Center for Development Studies, Winrock International Institute for Agricultural Development.

Singer, Hans W. 1950. "The Distribution of Trade Between Investing and Borrowing Countries." *American Economic Review* 40:470–85.

Timmer, C. Peter. 1992. "Food Price Stabilization: The Relevance of the Asian Experience to Africa." Draft paper for the International Conference on Agricultural Development Policy Options for Sub-Saharan Africa, August 23–25.

Tomich, Thomas. 1991. "Smallholder Rubber Development in Indonesia." In *Reforming Economic Systems in Developing Countries,* ed. Dwight Perkins and Michael Roemer. Cambridge, Mass.: Harvard Institute for International Development.

———. 1992. "Sustaining Agricultural Development in Harsh Environments: Insights from Private Land Reclamation in Egypt." *World Development* 20 (2): 261–74.

Tomich, Thomas, Hastuti, and Christopher P. A. Bennett. 1993. "Agricultural Intensification and Indigenous Technological Change: Policy Lessons from Smallholder Coffee in Highland Sumatra." HIID Development Discussion Paper. Harvard Institute for International Development, Cambridge, Mass.

Tomich, Thomas, Peter Kilby, and Bruce Johnston. 1995. *Transforming Agrarian Economies: Opportunities Seized, Opportunities Missed.* Ithaca, N.Y.: Cornell University Press. Forthcoming.

United Nations. 1992. *Energy Statistics Yearbook, 1992.*

Vincent, J. R. 1990. "Rent Capture and the Feasibility of Tropical Forest Management." *Land Economics* 66 (2): 212–23.

———. 1992a. "A Simple, Nonspatial Modeling Approach for Analyzing a Country's Forest-Products Trade Policies." In *Forestry Sector Analysis for Developing Countries,* ed. R. Haynes, P. Harou, and J. Mikowski. Seattle: CINTRAFOR, College of Forest Resources, University of Washington.

———. 1992b. "The Tropical Timber Trade and Sustainable Development." *Science* 256 (5064): 1651–55.

Vincent, J. R., and C. S. Binkley. 1992. "Forest-Based Industrialization: A Dynamic Perspective." In *Managing the World's Forests,* ed. N. Sharma. Dubuque, Iowa: Kendall/Hunt Publishing Co.

von Braun, Joachim, H. de Haen, and Juergen Blanken. 1991. "Commercialization of Agriculture under Population Pressure: Effects on Production, Consumption, and Nutrition in Rwanda." Research Report 85. International Food Policy Research Institute, Washington, D.C.

von Braun, Joachim, and Eileen Kennedy. 1986. "Commercialization of Subsistence Agriculture: Income and Nutritional Effects in Developing Countries." Working Papers on Commercialization of Agriculture and Nutrition, Number 1. International Food Policy Research Institute, Washington, D.C.

von Braun, Joachim, Detlev Puetz, and Patrick Webb. 1989. "Irrigation Technology and Commercialization of Rice in the Gambia: Effects on Income and Nutrition." Research Report 75. International Food Policy Research Institute, Washington, D.C.

The World Bank. 1992. *World Development Report 1992.* New York: Oxford University Press.

———. 1993. *World Tables 1992.* Baltimore: Johns Hopkins University Press, for the World Bank.

World Resources Institute. 1990. *World Resources 1990–91.* New York, Oxford: Oxford University Press.

———. 1992. *World Resources 1992–93.* New York, Oxford: Oxford University Press.

WWF Malaysia. 1992. *Malaysian National Conservation Strategy.* Volume 4: Natural Resource Accounting, Draft Report. Petaling Jaya: World Wide Fund for Nature Malaysia.

Yee, Yuen L., and John W. Longworth. 1985. "Biases in Research: The Case of Rubber Growing in Malaysia." *Journal of Agricultural Economics* 36 (January): 15–29.

CHAPTER 6

Patterns and Sources of Food Systems Development

Richard H. Goldman

Agriculture dominates the economies of most poor countries, in terms of employment and contribution to both gross domestic product (GDP) and, especially, net foreign exchange earnings. This was true for Southeast Asia in the earlier stages of its economic growth, and it is currently the case in most of Africa. Because of its dominance and its linkages with other sectors of the economy, agriculture exerts important leverage on the growth process. By providing rural incomes, development with agricultural growth also contributes to economic equity and directly alleviates nutritional poverty in rural households.

In addition, domestic food production is often a strategic element in food price stabilization and security strategies that impact on both rural and urban consumer welfare and on the rate of domestic investment. This chapter takes a comparative approach to analyzing the changing nature of food systems in Southeast Asia and Africa and the technical and economic features that influence these systems.

Contribution of Agriculture to Economic Growth

Agricultural growth, and particularly growth in food production for both domestic consumption and export, has played an important role in the economic development of Southeast Asian countries. The experience among

TABLE 6.1
Agriculture's Direct Contribution to Economic Growth

	Growth rate				Agriculture				
	Agriculture		GDP		Share of GDP, %			Contribution to GDP growth, %[a]	
	1965–80	1980–90	1965–80	1980–90	1965	1980	1990	1965–80	1980–90
Indonesia	4.1	3.3	7.6	5.6	50	27	21	18	14
Malaysia	5.8	3.8	7.3	6.2	30	26	22	23	17
Thailand	4.9	3.9	7.6	7.8	37	22	15	17	9
Philippines	4.5	1.3	5.8	1.8	31	26	25	22	18

NOTE: Table does not include indirect contribution through linkage to other economic sectors.
a. Based on $(Y_{A2} - Y_{A1})/(Y_2 - Y_1)$ where Y_i and Y_{Ai} equal GDP and the agriculture component of GDP during the relevant time period, respectively.
SOURCES: World Bank, *World Development Report 1992* (Washington, D.C., 1992a); World Bank, *World Tables 1992* (Washington, D.C., 1992b).

these countries has not been homogeneous. Growth has been led by different crops, irrigation has played a more critical role in some countries than in others, and economic policies have varied across countries and over time. Across Africa the performance of the agricultural sector has also varied, but nowhere has it been as dynamic as in the recent history of Southeast Asia.

The contribution of agriculture to general economic growth can be approached in various ways. The easiest measure is derived in Table 6.1 from a decomposition of gross domestic product (GDP). A rough approximation of the agricultural sector's contribution to the growth process is determined from the sector growth rate, weighted by the sector's share in GDP, relative to total GDP growth. In 1965, on the eve of the Green Revolution, agriculture accounted for almost half of GDP in Indonesia and between a quarter and a third of GDP in Malaysia, Thailand, and the Philippines. Between 1965 and 1980 agriculture grew at almost unprecedented rates in these countries, fueling, by this measure, 15 to 25 percent of economic growth. By 1980 the agriculture share of GDP had fallen dramatically in all countries because of the even more rapid growth of other sectors.[1]

Recent research (Hwa 1988; Haggeblade et al. 1991) suggests that the contribution of agriculture to growth is underestimated in the approach taken in Table 6.1 because of the failure of this technique to capture the effect of dynamic linkages, including rural consumption multiplier effects, which enable agricultural growth to foster growth in the rest of the economy. Also, the approach ignores completely the impact of agricultural growth on equity.

The economic role of agriculture varies across Africa, as shown in Table 6.2, where countries are divided into three groups according to the share of agriculture in GDP. Where agriculture is dominant, accounting for almost 50 percent of GDP, agriculture's importance in the economy is similar to what it was in Indonesia in the 1960s. These large agriculture countries account for almost half the African population, not including Nigeria and South Africa.[2] The group of countries where agriculture contributes about a third of GDP have initial conditions today similar to those of Malaysia, Thailand, and the Philippines in the 1960s. There is a third group of African countries, comprising about a quarter of the population (as measured above), where agriculture plays a diminished role in GDP—less than 30 percent. The economies of some of these countries are dominated by high-valued mineral production.

In each of these groups agriculture's contribution to foreign exchange earning is strategic: 85 percent in the countries with high agricultural shares and over 40 percent even in the countries where agriculture's contribution to GDP is relatively small. The large degree of exchange rate overvaluation that is prevalent in most African countries causes foreign exchange earned or saved through agricultural production to have a real economic value much greater than its measure in local currency. The GDP share measure, therefore, underestimates agriculture's importance in the African economies relative to those countries with similar GDP shares in Southeast Asia, where, with the exception of the Philippines, overvaluation is less of an issue.

The framework for measuring the sectoral contribution to economic growth in Southeast Asia in Table 6.1 is used in a growth projection context for Africa in Table 6.2. This sheds some light on the question of whether rapid economic growth can occur if agricultural growth remains slow. The right half of this table shows the results of a projection experiment where GDP is presumed to grow at an annual 5 percent rate for fifteen years. In each of the three subregions of Africa, two growth scenarios are shown—one where the agricultural sector is projected to grow at 3 percent and the other where it grows at 4 percent. These rates are higher than the recent sustained agricultural growth rates in Africa and somewhat below those for Southeast Asia during its period of most rapid growth. In these two scenarios, agri-

TABLE 6.2

Agriculture's Direct Contribution to African Growth under Various
Sector Share and Growth Rate Scenarios, Assuming a Target GDP
Growth Rate of 5.0 Percent

Share of agriculture in GDP by country group	Share of African population excluding Nigeria and South Africa	Average share of agriculture in foreign exchange earnings, 1990[a]	Average share of agriculture in GDP, 1990[b]	Growth scenarios: 15-year projection based on target GDP growth rate of 5%[c]			
				Agricultural growth rate assumptions	Required nonagricultural sector growth rate	Agriculture's contribution to GDP growth	Final share of agriculture in GDP
High[d]	49	84.8	48.9				
				3.0%	6.9	25.3	36.6
				4.0%	6.0	36.3	42.3
Medium[e]	26	58.1	32.9				
				3.0%	6.0	17.0	24.6
				4.0%	5.5	24.4	28.5
Low[f]	24	42.5	21.5				
				3.0%	5.5	11.1	16.1
				4.0%	5.3	16.0	18.6

a. Does not include indirect contribution through linkage to other economic sectors.
b. Group averages are weighted by intragroup population shares.
c. Based on $Y = \alpha Y_A + (1-\alpha) Y_N$ where Y, Y_A, and Y_N equal the growth rates of GDP and the agriculture and nonagriculture components of GDP, respectively, and α is the beginning period agriculture sector share of GDP.
d. High (41–67%): Burundi, Central African Republic, Côte d'Ivoire, Ethiopia, Ghana, Mali, Mozambique, Sudan, Tanzania, Uganda.
e. Medium (30–38%): Benin, Burkina Faso, Chad, Madagascar, Malawi, Niger, Nigeria, Rwanda, Sierra Leone, Zaire, Togo.
f. Low (3–28%): Angola, Botswana, Cameroon, Congo, Gabon, Guinea, Kenya, Lesotho, Mauritania, Namibia, Senegal, Zambia, Zimbabwe.
SOURCES: World Bank, *World Development Report 1992* (Washington, D.C., 1992a); World Bank, *World Tables 1992* (Washington, D.C., 1992b).

culture accounts for a quarter to just over a third of economic growth in the African countries where agriculture has a high GDP share. In the middle group, the contribution is between 17 and 25 percent. In the countries where agriculture is less important, the sector accounts for between 11 to 16 percent of the simulated growth performance.

The Southeast Asian experience confirms that where agriculture's contribution to the economy is relatively large, rapid agricultural growth has important leverage on the overall growth process. Other sectors of the economy, in the aggregate, must grow faster than agriculture for general rapid growth to be achieved, but the more dynamic of these sectors are likely to account for a small amount of economic activity and so will have less leverage at the beginning. A dynamic agricultural sector is probably even more critical to the future economic success of Africa than it was in Southeast Asia, as suggested by Table 6.2. Achieving rapid agricultural sector growth will be a major challenge in Africa. Yet if a 5 percent aggregate growth rate is to be achieved, anything lower than 3 to 4 percent in agriculture would seem to place an unrealistic burden on the nonagricultural sectors of many countries.

Much of agricultural growth in Africa will have to come from investment in rural infrastructure and technical change, which thus far has proceeded at a slower pace than in Southeast Asia. Finding an appropriate balance between food production and export agriculture, an issue that has been resolved differently among the Southeast Asian countries, may also have important ramifications. Finally, improved economic management is required to enhance the performance of markets and to raise incentives in the agricultural sector.

Food Production and Consumption Growth

The balance of this chapter focuses on staple food systems in an effort to understand the diversity of factors that have supported the growth of food production and consumption in Southeast Asia and the similarities and differences that are likely to prevail in Africa. Measured at a national level, food production and food consumption do not necessarily grow apace. At the interface between the two is economic policy, particularly pricing policy, and food imports and exports. An examination of the sources of food consumption provides useful insight into performance of food systems. Within Southeast Asia, for example, the role of rice production in consumption growth varies considerably. When Southeast Asia is compared with Africa, distinctly different patterns of dependence on food imports emerge.

Production/Consumption Patterns in Southeast Asia

Expansion paths that track over time the changing levels of and relationships between per capita production and consumption of calories are shown in

FIGURE 6.1
Calories Production and Consumption, 1962–1985, Log Scale

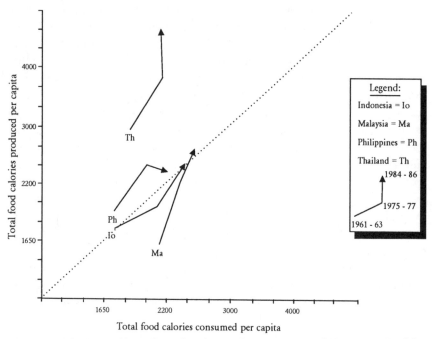

SOURCE: Richard H. Goldman, "Growth and Diversification in Asian and Near Eastern Food Systems" (Harvard Institute for International Development, word-processed document).

Figure 6.1.[3] Placements below the 45 degree line represent net import positions; those above reflect net exports or inventory accumulations. Expansion parallel to the 45 degree line depicts a constant share of imports in consumption; a vertical path shows import substitution or export expansion (the share of net imports in consumption falls); horizontal expansion represents import intensification.

Per capita food production grew rapidly in both periods (1961–1963 to 1975–1977 and 1975–1977 to 1984–1986) in all Southeast Asian countries except the Philippines, where it grew impressively in the first period and then fell back. Indonesia, which started from a position of severe calorie poverty, used its production improvements to raise capita consumption dramatically, and then in the second period moved to eliminate imports and build food security stocks while further improving per capita consumption.[4] Malaysia, by contrast, started the period with relatively high per capita food consump-

FIGURE 6.2
Rice Calories: Production and Consumption, 1962–1986, Log Scale

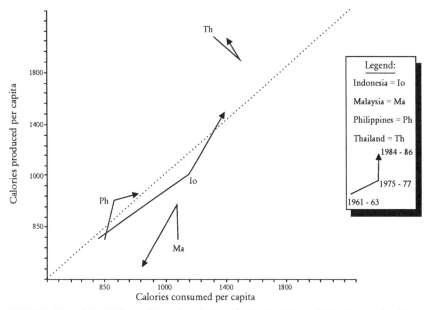

SOURCE: Richard H. Goldman, "Growth and Diversification in Asian and Near Eastern Food Systems" (Harvard Institute for International Development, word-processed document).

tion but was a large net importer. Food production growth was used mainly to save or earn foreign exchange, with only modest improvement in calorie consumption. Thailand followed a pattern similar to Malaysia's, except that it started as a net exporter of calories, a position that was greatly enhanced by the end of the period, with virtually no growth in per capita food consumption during the second period. The Philippines, where population grew faster than in the other countries, nevertheless achieved sufficient per capita production growth in the early period both to augment per capita consumption and to increase net exports. Food production slowed in the second period and net calorie exports fell.

Some of the experience depicted in Figure 6.1 is influenced by rapid growth in specialized food export activities. Expansion paths for rice, the dominant staple food, which are shown in Figure 6.2, give a clearer view of performance in the core food economy. The paths are similar to those in Figure 6.1 for all food in the cases of Indonesia and the Philippines, but they are dramatically different for Malaysia and Thailand. Per capita production of rice actually fell in Thailand in the first period, when per capita consumption was encouraged by a rice export tax that reduced domestic prices. Production picked up somewhat in the second period, but over the whole time span there was virtually no change in per capita rice consumption. Malaysia's drive toward rice self-sufficiency, supported by the large Muda Irrigation Project, is clearly revealed in the first period expansion path. The thrust was not sustained, however, in the face of steeply increasing marginal costs of irrigation investments (Goldman 1975). Imports increased, and per capita rice consumption, dampened by rising real prices and low income elasticity of demand, was actually lower at the end of the period than at the beginning.

The Green Revolution in rice has attracted the attention of those who hope to derive lessons from the Southeast Asian experience, but it is important to note that other food crops also made important contributions both to increasing domestic food consumption and to exports. A comparison of Figures 6.1 and 6.2 makes it clear that, particularly for Malaysia and Thailand, food commodities other than rice drove production growth: maize and cassava in Thailand and edible oil in Malaysia.[5]

Production/Consumption Patterns in Africa

Per capita food production in Africa has been subject to much variation over the past two decades, but the general trend has been downward, in part a reflection of the difficulty in improving per capita food production in the face of rapid population growth, which has been about 1.5 percentage points higher than that in Southeast Asia (see Turner et al. 1993). As the sample of countries shown in Figure 6.3 suggests, the total food production record is not uniform across Africa. Only four countries maintained food production growth in excess of 2.5 percent in both periods. While the largest group of countries in Figure 6.3 represents slow growers in both periods, a number of countries recorded food production growth in excess of 2.5 percent in the 1980s. Most of these countries were slow growers in the 1970s. Some of this improvement is probably due to better weather conditions in the latter half of the 1980s. There is important evidence, however, that economic factors played a role in the improved performance of food crops.

Per capita food consumption in Africa, as measured by food balance sheet records of available supply, is highly varied and not necessarily a reflection of food production, since food imports play an important role in national consumption. In most African countries, per capita calorie availability,

FIGURE 6.3

Change in African Food Production, Annual Growth Rates

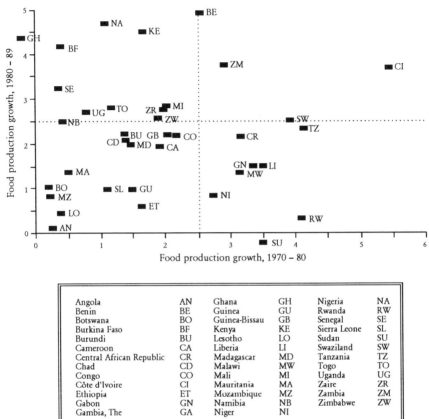

Angola	AN	Ghana	GH	Nigeria	NA
Benin	BE	Guinea	GU	Rwanda	RW
Botswana	BO	Guinea-Bissau	GB	Senegal	SE
Burkina Faso	BF	Kenya	KE	Sierra Leone	SL
Burundi	BU	Lesotho	LO	Sudan	SU
Cameroon	CA	Liberia	LI	Swaziland	SW
Central African Republic	CR	Madagascar	MD	Tanzania	TZ
Chad	CD	Malawi	MW	Togo	TO
Congo	CO	Mali	MI	Uganda	UG
Côte d'Ivoire	CI	Mauritania	MA	Zaire	ZR
Ethiopia	ET	Mozambique	MZ	Zambia	ZM
Gabon	GN	Namibia	NB	Zimbabwe	ZW
Gambia, The	GA	Niger	NI		

SOURCE: Data from the Food and Agriculture Organization of the United Nations, *Supply Utilization Accounts* (Rome: FAO, 1990).

which is measured on the vertical axis of Figure 6.4, is substantially higher in 1989 than it was in Indonesia and the Philippines two decades ago. Unlike the Southeast Asian countries where food consumption grew to exceed 2,200 calories daily, more than half of African countries have experienced a declining trend in food consumption, or fluctuation but no trend. In seventeen countries, those in the lower right hand part of Figure 6.4, food consumption is both above the 2,000-calorie level *and* has recorded substantial improvement over the past twenty-five years. In most of these countries,

FIGURE 6.4
Per Capita Calorie Availability and Growth in Africa

Level of calorie availability per capita, 1989 (calories)	Change in per capita calorie availability, 1965–89 (growth, %)[a]		
	Declining (−27 to −5)	Constant (−3 to 6)	Increasing (10 +)
Low (1667 to 1991)	Angola Burundi Chad Ethiopia Sierra Leone Zaire	Mozambique Namibia Rwanda Sudan	Somalia
Population share[b]	30, 23	13, 10	2, 1
Middle (2036 to 2299)	Madagascar Malawi Togo Uganda	Central African Republic Guinea Kenya Zambia	Zimbabwe *Burkina Faso* *Cameroon* *Ghana* *Lesotho* *Tanzania*
Population share	11, 8	11, 8	20, 15
High (2305 to 2685)		*Senegal* *Nigeria*	Benin Côte d'Ivoire *Botswana* *Congo* *Gabon* *Liberia* *Mali* *Mauritania* *Niger*
Population share	0, 0	2, 25	11, 9

a. Countries in italics are those that grew to medium or high per capita calorie consumption primarily through import growth.
b. Group population shares are calculated excluding Nigeria and including Nigeria, respectively.
SOURCE: World Bank, *World Development Report 1992* (Washington, D.C., 1992).

however, the growth in food consumption has been driven by food imports rather than by increases in per capita food production as it was in Southeast Asia. The exceptions are Côte d'Ivoire, Benin, and Zimbabwe, where per capita production growth complimented imports.

Food imports have played an important role in African food consumption, particularly since 1975. Cereal imports, commercial and concessionary, doubled between 1976 and 1981, representing an increase of almost 10 kilograms per person. Nigeria accounted for 30 percent and five other countries accounted for another 30 percent of the import growth. Jaeger (1992) has shown that the level of urbanization and changes in food import prices and per capita incomes explain a great deal of the variation in African food imports. Indeed, of the fourteen countries in Figure 6.4 where an increased import share of food consumption was the principal source of consumption growth to above the 2,000-calorie level (shown in italics in Figures 6.4 and 6.5), twelve had unusually high urban population shares and/or high rates of urban population growth in the decade of the 1980s.

In many African countries the level of urbanization and its growth rate are considerably higher than was the case for Southeast Asian nations twenty-five years ago (Figure 6.5). Urbanization in poor countries has historically been driven by labor demand supported by rapid technical change in nonagricultural economic activities (Kelly and Williamson 1984). In contrast, the recent rapid urbanization of Africa seems to be associated with general high rates of population growth (particularly in the younger age cohorts); with the collapse of the agricultural economy because of poor macroeconomic management and a worsening security situation; and with declining international terms of trade and publicly funded urban amenities, including cheap imported food supported by overvalued exchange rates (Jaeger 1992).

Rising per capita incomes generated by the export commodity booms of the mid-1970s and falling world prices for cereals, made even cheaper by overvalued exchange rates, were important factors supporting the growth in food imports. These factors reversed themselves in the 1980s. The collapse of world markets for African export commodities combined with exchange rate devaluations in many African countries have led to a reduction in per capita imports except in countries with food emergencies fostered by drought and civil war.

Although per capita cereal imports have declined somewhat from their early 1980s peak, they still make up a large share of consumption. Wheat and rice constitute the dominant share of these imports, most of which are consumed by the urban population. In both urban and rural areas the increase in wheat

FIGURE 6.5

Urban Population Shares and Growth in Africa

Urban population as percentage of total, 1990 (range)	Average annual growth rate of urban population, 1980–90 (range)[a]		
	Low (3.7–5.3)	Middle (5.5–6.5)	High (6.9–10.5)
Low (6–24)	Ethiopia Sudan Uganda *Burkina Faso* *Mali* (Indonesia)[b] (Thailand)	Burundi The Gambia Malawi	Kenya Rwanda *Lesotho* *Niger*
Population share[c]	30, 23	4, 3	11, 8
Middle (25–38)	Benin Namibia Sierra Leone *Ghana* *Senegal* (Malaysia) (Philippines)	Angola Chad Guinea Madagascar Zimbabwe *Nigeria*	Mozambique Swaziland Togo *Botswana* *Tanzania*
Population share	8, 6	12, 33	13, 10
High (40–50)	Central African Republic Côte d'Ivoire Zaire *Congo*	Zambia *Cameroon* *Gabon* *Liberia*	*Mauritania*
Population share	14, 11	6, 5	1, 1

a. Countries in italics are those that grew to medium or high per capita calorie consumption primarily through import growth.

b. For the Southeast Asian countries, the urban population share is for 1965 and the average annual growth rate of urban population is from 1965–80.

c. Group population shares are for Sub-Saharan Africa and are calculated excluding Nigeria and including Nigeria, respectively.

SOURCE: World Bank, *World Development Report 1992* (Washington, D.C., 1992).

and rice consumption is associated with the rise in female employment away from the home. These commodities require less home preparation and are more commonly sold by street vendors than are coarse grains (Kennedy and Reardon 1994). In 1988–1989 food aid accounted for between 15 and 30 percent of cereal imports in seven African countries and in excess of 30 percent in eighteen countries. This pattern of import-driven growth in urban cereals consumption contrasts with the Southeast Asia experience, where urbanization proceeded at a slower pace and consumption growth both induced and was driven by domestic production. The possible implications of this pattern for agricultural growth are discussed further below.

Sources of Food Production Growth

Rice is the dominant staple food in Southeast Asia, but its role in food production growth has varied within the region. The role of irrigation, which also has featured prominently in rice production growth, has been less important to the general growth in food production in some Southeast Asian countries than in others. From the perspective of African agriculture, it is important to acknowledge the critical role of technical change. It is also important that considerable agricultural growth has occurred on rainfed land and in crops other than rice, suggesting that the record of Southeast Asia holds promise for African countries, where opportunities for productive irrigation are very limited.

Food Production in Southeast Asia

Rice production grew rapidly in Southeast Asia following the introduction of modern rice varieties in the late 1960s. There has been sustained growth in Indonesia throughout the 1970s and 1980s. In the early and later period (Table 6.3), rice production growth is dominated by increases in output per hectare. During the 1970s growth was more evenly balanced between area and yield increases, as irrigation facilities were rehabilitated and expanded. Indonesia is the only country where high rates of growth were recorded in each of the time periods. In Malaysia, following a spectacular period of expansion driven by the completion of the Muda Irrigation Project in the early 1970s, rice production faltered. In the Philippines, rice yield improvements dominate the growth process; production grew rapidly throughout the 1970s but slowed dramatically in the most recent period. In Thailand, modern rice varieties have not been well adapted to the deep water and poor water control that characterize much of the growing environment.[6]

TABLE 6.3
Rice Production Growth Rates and Relative Contribution of Area and
Yield to Output Growth, 1967–1990

	1967–72			1972–77			1980–90		
Country	Output growth rate, %	Contrib-uted by area, %	Contrib-uted by yield, %	Output growth rate, %	Contrib-uted by area, %	Contrib-uted by yield, %	Output growth rate, %	Contrib-uted by area, %	Contrib-uted by yield, %
Indonesia	6.40	24	76	3.30	46	54	3.99	27	73
Malaysia	6.90	59	41	0.66	−177	277	−1.27	−88	188
Philippines	3.10	20	80	5.80	27	73	2.20	9	91
Thailand	2.00	75	25	3.80	86	14	1.62	71	29

SOURCES: Asian Development Bank, *Key Indicators of Developing Member Countries of ADB* (Manila, 1985); Asian Development Bank, *Key Indicators of Developing Asian and Pacific Countries* (Manila, 1991); Randolph Barker and Robert W. Herdt, *The Rice Economy of Asia* (Washington, D.C.: Resources for the Future, 1985); Food and Agriculture Association of the United Nations, *Supply Utilization Accounts* (Rome, 1990).

Throughout Asia rice is grown in a variety of agri-ecological environments. Irrigated rice accounts for less than half of rice area but substantially
more of production. Water availability and water control are closely associated with levels of fertilizer application and cereal yields. In the two countries
where rice production growth has been sustained since the late 1960s, Indonesia and the Philippines, irrigated area has grown at an average annual
rate of 2 to 2.8 percent (Table 6.4). By the mid-1980s more than 60 percent
of rice area was irrigated and almost three-quarters of the rice area was under
Green Revolution varieties in Indonesia. Fertilizer application had grown to
substantially more than 100 kilograms per hectare. In the Philippines, despite substantial growth in irrigated area, more than half of rice area is
rainfed. Although the share of modern rice varieties is high, the poor water
control and low solar radiation in rainfed areas reduce the productivity of
fertilizer. These factors combined with less favorable pricing policies result in
fertilizer application at half the Indonesian level.

The Malaysian share of rice area under irrigation is similar to that of
Indonesia; nevertheless, only 36 percent of its rice area is using modern rice
varieties. Modern rice varieties do not do well in the poor water control and
soil quality found in many Malaysian irrigation areas. Substantial price
subsidies, however, have encouraged high levels of fertilizer application even
on traditional varieties. Thailand's traditional comparative advantage in rice
production and its importance in rice export markets are the result of large

TABLE 6.4
Growth of Principal Rice Inputs

Country	Annual growth in irrigated area 1960–85, %	Gross rice area irrigated late 1970s, %	Share of acreage under high-yielding varieties, %	Fertilizer consumption per hectare of arable land, kg/ha	Average index of fertilizer consumption per hectare, 1989–90 (1970–71 = 100)
Indonesia	2.1[a]	63	72.8	116.6	877
Malaysia	2.8[b]	66	36.4	157.2	361
Philippines	3.5	43	83.5	67.4	235
Thailand	1.5	14	12.8	36.5	619

a. 1961–83 b. 1960–80
SOURCES: Randolph Barker and Robert W. Herdt, *The Rice Economy of Asia* (Washington, D.C.: Resources for the Future, 1985); International Rice Research Institute, *World Rice Statistics, 1987* (Los Banos, Calif., 1988); World Bank, *World Development Report 1992* (Washington, D.C., 1992).

areas of natural flooding in the Chao Phraya river basin. But water control is poor, and with only 14 percent of rice land irrigated, the area under modern varieties and level of fertilizer application is correspondingly low. Production growth in Thailand, particularly for cassava and maize, but also for rice, has been associated with a huge expansion of new road construction in the 1960s and 1970s and new cultivation following the deforesting of rainfed land. There has also been an ambitious irrigation investment program in the traditional rice zone, although the economic rates of return have been very low (Siamwalla et al. 1992).

The observation that rice was not the exclusive or, in some cases, even the dominant factor in food production growth in much of Southeast Asia is an important one from the perspective of judging the relevance of the experience for Africa. Although agricultural growth was rapid in all four countries prior to 1980, Indonesia and the Philippines were the only countries where the combination of water availability and control, modern varieties, and fertilizers were at levels high enough for rice to play a leading role. Irrigation was a critical feature in Southeast Asia, but its role should not be exaggerated. Oil palm, maize, and cassava all grew rapidly on rainfed land, accounting for much of Southeast Asia's food production growth.

Between 1980 and 1990 annual growth in maize production exceeded 3 percent in Indonesia, the Philippines, and Thailand. The record portrayed in Table 6.5 shows that improvements in maize output per hectare, generated

TABLE 6.5
Maize Production Growth

	Indonesia	Philippines	Thailand
Growth rate, 1980–90	5.2	3.0	3.6
Causes of growth (% contribution)			
Area	28	27	82
Yield	72	73	17
Maize production/rice production			
1978	0.13	0.40	0.17
1990	0.15	0.43	0.21

SOURCE: Asian Development Bank, *Key Indicators of Developing Asian and Pacific Countries* (Manila, 1991).

by modern varieties and fertilizer, dominated this growth in Indonesia and the Philippines, whereas in Thailand growth was driven by area expansion. The agri-ecological environments that supported this growth are similar to those found in much of the maize-growing parts of Africa (Byerlee 1992). But maize yields on rainfed land in Asia and Latin America have grown rapidly, as shown in Figure 6.6, in contrast to the slow growth in Sub-Saharan Africa.

Food Production in Africa

In Africa, agricultural sector growth has been slow and erratic (see Figure 6.3 for an example of the food production performance and Table 6.6 for agricultural sector estimates). In a study of African agriculture,[7] Block (1993) estimates that total factor productivity in African agriculture has grown only about 0.5 percent annually between 1963 and 1988 (Table 6.7). Eastern Africa, where subhumid and highland climatic zones play an important role, outperforms other regions (1.2 percent growth) and the Sahel (falling output) and Southern zones lag. Only the Eastern and Central zones escaped a protracted period of declining productivity sometime between 1968 and 1983. In each region there has been a notable recovery of productivity growth, averaging 1.6 percent annually, in the 1980s. In a follow-up analysis, Block (1994) develops econometric evidence explaining the recent period of growth in terms of improved weather, ten-year lagged

FIGURE 6.6
Evolution of Maize Yields by Developing Country Region, 1951–1990

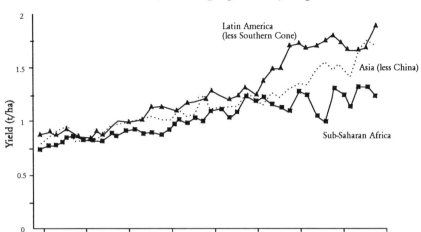

SOURCE: Derek Byerlee, "Strategies for Technical Change in Small-Farm Agriculture" (paper presented at Sasakawa-Global 2000 Conference on Agricultural Development Policy Options for Sub-Saharan Africa, 1992), 19.

TABLE 6.6
Average Annual Growth Rates of Agricultural Output (percentage per year in wheat units)

	1963–68	1968–73	1973–78	1978–83	1983–88	1963–88
Sub-Saharan Africa	2.9	1.9	1.1	2.1	3.2	2.2
Sahel	2.3	1.1	1.1	2.0	1.8	1.7
West	2.1	1.1	0.2	2.6	5.7	2.3
Central	2.7	2.9	1.1	1.9	2.5	2.2
East	4.6	2.5	3.8	3.1	2.9	3.4
Southern	3.4	3.1	0.1	0.4	2.4	1.9

SOURCE: Steven Block, "Agricultural Productivity in Sub-Saharan Africa" (Ph.D. diss., John F. Kennedy School of Government, Harvard University, 1993).

research expenditures, and real exchange rate depreciations, with the last two factors explaining about two-thirds of the improved growth performance.

Block's measures of aggregate agricultural land and labor productivity at various times between 1963 and 1988 are depicted in Figure 6.7. Although

TABLE 6.7
Region-Specific Agricultural Total Factor Productivity Growth Rates
(percentage per year)

	1963–68	1968–73	1973–78	1978–83	1983–88	1963–88
East	2.98	0.74	1.20	0.44	0.65	1.20
West	0.75	−0.35	−1.04	0.43	3.35	0.63
Sahel	0.45	−2.48	−0.82	0.17	1.76	−0.19
Central	1.40	0.34	−0.04	0.46	1.85	0.80
Southern	1.36	1.88	−1.25	−1.47	0.34	0.16
Sub-Saharan Africa	1.45	0.10	−0.46	−0.02	1.63	0.54

SOURCE: Steven Block, "Agricultural Productivity in Sub-Saharan Africa" (Ph.D. diss., John F. Kennedy School of Government, Harvard University, 1993).

labor productivity growth was slow in most regions (ranging from −0.1 to 1.4 percent per annum over the twenty-five years), it would have been even slower were it not for rapid urbanization of the population combined with expansion of the agricultural land frontier. An understanding of the modest improvement in land productivity (between 0.8 and 2.3 percent per annum), which has spillover effects onto labor productivity, is more elusive. Productive irrigation investments have been negligible and the overall level of fertilizer use is extremely low, with little per hectare growth recorded. Better weather conditions at the end of the period probably explain some of the gain. Increased rural population densities have also contributed. The impact of this on cultivation practices, including the reduction of fallow land in farm systems, will result in a measured improvement in land productivity, even if such intensification proves unsustainable in the longer run.

Changes in crop composition from lower- to higher-valued activities occurred in some African countries when restrictions imposed by colonial governments ended, contributing to land (and other factor) productivity. In the most recent period, similar changes may be occurring in a broader range of countries stimulated by economic structural adjustment reforms favoring export crops. Finally, although agricultural research may be contributing to the small enhancements in African factor productivity, the spread of improved maize varieties in the highlands of Eastern and Southern Africa in the late 1970s stands as almost a lone example of technical change similar in nature to that which propelled the increases in food production achieved in Southeast Asia.

FIGURE 6.7
Regional Partial Productivity Paths (output in wheat units)

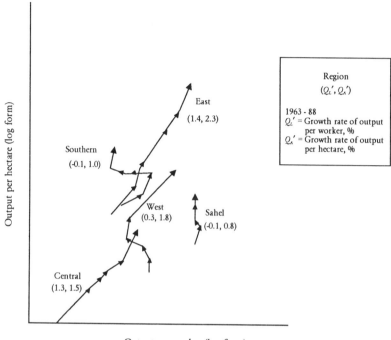

SOURCE: Steven Block, "Agricultural Productivity in Sub-Saharan Africa" (Ph.D. diss., John F. Kennedy School of Government, Harvard University, 1993).

Four features of African agriculture stand out as challenges to both the development and adoption of new agricultural technology: agri-climatic variability, unstable growing conditions, poor marketing infrastructure and limited opportunities for irrigation investments, and the large share of root crops in many African food systems. The economic rate of return to agricultural research is greatly influenced by the amount of land that actually comes under new technology. Since the effectiveness of agricultural technology is very sensitive to features of soil, temperature, humidity, and water availability, the classification of countries by broad agri-climatic regions (shown in Chapter 5, Table 5.4) provides some evidence of the difficulty faced by agricultural scientists in Africa. Most African countries are a mosaic of agri-climatic zones that have been resistant to research efforts (Grigg 1974). Research successes sometimes affect only small areas. Nevertheless, measured rates of return to agricultural research in Africa are high, suggesting that higher funding levels combined with organizational and management reforms may be effective as part of an accelerated growth strategy (Oehmke and Crawford 1993).

Unstable growing conditions are also characteristic of African agriculture, but the degree of impact on crop production varies. Instability influences the risk that farmers must evaluate when deciding whether or not to adopt a new technology or purchase inputs, such as fertilizer, to exploit the genetic potential of new seed varieties. Countries are classified in Table 6.8 according to the variability of cereals yield (measured as the standard deviations of differences from a time series trend in yields). These variability zones correspond generally to the agri-climatic regions defined in Chapter 5, with variability increasing along the humid to mixed to dry continuum. Compared with the lowest variability zone, which accounts for 36 percent of the African population excluding Nigeria, the medium and high zones are more unstable by a factor of two and four, respectively. A similar measure of instability was developed from a data time series of rice and maize yields in Southeast Asia. These measures are compared with those from Africa in Table 6.9. The last column of Table 6.9 shows the yield variability measure as an index relative to the low variability African group.

Rice, the dominant food crop in Southeast Asia, is about as stable (except in Malaysia) as cereals grown in the low variability African zone. The high level of water control in much of Southeast Asia is an important factor. However, most of the cereals in Africa are grown in the medium variability zone, which shows a yield instability double that of rice in Southeast Asia, and a significant amount is grown in the high variability zone. On the other hand, maize in Southeast Asia is generally as unstable as cereals in the medium variability zone of Africa, with the outstanding exception of the Philippines, where maize is a large crop with an instability index about half that of the low variability Africa zone.

TABLE 6.8
Cereals Yield Variability in Africa

	Population (% of total[a]), 1989		Cereals yield variability, 1970–90[b]	Index of cereals yield variability, 1970–90[c]
	Excluding Nigeria	Including Nigeria		
Low variability	36.4	27.4		
Liberia			0.015	28.0
Zaire			0.026	48.0
Madagascar			0.039	71.3
Rwanda			0.051	93.2
Guinea			0.058	105.7
Burundi			0.059	106.7
Gabon			0.062	113.0
Cameroon			0.070	127.2
Sierra Leone			0.074	134.0
Tanzania			0.077	139.3
Malawi			0.079	144.4
Burkina Faso			0.082	148.3
Average			0.055	100.0
Medium variability	41.2	55.7		
Togo			0.093	169.4
Côte d'Ivoire			0.098	177.7
Mozambique			0.102	184.5
Benin			0.102	185.0
Nigeria			0.112	203.5
Central African Republic			0.112	203.8
Kenya			0.114	207.6
Ethiopia			0.114	207.9
Mali			0.130	237.1
Guinea-Bissau			0.133	240.8
Niger			0.134	243.4
Chad			0.141	256.8
Zambia			0.150	273.1
Gambia			0.152	275.8
Congo			0.159	288.4
Average			0.115	208.2

Continued on next page

TABLE 6.8 (Continued)

	Population (% of total[a]), 1989		Cereals yield variability, 1970–90[b]	Index of cereals yield variability, 1970–90[c]
	Excluding Nigeria	Including Nigeria		
High variability	22.4	16.9		
Senegal			0.189	344.2
Sudan			0.192	349.7
Uganda			0.205	373.3
Ghana			0.216	392.9
Mauritania			0.230	417.4
Zimbabwe			0.287	521.0
Lesotho			0.291	529.6
Swaziland			0.294	535.0
Botswana			0.616	1118.8
Average			0.222	402.7

a. Excludes South Africa. b. Standard deviation of residuals of logged cereal yields from trend. Group averages are weighted by intragroup population shares. c. Index based on low variability group average = 100.
SOURCES: World Bank, *World Tables 1992* (Washington, D.C., 1992); William K. Jaeger, "The Effects of Economic Policies on African Agriculture" (World Bank Discussion Paper 147, 1992).

Production instability, generated by climatic conditions and pest populations, is clearly a problem in much of Africa. Agricultural science has had more success raising cereal yields and developing disease and pest resistance in stable and well-watered agri-climatic environments than it has had in stabilizing yields in the face of serious environmental constraints. Farmers, particularly those producing for subsistence, face a major barrier to adopting new technology requiring cash inputs when production outcomes are highly unstable (see Anderson 1991; Byerlee 1992).

Although attention was called above to the growth of rainfed agriculture in Southeast Asia, the relatively large share of irrigated cropland there is in stark contrast with Africa, where about 5 percent is irrigated. Moreover, the topology of much of Africa, limited water sources, relatively low rural population densities, and the administrative and cultural requirements of larger-scale irrigation systems ensure that irrigation will play a much smaller role in

TABLE 6.9
Cereals Yield Variability

	Crop	Cereals yield variability, 1970–90[a]	Index of cereals yield variability, 1970–90[b]
Indonesia	Rice	0.054	98.3
	Maize	0.117	213.0
Malaysia	Rice	0.113	205.3
Philippines	Rice	0.059	106.6
	Maize	0.032	58.2
Thailand	Rice	0.049	89.7
	Maize	0.127	230.2
Low Variability Africa	Cereals	0.055	100.0
Medium Variability Africa	Cereals	0.115	208.2
High Variability Africa	Cereals	0.222	402.7

NOTES: a. Standard deviation of residuals of logged cereal yields from trend. African groupings are as outlined in Table 6.5, with group averages weighted by intragroup population shares.
b. Index based on African low variability group average = 100.
SOURCES: Food and Agriculture Organization of the United Nations, *Supply Utilization Accounts* (Rome: FAO, 1990); William K. Jaeger, "The Effects of Economic Policies on African Agriculture" (World Bank Discussion Paper 147, 1992).

Africa's agricultural growth than it did in Southeast Asia's. Rising population density may provide a more conducive environment for irrigation and labor-intensive technologies in some parts of Africa in the coming decades (Binswanger and Pingali 1988; Turner et al. 1993). Seckler and his colleagues (1992), for example, call attention to the potential for smaller-scale pump and tank irrigation systems in "Mid-Africa." Nevertheless, the likelihood for irrigation playing a strategic role in rapid agricultural growth seems modest. Successful irrigation facilitates production stability and raises the productivity of fertilizer, new seed varieties, and other inputs. Because of its limited present and future role in Africa, a 3 to 4 percent annual growth rate may represent a sustained high-growth path for African agriculture, rather than the 4 to 5 percent record of Southeast Asia.

A program of strategic investments in transportation and marketing infrastructure might compensate for the limited irrigation potential. These facilities are much less developed in Africa now than was the case in Southeast Asia in the 1960s. Poor economic integration within rural areas and between rural and urban areas is an important constraint to agricultural and general economic growth throughout Africa (Haggeblade et al. 1987; Weber et al. 1988). Food price instability, unreliable and expensive input supply, and a low responsiveness to pricing policies, including trade and macroeconomic reforms, are all largely the result of undeveloped infrastructure and inappropriate market regulation. If urban growth continues at its projected pace in Africa, improvements in market integration will become even more strategic.

An additional feature of African agriculture that presents a challenge to technical change is the large share of root crops in the diets and production systems of many African countries. As with other factors discussed here, the relative importance of root crops varies substantially across Africa. A reclassification of countries according to the share of the diet supplied by root and plantain calories is shown in Table 6.10. Compared with maize, root crops such as yams and cassava are better adapted to the humid zones of Africa and to regions of high population density where their high calorie yield per hectare is prized by subsistence farm families. Productivity-enhancing technical changes for root crops have been less impressive than those for maize, rice, and wheat, the Green Revolution crops. The improvements that have been achieved around the world, and even on African research stations, have had little impact on farm productivity in Africa (see Seckler, Gollin, and Antoine 1992 for a summary).

Average cassava yields in Africa are about half those in Asia and Latin America, although there is a good deal of yield difference among African regions. Improved germ plasm has been developed, but adapting it to field conditions has been difficult. Much of the African cassava crop is damaged by cassava mosaic disease and mealybug in addition to other diseases and pests. Developing resistant varieties has been difficult. Although some cassava varieties currently undergoing extensive field tests in Nigeria show encouraging signs of progress on both the yield and resistance dimensions, significant impact on food production may be a decade away.

The current inventory of cereal crop technology, the fruits of intensive worldwide research culminating in the Green Revolution successes in Southeast Asia and other regions, probably holds more near-term promise for maize in Africa than does its counterpart for African tubers. The dominance of cereals in Southeast Asian food systems was an advantage in this regard. Although more rapid progress in adapting maize technology is likely in Africa, it appears that large parts of the African food system must await more fundamental root crop innovations before rapid productivity growth is possible.

The encouraging progress of rainfed agriculture in Southeast Asia com-

TABLE 6.10
Africa: Share of Roots and Plantains in Total Calorie Consumption

	Population (% of total[a]), 1989		Roots and plantains in total calories, %[b]	Index of root shares, 1983–85[c]
	Excluding Nigeria	Including Nigeria		
Low root share	26.4	20.0		
Mauritania			0.4	8.5
Senegal			0.5	10.0
Lesotho			0.6	11.7
Swaziland			0.7	13.8
Botswana			1.0	19.9
Gambia			1.3	24.6
Zimbabwe			1.4	28.0
Sudan			1.8	35.2
Burkina Faso			1.8	35.9
Mali			2.7	53.5
Ethiopia			3.1.	60.2
Niger			4.0	77.8
Zambia			4.8	94.1
Malawi			6.4	125.8
Sierra Leone			7.0	136.7
Kenya			9.1	177.4
Chad			16.2	317.9
Madagascar			19.8	387.3
Average			5.1	100.0
Medium root share	22.9	41.5		
Burundi			22.7	445.4
Liberia			23.3	456.3
Guinea			23.8	465.4
Cameroon			24.6	481.5
Togo			29.4	575.1
Tanzania			29.7	582.0
Nigeria			30.8	603.0
Angola			32.5	636.0
Côte d'Ivoire			34.5	675.2
Benin			35.6	697.9
Average			30.1	589.8

Continued on next page

TABLE 6.10 (Continued)

	Population (% of total[a]), 1989		Roots and plantains in total calories, %[b]	Index of root shares, 1983–85[c]
	Excluding Nigeria	Including Nigeria		
High root share	50.7	38.5		
Mozambique			41.8	817.9
Rwanda			44.3	867.1
Congo			45.2	885.5
Uganda			45.3	886.4
Ghana			49.6	972.1
Central African Republic			50.6	991.5
Gabon			50.8	995.2
Zaire			61.3	1200.0
Average			51.4	1006.2

a. Excludes South Africa. b. 1983–85. Group averages are weighted by intragroup population shares. c. Index based on low root share group average = 100.
SOURCES: World Bank, *World Tables 1992* (Washington, D.C., 1992); Food and Agriculture Organization of the United Nations, *Agriculture: Toward 2000* (Rome: FAO, 1987).

bined with a realistic assessment of the agri-ecological and technical constraints in Africa suggest that there is important scope for faster and more-sustained growth in African food production. The potential varies across Africa, however. In general, although food production should make an important contribution, rapid agricultural growth in many countries may depend more on performance of beverage and nonfood export crops than was the case in Southeast Asia.

Economic Policies in Southeast Asia

Although a good deal of the story of agricultural growth in Southeast Asia involves the advent of modern seed varieties, investments in irrigation, and rapidly increasing fertilizer applications, all of this took place within an economic environment influenced by government management of prices directly through trade policies and food security stocks and indirectly through macroeconomic policies.

Staple food self-sufficiency has been an important objective for all Southeast Asian governments except in Thailand, with its traditional rice export surplus. Malaysia has used public investment in irrigation, combined with price supports, to pursue this goal. The incremental cost in an economy where rice does not have a comparative advantage was judged too great, however, and the self-sufficiency program was abandoned. Malaysia nevertheless achieved rapid agricultural growth by emphasizing export crop production and importing food to facilitate both consumption growth and diet diversification. In the Philippines, irrigation and new rice technology drove the country to self-sufficiency in the 1970s. Technical change has stalled, however, and macroeconomic management has undermined the country's rice price policies, pushing it into the position of a marginal rice importer. Indonesia, by contrast, has moved from being the world's largest rice importer into a position of structural self-sufficiency. Irrigation investments, new rice technology, stable macroeconomic management, and rice price policy have all played important roles in this success story.

Price support policies aimed at keeping the domestic price of rice above the world market level have not been an important objective of economic policy in most Southeast Asian countries. Nominal protection coefficients (the ratio of the domestic to the world price) for rice fluctuate widely over time, caused mainly by year-to-year changes in the world price. Rather than introduce this instability into domestic markets, most governments have used border price policies or domestic inventory adjustment to insulate the domestic market from such variations (Timmer 1993). As a result, standard measures indicate negative protection during periods when the world price is rising and positive protection when the world market softens, as it has throughout much of the 1980s.

The security of staple food supply may have been a more strategic factor for economic growth than food production growth itself, although in some countries they were indistinguishable. Timmer (1993) argues that the main objective of rice price policies in Southeast Asia has been real price stability. Given the dominant role of rice in rural incomes, as an urban wage good, and in consumer budgets, stable rice prices have had a strategic impact both on economic growth, by reducing risk to investment, and equity, by insulating poor consumers from uncertainty in food markets.[8]

Price stabilization was important in all countries. In Indonesia, with its uneasy dependence on imports and its underlying comparative advantage in rice production, stabilization and rice self-sufficiency constituted a strategic alliance playing the key role in agricultural sector growth. The instruments employed to achieve pricing policy objectives vary among the Southeast Asian countries. Indonesia and the Philippines both use parastatal marketing organizations with buffer stock operations and monopoly control over imports, although Indonesia's Bureau of Logistics (BULOG) operates within a much less erratic administrative, financial, and policy framework than the National Food Authority (NFA) of the Philippines (Dawe and Timmer 1991). Malaysia procures rice from domestic producers through a marketing board and then requires private sector rice importers to purchase stipulated shares of domestic rice at an administered price. The process acts like a variable levy, with the offtake shares and price manipulated to achieve the desired degree of domestic price stabilization and support (Goldman 1975). Thailand, until recently, has varied its rice export tax to stabilize consumer prices (Siamwalla 1992).

Among the Southeast Asian countries, Indonesia's price policy has been most exclusively aimed at stabilization. Prior to becoming self-sufficient in rice, stabilizing during periods of high world prices resulted in high fiscal costs. Success in rice production has eliminated the need for imports in recent years. Floor and ceiling prices are set to achieve the stabilization objective, but narrow, policy-determined market margins result in the treasury, through BULOG, providing a subsidy for long-term rice storage (Piggot et al. 1993). Malaysia has generally supported rice producer prices above the world market level, but from year to year it has used its policy instruments to stabilize the domestic market. In both countries there has been a modest upward trend in the real price of rice since the mid-1970s. Thailand, the region's rice exporter, has employed negative protection through the export tax until very recently and has varied the tax to achieve domestic price stabilization. The export tax was eliminated during the 1980s in response to the slump in world prices. Producer prices, which had badly eroded earlier in the decade, began to rebound in the late 1980s.

A key feature in the agricultural success of Indonesia, Malaysia, and Thailand has been stable macroeconomic management. Conservative management of domestic public expenditure and the government budget constraint has resulted in low inflation and relatively little burden on the exchange rate. In these countries, the domestic agricultural terms of trade have not been eroded by inflation and overvalued exchange rates. Their good macroeconomic management stands in stark contrast to the Philippines and to the experience of many African nations.

The pattern of real prices and nominal protection in the Philippines has been highly erratic. But since the mid-1970s real rice prices have declined by over 30 percent. This performance is reflective of a policy stance aimed at rice price stabilization but without the financial or administrative means to counter the general inflation forces fueled by poor macroeconomic policies. David (1989), in a thorough study of the impact of sectoral and macroeconomic policies on food production in the Philippines, shows that during periods of deteriorating domestic terms of trade, net private capital outflows from agriculture represent about a fifth of agricultural value added. These flows fall by half during the few periods when price relationships were reversed. Agricultural growth can be robust, even in the face of worsening terms of trade, when previous infrastructure investments are coming on stream and new seed varieties are being introduced, which was the case in the Philippines in the 1970s. But as the capacity of these inputs is approached, agricultural growth will falter as price relationships discourage new investment. Management of the domestic terms of trade can be a strategic factor in promoting agricultural as well as general economic growth.

Economic Policies in Africa

Although reliable information on real food crop prices in Africa is scarce, Jaeger (1992) estimates that for an eighteen-country sample there has been no significant trend through the 1970s and 1980s. Relative to export crops, however, food crop prices rose substantially until the mid-1980s when real devaluations and reduced border taxes pushed export crop prices back to their 1970s parity with food crops. Oyejide (1993) and Jaeger (1992) show that food crops in many African countries received negative nominal protection throughout most of the 1970s, rising during the early 1980s to a modestly positive level. This superficial glimpse of food crop prices in Africa suggests a performance similar to that in Southeast Asia. Food markets in Africa, however, are much more fragmented than in Southeast Asia owing to poor marketing infrastructure and the important role of informal markets, whereas the statistical record is dominated by official urban market prices.

In contrast to most of Southeast Asia, real exchange rates appreciated rapidly in many African countries during the 1970s and early 1980s, with sustained real devaluations occurring only in recent years. The impact of macroeconomic policies on export crop incentives has been disastrous. The implications for food crops are more complicated, however, since much of the African food system is distorted by administrative interventions that separate urban and rural markets. In contrast to a prevailing assumption behind many macroeconomic adjustment programs, that the agricultural sector is dominated by tradables, there is important evidence from Africa

FIGURE 6.8

Change in Agricultural Terms of Trade and the Real Exchange Rate, 1986–1990/1975–1980

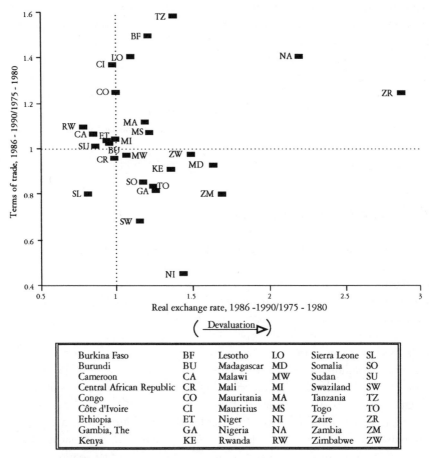

NOTE: Agricultural terms of trade equals the ratio of the domestic agricultural price index to the nonagricultural price index.

SOURCES: World Bank, *African Development Indicators* (Washington, D.C., 1991); World Bank, *World Tables 1992* (Washington, D.C. 1991).

that a significant share of agricultural output is nontradable, that is, its domestic price is not directly affected by world prices or exchange rate adjustments. Evidence developed by Mundlak and Larson (1992) shows that border price adjustments pass through with reasonable strength to domestic export crop prices in most African countries. It is foodcrops where the status of tradability is questioned.

One indication of the degree of nontradability in African food systems is the large share of root crops in food consumption, between 40 and 60 percent in many countries (see Table 6.10). These crops are generally nontradable in Africa because of their perishability and high transportation cost. Cereals, particularly sorghum and millet, but also maize in many cases, are also insulated from the direct effect of world prices because of poor infrastructure and high transportation cost. These conditions result in a wide gap between import and export parity prices, allowing domestic prices to fluctuate widely before unsubsidized international trade is induced. Kyle and Swinnen (1994), in an econometric study of this issue in Zaire, show that an important share of agricultural sector output is nontradable. It is not surprising, therefore, that successful macroeconomic reform leading to real exchange rate devaluations has not produced a consistently clear improvement in the agricultural terms of trade in Africa, as shown in Figure 6.8. Although nominal devaluations and export tax adjustments have improved incentives for export crop production, prices in the nontradable food markets are more influenced by economic contraction and the rise of official prices toward parallel market prices that occurs with less government intervention and improved market integration. In parts of West Africa the potential for export crop expansion may be limited by the competition for labor between tradable export crops and nontradable staple foods (Delgado 1992). As labor is absorbed by an expanding export sector, staple food prices rise, causing a rise in agricultural wages.

Many of the structural features that distinguish Africa from Southeast Asia come into play on the issue of food price stabilization. It seems plausible that African governments are at least as concerned about food price stability as their Southeast Asian counterparts. Levels of urbanization and urban growth rates are generally higher in Africa than they were in Southeast Asia when the latter had similar levels of per capita income. Food price stabilization is a particularly important political economic objective for governments facing large and poor urban populations whose food expenditures constitute a large share of income. In addition, the underlying level of cereal production instability is higher in most African countries than it is in Southeast Asia (see Table 6.9). Finally, governments have an added incentive to stabilize staple food prices when inflation is stimulated by macroeconomic imbalance, a condition that has been more present in Africa than in Southeast Asia.

Southeast Asian countries were able to use border taxes, domestic buffer stocks, and relatively modest fiscal resources to stabilize domestic rice prices successfully because rice is tradable in all Southeast Asian countries and, with the exception of the Philippines, commodity price stabilization did not have to lean against the dominant force of general inflationary pressure. When such pressures emerged in Indonesia, fiscal and exchange rate policies were employed to dampen inflation and take the burden off rice price policy.

Stabilization is more difficult to implement in Africa. With important parts of the food system dominated by nontradables and fragmented markets, using imports and border price policies to achieve stabilization beyond coastal urban markets is problematic. This is exacerbated by the fact that maize and root crops are the principal sources of domestic production instability, on the one hand, and scarce foreign exchange is used to import mainly wheat flour and rice, on the other. Substitution and cross-price effects extending into upcountry markets may be relied upon to a degree, but because of market regulation and poor infrastructure they are probably not very strong.

Using commodity stabilization policy in an effort to offset inflation presents additional difficulties. General excess demand puts pressure on nontradable food prices. This is true even for imported foods in domestic markets when supply is rationed because of scarce foreign exchange. Governments generally target nominal food prices for stabilization. The fiscal resources required to make up the growing gap between the target price and the latent price become excessive. This is compounded by sporadic and unplanned exchange rate devaluations, which raise the import parity price of food and upset any fiscal plan that may have been developed to finance imported food in the stabilization effort. For all of these reasons, African stabilization efforts often result in policy failure.

A common response to the mismatch between general price stabilization objectives and available fiscal and administrative resources is to concentrate these programs and resources on urban markets. Administrative interventions and the naturally poor market integration that comes with deteriorating rural infrastructure combine to delink urban from rural markets. The result is urban price stability at the expense of increased rural market instability; this has occurred in much of Africa.

Conclusions

Rapid economic growth will be achieved in Africa only if agricultural growth is stimulated, as it was in Southeast Asia. The two regions differ in important ways, but the platforms for growth in Southeast Asia—agricultural technical change, good marketing infrastructure, and stable macroeconomic policies—are also strategic factors in Africa. The generation of new agricultural technology for African food crops will be a more challenging and protracted process than that which stimulated the more successful rice economies of Southeast Asia. Therefore growth in Africa must come more from infrastructure investments and economic reforms. This strategy will promote growth in the medium term as well as provide a supportive environment for the more promising food crop technologies now in the development pipeline. Poor market integration in African agriculture is a strategic constraint. Without developments in this area, involving both physical investments and financial market and regulatory reform, the impact of improved pricing and macroeconomic policies will be limited. Reducing transportation costs, particularly between potential food surplus producing areas and urban areas, will promote market integration and result in improved incentives for producers and lower, more stable prices for consumers.

The underlying instability of crop production and the large share of root crops in African food systems contrast sharply with Southeast Asian conditions. Although technical change is a strategic factor in agricultural growth, these features present major challenges to agricultural research. Research strategies aimed at building resistance to environmental conditions rather than genetic yield potential may have higher payoff in Africa than in Southeast Asia. In African food systems where maize is the staple crop, food production is likely to grow faster than in other regions, based on the high-yield and high-input model followed by Southeast Asian countries.

Relative to the recent history of Southeast Asia, the level and rate of growth of urban populations in much of Africa is higher and presents major issues regarding food demand and supply. The current import dependence of urban areas may not be sustainable without improvements in foreign exchange availability or increasing food aid. On the other hand, facilitating urban food consumption through domestic production will require substantially more agricultural technical change than has been forthcoming thus far, improved marketing infrastructure, and enhanced producer incentives. If African urbanization continues to occur in an economic environment characterized by low labor productivity, then insufficient purchasing power will threaten urban food security. Governments will be under great pressure to provide relief through price subsidies and cheap imports. This will conflict with the incentives required to encourage domestic food production. A successful strategy that focuses on cost-reducing technical change, infrastructure investments to promote greater integration between urban and rural areas, and market system reforms will lessen the burden on pricing policies to produce desirable outcomes for both producers and consumers.

Although sustained growth in agriculture is a prerequisite for general economic growth in much of Africa, the contribution of food production relative to that of export crops may vary. The Southeast Asian experience is instructive on this issue. The contrast between Indonesia and Malaysia is particularly striking. In Indonesia, staple food production played a dominant role in agricultural growth, whereas Malaysia abandoned its high-cost rice self-sufficiency strategy. Rapid agricultural growth was driven by export crops, while food imports and pricing policy facilitated both consumption growth and price stability. African countries, where the balance of comparative advantage between food and export crops varies, may face a similar choice between agricultural growth strategies.

For most African countries such a choice need not be imminent. In cases of rapid technical change in foodcrops the threshold of comparative advantage relative to export crops will shift toward the former. Also, macroeconomic management improvements, marketing system reforms, and transportation infrastructure development can promote both food and export crop production. Where the two compete for resources, however, the experience of Southeast Asia suggests that agricultural strategy should be guided mainly by comparative advantage.

NOTES

The author wishes to thank Daniel Gilligan for his assistance with research and for his advice on many substantive issues as this chapter was developed.

1. Agricultural growth slowed to moderately high levels in Malaysia, Thailand, and Indonesia and virtually stalled in the Philippines during the 1980s. Nevertheless, during the fifteen-year period prior to 1980 when real per capita incomes in Southeast Asia almost doubled, the agriculture sector played an important role in the growth process.

2. These two large countries so dominate African demographics that a clearer view of the distribution of characteristics across Africa is more accessible when Nigeria and South Africa are excluded from share calculations.

3. This figure depicts the following food system identity:

$$Q/N = C/N * Q/C$$

Change in per capita calorie production (Q/N) must be allocated between change in per capita consumption (C/N) and change in the domestic production share in consumption (Q/C) (Goldman 1993).

4. There is some evidence from national sample surveys (SUSENAS) on rice consumption that the second period growth of both consumption and production shown in Figure 6.2 may be overstated (Piggot et al. 1993, 86–88).

5. Although these commodities have led agricultural exports in both countries, domestic food consumption has also diversified. Since the mid-1970s rice production has driven per capita food consumption growth only in Indonesia. In the Philippines, a third of consumption growth has been supplied by rice calories. Almost half the consumption increment came from domestic root crops, fruits, and vegetables. In Malaysia and Thailand, per capita rice consumption actually declined. Increases in production of palm oil in Malaysia and Indonesia are reflected not only in exports but in the diversification of domestic consumption as well. These calorie figures for all Southeast Asian countries mask increases in per capita consumption of meat protein, particularly from poultry and pork. This has been supported by increases in maize production and other animal feed sources.

6. Until recently, farm prices have also been depressed first by a rice export tax and, in the 1980s, by a falling world price.

7. Block (1993) estimates total factor productivity based on a "wheat units" measure that aggregates physical production of different crops with initial weights based on a common set of relative prices. Although this approach is not perfect, it is free of various measurement biases that taint other measures of productivity, particularly those that use a common currency and require exchange rate conversion.

8. The performance of real domestic rice prices over time, therefore, provides greater insight into domestic policy objectives than nominal protection measures, which are a statistical residual of policy decisions aimed at stabilization objectives.

BIBLIOGRAPHY

Anderson, Jock. 1991. "A Framework for Understanding the Impact of 'Improved' Agricultural Technologies in Africa." In *Agricultural Technology in Sub-Saharan Africa: A Workshop on Research Issues,* ed. Suzanne Gnaegy and Jock R. Anderson. World Bank Discussion Paper 126.

Anderson, Jock, with Robert W. Herdt and Grant M. Scobie. 1988. *Science and Food: The CGIAR and Its Partners.* Washington, D.C.: The World Bank for CGIAR.

Asian Development Bank. 1985. *Key Indicators of Developing Member Countries of ADB.* Manila.

———. 1991. *Key Indicators of Developing Asian and Pacific Countries.* Manila.

Barker, Randolph, and Robert W. Herdt. 1985. *The Rice Economy of Asia.* Washington, D.C.: Resources for the Future.

Berthelemy, J. C., and C. Morrison. 1989. *Agricultural Development in Africa and the Supply of Manufactured Goods.* Paris: Development Centre of the Organisation for Economic Cooperation and Development.

Binswanger, Hans, and P. Pingali. 1988. "Technological Priorities for Farming in Sub-Saharan Africa." *World Bank Research Observer* 3(1): 81–98.

Block, Steven. 1993. *Agricultural Productivity in Sub-Saharan Africa.* Ph.D. dissertation, John F. Kennedy School of Government, Harvard University.

———. 1994. "A New View of Agricultural Productivity in Sub-Saharan Africa." *American Journal of Agricultural Economics, Proceedings* (August).

Byerlee, Derek. 1992. "Strategies for Technical Change in Small-Farm Agriculture: Lessons and Challenges, with Particular Reference to Maize in Sub-Saharan Africa." Paper presented at Sasakawa-Global 2000 Conference on Agricultural Development Policy Options for Sub-Saharan Africa.

Chhibber, Ajay. 1989. "The Aggregate Supply Response: A Survey." In *Structural Adjustment and Agriculture,* ed. Simon Commander, 55–68. London: Overseas Development Institute.

———. 1992. "Exchange Reforms, Supply Response, and Inflation in Africa." In *Open Economies: Structural Adjustment and Agriculture,* ed. Ian Goldin and L. A. Winters. Paris: Development Centre of the Organisation for Economic Cooperation and Development.

David, Christina. 1989. "Philippines: Price Policy in Transition." In *Food Price Policy in Asia,* ed. Terry Sicular, 154–84. Ithaca, N.Y.: Cornell University Press.

Dawe, David, and C. Peter Timmer. 1991. "Rice Price Stabilization: Contrasting Experience in the Philippines and Indonesia." Agricultural Policy Analysis Project Research Report 339.

Delgado, Christopher. 1992. "Why Domestic Food Prices Matter to Growth Strategy in Semi-Open West African Agriculture." *Journal of African Economies* 1(3): 447–71.

Food and Agricultural Organization of the United Nations (FAO). 1987. *Agriculture: Toward 2000.* Rome: FAO.

———. 1990. *Supply Utilization Accounts.* Rome: FAO.

Goldman, Richard H. 1975. "Staple Food Self-Sufficiency and the Distribution Impact of Malaysian Price Policy." *Food Research Institute Studies* 14: 3.

———. 1993. "Growth and Diversification in Asian and Near Eastern Food Systems." Presented at Harvard Institute for International Development research conference, (May).

Gonzales, Leonardo A., F. Kasryno, N. Perez, and M. Rosegrant. 1993. "Economic Incentives and Comparative Advantage in Indonesian Food Crop Production." International Food Policy Research Institute, Research Report 93.

Grigg, David B. 1974. *The Agricultural Systems of the World: An Evolutionary Approach.* Cambridge: Cambridge University Press.

Haggeblade, S., J. Hammer, and P. Hazell. 1991. "Modeling Agricultural Growth Multipliers." *American Journal of Agricultural Economics* 73(2): 361–74.

Haggeblade, S., P. Hazell, and J. Brown. 1987. "Farm/Nonfarm Linkages in Rural Sub-Saharan Africa: Empirical Evidence and Policy Implications." *World Development* 17(8): 1173–1201.

Hwa, Erh-Cheng. 1988. "The Contribution of Agriculture to Economic Growth: Some Empirical Evidence." *World Development* 16(11): 1329–39.

International Rice Research Institute (IRRI). 1988. *World Rice Statistics, 1987.* Los Banos, Calif.: International Rice Research Institute.

Jaeger, William K. 1992. "The Effects of Economic Policies on African Agriculture." World Bank Discussion Paper 147.

Kelly, Allen C, and Jeffrey G. Williamson. 1984. "Population Growth, Industrial Revolutions, and the Urban Transition." *Population and Development Review* 10(3): 419–41.

Kennedy, Eileen, and Thomas Reardon. 1994. "Shift to Non-traditional Grains in the Diets of East and West Africa: Rise of Women's Opportunity Cost of Time." *Food Policy* 19(1): 45–56.

Krueger, Anne O., M. Schiff, and A. Valdés. 1988. "Agricultural Incentives in Developing Countries: Measuring the Effects of Sectoral and Economy-wide Policies." *The World Bank Economic Review* 2(3).

Kyle, Steven C. 1992. "Pitfalls in the Measurement of Real Exchange Rate Effects on Agriculture." *World Development* 20(7): 1009–19.

Kyle, Steven C., and Johan Swinnen. 1994. "The Theory of Contested Markets and the Degree of Tradedness of Agricultural Commodities: An Empirical Test in Zaire." *Oxford Journal of African Economies* (forthcoming).

Lele, Uma. 1989. "Sources of Growth in East African Agriculture." *The World Bank Research Review* 3(1): 119–44.

Mundlak, Yair, and Donald F. Larson. 1992. "On the Transmission of World Agricultural Prices." *World Bank Economic Review* 6(3): 339–422.

Oehmke, James F., and Eric Crawford. 1993. "The Impact of Agricultural Technology in Sub-Saharan Africa: A Synthesis of Symposium Findings." Michigan State University, Department of Agricultural Economics, International Development Paper No. 14.

Oyejide, T. Ademola. 1993. "Effects of Trade and Macroeconomic Policies on African Agriculture." In *The Bias against Agriculture: Trade and Macroeconomic Policies in Developing Countries,* ed. Romeo M. Bautista and A. Valdés. San Francisco: International Center for Economic Growth, 241–62.

Panayotou, Theodore. 1989. "Thailand: The Experience of a Food Exporter." In *Food Price Policy in Asia,* ed. Terry Sicular, 65–108. Ithaca: Cornell University Press.

Piggot, R. R., K. A. Parton, E. M. Treadgold, and B. Hutabarat. 1993. *Food Price Policy in Indonesia.* Canberra: Australian Centre for International Agricultural Research.

Seckler, David, D. Gollin, and P. Antoine. 1992. "Agricultural Potential of Mid-Africa: A Technological Assessment." Winrock International Institute for Agricultural Development, Center for Economic Policy Studies, Discussion Paper No. 5.

Siamwalla, Ammar, S. Setboonsarng, and D. Patamasiriwat. 1992. "Thai Agriculture: Resources, Institutions and Policies." Thailand Development Research Institute. Word-processed document.

Timmer, C. Peter. 1989. "Indonesia: Transition from Food Importer to Exporter." In *Food Price Policy in Asia,* ed. Terry Sicular, 22–64. Ithaca, N.Y.: Cornell University Press.

———. 1991a. "Food Price Stabilization: Rationale, Design, and Implementation." In *Reforming Economic Systems in Developing Countries,* ed. Dwight H. Perkins and Michael Roemer, 219–48. Cambridge: Harvard Institute for International Development.

———. 1991b. "Agricultural Employment and Poverty Alleviation in Asia." In *Agriculture and the State: Growth, Employment, and Poverty in Developing Countries,* ed. C. Peter Timmer, 123–55. Ithaca, N.Y.: Cornell University Press.

———. 1993. "Food Price Stabilization: The Relevance of the Asian Experience in Africa." In *Agricultural Development Policy Options for Sub-Saharan Africa,* ed. G. Edward Schuh. Mexico, D.F.: CASIN/SSA/Global 2000.

Tomich, Thomas P. 1992. "Survey of Recent Developments." *Bulletin of Indonesian Economic Studies* 28(3): 3–39.

Turner, B. L. II, Goran Hyden, and Robert Kates, eds. 1993. *Population Growth and Agricultural Change in Africa.* Gainsville: University Press of Florida.

United Nations Development Program. 1992. *Human Development Report 1992.* New York: United Nations.

Weber, Michael T., J. Staatz, J. Holtzman, E. Crawford, and R. Bernsten. 1988. "Informing Food Security Decisions in Africa: Empirical Analysis and Policy Dialogue." *American Journal of Agricultural Economics.* (December), 1045–52.

World Bank. 1991. *African Development Indicators.* Washington, D.C.

———. 1992a. *World Development Report 1992.* Washington, D.C.

———. 1992b. *World Tables 1992.* Washington, D.C.

CHAPTER 7

Industrial Strategies: Outward Bound

Michael Roemer

Over the past quarter century, the most rapidly industrializing countries in the world have been in East and Southeast Asia. The stories of rapid economic growth in Japan, followed by those of South Korea, Taiwan, Hong Kong, and Singapore, are well known.[1] As Table 7.1 shows, the "four tigers" or newly industrialized countries (NICs) of East Asia sustained growth rates of manufacturing value added in excess of 11 percent per year from 1965 to 1990, rates that may have been unprecedented in history. It has only recently become apparent that three countries in Southeast Asia—Indonesia, Malaysia, and Thailand—have also enjoyed sustained, rapid growth of manufacturing value added at rates comparable to the NICs and seem to be on a similar path of industrial transformation.

Africa, in contrast, has industrialized relatively slowly. Among the sixteen countries for which there are data in Table 7.1, in only four—Botswana, Cameroon, Kenya, and Nigeria—did manufacturing value added grow faster than 5 percent per year from 1965 to 1990. And in all except Cameroon, manufacturing growth slowed to 5 percent or less during the 1980s, a decade during which the Asian countries maintained or accelerated their pace of industrialization.

What explains this difference in performance? Previous chapters have supplied some of the reasons. The Asian countries, especially those in East Asia, were better endowed with experienced entrepreneurs and educated labor forces. During the 1960s many Asian governments went through political changes that brought more competent, developmentally focused

TABLE 7.1

Manufacturing Performance, Asia and Africa, 1970–1990

	Manufacturing value added		Manufactured exports[a]		
	% of GDP 1990	Growth (% per anum), 1970–90	Share (%) of total exports 1970	1990	Growth (% per anum), 1970–90
East/Southeast Asia					
Korea	32	13.7	77	94	18.6
Taiwan	34	10.8	54	57	13.4[e]
Hong Kong	18	—	96	96	7.8
Singapore	31	8.9	31	73	17.6
Indonesia	19	12.9	1	35	30.1
Malaysia	28	10.5	7	44	19.1
Philippines	25	3.4	8	62	16.5
Thailand	26	9.6	8	64	24.9
East/Southeast Asia Average	**26**	**8.7**	**37.5**	**72.5**	**11.0**
Sub-Saharan Africa					
Botswana[b]	6	10.1	—	—	—
Cameroon	13	8.8	9	16	5.9
Chad[b]	14	−0.3[c]	3	8	—
Côte d'Ivoire	15	3.0[c]	6	11	5.9
Ethiopia	11	3.3	2	3	1.4
Ghana[b]	9	3.0	1	1	−.1
Kenya	10	8.2	13	11	1.6
Mali[b]	8	4.8[c]	3	—	9.7
Mauritius	21	8.0	2	30	25.4
Nigeria	7	8.2	1	1	5.6
Senegal	13	4.5	19	23	3.1
Sudan	9	3.5	—	1	7.9
Tanzania	7	1.6	13	11	−5.3
Uganda[b]	4	−0.2	1	—	−2.8
Zaire	8	−1.2	7	8	−3.1
Zambia	31[d]	3.2	0	3	—
Zimbabwe[b]	26	2.5[c]	29	—	—
Sub-Saharan Africa Average	**11**	**4.7**	**4.3**	**6.2**	**3.7**

NOTE: Dash = not available.

a. Shares in current dollars; growth rates in constant dollars calculated from current dollar values deflated by U.S. wholesale price index.

b. 1965–90.   c. 1970–1988 from UNIDO (1991b).   d. Probably includes mining.   e. 1965–89.

SOURCES: China, Government of the Republic of, *Taiwan Data Book, 1992* (Taipei, 1992), 213, 317–18; UNIDO, *African Industry, in Figures 1990* (Vienna, 1991b); World Bank, *World Development Report 1992* (Washington, D.C., 1992), 220–23, 244–45, 248–49.

regimes, a revolution that has touched only a few African countries. These new or reformed Asian regimes instituted stabilizing macroeconomic policies with incentives that encouraged investment in industry, especially in export manufacturing, and maintained macroeconomic balance through the world economic shocks of the 1970s and 1980s. African governments operated balanced economies until the shocks, but they then tried to finance their deficits without adjusting; controls dominated, the investment climate deteriorated, and industrial growth slowed.

Beyond endowments, governments, and macroeconomic stability, Asian countries simply adopted and implemented more productive industrial strategies than those in Africa. Japan hitched its "miracle" of recovery from wartime devastation to the engine of export growth. Protectionist to an extreme, interventionist in its industrial policies, the Japanese government nevertheless challenged its large firms to export or fail. Korea followed the Japanese blueprint through the 1970s. Other countries in East and Southeast Asia used different approaches, ranging from the *dirigiste* (controlled) to the nearly laissez faire. But all of these countries followed the contours of their comparative advantage, emphasized manufactured exports as the principal engine of growth, and put government energy and resources behind these strategies.

Africa took a different path. Like the Asian countries, its first postindependence strategy was import substitution. Unlike the Asian countries, Africa's governments continued with inward-looking strategies long after they had ceased producing industrial growth. With the exception of Mauritius, export orientation never figured prominently in promoting manufacturing. Unproductive government policies and industrial practices became entrenched and difficult to change without daunting social and economic costs, especially in stagnant economies.

This chapter traces Asia's varied approaches to industrialization in hope of finding a path that African countries could follow. The first section reviews industrial performance in the two regions. The next section examines the differing industrial strategies in East and Southeast Asia, comparing these with Africa's approach, and the concluding section draws lessons for African industrialization.

Three major themes emerge from this chapter. *First,* there is no single Asian strategy for manufacturing, but a continuum of approaches that are all focused on export-led growth. *Second,* it is to Southeast Asia, rather than the "Gang of Four" newly industrialized countries, that Africa should look for guidance in industrial strategy. *Third,* because African governments, like those in Southeast Asia, have limited capacity to manage direct interventions into manufacturing development, prescriptions for industrial strategies should emphasize market orientation and keep government involvement to a minimum.

Patterns of Industrialization

Manufacturing growth in East and Southeast Asia has been swift, as already noted; it has depended heavily on exports; it has followed the dictates of comparative advantage; and it has generated a virtuous circle of productivity gains that reinforce export competitiveness. In none of these respects has African manufacturing development been comparable with the Asian pattern.

Manufacturing Growth

Rapid industrialization for twenty-five years in Asia raised the manufacturing share of gross domestic product into the range of 20 to 30 percent in 1990 (see Table 7.1). The leaders, Korea and Taiwan, had manufacturing shares of less than 20 percent in 1965 but over 30 percent in 1990. Singapore, Thailand, and Indonesia roughly doubled their shares.

Most African countries sustained small gains in manufacturing. Cameroon, Kenya, Mauritius, and Nigeria managed growth of 8 percent per year in manufacturing value added from 1970 to 1990, but other countries in Table 7.1 had much slower growth. Only in Mauritius, Zambia, and Zimbabwe did manufacturing account for 20 percent or more of GDP in 1990. Of these, Zambia's high share may be due to a statistical anomaly,[2] Zimbabwe's manufacturing sector flourished in a hothouse environment during the UDI period,[3] and only Mauritius experienced rapid manufacturing growth by competing in world markets.

Export Orientation

It has been well established that, in the East Asian NICs, industrialization was based on rapid export growth. Table 7.1 shows that, among the East Asian NICs, the growth of manufactured exports in constant dollar values ranged from 8 percent per year for Hong Kong to 19 percent for Korea over twenty years. Among the Southeast Asian industrializers, starting from a lower base in 1970, growth rates ranged from 17 to 30 percent per year. These ASEAN countries were overwhelming primary exporters in the 1960s and 1970s, with manufacturing exports responsible for 8 percent or less of total commodity export earnings in 1970. By 1990, manufacturing exports earned 35 percent (in Indonesia) to 64 percent (in Thailand) of total export earnings.

Sub-Saharan Africa remains predominantly a primary-exporting continent. For the region as a whole, the manufacturing share of commodity exports was only 6 percent in 1990. Cameroon, Chad, and Côte d'Ivoire made substantial gains during the two decades to 1990, and Mauritius was an outstanding performer. But other countries made meager progress. Even for Côte d'Ivoire and Kenya, two of the most advanced countries of the region, only 11 percent of commodity export earning came from manufactures in 1990, and in Nigeria the contribution was negligible. Zimbabwe is an important exception: it became an exporter of manufactures under the Rhodesian federation and 29 percent of its export earnings came from manufactures as early as 1965.

East Asia, and to a lesser extent Southeast Asia, were fortunate in riding the crest of rapidly growing world markets through the 1970s. But they did not depend only on growth in world demand. According to data from UNIDO (1991a, Table 1.8), East and Southeast Asia's share of world manufactured exports (SITC categories 5–8) rose from 3.5 percent in the 1970s to 12 percent in 1988.[4] Africa as a whole has just been able to maintain its world market share of manufactured exports at a minuscule 0.5 percent. But the Sub-Saharan countries have fallen far behind other developing countries, as Africa's share of manufactured exports among developing countries fell from 8 percent in 1970 to only 3 percent in 1988 (UNIDO 1991b, 31).[5]

Comparative Advantage

Although the Asian countries have undergone dramatic structural changes in the composition of their exports, they have adhered closely to their comparative advantage in world trade. Korea, Hong Kong, and Singapore, poorly endowed with land and natural resources, began their export drives with labor-intensive manufactures. Taiwan's early growth depended more on agricultural exports in the 1950s but moved quickly toward labor-intensive manufactured exports. As these countries exhausted their labor surpluses and accumulated both human and physical capital, they moved toward exports that were more intensive in skills, capital, and technology. As we shall see,

FIGURE 7.1

Revealed Comparative Advantage: Unskilled Labor–Intensive Goods

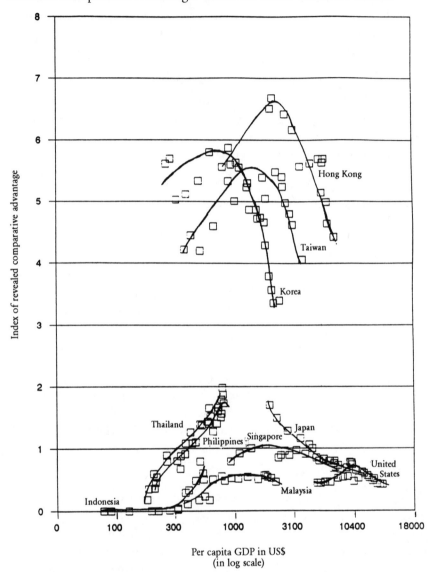

SOURCE: Seiji Naya, William E. James, and Michael Plummer, *Pacific Economic Cooperation in the Global Context: Macroeconomic Structural Issues of Trade, Finance and the Adjustment Process.* (Honolulu: East-West Center, 1989).

economic policies encouraged these shifts in the composition of exports but, especially in Korea during the 1970s, sometimes pushed them faster than the market and existing comparative advantage might otherwise have indicated.

The Southeast Asian countries, richly endowed in natural resources, were and to a considerable extent remain primary exporters. Their comparative advantage has been shifting, however, toward labor-intensive manufacturers and, for Malaysia, toward more capital- and skill-intensive exports.

Shifts in comparative advantage are traced systematically for East and Southeast Asian countries by Naya, James, and Plummer (1989) over the period from 1970 to 1986. They plot changes in *revealed comparative advantage* (RCA), an indicator that compares the shares of a commodity or commodity group within a single country's exports to the same share in world markets. If the ratio for textiles, for example, exceeds one, then the country is said to have a revealed comparative advantage in textiles. Naya et al. divide commodities into three categories: unskilled labor–intensive, human capital–intensive, and technology-intensive commodities. Their graphs are reproduced in Figures 7.1 to 7.3.

The patterns are striking. As their incomes rise, Korea, Taiwan, and Hong Kong reveal a sharp rise in RCA for unskilled labor–intensive goods, followed by an equally sharp decline, although the RCA remains high, over 3.0 for all countries.[6] Thailand, the Philippines, and Indonesia, however, remain on the sharply rising portion of their curves, while Singapore and Malaysia show gently declining RCAs. All the Southeast Asian countries have much lower RCAs for unskilled labor–intensive goods, presumably because of their even greater comparative advantage in resource-intensive goods, not plotted by Naya et al.

As expected, the four ASEAN countries have little or no revealed comparative advantage in human capital. It is the technology-intensive curves that show the tightest pattern: all countries, from Indonesia to Japan and the United States, appear to be on the same path of rising RCA in high-tech exports, even though the ASEAN four remain very close to zero, as expected. Singapore has gone the farthest of the Asian countries in exporting technology-intensive goods, followed closely by Hong Kong, and then Taiwan and Korea. Even Malaysia is moving up toward a ratio of one, evidently because of its success in electronics.[7]

The resource endowments of most African countries suggest a comparative advantage in smallholder primary exports, which are land and labor intensive (see Chapter 5); and, eventually if not already, in unskilled labor–intensive manufacturing. The scanty evidence available does not suggest that

FIGURE 7.2
Revealed Comparative Advantage: Human Capital–Intensive Goods

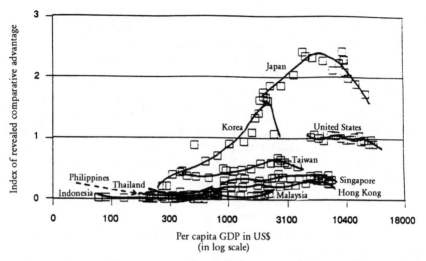

SOURCE: Seiji Naya, William E. James, and Michael Plummer, *Pacific Economic Cooperation in the Global Context: Macroeconomic Structural Issues of Trade, Finance and the Adjustment Process* (Honolulu: East-West Center, 1989).

African countries are investing heavily in labor-intensive manufacturing, however. During the 1980s, the share of labor-intensive industries in total manufacturing value added fell in ten of the twelve most industrialized countries (UNIDO 1991b, 98).

Employment and Productivity Gains

A notable feature of Korean and Taiwan growth from the start has been rapid growth of employment, productivity, and wages in manufacturing. Table 7.2 shows that this trend carried over to other Asian exporters and extended into the 1980s, the only decade for which we have data. Indonesia's rapid growth of employment (albeit from a small base), of productivity, and of real wages was remarkable. The performances of Malaysia and Thailand were also strong.

For the twenty-nine Sub-Saharan countries listed by UNIDO (1992, 78), some of which are included in Table 7.2, total manufacturing employment gained only 13 percent from 1980 to 1990.[8] Even these modest gains were seriously compromised by declines in productivity. Only five of the twenty-

FIGURE 7.3
Revealed Comparative Advantage: Technology-Intensive Goods

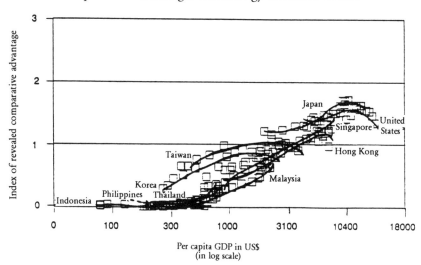

SOURCE: Seiji Naya, William E. James, and Michael Plummer, *Pacific Economic Cooperation in the Global Context: Macroeconomic Structural Issues of Trade, Finance and the Adjustment Process* (Honolulu: East-West Center, 1989).

nine countries—Burkina Faso, Burundi, Mauritius, Zambia, and Zimbabwe—gained significantly in both employment and labor productivity in manufacturing. Of the remaining twelve countries with employment gains, ten did so at a significant cost in reduced productivity, while productivity stagnated in the other two. Overall, productivity declined or remained stagnant in nineteen of the twenty-nine countries. Given employment and productivity trends, it is not surprising that real wages in African manufacturing grew slowly or even declined during the 1980s. The picture would probably not be as bleak if the data could be extended back to the 1960s to cover the years of rapid industrialization. But whatever momentum was gained in the postindependence period, it had certainly been lost by the end of the 1980s.

Industrialization Strategies

Industrialization, although it focuses on the growth and development of manufacturing, is an especially broad topic with close links to almost every

TABLE 7.2
Employment and Labor Productivity Growth in Asian Manufacturing,
1980–1990, (% per annum)

Country	Manufacturing employment	Labor productivity	Real wage
East/Southeast Asia			
Korea	5.0	6.0	5.6
Taiwan	1.9	4.9	7.2
Hong Kong	1.7	3.7	4.5
Singapore	2.1	5.3	5.2
Indonesia	8.9	3.6	4.7
Malaysia	2.5	3.6	2.5
Philippines	−2.3	2.1	4.1
Thailand	3.8	3.1	1.3
Sub-Saharan Africa			
Botswana	14.3	−2.1	−6.6
Cameroon	−0.2	2.8	2.1
Côte d'Ivoire	−2.7	2.9	6.5
Ghana	−1.2	9.9	5.0
Kenya	2.8	0.7	0.9
Mali	4.1	−3.6	−2.1
Nigeria	−0.9	−2.0	−2.7
Senegal	3.2	−2.3	−0.5
Tanzania	1.5	−5.0	−3.8
Zambia	0.7	3.5	4.4
Zimbabwe	1.8	1.7	0.6

SOURCE: UNIDO, *Industry and Development Global Report 1992/1993* (Vienna, 1992), 78, 103.

other aspect of economic development. This chapter focuses on topics narrowly related to industrial strategy: trade policy, interventions to accelerate manufacturing development, and technology policy. But this section begins with a brief review of the preconditions that, in Asia at least, have seemed essential to support sustained industrialization. Thereafter, this section deals with Hong Kong and Singapore, the two examples of nearly neoclassical, outward-looking strategies; with Korea and Taiwan, which mixed purposive intervention with market-oriented development; with Southeast Asia, where export industries were insulated from the distortions and rent-seeking of protection; and with Africa, which has yet to emerge from largely ineffectual, inward-looking strategies.

Preconditions for Industrialization

Five conditions identified in other chapters for accelerated economic development in Asia apply with equal force to rapid, sustained industrialization historically in Asia and, prescriptively, in Africa.

- *Stable regimes* put economic development in general, and industrialization in particular, high on the national agenda, with economic policy entrusted to teams of economists who are insulated from politics and rent-seeking (see Chapters 2 and 3).

- Prudent *macroeconomic policies* kept exchange rates in line with changes in world and domestic prices and avoided large fiscal deficits, excessive money growth, and rapid inflation (see Chapter 4).

- Especially in Southeast Asia, investment in research, infrastructure, and human capital encouraged productivity gains in *food and export agriculture,* releasing labor to industry, keeping urban wages competitive in world markets, providing foreign exchange and investible resources to support industrialization (see Chapters 5 and 6).

- *Factor markets* were relatively free to adjust to market forces. Labor markets were not inhibited by regulation. Although financial markets were repressed, informal credit markets (in Korea and Taiwan) or relatively open capital accounts (in the other countries) permitted firms to obtain credit on market terms (see Chapters 8 and 9).

- In Southeast Asia, where indigenous entrepreneurship was not abundant or experienced, *ethnic minority entrepreneurs and foreign investors* were engaged in development while government acted to reduce the animosity of the ethnic majority (see Chapters 2 and 8).

A sixth condition may have been *geography:* East and Southeast Asian countries may have been favored because they developed in the shadow of Japan. Japan was a model for Korea especially and gave other East Asian countries confidence in their capacity to industrialize. East Asian growth then offered Southeast Asian countries reinforcing reasons to follow similar paths. More tangibly, Japan pioneered export markets that they later abandoned, making way for the later industrializers. In the early stages of development in Southeast Asia, Japanese firms provided a significant share of the investment needed. Now Korean and Taiwanese manufactures literally move their plants to lower-wage countries in Southeast (and South) Asia (see Chapter 10).

Although geography was a help in Asia, it is not an impassible barrier for Africa. It is true that, with the possible exception of Mauritius, African industrializers have no obvious model from their own continent. But it is the principal thesis of this book that they could emulate much of the approach of countries in Southeast Asia. Geography imposes no great disadvantages in market access, as Mauritius shows: all of Africa lies closer to Europe than does East Asia, and much of it is closer to North America. Africa itself is not, at present, a promising market for its own commodities, as Asia has become. But a resurgent Nigeria and a politically settled South Africa could eventually become engines for the growth of many of their neighbors. The periods of vigorous (though not always efficient) industrialization in Southern Rhodesia (Zimbabwe) and Kenya in the past, and Botswana today, were made possible by their membership in a customs union.

Open Economies: Hong Kong and Singapore

The orthodox, neoclassical, *outward-looking strategy* for trade and industrial development begins with the policy preconditions just discussed, especially the management of exchange rates to avoid overvaluation and the maintenance of flexible markets for labor and capital. In addition, it prescribes an incentive structure that approaches free trade, with domestic goods prices reflecting world prices.

First, this implies that the incentives provided by subsidies, tariffs, income and corporate taxes, and subsidized credit should be very low and as nearly the same as possible for every industry, with no distinction between exports and import substitutes. If there is any bias, it should favor exports. This overall incentive is frequently measured by the *effective rate of subsidy,* or ERS (Balassa et al. 1982).[9] *Second,* these world prices and uniform incentives should, working through the market, be the principal determinants of economic activity. The neoclassical, outward-looking strategy counsels against direct government intervention to promote industrialization. *Third,* infant industry protection, if any, should be based strictly on tariff protection or direct subsidies, which should be moderate (to limit high costs) and temporary (to promote rapid learning and productivity gains).

Hong Kong and Singapore are wide open to world trade, and their internal markets reflect world prices. Balassa et al. (1982, Table 1-5) report that Singapore's effective rate of subsidy was close to zero for both import-competing manufacturing and manufactured exports in 1967. The colonial government of Hong Kong avoided market intervention, even encouraging private financing, construction, and management of infrastructure.

Singapore's government ruled the economy with a heavier hand, however. At times government tried to force the pace of changing comparative advantage by intervening in wage setting and guiding private investment decisions, though always with world market competitiveness as its goal. Singapore is unusual in having a large, modern, efficient, export-oriented service sector that is, however, largely owned by government, including shipping, airport, airline, and telecommunications companies (Lee 1992, 238).

The core lesson from the two city-states is that wide open economies can develop very rapidly, with or without government intervention. If intervention is used, it must also be export focused. However, the highly urbanized, very open nature of these economies, with no natural resource base or agricultural hinterland and with well-educated labor forces, makes Hong Kong and Singapore questionable models for African countries, even very small ones such as Mauritius, Togo, and The Gambia.

Market-Disciplined Interventions: Korea and Taiwan

Korea and Taiwan, which are often held as examples to other countries, present more complex cases. Both managed their exchange rates to avoid overvaluation and both operated flexible labor markets in which wages remained low, reflecting labor surplus, until the rapidly rising, export-led demand for workers drove real wages up. During the late 1960s, both countries also maintained effective rates of subsidy that were moderate on average and either the same for export sales and home market sales, as in Korea, or favorable to exports, as in Taiwan (Balassa et al. 1982, Table 1-5).[10] In this they contrasted with the pattern of import substitution, common in developing countries at that time, that placed much higher incentives on import substitutes and discriminated against exports.[11]

The orthodox, outward-looking approach is more stringent, however: it prescribes both low and roughly uniform incentives for all individual commodities. In this respect Korea and Taiwan were neither orthodox nor so different from import-substituting countries such as Colombia and Argentina. Wade (1990, Table 3.2) uses Balassa's results to show that the dispersion of effective rates of subsidy within Korean manufacturing was about as

TABLE 7.3
Deviations from International Prices, 1975 (coefficients of variation[a])

	All goods and services	Tradable goods only
Sri Lanka	1.22	1.03
Zambia	1.11	1.04
Philippines	.87	.76
Colombia	.86	.71
India	.84	.69
Korea	.79	.69
Thailand	.76	.65
Malawi	.74	.62
Malaysia	.66	.55
Kenya	.63	.52
Mexico	.62	.53
Brazil	.61	.48
Germany	.40	.38

a. The coefficient of variation is the standard deviation of the difference between domestic prices and purchasing power parity prices divided by the mean of PPP prices.
SOURCE: Dwight Perkins, "Economic Systems Reform in Developing Countries," in Dwight Perkins and Michael Roemer, eds., *Reforming Economic Systems in Developing Countries* (Cambridge: Harvard University Press, 1991), 220.

great in Korea as in Colombia or Argentina, and within import-competing manufacturing in Taiwan the dispersion was about two-thirds that of Argentina.

Table 7.3 reports a measure of the deviation of domestic prices from world prices (based on purchasing power parity, or PPP) for thirteen economies. Korea ranks in the middle of that sample, with coefficients about midway between Sri Lanka, the country with the greatest deviation from world prices in this sample, and Germany, with the least deviation.[12] Such import-substituting countries as Mexico and Brazil actually came closer to this measure of the neoclassical standard than did Korea, as did two of the three African countries in the sample, Malawi and Kenya. The ERS and PPP deviations suggest that the governments of Korea and Taiwan did intervene to favor some industries over others, even though, on average, the incentives facing export industries were comparable to those facing import-competing industries.

Korea and Taiwan did not use tariffs alone to impose protection for infant industries. Despite Korea's low average rates of protection, visitors to the country during the 1970s were not impressed with the availability of imported goods. Luedde-Neurath (1986) documents the elaborate web of trade associations that had exclusive rights to import commodities of interest to their members, who generally produced import-competing goods. Officials in Taiwan argued from the start of industrialization that import controls were more flexible and more easily targeted than protective tariffs. As recently as 1984 restrictions applied to more than half of Taiwan's imports by value (Wade 1990, 128–36).

Both countries also deviated from the neoclassical prescription in the management of their financial markets. Throughout the period of rapid growth until the 1980s, the government of Korea maintained control over both the rate of interest and the allocation of credit through the state-owned banking system. For much of this period, with some exceptions, real interest rates on bank loans were negative. The large conglomerates, or *chaebol,* had access to subsidized bank loans, while smaller firms were forced to borrow, at much higher interest rates, on the semilegal, informal credit or curb market. From 1972 to 1978, for example, borrowers from the banks paid 15.5 to 17.7 percent per year, while borrowers on the curb market paid 33 to 43 percent per year (Cole and Park 1983, 312–13).

Taiwan set bank loans at relatively high rates from the start of its industrialization, but in other respects its financial system was similar to Korea's. Even the positive real rates on bank loans did not clear the market, and small firms were forced to borrow on the informal market at rates that, for example, reached 35 percent in 1981, compared with 15 percent on bank loans (Wade 1990, 58–59). Taiwan's government supported the curb market by ruling that postdated checks, the most important credit instrument in the market, constituted an enforceable contract, recognized by the courts (Biggs 1991).

How, in the face of these deviations from the orthodox, outward-looking strategy, would a neoclassical economist explain Korea's and Taiwan's dramatic export-led growth? A possible explanation has two parts: comparative advantage and export-oriented interventions by government.

Through much of the first two decades of rapid industrialization in Taiwan and Korea, exports were primarily labor-intensive manufactures such as textiles, clothing, footwear, processed foods (in Taiwan), and plywood (in Korea), which were produced in small and medium-sized firms. The neoclassical policies of Korea and Taiwan—a well-managed exchange rate, market-determined wages, and low average protection, especially on industrial inputs—supported these industries. High interest rates on the curb market were not especially damaging to labor-intensive industries and, most important, the curb market did make credit widely available to firms not able to borrow at subsidized rates from the banks.

Because comparative advantage lay with firms in multifirm industries, even the protected domestic market did not dull the incentive to compete at home through cost cutting, which prepared firms to compete abroad. Thus, while Korea and Taiwan retained a comparative advantage in labor-intensive goods, government policies, market signals, and market structure promoted exports, despite price distortions in goods and credit markets.

Government interventions in both countries also supported export growth. In Korea the government bestowed economic favors on the *chaebol*. Westphal (1987, 85; 1990, 50–51) observes that, for established industries, Korean export subsidies did little more than achieve a neutral incentive system, overcoming a modest exchange rate overvaluation and other distortions. But an arsenal of infant industry protection was conferred on a narrow group of industries that were targeted as future exporters: access to cheap credit through government-owned banks, access to controlled imports with duty drawbacks, access to protected domestic markets, relaxed enforcement of income tax payments, and the public approval of the government. These advantages depended, however, on the firms' ability to meet ambitious export goals, even for new products. Export targets were set in consultation with the protected companies and closely monitored by officials, who could remove protection from firms that did not comply. For the most part these infant industries achieved rapid productivity growth and succeeded in export markets (Westphal 1990, 47–49).

This pattern reached its peak during the heavy and chemical industries (HCI) drive of the 1970s, when government moved decisively away from Korea's existing comparative advantage by pushing the *chaebol* to produce autos, steel, fertilizer, chemicals, and other capital-intensive products. Many of these industries eventually were able to export. Amsden (1989, 58) documents the rising share of heavy and chemical industries in Korea's total exports, from 14 percent in 1970 to 60 percent in 1984. But the dislocations of the HCI drive led the government to abandon it for a return to more market-based policies after 1979. Writing from a neoclassical perspective, Stern et al. (1992) conclude from a limited sample of case histories that, by and large, government did not promote any successful HCI that might not in any case have been promoted by market forces. In this view, Korea's comparative advantage was shifting anyway, as unskilled labor become more scarce, skills were being acquired, and capital was being accumulated. Government's HCI drive simply hurried this process.

Taiwan has used a similar range of interventions, but with two major differences. *First,* direct interventions to promote heavy industry were primarily through state-owned firms, not private conglomerates. *Second,* because small firms remain the backbone of Taiwan's export capacity, broad market forces rather than direct persuasion have been more important in Taiwan than in Korea. Amsden (1989, 123) documents this difference: the top fifty industrial firms in Taiwan shipped 16 percent of total production in 1980, whereas in Korea the share in 1982 was 38 percent.

This neoclassical perspective on the interventionist but "market-conforming" approach of Korea and Taiwan has been broadened and challenged by a group of writers including Westphal (1987), Amsden (1989), and Wade (1990). Observing the same phenomena (many of which they helped bring into focus), these observers suggest more far-reaching conclusions.

Westphal, who writes in the neoclassical tradition, emphasizes Korea's deliberate policies to upgrade technological capacities in industry, something outside the ken of neoclassical strategy. He identifies two patterns: an "apprenticeship" in which industries such as petrochemicals and steel would be started with foreign technology, sometimes in turnkey plants with foreign technicians, and then gradually turned over to Korean engineers and managers who would become increasingly proficient in running the plants; and "imitatorship," in which industries such as machinery, led by increasingly sophisticated Korean engineers and managers, would acquire and apply technical information that was freely available on world markets.

Westphal (1990, 55) offers neoclassical arguments to justify government subsidies and other interventions that speed technology transfer. Technology is not perfectly tradable and can be costly for a firm to acquire and learn to use. Although the returns can be great, not all of them are captured by the firm, as followers can copy leaders at much lower cost and can acquire skilled personnel from leading firms. Westphal (1987, 81–82) suggests that, for the four NICs, "technological development has been far more important than the advantage they have derived from low wage rates."

Amsden (1989, 3–18) argues that the development of Japan, Korea, and Taiwan exemplifies a new paradigm of "late industrialization." Learning—to acquire, rather than invent, and use new production technologies, management techniques, and other aspects of large, modern firms—is characteristic of late industrialization. To promote learning, the state plays a central role, offering subsidies (in contrast to tariffs) in return for performance standards (export targets), and exercises strong discipline over private firms. Salaried engineers are the instrument of technology transfer, and workforces are relatively well educated. Market incentives take a back seat to government interventions; when actively used, prices are often deliberately gotten "wrong"—different from the neoclassical prescription—to achieve development goals.

Wade (1990, 25–29), writing in a similar vein about Taiwan, speaks of a "governed market," in which an authoritarian government exercises "corporatist relations" with private firms. Taiwan has used highly selective and targeted controls and tax incentives, subsidized credit, investment in research, moral suasion, and other means to foster an export-oriented economy, especially among larger firms. Government augmented investible resources, socialized the risks of investing in developing markets, and steered private investment allocations to achieve development goals. The notion of a government-managed market may be more apt for Korea, however, than for Taiwan, where small firms still dominate production and exports.

Although neoclassical economists and their critics take different lessons from the same phenomena, there appears to be a consensus among both groups on the conditions necessary to make government intervention an effective tool of rapid and sustainable industrialization.

First, interventions must be targeted to promote exports, with export growth the inescapable measure of success. Amsden (1989, 146–47) concludes that, because export targets were "an objective, transparent criterion by which firm performance is easily judged . . . big business groups had to deliver" to justify the many advantages government bestowed upon them.

Second, interventions may push the market to work faster, but they cannot be effective if they stray too far from the direction of market forces. Governments can force the pace of shifting comparative advantage, but they cannot move in an unrelated direction or move too fast.

Third, the civil service managing such interventions must be disciplined enough to keep rent-seeking within tight bounds and must be efficient enough to manage some complex interventions involving subsidies, controls, and moral suasion.

Industrial Strategies in Southeast Asia

The governments of the four ASEAN countries thus far have not met all three of these conditions, and this is an important reason why they offer more relevant models for Africa. Governments in Indonesia, the Philippines, and Thailand depend to a considerable extent on a reciprocal system called *clientelism,* in which a regime derives support, political and especially financial, from private firms, families, and individuals who in turn receive economic favors from the government, such as protection, low-interest credit, and monopoly licenses (see Chapter 3). In clientelistic states, intervention in market forces is far more likely to point toward protected positions and rent-seeking than toward rapid export growth. Malaysia's government, while not so obviously a clientelistic one, has intervened to pursue distributional goals rather than export-led growth.

Interventions that, in Korea or Singapore, would lead quickly to new export industries more often have other outcomes in the ASEAN four. Treecrop exports are cartelized, ostensibly to stabilize domestic prices, but actually to protect processors by reducing prices to farmers. Log exports are banned or heavily taxed to promote cartelized plywood industries that use political influence to retain their protection. Steel mills and cement plants are constructed by clients of the regime, or by the regime itself, behind high protective barriers that remain in place long after the industry is mature, stifling export growth from downstream industries. Technological advances, such as the auto industry in Malaysia and the airplane industry in Indonesia, are disciplined neither by competition nor by ambitious export targets. Many public enterprises are notably inefficient, with little prospect of selling overseas.

Yet, although these interventions frequently go sour, three of the ASEAN countries have been outstandingly successful in pursuing export-led growth. How have they managed it?

First, the ASEAN three, like the four NICs, have met the *policy preconditions* for sustained industrialization discussed above. The governments of Indonesia and Malaysia have been stable and developmentally oriented; policies to further economic growth have been popular and are seen to promote regime survival. Both Indonesia and even the revolving door governments of Thailand entrusted macroeconomic policy to groups of technocrats who kept their economies in external and internal balance. Rent-seeking goes on in Indonesia and Thailand, but if it begins to interfere seriously with growth, it is curbed. When the debt of Pertamina (the national oil company) threatened macroeconomic stability in 1974, the company president, a close associate of President Suharto, was removed; when rent-seeking customs officials seriously compromised Indonesia's competitiveness in 1985, a private foreign company was called in to take over many customs procedures. In Malaysia, when the redistributive features of the New Economic Policy dampened investment, the policies were curtailed and eventually shelved.

The ASEAN three have built a productive primary base, investing heavily in both food and export agriculture and encouraging (mostly foreign) investment in petroleum and mining. Labor markets were not inhibited by regulation or strong unions, leaving wages free to adjust to changing circumstances. Although domestic financial markets were repressed for many years, currency convertibility and relatively open capital accounts permitted access to world capital markets for the largest or most competitive borrowers.

Second, export manufacturing was insulated from the costs of substantially inward-looking trade regimes. Although Southeast Asian governments would not have been able to employ Korea's intricate methods for neutralizing the disadvantages of export manufacturing in a protected economy, they found simpler ways of accomplishing the same thing.

Indonesia only began to dismantle its myriad of import and investment controls in the mid-1980s and still maintains a highly differentiated tariff schedule. A study of effective protection based on 1980 data found high and highly differentiated rates (Poot, Kuyvenhoven, and Jansen 1990, 443–51). Among import-competing industries, ERPs averaged 63 percent on consumer nondurables and 46 percent on consumer durables, followed by 31 percent on intermediate goods and only 4 percent on capital goods. Seventeen of sixty-six import-replacing industries had either negative value added at world prices or ERPs over 100 percent, while twenty-five branches had ERPs below 25 percent and nine of these were slightly negative. These results incorporate only import duties and sales taxes; had import restrictions been included, many of the rates could have been considerably higher.

Considerable progress was made on deregulating imports and other controls from 1985 on. The most far-reaching and innovative reform was to employ a private foreign company to inspect imports and assess duties, which dramatically reduced importers' costs and uncertainties from 1985 on. Despite continuing deregulation, the protective tariff regime persisted through the late 1980s. A recent study shows that the average rate of effective protection for industry, including the effects of both tariffs and licensing, has been declining since 1975 but remains high, 59 percent in 1990 (World Bank 1993, 299). Had nontraditional export growth depended on general trade reform, it seems unlikely that manufactured exports would have expanded by 35 percent per year from 1985 to 1992. Unwilling to wait for general deregulation to take effect, Indonesia's technocrats initiated trade reform, in May 1986, with a scheme to exempt manufacturing exporters from all import restrictions and to establish a duty drawback scheme. Both were housed in an effective special agency of the Ministry of Finance, under the supervision of the reforming technocrats.

Malaysia's industrial policy actually became much more protectionist as it moved from virtually free trade of the 1960s to the New Economic Policy of the 1970s, and the government invested in inefficient state enterprises well into the 1980s. During the 1970s, effective rates of protection on domestic sales were more uniform across categories than in Indonesia, varying from 28 percent on capital goods to 50 percent on consumer goods, but they were highly disadvantageous for exports of all kinds and showed the wide variance across industries characteristic of import-substituting regimes (Hoffmann and Tan 1980, 52–84). But the government encouraged investors, especially foreign firms, to set up export industries in duty-free zones with tax incentives and subsidized services, neutralizing the anti-export bias of the tariff regime. Most labor-intensive textile and electronic exports were launched from these "export platforms" (Gan 1992, 222–23). (Hill describes these and other export-promoting interventions in greater detail in Chapter 11 of this volume.) During the 1980s, policies appear to have reduced effective protection substantially compared to values prevailing in the 1970s (World Bank 1993, 298).

Thailand's trade regime looks similar to those of Indonesia and Malaysia. Although Thailand used import restrictions sparingly, its tariff structure is highly protective and differentiated. Even export sectors average high ERPs, from 11 to 36 percent depending on how nontraded goods are handled, but import-competing sectors enjoy comparably measured average ERPs of 36 to 87 percent. Moreover, these rates have been increasing and the bias in favor of import-replacing branches has been widening (Paitoon, Chintayarangsan, and Thongpakde 1989). Exporters, especially foreign investors, are typically insulated from the protective structure through duty exemptions on capital equipment and recurrent inputs, granted by the Board of Investment.[13] However, Thailand's rapid export growth since the mid-1980s has been due primarily to fundamental changes in economic structure. Falling agricultural prices intensified the migration of low-wage labor to industry; a government stabilization program reduced domestic demand, freeing up existing capacity for export; and a major devaluation provided a strong additional incentive for manufacturers to seek overseas markets (Narongchai, Dapice, and Flatters 1990, 22).

The *third* factor contributing to rapid industrialization is that all three economies have *established programs of reform* to move gradually toward outward-looking policies in trade, investment, and financial markets. None of these countries needed shock treatment, but they acted decisively when economic conditions worsened in the mid-1980s and have maintained momentum of both policy and performance. Central to these reforms has been an end to controls over imports, investment, and credit, giving investors and producers greater freedom to make their own decisions and implement them. As reforms continued and gained credibility, more investors began to bet on profits in exports, reinforcing the momentum toward outward-looking development.

Asian economies thus display a continuum of successful industrialization strategies. Hong Kong, and to some extent Singapore, come close to the market-based, open economy model of neoclassical economics. In Korea, and to a lesser extent in Taiwan and Singapore, effective government interventions generally push in the same direction as market forces. Three Southeast Asian countries have been able to generate export-led growth by managing two interventions that seem essential—sound macroeconomic policies and the insulation of exports from the disincentives of protection and rent-seeking—and by implementing gradualist reform programs to deregulate their economies.

Inward-Looking Industrialization in Africa

Africa, like Asia, went through a stage of pronounced import substitution, beginning with independence and lasting through the 1970s. Rapid industrialization occurred in some countries: Botswana, Cameroon, The Gambia, Kenya, Nigeria, Rwanda, and Swaziland enjoyed growth rates in manufacturing value added of 7 to 15 percent for a decade or more (World Bank 1992a; UNIDO 1992). Unlike East and Southeast Asia, however, import substitution came to a dead end, producing the slower growth rates in the 1980s. It did not lead to competitive industries, exports, productivity gains, or any kind of sustainable structural transformation.

Evidence for Africa's inward-looking industrialization comes from Riddell (1990), who has compiled seven studies on African industry, covering the most industrialized economies in Sub-Saharan Africa.[14] The predominant source of growth for manufactures in these countries was the expansion of domestic demand, with import substitution a significant second; export expansion was hardly a factor. Where import substitution did occur,[15] it did not create linkages with other industries and did not cause a fall in the absolute level of imports of consumer goods (Riddell 1990, 33–38).

Too much of African manufacturing in countries such as Cameroon, Côte d'Ivoire, Kenya, and Zambia remained inefficient behind high protective tariffs and import controls. In Cameroon, for example, the average nominal rate of protection for import-competing industries was 70 percent; two-thirds of all manufacturing branches had domestic resource costs (DRC) greater than 1.6 and one-third of the branches were well over 2 (Karmiloff 1990, 136).[16] Zambia's ERP in 1975 ranged from an average 30 percent on heavy intermediate goods to 180 percent on light intermediates and consumer durables (Karmiloff 1990, 310–11). Only in Zimbabwe did manufacturing appear to be efficient (Riddell 1990, 350), apparently a rare case in Africa where generally competitive industries have emerged despite high protection (Robinson and Somsak 1993, 15–17).

The spotty to poor results noted by Riddell come from some of the most industrialized and most promising countries in Africa. Had the sample been larger, it is likely to have produced worse outcomes. Equally disturbing, the textile, clothing, and allied branches, in which Africa ought to be approaching competitiveness in world markets, showed among the worst results in the studies where it was identified. There were exceptions of efficient industries within each country, and other authors cite African industries that can compete in world markets.[17] The overwhelming impression from these case studies, however, is that few if any of the most industrialized countries in Africa are on the verge of following the Southeast Asian countries into world markets for manufactures.

Unable to compete in world markets, African industry was forced to turn inward to small and slowly growing domestic markets. Only a few African economies are, in the 1990s, large enough to undertake the kind of import substitution that most Asian countries had well underway in the mid-1960s. Even those that have large enough markets are not growing fast enough, and they have not hitched import substitution sufficiently to export growth to generate the kind of productivity gains and growth dynamics seen in Asia.

The rates of protection and inefficiencies found by Riddell and his co-authors are not so different from those cited above for Indonesia, Malaysia, and Thailand. But the ASEAN three, as well as Korea and Taiwan, found ways to compensate for trade distortions and establish conditions approaching free trade for export industries. In East Asia the means were a complex set of subsidies, protection tied to export performance, and government favors. In Southeast Asia the mechanisms encompassed a narrower range: duty drawbacks, exemptions from import restrictions, export processing zones, or a combination of these. Many of these mechanisms have been tried in Africa, with poor results.

In Kenya, for example, an export compensation (subsidy) scheme, intended to offset taxes paid in lieu of a duty drawback scheme, was highly discounted by exporters because of long delays and great uncertainty in payments. Similar problems have haunted duty and sales tax rebate schemes. Duty-free zones may provide better insulation, but they are often subject to initial clearance by senior officials and, once in operation, to interference by customs and other authorities. These vestiges of rent-seeking reduce the value of export zones, especially in countries where government's credibility with investors is poor. Hill explores these issues in Chapter 11. Her basic point is that, in the absence of sound supporting policies, notably an exchange rate keyed to export growth, special export incentives have limited impact in Africa or in Asia.

Mauritius has demonstrated that if strong export incentives are combined with sound macroeconomic policies, African countries are capable of export-oriented industrialization. Manufactured exports, negligible in the early 1970s, accounted for 60 percent of total exports by the late 1980s, due largely to the growth of clothing exports. During the 1980s, merchandise exports grew by 9.6 percent per year and GDP by 6 percent per year. The ingredients for export-led growth were an incentive system, installed in the 1970s, that included an export processing zone and essentially gave exporters free trade status; a decisive adjustment program in the early 1980s, a response to lower sugar prices that included devaluation and an incomes policy; and an openness to foreign investors, especially from Hong Kong (World Bank 1992a and 1989, 111; Robinson and Somsak 1993, 15).

Thus Africa's industrialization strategies have failed so far because macroeconomic preconditions for growth have not been met; because policies have been inward looking without providing incentives for firms to increase productivity and turn outward; because strategies have been interventionist without the discipline of export targets; because rent-seeking has been allowed to dominate economic concerns; and because export promotion has been halfhearted, carried on within an unsupportive economic and political environment.

An Outward-Looking Industrial Strategy for Africa

The discussion to this point suggests three basic premises for African industrial strategies.

First, Africa has to establish an economic environment that meets the six preconditions for rapid, export-led industrialization: stable, development-oriented governments; sound macroeconomic management; a productive agricultural base; flexible factor markets; an accommodation with entrepreneurially gifted ethnic minorities and foreign investors; and access to growing markets. Few African countries met all or even most of these conditions over the past two decades. However, determined and reformist African countries such as The Gambia, Ghana, and Uganda (and South Africa) are capable of establishing the economic environment needed to resume industrialization.

Second, African industrialization should follow the path of comparative advantage, using outward-looking strategies, as Asia's exporters did. For the next decade or more, most countries will have to build a foundation for industrial growth by reinvesting in primary exports and food agriculture, as the Southeast Asian countries did. Simultaneously, governments need to encourage labor-intensive manufacturing for export and the processing of a few (by no means all) primary exports[18] as the most likely emerging sources of comparative advantage.

Third, and perhaps more controversial, African governments should seek industrial strategies requiring as little intervention as possible. The history of African states suggests that governments are not yet capable of sustaining interventions anywhere near as complex or demanding as those used in East Asia. A basic appeal of the Southeast Asian model is that those governments, recognizing their limitations, concentrated on macroeconomic policies and chose minimalist interventions to promote manufactured exports.

The second and third premises have strong implications for industrial trade strategy and technological development.

Trade Strategy

Africa, like Asia, must find ways to establish a free trade environment for export industries within economies characterized by protection, controls, and rent-seeking. The alternative is to deregulate the economy, scale down protection and other price distortions, and so reduce the opportunities for rent-seeking. The more market- and outward-oriented an economy is, the less are special export incentives required, the less difficult it becomes to manage them, and the less rent-seeking distorts efforts away from productivity.

In Africa, recent history and current conditions argue for even more market-oriented strategies, with less need for intervention, than were adopted in Southeast Asia. Even if African governments could effectively manage a range of export-insulating devices, it might not be enough to attract investors into exports. A decade or more of economic stagnation or retrogression, poor macroeconomic management, governments that have been unable to deliver on policy reforms, and hostility to many entrepreneurially talented groups have made domestic and foreign investors especially skeptical. To gain policy credibility and win back investors, it may be necessary to undertake fairly radical outward-looking reforms of trade policy.

An outward-looking stance would have two components. *First,* controls of all kinds—over imports, exports, investment, production and employment decisions, repatriation of capital—would be radically eased and, if possible, eliminated. *Second,* tariffs would be generally reduced and made more uniform. In tariff reform, revenue would be a more important consideration than protection, though even a uniform revenue tariff would provide some effective protection of value added. Such a radically different trade structure is not a fanciful idea. Ghana and The Gambia have approached it in their reforms and Kenya recently eliminated import controls.

Technological Development and Infant Industries

There is a body of opinion, including some neoclassical economists, arguing that Africa should not move toward such a nearly free trade posture, because comparative advantage will not evolve rapidly enough under strictly market-based incentives to help African countries diversify production and escape their role as primary exporters. If exposed to international competition, fledgling African industries will not be able to move up the ladder of more advanced technologies because of their late start. What role can an interventionist technology policy play in a liberalized trade regime?

It seems generally agreed by economists that great technological leaps do not work. Rather, technological change evolves through deliberate but gradual improvements in a country's existing capacity to manage industrial technology (Westphal 1990; Lall 1992; Pack 1993). This has been the experience in East and Southeast Asia, even in Korea during its heavy and chemical industries drive in the 1970s, which was spearheaded by Korean engineers (Westphal 1987). China's failed attempt at a "great leap forward" in the 1950s cautions against revolutionary technological change.

In Africa, the realities are that indigenous mastery of production techniques is largely in agriculture, trading, and small-scale manufacturing; that efficient, modern manufacturing is confined to the early, labor-intensive industries such as food processing and textiles; and that workers are not well educated by international standards and lack experience in modern manufacturing. Technological advancement must evolve from this base.

Advancing from this base, or even improving productivity within existing capabilities, requires new ways of doing things, with and without technologies embodied in new capital, and requires learning by all concerned: workers, engineers, managers, entrepreneurs, government, and society in general. Bruton (1989) reminds us that the core of well-conceived import substitution is to protect such learning, which is a process of trial and error, because new pursuits, including new industries, cannot begin at internationally competitive costs.

Even advocates of free trade recognize this legitimate need for protection of *infant industries*. Infant industry protection (or subsidy) is justified if (1) the net long-run benefits to the economy from a competitive industry outweigh the net costs of inefficient production during the startup or learning period and (2) private firms cannot capture sufficient benefits to make learning profitable or (3) they cannot finance the high startup costs because they lack access to sufficiently advanced financial markets. These conditions are likely to prevail in most African countries for at least some new industries.

Westphal (1990, 57) has emphasized that protection of industrial learning (infant industries) must be narrowly targeted to be meaningful. The problem with import substitution as widely practiced, certainly in Africa, has been its indiscriminate, long-lived, almost wanton protection for any and every start-up industry (Lall 1992, 124). The consequence is that, although broad classes of manufacturing are protected at the expense of exports, agriculture, and capital goods production, in fact no single industry is well protected because so many are laying claim to scarce resources, including skilled labor, capital, and the support of overworked government officials.

Pack (1993) argues that for Africa the most productive new lines of manufacturing will be in process industries requiring relatively unskilled labor, such as food processing, textiles, and clothing. Industries that require engineering skills, rapid product changes, rapid technology changes, or tight linkages to other domestic industries are less likely to succeed in Africa for some time.

A disciplined policy to upgrade industry and increase technological sophistication would be to evaluate existing capabilities and the potential for moving into new, but closely related, fields, and then announce a set of infant industry tariffs or other incentives for all investors in these new activities. Direct subsidies are often considered the ideal arrangement because they are evident in the budget and thus self-limiting. Tariffs can be equally effective, however, if they are moderate, to limit the cost and discourage very inefficient infants; temporary, to encourage rapid learning and productivity gains; and not subject to extension, so the limited duration is credible to investors. A practical trigger mechanism would be to start the clock on temporary protection once the first firm begins production in the target industry. Thus pioneers get the longest period of protection, but they do not get such an advantage that they, in effect, have a monopoly.

Lall (1992) subscribes to this approach, set within a basically liberal, market-oriented trade strategy. But he also lists the stiff requirements for governments to succeed at industrial targeting and, like Pack, is skeptical that many African governments will have the discipline to manage such a policy. Riddell (1990), who also endorses targeting, is less critical of government capacities, not only to pick winners, but also to intervene with managements to help solve problems at the industry or even firm level.

Such an idealized approach to infant industry protection has probably never been implemented anywhere. Korea, with its industrial targeting, export targets, and complex incentives, has approximated it. But nothing like this approach has been tried in Southeast Asia, where protection has been indiscriminate, as it has in Africa. Even a targeted approach can be very costly to the economy. Jacobsson (1993) observes that the learning period may be much longer than expected: in Korea, some advanced engineering firms took one to two decades to become competitive at world prices. Although African countries are generally dealing with simpler technologies, they start with fewer industrial skills and may also face long and costly periods of infancy. If, as seems likely, African governments are unable to implement such targeted infant industry protection or are unable to bear the costs of long learning periods, the next-best approach is probably closer to a free trade policy.

The Small Industry Alternative

Given the narrow foundation of technological mastery in Africa, the requirements for managing a carefully targeted infant industry program, and the high costs of supporting infants through long periods of learning, African countries may seek a more accessible approach to industrialization. Most economists accept that developing nations must eventually master large-scale, modern manufacturing, however gradually, if only because such industry is the most important long-term source of productivity growth in modern economies. Taiwan, however, managed to enter world markets through the exports of smaller, more traditional firms. Some writers on Africa hold that small-scale industry is a natural vehicle for learning by doing in Africa, precisely because, with the exception of farming, African entrepreneurship and management has been most productive in the informal manufacturing and trading sectors.

The essence of the informal sector is that it thrives in spite of, not because of, government intervention. In summarizing recent studies of medium- and small-scale enterprise in developing countries, Snodgrass and Biggs (1994) conclude that, on balance, government interventions discourage small firms more than large ones. Large and powerful enterprises tend to obtain better access to import and investment licenses, subsidized credit, and zoning permissions when these are tightly rationed by officials. It is true that small firms often gain advantages over large enterprises by circumventing taxes and labor regulations. But they generally seem to do best in deregulated markets and to benefit, along with all other producers, from improvements in infrastructure and development of market institutions.

In Taiwan, for example, small companies had access to a large, unregulated, informal credit market, which helped to finance their exports. When government intervened, it was to improve the functioning of the curb market: most small firms obtained credit by issuing postdated checks and government made these instruments more secure by allowing creditors to enforce them through the courts (Biggs 1991). One of the most successful financial reforms in Indonesia was the creation of a credit scheme for small borrowers, housed in a government bank but run on commercial principles, with loans made at interest rates that fully covered costs and earned a profit for the bank. These Asian innovations suggest that market deregulation and the improvement of market institutions can be effective in promoting small (as well as large) firms.

Snodgrass and Biggs (1994) find little support, however, in the hope of a widespread transition from small, traditional firms to modern, large firms. To make the leap from the informal to the formal sector, small enterprises have to begin paying taxes and obeying regulations that add substantially to their costs. This barrier to growth is an important reason for the "missing middle" of intermediate-sized firms in most economies (Biggs and Oppenheim 1986).

From their review of programs in Asia and Africa, Snodgrass and Biggs conclude that aid targeted to small firms—including subsidized and directed credit, managerial assistance, and marketing advice—has not delivered widespread benefits to the firms or their economies. This fact, combined with Africa's shortage of managerial skills within government, implies that programs aimed at small-scale industry may be misdirected. A better approach would be to deregulate the economy, moving toward a less protected, more outward-looking environment; to improve market institutions in general; and then to allow small-scale industries to find their niche without specific assistance from government.

Transition Policies

How would an African country make the transition to a more outward-oriented trade policy without causing bankruptcies and unemployment? It is probably impossible to avoid some of both, but the effects can be minimized through gradual implementation of reforms. Import controls can be eliminated and, if necessary, partly compensated by higher tariff protection, an approach that has become standard in reforming countries, including Indonesia. Then the general reduction in tariffs can be implemented over a long period, up to a decade, on a schedule that is legislated, is announced publicly, and cannot legally be changed by officials. This approach gives firms time to adjust, much as infant industries should, but it also gives credibility to the reforms because they are beyond intervention by the authorities. New investors would be discouraged unless they can make profits at the reduced rates of protection.

Although this more outward-looking trade regime would reduce the need for *export-promoting interventions,* these would still be necessary during the transition, when vestiges of protection and rent-seeking may remain strong. Even under the fully reformed regime, as long as there is a revenue tariff, an infant industry tariff, or some form of domestic sales tax (including a value added tax), some form of relief to exporters would reduce their costs and make them more competitive. Thus the duty drawback or exemption schemes and export processing zones that were used effectively in Asia should retain some appeal for African industrializers.

Conclusion

For African countries wishing to industrialize, the choice from a wide range of Asian strategies is, in practical terms, rather narrow. The immediate priorities should be to achieve those preconditions that are amenable to policy: macroeconomic balance, including a realistic and flexible exchange rate; free credit markets; and accommodations with entrepreneurially gifted ethnic minorities and foreign investors.

As these goals are being accomplished, planners should design and implement a reform program that moves the economy gradually from its controlled, inward orientation to a deregulated, outward-looking environment with less protection and minimal need for complex interventions. Within a market-oriented setting, two kinds of interventions would be advantageous, however: narrowly focused infant industry protection and mechanisms to insulate exporters from the vestiges of protection and rent-seeking.

The lines of industrialization and the targets for infant industry protection should evolve from Africa's existing comparative advantage in smallholder agriculture and an evolving comparative advantage in labor-intensive industry. It is essential not to abandon agriculture, but to ensure its rising productivity as the base for sustained industrialization. Attempts to upgrade technologies and skills will have to be supported by improvements in education and learning on the job. Great leaps into new industries or technologies, well beyond existing capacities, have not worked in Asia and will not in Africa.

An industrial miracle is unlikely in Africa. The best approach will be to put in place a set of policies like those described and to maintain them in place for many years. Wide swings in incentives can discourage investors as much as bad policies.

NOTES

1. Research and publication on rapid industrialization in Korea has been a growth industry itself, beginning with Cole and Lyman (1971), continuing with studies by Frank, Kim, and Westphal (1975) and a ten-volume study by the Harvard Institute for International Development and Korea Development Institute (Mason et al. 1980); and burgeoning in the 1980s with studies by Luedde-Neurath (1986), Dornbusch and Park (1987), Westphal (1987), the World Bank (1987a), Collins and Park (1989), and Amsden (1989). Work on Taiwan, though less plentiful, has many notable contributors, including Ranis (1973), Lau et al. (1990), and Wade (1990).

2. The data suggest that between 1965 and 1990 a large part of mining value added was reclassified as manufacturing. This could have been a real shift (if copper output had been more fully processed before export) but probably is a statistical artifact.

3. During the 1970s, the Smith government made its unilateral declaration of independence (UDI) and Southern Rhodesia became an international pariah, trading only with South Africa. This industrial base is, according to Riddell (1992, 226), still "one of the most advanced and diversified in Sub-Saharan Africa."

4. The ASEAN countries as a group increased their world market share from 0.7 percent in 1965 to 2.7 percent in 1989 (UNIDO 1991a, 13).

5. This decline was general, affecting every category of export, including food, beverages, and tobacco. For exports as a whole, Africa's share fell from 22 percent to 10 percent (UNIDO 1991b, 31).

6. That is, the share of unskilled labor–intensive exports in each country's total exports by value is over three times the average share of these commodities in world trade.

7. There is a possible ambiguity in the Malaysian case, because electronic components are both technology and labor intensive. In recent years, however, the labor content of semiconductor manufacturing has declined with automation; labor costs have fallen to a range of 5 to 10 percent of total costs (Chalmers 1991, 204).

8. If Nigeria is excluded, the gain is 22 percent, or 2.0 percent a year.

9. The *effective rate of subsidy* (ERS) is derived from the *effective rate of protection* (ERP) and uses a similar formula. The ERP is the percentage by which value added, measured at domestic prices including protection, exceeds value added measured at world prices, without protection. It is a measure of the degree to which tariffs (and, depending on the way it is measured, import restrictions) permit domestic factors of production to exceed the payments to internationally competitive factors of production in the same industry abroad. The ERS includes, in addition to tariff and quota protection and direct subsidies paid to producers, any differences in internal taxes and interest rates paid by producers in different industries.

10. When manufacturing is taken alone, the effective subsidies averaged 8 percent in Korea, averaged 18 percent in Taiwan, and favored export sales in both countries.

11. Balassa included three other countries in his sample, all with strong biases toward protection of domestic sales. Their effective rates of subsidy in manufacturing, all during the late 1960s, were as follows: Argentina, −29 percent for exports, 116 percent for domestic sales; Colombia, 10 percent for exports, 32 percent for domestic sales; and Israel, 38 percent for exports, 82 percent for domestic sales.

12. The coefficient of variation reported in Table 7.3 is the standard deviation of the difference between domestic and international (PPP) prices divided by the mean of PPP prices. A coefficient of 1.00 means that 32 percent of the sample of prices (the share of a normal distribution not encompassed by one standard deviation) differs from the PPP price by at least 100 percent.

13. Telephone communication with David Dapice, August 1994.

14. The case studies cover Botswana, Cameroon, Côte d'Ivoire, Kenya, Nigeria, Zambia, and Zimbabwe.

15. In Nigeria, 30 percent of output growth was attributed to import substitution from 1963 to 1973; in Botswana, 37 percent from 1974 to 1985; and in Kenya, 18 percent from 1970 to 1975 (Riddell 1990, 38).

16. Domestic resource cost is the ratio of domestic costs (value added) to net foreign exchange earned or saved at the official exchange rate. A ratio over one suggests that the industry cannot compete at the official exchange rate unless it is protected. (Of course, if the exchange rate is overvalued, it might be able to compete at the higher equilibrium rate.)

17. Pack (1993, 10), for example, notes that in Kenya and Zimbabwe, foreign-owned "integrated textile mills have achieved production engineering performance close to that of best practice plants in the developed countries."

18. A country does not always, or often, have a competitive advantage in processing its own primary exports, so this route needs to be approached with caution (Chapter 5; Roemer 1979).

BIBLIOGRAPHY

Amsden, Alice. 1989. *Asia's Next Giant: South Korea and Late Industrialization.* New York: Oxford University Press.

Balassa, Bela, et al. 1982. *Development Strategies for Semi-Industrialized Countries.* Baltimore: Johns Hopkins Press for the World Bank.

Biggs, Tyler. 1991. "Heterogeneous Firms and Efficient Financial Intermediation in Taiwan." In *Markets in Developing Countries: Parallel, Fragmented, and Black,* ed. M. Roemer and C. Jones. San Francisco: ICS Press, 167–97.

Biggs, Tyler, and Jeremy Oppenheim. 1986. *What Drives the Size Distribution of Firms in Developing Countries?* EEPA Discussion Paper No. 6, Cambridge, Mass.: Harvard Institute for International Development.

Bruton, Henry, et al. 1992. *The Political Economy of Poverty, Equity, and Growth: Sri Lanka and Malaysia.* New York: Oxford University Press for the World Bank.

Chalmers, Ian. 1991. "International and Regional Integration: The Political Economy of the Electronics Industry in ASEAN." *ASEAN Economic Bulletin* 8–3 (November), 194–209.

China, Government of the Republic of. 1992. *Taiwan Data Book, 1992.* Taipei.

Cole, David C., and Princeton N. Lyman. 1971. *Korean Development: The Interplay of Politics and Economics.* Cambridge, Mass.: Harvard University Press.

Cole, David C., and Yung-chul Park. 1983. *Financial Development in Korea, 1945–1978.* Cambridge, Mass.: Council on East Asian Studies, Harvard University.

Collins, Susan M., and Won-Am Park. 1989. "External Debt and Macroeconomic Performance in Korea." In *Developing Country Debt and Economic Performance*, Volume 3, ed. J. D. Sachs and S. M. Collins. Chicago: Chicago University Press, 151–369.

Dornbusch, Rudiger, and Yung Chul Park. 1987. "Korean Growth Policy." *Brookings Papers on Economic Activity* 2:389–454.

Forrest, Tom. 1992. "The Advance of African Capital: The Growth of Nigerian Private Enterprises." In *Alternative Development Strategies in Sub-Saharan Africa*, ed. Francis Stewart, Sanjaya Lall, and Samuel Wangwe. New York: St. Martin's Press, 368–401.

Frank, Charles R., Kwang Suk Kim, and Larry E. Westphal. 1975. *Foreign Trade Regimes and Economic Development: South Korea*. New York: Columbia University Press.

Gan Wee Beng. 1992. "Industrialization and the Export of Malaysian Manufactures." In *The Dangers of Export Pessimism: Developing Countries and Industrial Markets*, ed. Helen Hughes. San Francisco: ICS Press, 202–23.

Helleiner, Gerald K. 1992. "Structural Adjustment and Long-Term Development in Sub-Saharan Africa." In *Alternative Development Strategies in Sub-Saharan Africa*, ed. Francis Stewart, Sanjaya Lall, and Samuel Wangwe. New York: St. Martin's Press, 48–102.

Hoffmann, Lutz, and Tan Siewee. 1980. *Industrial Growth, Employment, and Foreign Investment in Peninsular Malaysia*. Kuala Lumpur: Oxford University Press.

Jacobsson, Stefan. 1993. "The Length of the Infant Industry Period: Evidence from the Engineering Industry." *World Development* 21–3: 407–19.

Karmiloff, Igor. 1990. "Zambia." In *Manufacturing Africa*, ed. Roger C. Riddell. London: Overseas Development Institute, 297–336.

Lall, Sanjaya. 1992. "Structural Problems of African Industry." In *Alternative Development Strategies in Sub-Saharan Africa*, ed. Francis Stewart, Sanjaya Lall, and Samuel Wangwe. New York: St. Martin's Press, 103–31.

Lau, Lawrence J., ed. 1990. *Models of Development*. San Francisco: ICS Press.

Lee Tsao Yuan. 1992. "Singapore: The Role of the Government in Export Success." In *The Dangers of Export Pessimism: Developing Countries and Industrial Markets*, ed. Helen Hughes. San Francisco: ICS Press, 224–49.

Luedde-Neurath, R. 1986. *Import Controls and Export-Oriented Development: A Reassessment of the South Korean Case*. Boulder, Colo.: Westview Press.

Mason, Edward S., M. J. Kim, D. H. Perkins, K. S. Kim, and D. C. Cole. 1980. *The Economic and Social Modernization of the Republic of Korea*. Cambridge, Mass.: Council on East Asian Studies.

Narongchai, Akrasanee, David Dapice, and Frank Flatters. 1990. *Thailand's Export-Led Growth: Retrospect and Prospects*. Bangkok: The Thailand Development Research Institute.

Naya, Seiji, William E. James, and Michael Plummer. 1989. *Pacific Economic*

Cooperation in the Global Context: Macroeconomic Structural Issues of Trade, Finance and the Adjustment Process. Honolulu: East-West Center.

Pack, Howard. 1993. "Productivity and Industrial Development in Sub-Saharan Africa." *World Development* 21–1 (January): 1–16.

Paitoon, Wiboonchutikula, Rachain Chintayarangsan, and Nattapong Thongpakde. 1989. "Trade in Manufactured Goods and Mineral Products." Background Paper No. 4, Thailand Development Research Institute, Year-End Conference.

Perkins, Dwight. 1991. "Economic Systems Reform in Developing Countries." In *Reforming Economic Systems in Developing Countries,* ed. Dwight Perkins and Michael Roemer. Cambridge: Harvard University Press, 11–53.

Poot, Huib, Arie Kuyvenhoven, and Jaap C. Jansen. 1990. *Industrialization and Trade in Indonesia.* Jogyakarta, Indonesia: Gadjah Mada University Press.

Ranis, Gustav. 1973. "Industrial Sector Labor Absorption." *Economic Development and Cultural Change* 21:347–408.

Riddell, Roger C. 1990. *Manufacturing Africa.* London: Overseas Development Institute.

———. 1992. "Manufacturing Sector Development in Zimbabwe and the Côte d'Ivoire." In *Alternative Development Strategies in Sub-Saharan Africa,* ed. Francis Stewart, Sanjaya Lall, and Samuel Wangwe. New York: St. Martin's Press, 215–37.

Robinson, Peter B., and Somsak Tambunlertchai. 1993. *Africa and Asia: Can High Rates of Economic Growth be Replicated?* International Center for Economic Growth, Occasional Paper No. 40. San Francisco: ICS Press.

Roemer, Michael. 1979. "Resource-Based Industrialization in Developing Countries: A Survey." *Journal of Development Economics* 6–2:163–202.

———. 1982. "Economic Development in Africa: Performance Since Independence and a Strategy for the Future." *Daedalus* (Spring), 125–48.

Snodgrass, Donald R., and Tyler Biggs. 1994. *Industrialization and the Small Firm: Patterns and Policies.* Cambridge, Mass.: Harvard Institute for International Development. Forthcoming.

Stern, Joseph J., Ji-hong Kim, Dwight H. Perkins, and Jung-ho Yoo. 1992. "Industrialization and the State: The Korean Heavy and Chemical Industry Drive." (Manuscript).

United Nations Industrial Development Organization (UNIDO). 1991a. *ASEAN Industry in Figures.*

———. 1991b. *African Industry in Figures 1990.* Vienna.

———. 1992. *Industry and Development Global Report 1992/1993.* Vienna.

Wade, Robert. 1990. *Governing the Market: Economic Theory and the Role of Government in East Asian Industrialization.* Princeton, N.J.: Princeton University Press.

Westphal, Larry E. 1987. "Industrial Development in East Asia's 'Gang of Four.'" *Issues in Science and Technology* 3–3 (Spring): 78–88.

————. 1990. "Industrial Policy in an Export-Propelled Economy: Lessons from South Korea's Experience." *The Journal of Economic Perspectives* 4–3 (Summer): 41–95.

World Bank. 1987. *Korea: Managing the Industrial Transition,* Volume 1. Washington, D.C.

————. 1989. *Sub-Saharan Africa: From Crisis to Sustainable Growth.* Washington, D.C.

————. 1992a. *World Development Report 1992.* Washington, D.C.

————. 1992b. *World Tables 1992.* Washington, D.C.

————. 1993. *The East Asian Miracle.* Washington, D.C.

CHAPTER 8

Can African Labor Compete?

David L. Lindauer and Ann D. Velenchik

Alternative accounts for Asia's success and Africa's failure in developing a manufacturing sector read like the contents of a textbook on development economics. Politically, Asian countries have been relatively stable and increasingly characterized by growth-oriented governments. This has created an environment conducive to the long-term investments required for success in manufacturing. By comparison, Africa has been torn by civil war and victimized by governments that have ranged from near feudal states to African socialism to more liberal regimes for whom economic growth was secondary to other objectives. African countries have more often (or to a greater degree) than their Asian counterparts looked inward rather than outward, suffered from severe fiscal mismanagement, and relied on government intervention as much as the market for the allocation of resources. Lastly, Africa's relatively dismal performance in manufacturing can be explained by more microeconomic factors including the inferiority of capital, both physical and human, and the absence of an institutional environment supportive of industrial activities.

This list of explanations is long and certainly not exhaustive. Rather than attempting a comprehensive survey of why manufacturing has not yet developed in Africa, we examine the performances of Africa and Asia from the vantage point of the labor market. Our goal is to present competing hypotheses and to elevate the comparison of Africa and Asia beyond the all-too-frequent cultural stereotyping of each region's workers—Asia's as disciplined and hard-working, Africa's as lazy and unproductive.

In the next section we introduce unit labor costs as an organizing framework, one that emphasizes the relationship between wages and productivity as well as the exchange rate as core determinants of competitiveness. Once African manufacturing is established as facing relatively high wages and low productivity compared to Asian economies, competing explanations for these outcomes are offered. On the wage side we consider the significance of government wage policies either as tools of "wage repression" in Asia or as instruments of "rent creation" in contemporary Africa. We also draw attention to factor endowments, especially of labor and land, as an alternative explanation for differential wage outcomes. Turning to productivity, we view the respective stocks of physical and human capital as alternatives to any innate qualitative differences in labor's abilities. The policy relevance of our findings is presented in the concluding section.

Unit Labor Costs: An Organizing Framework

Theory

Why has Africa been unable to produce manufactured goods at internationally competitive prices? Unit labor cost, which measures total labor costs per unit of output in a common currency, serves as an organizing framework for a discussion of possible answers to this question. Unit labor cost (ULC) is defined as

$$ULC = \left(\frac{wL}{Q}\right)\left(\frac{1}{e}\right) \tag{8.1}$$

where w is the manufacturing wage, L the amount of labor employed, Q a physical measure of output, and e the exchange rate defined as domestic currency per dollar. Theoretically, it should be possible to compare ULCs across countries, at least for homogenous outputs, with lower ULCs predicting superior performance in the sale of manufactured goods.

It is useful to rewrite Equation (8.1) as

$$ULC = \left(\frac{W}{Q/L}\right)\left(\frac{1}{e}\right) = \left(\frac{W}{AP_L}\right)\left(\frac{1}{e}\right) \tag{8.2}$$

which reveals two major factors influencing competitiveness: the ratio of wages to productivity (AP is the average product of labor) and the exchange rate. The importance of a properly valued exchange rate is a common theme throughout this volume. The unit labor cost formulation echoes this conclusion, suggesting that in addition to the qualities of a nation's labor force, an overvalued exchange rate will reduce competitiveness.

More directly related to this chapter's focus on labor market outcomes, the first term in Equation (8.2) indicates that unit labor costs are driven by the ratio of wages to productivity. This implies that low ULCs, and hence competitive performance, can occur both in high wage/high productivity as well as in low wage/low productivity economies. In other words, it should be no surprise that both Taiwan (high wage/high productivity) and China (low wage/low productivity) simultaneously can be internationally competitive. The worst performers, common to Africa, will be countries with relatively high wages and low labor productivity.

The ULC formulation provides a mechanism for organizing and classifying several different hypotheses about how and why manufacturing in Africa has been less successful than in Asia. To the extent that labor market factors have been a cause of differential performance, the wage/productivity ratio must be higher in Africa than Asia. The causes of this difference can be classified in two groups, though the true explanation is probably a combination of both.

For heuristic purposes, assume African and Asian manufacturing sectors face identical production functions. Differences in the wage/productivity ratio, then, would be due entirely to differences in wages. This case is illustrated in Figure 8.1. Identical production technologies and capital endowments generate identical functions of average and marginal product of labor, but differences in real wages between Africa and Asia yield different levels of employment and thus productivity. As indicated in Figure 8.1, the manufacturing industry facing the greater wage has a higher ratio of wages to average product, and hence higher ULCs. This must be the case because the smaller the difference between the wage and average product (that is, the vertical distance between them in Figure 8.1), the higher is the ULC.[1] Alternative explanations for higher wages in Africa, considered in more detail below, include government interventions that directly raise wages (for example, minimum wage legislation) and factor endowment patterns that increase the opportunity cost of labor available to manufacturing.

Now assume that wages in the two regions are equal but productivity differs. Figure 8.2 illustrates this situation. Explanations for higher labor

FIGURE 8.1
Identical Productivities, Different Wages

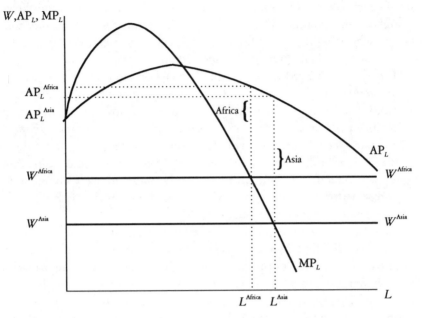

productivity in Asia at all levels of employment include differences in technology as well as differences in the quantity and quality of physical and human capital. If, as depicted, labor productivity is lower in Africa than in Asia, at any common wage Africa will have a higher wage/productivity ratio (again, a shorter vertical distance between wages and average products), higher ULCs, and a more poorly performing manufacturing sector.

Measurement

The existence, size, and potential explanations of interregional differences in the wage/productivity ratio are empirical matters. Examination of Equation (8.2) suggests that an appropriate strategy would be, first, to calculate values for ULCs in some representative Asian and African countries, and then to decompose the differences between the ULCs into the differences in their component parts. This would provide an empirical measure of the relative importance of the various explanations just noted for the divergent wage/productivity ratios.

Unfortunately, such a strategy cannot be pursued. Two problems present

FIGURE 8.2
Identical Wages, Different Productivities

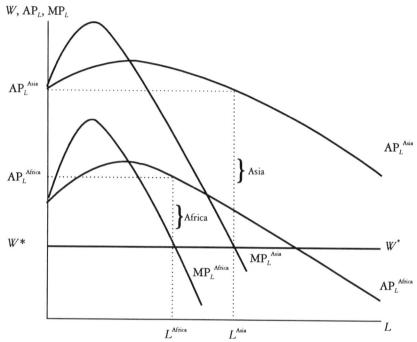

themselves. First, the ULC calculation in Equation (8.2) is based on *physical* measures of output and productivity. Making international comparisons of physical productivity requires a cross-country index of output in physical units that captures differences in the composition and quality of manufactured goods in the nations being considered. Not only is such an index unavailable, but it is difficult to imagine constructing one. As an alternative, comparisons could be made for single homogeneous products, but even here quality differences in output might make physical measures of relative productivity misleading. The only readily available, internationally comparable measure of productivity in manufacturing, value added per worker, cannot be substituted for physical productivity in Equation (8.2). If value added per worker replaces physical output per worker, ULC can no longer be expressed in a common currency and, hence, loses all meaning for comparative purposes. (See Appendix 8.1 for further discussion of the measurement of ULC.) Second, a separation exercise depends upon the assumption that the two components of ULC can be treated as independently determined. To the extent that movements in the exchange rate affect nominal wages and/or productivity levels, the separation does not hold. We return to this point in our discussion of exchange rates below.

Although ULCs are theoretically appealing as a means for assessing cross-country competitiveness, they cannot be readily computed for this purpose. The basic framework derived from the ULC equation, however, does suggest an empirical strategy for assessing the competing hypotheses on why African manufacturing has performed so poorly relative to Asia. We can examine the implications of currency overvaluation for external competitiveness and then inspect differences in wage/productivity ratios. Although the proportional influence of wage and productivity differences between Africa and Asia in determining the differences in the wage/productivity ratio cannot be quantified precisely, data on these two factors can be used to give impressionistic evidence on wage and productivity differentials between the two regions.

Exchange Rates

Exchange rates play an important role in generating differences in ULCs across countries because of a strong tendency for African countries to overvalue their currencies. This practice has not been common in East and Southeast Asia, at least in recent decades.

The consequences of overvaluation for ULCs, and hence competitiveness, can be portrayed as follows. The exchange rate, e, employed in the definition of ULCs (Equation [8.1]) is the rate at which international transactions involving manufactured goods take place. For most manufactured exports this is a nation's official exchange rate rather than the parallel market rate. When the official exchange rate is overvalued, ULCs may be higher than they would be if the exchange rate were permitted to reach its equilibrium value, and competitiveness declines.

We define

$$k = \frac{e_q}{e} \qquad (8.3)$$

where e_q is the equilibrium exchange rate and e is the official exchange rate. The equilibrium exchange rate, e_q, is defined as the rate at which the market for foreign exchange clears, regardless of whether the current account is in deficit or surplus. k is an index of the degree of official overvaluation or undervaluation of the domestic currency, where for values of $k > 1$ the official exchange rate is overvalued.

Substituting Equation (8.3) into the ULC definition yields

$$\text{ULC} = \frac{w}{\text{AP}_L}\left(\frac{1}{e_q/k}\right) \tag{8.4}$$

or

$$\frac{1}{k}(\text{ULC}) = \frac{w}{\text{AP}_L}\left(\frac{1}{e_q}\right) \tag{8.5}$$

Equation (8.5) indicates that if the official exchange rate is not an equilibrium rate but is overvalued, then under the equilibrium exchange rate, e_q, ULCs would be lower than they would be under the official and overvalued exchange rate, e. How much lower depends, in part, on the impact of nominal devaluation on the ratio of wages to average products. If, for example, wages are completely flexible and physical productivity is exogenous, then the effects of the devaluation will be completely captured in rising nominal wages, and ULCs will remain unchanged.[2] However, if there is some stickiness in nominal wages, or if devaluations lead to factor substitutions and influence productivity levels, then the effect of the devaluation on one component of ULCs $(1/e)$ may not be fully offset by an increase in the other (w/AP_L). This suggests that the degree of nominal overvaluation of the currency defines at least an upper bound to the size of the effect of a nominal devaluation on ULCs. Claims that African economies are uncompetitive because high wages and low productivity drive up costs must be tempered by the knowledge that grossly overvalued exchange rates also may be a culprit.

An assessment of the empirical significance of exchange rate policies on ULCs in Asia and Africa begins by comparing official exchange rates with a proxy for e_q, since e_q cannot be observed directly. What often can be measured is the parallel market rate for foreign exchange, e_p. Such rates are not identical to e_q for several reasons. If parallel market dealings in hard currencies are illegal, e_p will contain a risk premium reflecting the probability of getting caught, the extent of fines and other punishments, and the higher costs of operating in a thin market. In addition, since some transactions involving manufactured goods take place both at the official as well as the black market rate, e_q must lie between e and e_p. Thus e_p may be considered an upper bound of e_q and, although an imperfect estimate, the ratio e_p/e may be considered a proxy for k. Estimates of e_p/e offer some insight into the range of ULC increases due to the alternative exchange rate regimes pursued in Africa as compared with Asia.

Table 8.1 presents evidence on the extent of currency overvaluation, by decade, for a number of Asian and African economies. Specifically, the mean ratio of the black market to the official exchange rate is reported for the 1960s, 1970s, and 1980s.[3] What is immediately apparent from Table 8.1 is that for the past twenty-five years the successful economies of East and Southeast Asia have maintained official exchange rates at or relatively close to market clearing levels.[4] Not only does the median value of the ratio, e_p/e, equal 1.01–1.02 in Asia for all three decades, but individual Asian country estimates show remarkably little variation around this level—Korea during the 1970s is the lone outlier at 1.10.

Whereas successful Asian economies apparently have kept the exchange rate close to its equilibrium value, African economies have pursued the opposite course. Overvaluation (in relative terms) was modest in some nations in the 1960s but became both extreme and ubiquitous during the 1970s. The 1980s witnessed some moderation from the previous decade, especially following such recent and massive devaluations as in Ghana in 1983; by Asian standards, however, overvaluation of domestic currency remains extraordinarily high throughout much of Africa.

Beyond the eight African economies contained in Table 8.1, we should also call attention to those nations, members of the CFA zone, for whom $e_p/e = 1$.[5] At first glance, these nations might be thought to have followed exchange regimes common to East and Southeast Asia, but this is not the case. With fixed exchange rates tied to the French franc, the CFA zone operates under a different monetary regime. If these economies had equilibrium exchange rates below the official rate, set at 50 CFA francs to the French franc since 1948, excess demand for foreign exchange did not spill over into a black market but instead was supported by official capital inflows from France. In sum, overvaluation could and probably did exist, and ULCs in manufacturing were higher than they would have been at e_q, but the market signal of overvaluation was not the level of e_p but the amount of balance of payments support from Paris.[6]

We recognize that parallel market exchange rates are an imprecise measure of the extent of nominal overvaluation, and that the wage/productivity ratio

TABLE 8.1
Ratio of Parallel Market to Official Exchange Rate (mean values by decade)

	1960s[a]	1970s	1980s[b]
East Asia			
Hong Kong	1.00	1.00	0.99
Korea	1.06[c]	1.10	1.05
Singapore	na	1.01	1.01
Taiwan	na	1.05	1.04
Southeast Asia			
Indonesia	na	0.97	0.94
Malaysia	1.02	1.01	1.01
Thailand	1.01	0.99	0.97
Africa			
Botswana	na	na	1.21
Ghana	1.63	2.93	2.39[d]
Kenya	1.21	1.21	1.17
Nigeria	na	1.35	2.68
Tanzania	1.21	2.02	3.17
Zaire	na	2.36	1.59
Zambia	0.95	2.06	1.53[e]
Zimbabwe	na	1.53	1.60
Asia (Median)	1.02	1.01	1.01
Africa (Median)	1.21	2.02	1.60

a. Mean values for the 1960s are included as long as at least four years' worth of observations were available.
b. The 1980s refers to 1980–88 only.
c. 1965–69 only.
d. 1980, 1983–88 only.
e. 1980–87 only.
SOURCE: *World Currency Yearbook* (Brooklyn, N.Y.: International Currency Analysis, Inc.), various years.

is not independent of the nominal exchange rate. The extent and persistence of currency overvaluation, however, as well as the existence of structural rigidities in the labor market, suggest that exchange rate management in Africa has handicapped the region's efforts both to sell manufactured goods in third markets and to compete with manufactured imports at home.

The Wage/Productivity Relationship

We now turn our attention to a comparison of the ratio of wages to productivity in manufacturing between Africa and Asia. Data on both wages
and productivity are available from surveys and censuses of manufacturing
establishments, which are undertaken periodically in many countries.[7] Although these survey instruments vary in terms of information collected,
coverage by firm size, and accuracy, reported findings on earnings and
productivity levels in the manufacturing sector, we hope, are sufficiently
robust for our purposes.

Establishment surveys provide information reported by employers on
total labor costs. Usually included are wages, salaries, allowances, and benefits, sometimes including an estimate of the cash equivalent of payments-
in-kind. The definition of wages we employ is total labor costs divided by
total number of workers engaged, which includes unpaid family workers.
Productivity is defined as value added in manufacturing per worker engaged.
Because we are interested in the ratio of wages to productivity, no exchange
rate conversion to a common currency is required for cross-country comparisons.

Note we are no longer employing a physical measure of productivity.
Value added measures differ from physical productivity measures in two
dimensions. First, they convert physical units to monetary units by multi-
plying output quantities by prices, implying that the ratio of wages to value
added is a pure number without units. Second, value added measures are
based on the difference between output and input values and hence are
influenced by the structure of tariff and quota protection. If wage/produc-
tivity ratios are an important factor driving differences in competitiveness,
then we assume that a ratio based on wages and productivity measured in
value terms can act as a proxy. The ratio of wages to value added per worker,
although not a measure of costs per unit output, should approximate the size
of the vertical distance between wages and average products shown in Figures
8.1 and 8.2.

In contrasting the wage/productivity ratio between Africa and Asia, it was
important to decide which years were most appropriate to compare. Within
the limitations imposed by available data, the alternatives were to compare
Africa today with Asia today, or to compare Africa today with Asia of ten to
twenty years ago. The former comparison would have required considering
differences in the wage/productivity ratio between Africa and its current
competitors. In Asia this might include Bangladesh, China, and India, but

probably not the Asian NICs (or soon-to-be ASEAN NICs) who have already graduated to production of higher value added manufactured products and who no longer represent Africa's direct competition.

ULC comparisons between Africa and China or South Asia would be revealing, but instead we choose to compare the current situation in African countries with the historical experiences of the already successful Asian economies. Our intention is to consider Asian countries at points in time when their economic circumstances, particularly with respect to per capita income, were roughly similar to Africa today. Since we are interested in the ability of African countries to follow the industrialization patterns experienced in East and Southeast Asia, it is more appropriate to compare modern Africa with historical East and Southeast Asia than to compare the two regions' current performance.[8]

Table 8.2 reports the ratio of wages to productivity in manufacturing for a number of Asian and African economies. The results support the hypothesis that wages in Africa are "high" relative to labor productivity (alternatively, that productivity is "low" relative to wages) when compared to the historical experience of Asia's most successful economies. Specifically, for the thirteen African countries included in Table 8.2, the median value of the w/AP_L ratio is 0.37; the range 0.20–0.59. For the six Asian nations the median, 0.25, is lower by a third, and the range only 0.16–0.35.[9]

There is an overlap in the value of the ratio between the two regions. Figure 8.3 puts in sharper perspective the basic differences that distinguish Asia's historical experience from Africa in the 1980s. Mapping w/AP_L against per capita income, with the latter measured in constant 1975 ICP prices, reveals that the Asian countries as a group had a wage/productivity level well below that of the majority of African economies when countries from both regions were at roughly equivalent stages of development. Asian countries were already successful producers (and exporters) of manufactured goods at levels of per capita income comparable to much of Africa in the 1980s, which suggests, as predicted, that low wage/productivity ratios are consistent with competitiveness in manufacturing.

Some of the outliers in Figure 8.3 do present a challenge. Ghana and Nigeria, for example, display w/AP_L ratios comparable to those in Indonesia, Korea, and Taiwan, yet neither Ghana nor Nigeria had achieved any success in manufacturing by the early 1980s.[10] Similarly, Singapore displays a w/AP_L ratio of .035 in 1963, identical to Tanzania in 1983. Yet Singapore was already experiencing success in manufactures, whereas Tanzania has never done so.

TABLE 8.2
Ratio of Wages to Productivity

	Size cutoff	Year	w/AP
Africa			
Botswana	1 employee	1990	.39
Cameroon	not listed	1978	.39
Côte d'Ivoire	12 million CFA[a]	1982	.31
Ghana	30 employees	1983	.23
Kenya	50 employees	1988	.41
Madagascar	not listed	1984	.36
Malawi	100,000 kwacha[b]	1983	.59
Mauritius	10 employees	1987	.50
Nigeria	not listed	1983	.20
Senegal	not listed	1984	.43
Sierra Leone	10 employees	1986	.31
Tanzania	10 employees	1985	.35
Zimbabwe	2,000 dollars[c]	1987	.37
Asia			
Indonesia	20 employees	1981	.21
Korea	5 employees	1963	.26
Malaysia	5 employees	1970	.27
Singapore	10 employees	1963	.35
Taiwan	no cutoff	1961	.16
Thailand	10 employees	1970	.24

a. U.S. $36,000.
b. U.S. $85,000.
c. U.S. $1,000.
SOURCES: United Nations, *Yearbook of Industrial Statistics* (New York), various years. United Nations, *African Statistical Yearbook, 1987* (New York).

The outliers pose interesting cases, but the basic trends suggest that the combination of exchange rates close to equilibrium levels and a low ratio of wages to productivity characterize the East and Southeast Asian economies that have been most successful in developing their manufacturing sectors.[11] In Africa, overvalued exchange rates, high wage/productivity ratios, and poor manufacturing performance have been the norm. In terms of lessons for Africa, exchange rate management is clearly a matter for policy attention (discussed in Chapter 4), but can the same be said of the determinants of the

FIGURE 8.3

w/AP Ratios and Per Capita Income

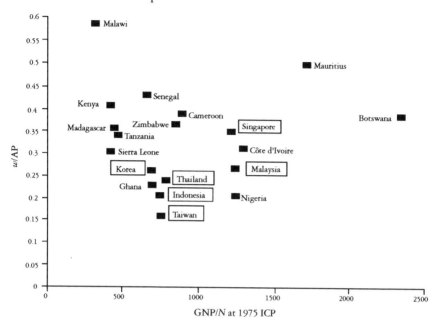

wage/productivity relationship? In order to answer this question we need to examine alternative explanations for why Africa exhibits higher w/AP_L levels.

Relative Wages and Relative Productivities in Africa and Asia

Although there is no empirical mechanism for making a precise decomposition of differences in the w/AP_L ratio into differences in its components, an examination of the levels of wages and productivity in Africa and Asia provides some insight into the relative importance of the two factors.

Levels of wages and value added per worker, calculated at both official and parallel market exchange rates and converted to 1982 dollars, are reported in Table 8.3. The data show a wide range of values for both wages and productivity for both regions, and there is substantial overlap across regions in these values. The median value of annual earnings in Africa measured at official exchange rates is $1,853, while conversion at parallel rates lowers this value to $1,711. For Asia, median earnings are $1,037 at official rates and $1,017 at parallel ones. The ratio of the African to Asian medians is 1.78 and 1.68 evaluated at official and parallel rates, respectively.

TABLE 8.3
Annual Manufacturing Wages and Value Added per Worker—Official
and Parallel Rates (U.S. dollar equivalent)

	Year	Wages		Value added/worker	
		Official	Parallel	Official	Parallel
Africa					
Botswana	1990	1853	1818	4788	4697
Cameroon	1978	5513	5099	14205	13136
Côte d'Ivoire	1982	4407	4453	14181	13547
Ghana	1983	723	283	3133	1228
Kenya	1988	1524	1510	3729	3695
Madagascar	1984	1013	664	2837	1859
Malawi	1983	1036	676	1766	1152
Mauritius	1987	1905	1711	3799	3411
Nigeria	1983	4419	1776	21605	8683
Senegal	1984	2457	2357	5684	5452
Sierra Leone	1986	821	420	2685	1373
Tanzania	1985	1072	266	3033	752
Zimbabwe	1987	3625	2319	6295	4027
Median		1853	1711	3083	2635
Asia					
Indonesia	1981	907	873	4332	4170
Korea	1963	924	511	3523	1949
Malaysia	1970	1700	1687	6341	6295
Singapore	1963	2813	2784	8034	7956
Taiwan	1961	463	463	2907	2907
Thailand	1970	1151	1161	4813	4855
Median		1037	1017	4573	4512

NOTE: The 1982 U.S. dollar equivalents were calculated by first converting from domestic currency into dollars at the current year's exchange rate and then using the U.S. consumer price index to find the appropriate value in 1982 dollars.
SOURCES: United Nations, *Yearbook of Industrial Statistics* (New York), various years. United Nations, *African Statistical Yearbook, 1987* (New York). United Nations and World Bank, *African Development Indicators* (New York, 1992).

The inclusion of three CFA zone countries, for whom parallel rates are not an effective measure of the degree of overvaluation, implies that the use of parallel rates does not decrease the median value of wages (or productivity) by as large a proportion as would be the case were they excluded. A sample of only non–CFA zone African countries yields median earnings of $1,298 at official rates and $1,093 at parallel rates, and the ratio of African to Asian wages drops to 1.25 at official rates and 1.07 at parallel ones. This is a more accurate measure of the proportional difference between the measurement at official and parallel rates, but a less accurate measure of the level of the pan–Africa/Asia ratio, since it omits the higher-wage African countries from the sample. In order to make the CFA zone countries more comparable with the rest of the Africa sample, we inflate CFA country earnings by 15 percent, the relative wage ratio suggested by the non–CFA zone sample. The median value of African earnings at parallel rates for the entire sample, then, is $1,575, and the pan–Africa/Asia ratio of relative wages ranges from 1.78 at official exchange rates to 1.55 at the imputed parallel rates. Applying the same approach to estimating the ratio of productivity between Africa and Asia, that is, of value added per worker, yields 0.83 at official exchange rates and 0.71 at the imputed parallel rates.

It appears, then, that earnings in Africa are about two-thirds higher than was the case historically in Asia, and African productivity is about one-fourth lower. This implies that higher wages are more important determinants of high wage/productivity ratios in Africa than is low productivity, but both factors are important. However, these results must be interpreted with considerable caution. They apply only to median values for each region with pairwise comparison of individual countries yielding a vast range of relative wage and productivity outcomes.

Wages and Competitiveness

In discussions of Africa's inability to compete in manufactured goods, it is not uncommon to hear that "African wages are too high." By itself, this statement is not especially revealing: after all, our concern is not that African workers are too rich. What needs to be considered is why African wages are "high" relative to African productivity levels, why this relationship persists, and why Asian experience has been different. This section focuses on wage determination; the next section examines differences in productivity levels.

One explanation for "higher" wages in Africa is the greater role of institutional wage determination. Powerful trade unions and progressive government labor regulations, covering everything from prohibitions on dismissals to generous maternity benefits, are alleged to have raised labor costs throughout Africa. In contrast, wage determination in Asia is associated more often with market forces. To the extent that Asian governments have intervened in their labor markets, policies to suppress rather than support worker demands have been followed. A second and different explanation for higher wages in Africa than in Asia considers factor endowments, particularly man/land ratios, and concludes that Africa's "higher" wages are due to Africa's relative abundance of land.[12]

Unionization and Labor Regulations

If institutional forces raise manufacturing wages above the level dictated by market forces, with no offsetting increase in productivity, w/AP_L ratios will rise and competitiveness will decline. The question, therefore, is whether unions and government regulations have had more of this effect in Africa than in Asia.

There is considerable variance in experience within each region, as well as between them, but the basic contours of wage determination are as follows. In Asia, especially in the early periods of industrialization, independent unions were repressed, labor codes and protective labor legislation were minimal, and institutions for dispute resolution (for example, wage councils, labor courts, and legal protection for collective bargaining) strongly favored capital over labor.

Korea did not even have the equivalent of a Ministry of Labor until 1980; before then labor matters were handled by the domestic security apparatus. Legal restrictions on labor protest were abundant and force was frequently used to end labor disturbances. Representative of Korea's approach toward protective labor legislation is minimum wages, which were not promulgated until 1988, when Korea was already an upper middle-income economy.

In Taiwan, the trade union movement long has been under government control, a policy enforced by legally permitting only one union per establishment, the union associated with the ruling party. Protective labor legislation is not well developed and even if it were, the preponderance of small establishments in Taiwan makes enforcement of any labor code problematic. In Singapore, strikes were outlawed in 1968. Much of the power to determine wages is vested in Singapore's National Wages Council, which, although tripartite in structure, is effectively controlled by an authoritarian government. At various times the National Wages Council has acted both to keep wage increases below productivity growth (1972–1979) and to do the opposite (1979–1982). An important exception to the East Asian model of strict government control over labor is Hong Kong. Although the union movement has long been weak, it has not been repressed. Hong Kong has retained its laissez-faire character, letting the market determine wages and employing a minimalist labor code.[13]

Less has been written on wage determination in the ASEAN nations, but our impressions are that Indonesia is following a more repressive strategy toward labor, and Malaysia and Thailand one somewhat less so. However, in none of these economies would it be suggested that labor is a powerful force in either economic or political decision making.

The labor movement in Africa, as in Asia, is not especially strong, but for different reasons. While independent trade unions were repressed and often crushed in Asia, African labor movements were co-opted by the state or became partners in the Africanization of economies. Union demands in foreign firms or in state enterprises received government support and were part of a general strategy for distributing economic rents. But the failure of the economy to industrialize deprived African unions of an essential source of power, namely, a growing industrial workforce and expanding union membership. In the face of economic decline, union power lost its credibility. Zambia provides a telling example. It once had a large, independent, and powerful trade union movement based on organized mine workers. But even here, the long-term demise of copper eviscerated labor's strength.

If institutional wage determination remains important in Africa, it is more likely to be the result not of union behavior, but of labor legislation. A cursory review of labor law in a number of African countries reveals several common features. Industrial wages often are determined by industrial boards or tripartite commissions. These boards set wages, often at a detailed occupational and experience level, for firms in the "formal" sector, which can include establishments with as few as ten employees. Protective labor codes, such as rules governing the employment of women, are common. Maternity leave requirements, fourteen weeks in Cameroon, can be more generous than in some industrialized countries. Labor legislation also places restrictions on how workers are hired and fired. In Senegal, Ghana, Mauritius, and Nigeria, firms are required to recruit workers through a government labor office. Firms must often present the government with justification for their proposed release of workers, demonstrating that sales have fallen in order to receive government permission for dismissals.

This review of institutional factors in wage determination suggests that African economies have more protective labor legislation on the books, and at an earlier stage of development, than Asia has had. Organized labor also appears to have played a more influential role in government policy making. Higher wage/productivity ratios in Africa as compared to Asia undoubtedly reflect these tendencies. How significant a factor are these institutional arrangements in wage determination? Although we have little empirical evidence on this question, we can offer some further impressions on the role of institutions, first, in repressing wage growth in Asia and, second, in inflating wages and reducing competitiveness in Africa.

Did policies of labor repression reduce ULCs in Asia? Wage repression, a policy of depressing wage rates below market clearing levels, does not appear to have been employed in most successful Asian economies. Singapore, the lone exception, did aggressively manage wages, but these policies are not seen as one of the city-state's better strategies. In Korea, there is a debate over the role and effectiveness of wage guidelines intended to keep wage increases below productivity growth. But since Korea has achieved, perhaps, the fastest rate of sustained real wage growth of any country for which we have data, it is difficult to argue that wage restraint has been a major element of government policy. Rapidly increasing real wages throughout East and Southeast Asia suggest the same conclusion.[14]

If wage repression was not a significant element in wage determination, what about the indirect effects of the repression of labor unions? In other settings we know that unions are successful in raising wages. Had unions been permitted to flourish in Korea, Taiwan, Indonesia, and elsewhere, would there have been a union wage effect, and if so, how large?[15] We cannot answer this counterfactual, but we conjecture that any union wage effect would have been tempered by market forces. Wage increases negotiated by Asian unions would have constantly been pressured by competition from the "endless supply" of cheap labor in these labor-abundant economies with enormous reservoirs of unskilled labor.

Do institutional factors significantly raise wages in Africa? Once again, empirical evidence is woefully inadequate. Our impression is that the set of labor institutions described earlier had a bigger impact on wage outcomes in the 1960s and early 1970s than they have had since then, particularly in the Anglophone countries. With declining resources, falling labor demand, and a growing supply of workers, real wages have dropped throughout Sub-Saharan Africa (see Chapter 7, Table 7.2) and protective labor legislation has neither been complied with nor been enforced. Once the economic rents of the earlier period, rents based on primary product exports and aid flows, were dissipated, institutions designed to transfer economic rents to workers could not overcome market fundamentals.

Kenya provides a useful example. Tripartite agreements in the 1960s have been cited as examples of institutional interventions responsible for raising labor costs. However, starting in 1975, government wage guidelines mandated less than cost-of-living increases for all collective bargaining agreements. From 1979 through mid-1982 the mandated ceiling was only 50 percent of the annual increase in the CPI! The extent to which these guidelines were enforced is not known, but they do suggest that the tripartite mechanism was no longer accommodating labor to the exclusion of all other concerns. Further evidence on the direction of institutional intervention comes from minimum wages. During the 1980s the value of the Kenyan real minimum wage fell by more than 7 percent per year. Similarly, the late 1970s and early 1980s saw a substantial decline in the real value of the minimum wage in Ghana, where by 1984 the real minimum wage was only one-quarter as high as it had been ten years earlier.[16] In sum, the strength of prolabor institutional interventions, at least in Anglophone Africa, appears to have waned under the pressure of economic stagnation and decline.

In contrast, the effects of labor legislation and tripartite wage setting mechanisms in the Francophone countries appear to have persisted longer. The evidence in Table 8.3 indicates that wages in Cameroon, Côte d'Ivoire, and Senegal were generally much higher than in the Anglophone countries. Unlike the Kenyan and Ghanaian cases described above, there was no substantial change in government policies toward labor during the 1970s and 1980s in the Francophone countries, so that wages in these countries may continue to reflect rigidities imposed by government intervention.[17]

Factor Endowments

Another important potential source of relatively high manufacturing wages in Africa is differences in labor endowments. Although both African and Asian countries are labor abundant in comparison with their *capital* endowments, differences in *land* endowments across the two regions may help explain the relatively higher level of wages in Africa.

African countries in general have larger endowments of land per agricultural worker than do Asian countries. Data on cropland per agricultural worker in the African and Asian countries for the years in our sample are presented in Table 8.4. Although there is some overlap across the regions, the median value for Asia, at 0.6, is almost half the 1.14 median for the African countries. As discussed elsewhere in this volume (see Chapter 5), this has had an important influence on the nature of the agricultural develop-

TABLE 8.4
Hectares of Agricultural Land per Agricultural Worker

Country	Year	Hectares/Worker
Africa		
Botswana	1990	5.19
Cameroon	1978	2.39
Côte d'Ivoire	1982	1.20
Ghana	1983	1.24
Kenya	1988	0.34
Madagascar	1984	0.81
Malawi	1983	0.99
Mauritius	1987	1.41
Nigeria	1983	1.84
Senegal	1984	1.14
Sierra Leone	1986	2.01
Tanzania	1985	0.56
Zimbabwe	1987	1.13
Asia		
Indonesia	1981	0.57
Korea	1963	0.41
Malaysia	1970	1.72
Taiwan	1961	0.58
Thailand	1970	1.04

SOURCE: Food and Agriculture Organization, *FAO Production Yearbook* (Rome), various years.

ment experiences in the two regions, and on the ability of Africa, like Southeast Asia, to use exports of agricultural products in its overall development strategy. Land/labor ratios also exert an influence on manufacturing wages and on the relationship of these wages to earnings in the agricultural sector.

The source of labor for manufacturing must be the agricultural sector, and manufacturing wages must be high enough to draw people out of agriculture and induce them to move to urban areas for manufacturing jobs. Manufacturing earnings will therefore be a function of agricultural earnings and should be higher when these earnings are higher. In smallholder-based agricultural systems of the kind seen in much of Africa and Asia, the average

FIGURE 8.4

Factor Endowments and Labor Productivity

Quantity/Land

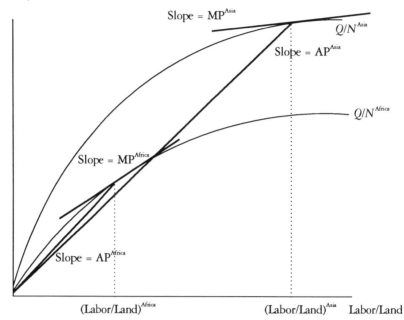

product of labor is probably a good approximation of what agricultural workers receive. However, if migration decisions are household based, which also seems to be a reasonable assumption, then the opportunity cost of having a family member leave the farm to seek a manufacturing job is the *marginal product* of labor in agriculture. Higher land/labor ratios in Africa will increase the marginal product of African labor and will therefore require higher wages to attract this labor into manufacturing. This will hold even if superior agricultural technology in Asia causes *average* labor productivity in Asian agriculture to be higher than it is in Africa.

Figure 8.4 provides a graphical illustration of this argument. Higher overall productivity in Asia is reflected in the higher production function for Asia. The difference in labor/land ratios, with Africa's lower than Asia's, gives rise to a situation where average product of labor per unit land is higher in Asia, while marginal product of labor per unit land is higher in Africa. This implies that if manufacturing wages are a markup on marginal products of labor in agriculture, manufacturing wages will be higher in Africa, as will

FIGURE 8.5
Wages versus Land/Labor Ratios

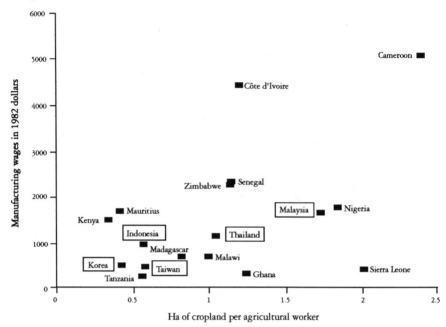

the ratio of manufacturing wages to agricultural earnings (average product). This relatively high opportunity cost of labor in African manufacturing raises unit labor costs and reduces manufacturing competitiveness.

One way of verifying this hypothesis is to compare manufacturing wages with land/labor ratios in agriculture. Figure 8.5 plots manufacturing wages, measured in 1982 dollars, against measures of cropland per agricultural worker drawn from Table 8.4. The figure indicates that in countries where there is more available land, manufacturing wages are higher, although the correlation is far from perfect[18] and, as pointed out in Chapter 5, Africa's situation is changing rapidly under the pressure of rapid population growth.

The impact of factor endowments on ULCs is also captured by the role of female labor in African and Asian economies. In Asia, where land is relatively scarce and ownership and cultivation rights are generally vested in men, the marginal productivity of female members of the household is quite low. In contrast, relative land abundance and land allocation practices that give cultivation rights to women as well as men cause the productivity of female labor in African agriculture to be substantially higher. This implies the existence of a relatively large supply of female labor for Asian manufacturing that is not paralleled in the African context. Since women are generally less expensive labor than men (due in part to the lower opportunity cost and reservation wages of women, as well as to gender discrimination), the available female labor force in Asia has helped to reduce average manufacturing wages. Because of both factor endowments and customs, the low-wage, young female factory workers that have fueled Asian manufacturing sectors are neither present in nor necessarily available (at low wages) to the industrial sector in African economies.

Productivity and Competitiveness

The limitations of empirical explanations for productivity trends are well known. Two examples are the size of the residual in sources-of-growth analysis and the failure to account for the recent productivity slowdown in the advanced industrial economies. It comes as no surprise, then, that we have little in the way of empirical understanding of why African productivity levels tend to lag behind those of Asia's historical experience. What we can provide is a set of explanations that go beyond cultural stereotypes. Specifically, differences in both the quantity and quality of physical capital as well as in the level of acquired human capital can account for productivity differences between the two regions. Since African endowments of both physical and human capital are generally lower than those of historical Asia, these factors are likely causes of lower productivity in Africa.

Physical Capital

Available physical capital in manufacturing can be characterized along three dimensions: the size of the capital stock; the quality of this capital, particularly the sophistication of the technology embodied in it; and the availability and reliability of social overhead capital and infrastructure. Africa lags behind Asia in all three dimensions, both today and in comparison with East and Southeast Asia's historical experience.

Lacking a reliable measure of the stock of physical capital, differences in investment rates across the two regions can serve as a rough proxy for capital formation. Gross domestic investment in Sub-Saharan Africa accounted for

15 percent of GDP in 1965 and 16 percent in 1990, compared with 22 percent and 37 percent, respectively, for Asia. Gross domestic investment in Africa grew at an average annual rate of 4.2 percent between 1965 and 1980, declining to a rate of 0.8 percent per year in the 1980s. Investment growth rates in Asia, conversely, were nearly constant since the 1960s, averaging 6.2 percent per year.[19] To the extent that lower investment rates indicate lower rates of capital formation and smaller capital stocks, capital/labor ratios, and hence labor productivity, would be lower in Africa.

In general, the capital goods in African manufacturing are also of lower quality, and embody less efficient technology, than that available in Asia. Foreign direct investment is a primary source of technology transfer to poor countries, as well as a means of increasing the size of the capital stock. African countries have done substantially less well in attracting this investment than have their Asian counterparts. Consequently, the African countries' manufacturing sectors often have not benefited from inflows of productivity-enhancing technology that accompany foreign firms. In Ghana, some textile firms are still using equipment imported secondhand twenty-five or thirty years ago. Although this machinery may well be of the same vintage as that used in Asia in the 1960s, thirty years of use and chronic shortage of spare parts have reduced its efficiency. On the other hand, when foreign investment has been forthcoming, as in the textile sector in Kenya and Zimbabwe, detailed analyses of productivity indicate "production engineering performance close to that of best practice plants in the developed countries."[20]

Growth in manufacturing also is dependent upon the ability of firms to develop, adapt, and use technology. This technological capability depends in large measure on the presence of scientific and engineering manpower, which is in distinctly short supply in Africa.[21] Finally, in addition to the capital stock within the firm, worker productivity also depends upon the availability of infrastructure and social overhead capital. The quality and quantity of such services as electricity, ports, roads, and water will have a direct impact on the output of manufacturing firms, and therefore on measured labor productivity. African economies are characterized by underprovision of these services. In particular, erratic supplies of electrical power are repeatedly cited as serious constraints on efficient firm operation. To the extent that African governments have been less able to create and maintain effective infrastructure service to their manufacturing sectors, worker productivity remains low.

Human Capital

There is an extensive theoretical and empirical literature about the relationship between human capital acquired through training and schooling and worker productivity. African workers have generally acquired much less human capital than Asians, even in comparison with historical Asian experience. Although direct measures of the stock of human capital in a country are not widely available, school enrollment rates and adult literacy rates may serve as proxies. Table 8.5 gives data on literacy rates and secondary school enrollment rates for the countries in our sample. The data provide a comparison between modern-day Africa and historical Asia. In general, African populations, with a few exceptions, are less literate and less well educated than the Asian populations were at similar points in their countries' development (see the appendix to Chapter 2). This is especially apparent when the better African performers in our sample (Botswana, Mauritius, and Zimbabwe) are excluded. Seven of the remaining ten African countries exhibit secondary school enrollment rates and adult literacy rates lower than any of our Asian countries exhibited ten to twenty-five years earlier. To the extent that manufacturing work requires a minimum level of human capital, and particularly where literacy is important, workers in African manufacturing would be less productive than Asian workers.

Can African Labor Compete?

Can African labor compete in the production of manufactured goods? The simple answer to this question is no, at least not if the conditions that determined ULCs in the 1980s prevail. We draw this conclusion based on a comparison of the determinants of ULCs between Africa and the historical experience of Asia's most successful economies. In the 1980s African countries generally exhibited higher wages relative to productivity levels and more overvalued exchange rates than was the case during the early phases of industrialization in East and Southeast Asia. Not only does this suggest that Africa was not yet in a position to follow the path of the successful Asian economies, but that African economies might not be able to meet the expected challenge of Asia's latecomers, including China.

Could African labor compete in the production of manufactured goods? Here we offer a more positive response. If Africa reforms those policies that

TABLE 8.5
Literacy and School Enrollment Rates (%)

Country	Year	Secondary school enrollment rates	Adult literacy rate[c]
Africa			
Botswana	1990	37	71
Cameroon	1978	16	56
Côte d'Ivoire	1982	17	43
Ghana	1983	38	53
Kenya	1988	23	59
Madagascar	1984	36	67
Malawi	1983	5	41
Mauritius	1987	51	83
Nigeria	1983	29	42
Senegal	1984	13	28
Sierra Leone	1986	18	29
Tanzania	1985	3	na
Zimbabwe	1987	45	84
Asia			
Indonesia	1981	30	74[d]
Korea	1963	35[a]	71
Malaysia	1970	34[b]	60
Singapore	1963	45[a]	75[e]
Taiwan	1961	27[f]	na
Thailand	1970	30[b]	79

a. Value is for 1965.
b. Value is midpoint of values for 1965 and 1975.
c. Literacy rates for Africa are for 1985.
d. Value is for 1985.
e. Value is for 1975.
f. Value was calculated as the number of secondary students divided by two-thirds of the population aged 10–19.
SOURCES: World Bank, *World Development Report* (New York), various years. United Nations, *Human Development Report, 1992* (New York). Republic of China, *Taiwan Statistical Data Book, 1991* (Taipei).

have been detrimental to manufacturing, we see no reason why industrialization could not establish a foothold in the Sub-Saharan region. In order to appreciate the policy agenda suggested by Asian experience as required to achieve competitiveness, it is important, first, to understand the constraints facing Africa's manufacturing sector and, second, to identify those factors most amenable to policy intervention.

Higher ULCs in Africa relative to Asia's experience are due, in part, to different factor endowments. High land/labor ratios in many African countries suggest a relatively high opportunity cost of labor available to manufacturing, and result in high wage/productivity ratios. Where these relationships hold, competitiveness in manufacturing will not be immediately forthcoming, as it was in East Asia. Instead, the Southeast Asian model holds more promise. The experience of the ASEAN nations recommends continued exploitation of a diversified portfolio of primary products until such time as productivity improvements enable the economy to become more competitive in industrial activities.

A second dimension of factor endowments concerns Africa's stock of human capital, measured in terms of adult literacy or in the numbers of school graduates. Evidence presented earlier indicates that as of the late 1980s most African economies, especially those with stagnant economies, had accumulated far less human capital than was the case in Korea, Singapore, and Taiwan by the 1960s, and in Indonesia, Malaysia, and Thailand by the 1970s. To the extent that human capital is a determinant of productivity levels in manufacturing, most African economies will not yet have accumulated sufficient stocks of educated workers to achieve a competitive position. Policy can have an influence on the stock of human capital, for example, by increasing expenditure on education and training to develop human capital. But the gestation period of such policies is long and support of industrialization may be achieved more quickly by policies designed to influence some of the other determinants of ULCs.

All the successful Asian economies had exchange rates at or near their equilibrium levels, whereas African countries, with virtually no exceptions, overvalued their currencies, often by considerable percentages. Neither foreign direct investors nor domestic import-competing firms will be attracted to manufacturing under such exchange rate regimes. With overvalued exchange rates manufacturing can proceed only if significant and guaranteed subsidies and/or protection are offered. But to use such countervailing policy measures sets in motion the problems of rent-seeking, which are already endemic to Africa and other inward-looking economies and which seem to frustrate rather than promote industrial growth. It would be far better to follow Asian experience, which has relied in part on realistic exchange rates to encourage competitive manufactures.

Assuming the exchange rate regime supports manufacturing, the next step is to avoid those policies that raise the wage/productivity ratio. On the wage side, our impression is that the market eventually dominated any attempt to undervalue wages in Asia, and at least in Anglophone Africa ultimately rejected imposition of wages and conditions of employment the economy could not sustain. The lesson Africa should learn from Asia, let alone from its own experience, is that government interventions in wage determination should not be targeted toward raising wages above the opportunity cost of labor. Part of East Asia's "economic miracle" has been to let the labor market generate rapid increases in real compensation following the expansion of employment opportunities. African workers would be well served if their governments permitted the labor market to do the same.

Improving labor productivity involves far more than making investments in human capital. A suitable environment for private investment must be established to raise both the quantity and quality of physical capital. Public investments in infrastructure as well as education are critical as both are positively correlated with labor productivity. The difficult question is how to allocate scarce resources among these competing claims, all of which enhance output per worker. Since our empirical understanding of the linkage between labor productivity and the accumulation of physical and human capital is weak, we can only recommend traditional cost-benefit methodologies for sorting out the best investment opportunities.

In conclusion, the policy lessons Asia has to offer Africa concerning the labor market are not novel. Let the labor market determine wages and employment, and increase worker productivity by providing labor with physical and human capital. If African economies adopt similar strategies, African labor can compete.

APPENDIX 8.1

Measuring Unit Labor Costs

Computation of ULCs requires measuring productivity (or output) in physical terms. This becomes evident when one substitutes the appropriate units of measurement for each of the variables in the definition of ULCs:

$$\text{ULC} = \left(\frac{w}{\text{AP}_L}\right)\left(\frac{1}{e}\right)$$

$$= \frac{\text{sh}}{\text{hr}}/\frac{\text{ton}}{\text{hr}}\left(\frac{1}{\text{sh.}/\$}\right) \qquad (8\text{A.1})$$

$$= \frac{\$}{\text{ton}}$$

where shillings (sh.) is the domestic currency, dollars ($) the foreign currency, and tons the unit of physical output. If value added is substituted as the measure of productivity, the calculation of ULCs becomes

$$\text{ULC} = \left(\frac{w}{\text{VA}/L}\right)\left(\frac{1}{e}\right)$$

$$= \frac{\text{sh}}{\text{hr}}/\frac{\text{sh}}{\text{hr}}\left(\frac{1}{\text{sh.}/\$}\right) \qquad (8\text{A.2})$$

$$= \frac{\$}{\text{sh.}}$$

and ULC cannot be meaningfully interpreted.

These measurement problems are well recognized and, no doubt, account for the limited comparisons of levels of ULCs available in the literature. ULCs are more commonly employed in comparing changes over time in labor costs relative to productivity changes. Even in the United States, for example, levels of ULCs on aggregate or for specific industries are not reported. Instead, the U.S. Department of Labor annually publishes reports on how America's ULCs have changed relative to those of its major competitors and decomposes each nation's changes into movements in productivity, wages, and exchange rates. This can be done because changes in physical productivity over time within an individual country are approximated by subtracting changes in the domestic price level from changes in the value of manufacturing output per worker. Formally, Equation (8A.2) is transformed as

$$\%\Delta(\text{ULC}) = \%\Delta(w) - \left[\%\Delta\left(\frac{\text{VA}}{\text{worker}}\right) - \%\Delta(\text{PPI})\right] - \%\Delta(e) \quad (8\text{A}.3)$$

where PPI is the producer's price index and the $\%\Delta(e)$ measures the appreciation or depreciation of the domestic currency. This method does not require, nor does it include, any calculation or comparison of levels of ULCs across countries or even within each country over time. The decomposition is based on rates of change, abstracting completely from levels. Discussion of movements in ULCs in the United States and in other OECD countries can be found in Neef (1986), Neef and Thomas (1988), and Yamamoto (1989/90). There is no parallel process for making cross-country comparisons of ULCs.

APPENDIX 8.2

Physical Productivity, Value Added, and Effective Protection

This appendix shows that a value-added-based measure of the wage/productivity ratio is equal to the physical-productivity-based measure inflated by the effective rate of protection.

Notation

Q	=	Physical output in manufacturing
VA	=	Value added per unit output in manufacturing at domestic prices
VA*	=	Value added per unit output at world prices
a_i	=	Input required to produce a unit of output; a constant
P	=	Domestic price of output
P_i	=	Domestic price of input
P^*	=	World price of output
P_i^*	=	World price of input

t =   Tariff on output

t_i =   Tariff on input

w =   Manufacturing wage

L =   Manufacturing labor force

r =   Effective rate of protection

F =   Africa

S =   Asia

Define the following:

M_1 = wL/Q = Physical wage/productivity ratio

M_2 = $wL/(\text{VA} \times Q)$ = Value added wage/productivity ratio

r = $(\text{VA}/\text{VA}^*) - 1$ = Effective rate of protection

VA = $P - a_iP_i = P^*(1 + t) - a_iP_i^*(1 + t_i)$

VA^* = $P^* - a_iP_i$

For each country, we can show the relationship between M_2, the measure we use in this paper, and M_1, the measure implicit in the unit labor cost formula [Equation (8.2)] as follows:

$$M_2 = \frac{wL}{\text{VA} \times Q} = \frac{wL/Q}{P - a_iP_i} = \frac{M_1}{P - a_iP_i}$$

$$= \frac{M_1}{P^*(1 + t) - a_iP_i^*(1 + t_i)}$$

$$= \frac{M_1}{(1 + r)VA^*}$$

This indicates that a value-added-based measure not only converts physical output into a value measure, but also incorporates the effect of differences in the level of protection between inputs and outputs.

The effect is best illustrated by taking the ratio of the value added measures in Africa and Asia, which are the numbers presented in Table 8.2, and illustrating how it is related to the ratios that would be generated if we had productivity-based measures. This can be seen in the following:

$$\frac{M_2^F}{M_2^S} = \frac{M_1^F/[(1 + r^F)/VA^*]}{M_1^S/[(1 + r^S)/VA^*]} = \frac{M_1^F}{M_1^S}\left(\frac{1 + r^S}{1 + r^F}\right)$$

The ratio of the value added measures in Africa to the value added measure in Asia is equivalent to the ratio of the physical productivity ratios multiplied by the ratio of Asian to African effective rates of protection. If, as is probably the case, African rates of effective protection are greater than those in place in Asia at the relevant period of history, then the value-added-based measures will underestimate the difference between African and Asian wage/productivity ratios, and hence underestimate the difference in unit labor costs. (We thank Michael Roemer for pointing out this relationship.)

NOTES

We would like to thank Paul Collier and Michael Roemer for their valuable comments.

1. This is the case because if real wages equal marginal products, then the wage/average product ratio also equals the ratio of marginal to average products. As drawn in Figure 8.2, marginal products fall more quickly than do average products; thus the ratio between the two falls as one moves down the product curves. This would not be the case if the underlying production function were Cobb-Douglas (where the ratio of MP_L/AP_L is a constant) but is true, for example, for the generalized CES production function.

2. This is a theme in some of the open-economy macro literature. See, for example, Dornbusch (1980, Chapters 6 and 8).

3. Parallel market rates are reported in the *World Currency Yearbooks* (various issues). Since parallel markets, by definition, are illegal, more than the usual caveats about sampling bias and the reliability of data are in order. The *World Currency Yearbook,* the standard reference on parallel market exchange rates, does not even indicate its sources, although they are rumored to be reports from airline pilots and flight attendants.

4. A ratio of $e_p/e < 1$ requires further explanation. Theoretically, undervalua-

tion of a currency creates conditions of excess supply, which should depress market rates to below official levels. If the government stands behind the official rate, however, and acquires enough domestic currency to satisfy all foreign exchange transactions, it is hard to see why any parallel market transactions would occur. In essence, why would anyone exchange dollars for domestic currency at less than the government's going rate? Anticipation of future currency devaluations could create a futures market in foreign exchange at a rate below the prevailing official rate, but why would a spot rate, with $e_p < e$, develop? An alternative explanation for why $e_p/e < 1$ can arise is based on "black money," that is, foreign exchange acquired illegally as a result of smuggling, sale of illicit goods (such as guns and narcotics), or tax evasion. Money "laundering" schemes then can create the demand side for a parallel market in foreign exchange where the parallel rate is less than the official one. (We are not sufficiently aware of the specifics of either the Indonesian or Thai cases to explain why either of these countries persistently displays $e_p/e < 1$.)

5. The CFA zone countries are Benin, Burkina Faso, Cameroon, Central African Republic, Côte d'Ivoire, Gabon, Mali, Niger, Senegal, and Togo. For these countries, e_p/e may not exactly equal one owing to the "black money" issues discussed in the previous note.

6. Further discussion of monetary management in CFA zone countries can be found in Deverajan and de Melo (1987).

7. Compilations of some of the information contained in these surveys can be found in United Nations, *Yearbook of Industrial Statistics,* and in United Nations, *African Statistical Yearbook.* Alternatively, published reports from the primary sources often are available.

8. As an empirical matter, the correspondence between Africa and historical Asia is not perfect. The data on wages and productivity are drawn from industrial surveys that are not conducted in all possible years, but we have attempted to choose representative years in which the Asian countries were relatively early in their industrialization process. As for Africa, the most recently available manufacturing surveys were used.

9. The use of value added as a productivity measure implies that the relative values of the African and Asian wage/productivity ratios are probably closer together than they would be if physical measures of productivity were used. Value added measures are based on the difference between output values and input values at *domestic prices* and therefore incorporate domestic tariffs. Positive effective rates of protection will inflate value added measures and therefore decrease the measured value of the wage/productivity ratio. If effective rates of protection in Africa are greater than they were in Asia during the relevant period, this would cause the wage/value added ratios to be closer in value than wage/physical productivity ratios would be. (See Appendix 8.2 for a detailed explanation of the relationship between physical productivity measures and effective rates of protection.)

10. In Nigeria, the petroleum and chemical industries, which are a substantial

fraction of total manufacturing, exhibit wage/productivity ratios of approximately .11, since they are dominated by capital-intensive and technologically sophisticated firms. This has the effect of reducing the overall ratio for the sector.

11. At the subsector level, an examination of African and Asian performance in the textile sector confirms the basic findings. The African countries display much higher wage/productivity ratios and much poorer export performance than do their Asian counterparts.

12. We do not contend that these ideas are novel. For example, the influential 1981 World Bank document, *Accelerated Development in Sub-Saharan Africa: An Agenda for Action,* commonly known as the Berg report, stated the following: "African wages are high compared with those of Asia. An ILO survey in 1979 showed that the median wage for textile workers in 10 African countries was 50 percent higher than in Pakistan and more than twice as high as in Bangladesh. Higher African wages reflect both government wage policy, which in many countries sets industrial wages above the level they would otherwise be, and better opportunities for agricultural employment" (p. 92).

13. An overview of wage-setting institutions in the NICs is contained in Fields and Wan (1989). Vogel and Lindauer (1991) focuses on industrial labor relations in Korea, including references to much of the work on labor law and regulations in Korea.

14. In the period from 1966 to 1984, real earnings in Korea grew at an average of 8.1 percent per year, which is faster than in Taiwan during the same period and in Japan during its high growth period in the 1950s and 1960s (Lindauer 1991, Table 3.6).

15. In addition, unions would have pressured for a shorter work week and greater occupational health and safety, measures that also would have raised labor costs.

16. Younger 1989, Table A3.1. The 1980s also witnessed declining real minimum wages in a number of other African countries, including Côte d'Ivoire, Nigeria, Senegal, and Tanzania.

17. See Terrell and Svejnar (1989) for a discussion of labor market institutions and their impact on wages in manufacturing in Senegal.

18. A regression of wages on cropland per agricultural worker for the entire sample in Figure 8.5 is:

$$\text{Wage} = 219 + 1520.79 \text{ ha/worker}$$
$$(503.65)$$

where the standard error is given in parentheses. R^2 for this regression is .24. The diagram excludes Botswana, but the observation for Botswana is included in the regression. These data are for the same variables and from the same source as that reported in Chapter 5, Table 5.4. Differences between our values and the ones reported in Table 5.4 are due to the different years for which the two tables were generated.

Overall, these data understate the difference between Africa and Asia. The arable land measure includes only land cultivated or lying fallow, but it does not include land in reserves that has not yet been brought into cultivation. In many of the African countries, substantial land areas remain as potentially cultivable reserves. If land reserves were included, the difference between Asian and African land/labor ratios would be larger, and the positive relationship between factor endowments and manufacturing wages shown in Figure 8.5 would be stronger.

19. *World Development Report, 1992,* Tables 8 and 9. The Asian figures refer to averages for East Asia and the Pacific.

20. Pack (1993, 10).

21. See Pack (1993) for a discussion of the role of technological capability.

BIBLIOGRAPHY

Deverajan, Shantayanan, and Jaime de Melo. 1987. "Adjustment with a Fixed Exchange Rate: Cameroon, Côte d'Ivoire and Senegal." *World Bank Economic Review* 1(3): 447–86.

Dornbusch, Rudiger. 1980. *Open Economy Macroeconomics.* New York: Basic Books.

Fields, Gary, and Henry Wan. 1989. "Wage-Setting Institutions and Economic Growth." *World Development* 17(9): 1471–83.

Food and Agriculture Organization. Various years. *FAO Production Yearbook.* Rome.

Lindauer, David. 1991. "Labor Market Performance and Worker Welfare." In "Korea: The Strains of Economic Growth," ed. David Lindauer. Harvard Institute for International Development. Unpublished.

Neef, Arthur. 1986. "International Trends in Productivity: Labor Costs in Manufacturing." *Monthly Labor Review* 109(12): 12–17.

Neef, Arthur, and James Thomas. 1988. "International Comparisons of Productivity and Unit Labor Cost Trends in Manufacturing." *Monthly Labor Review* 111(12): 27–33.

Pack, Howard. 1993. "Productivity and Industrial Development in Sub-Saharan Africa." *World Development* 21(1): 1–16.

Republic of China. 1991. *Taiwan Statistical Data Book.* Taipei.

Terrell, Katherine, and Jan Svejnar. 1989. *The Industrial Labor Market and Industrial Performance in Senegal: A Study in Enterprise Ownership, Export Orientation, and Government Regulation.* Boulder, Colo.: Westview Press.

United Nations. 1987. *African Statistical Yearbook.* New York.

———. 1992. *Human Development Report.* New York.

———. Various years. *Yearbook of Industrial Statistics.* New York.

United Nations and World Bank. 1992. *African Development Indicators.* New York.

Vogel, Ezra, and David Lindauer. 1991. "Toward a Social Contract for Korean Labor." *Korea: The Strains of Economic Growth.*

World Bank. Various years. *World Development Report.* New York.

Yamamoto, Shin'ichi. 1989/90. "Japan's Trade Lead: Blame Profit-Hungry American Firms." *The Brookings Review* 1989/90 (Winter): 14–18.

Younger, Stephen. 1989. "Ghana: Economic Recovery Program, A Case Study of Stabilization and Structural Adjustment in Sub-Saharan Africa." In *Successful Development in Africa: Case Studies of Projects, Programs, and Policies,* EDI Development Policy Case Series, Analytical Case Studies, Number 1. Washington, D.C.: World Bank.

CHAPTER 9

Financial Development

David C. Cole and James S. Duesenberry

A Common Heritage

Until the end of World War II the formal financial systems of most Asian and African countries were similarly structured to serve the needs of the colonial (or quasicolonial in China and Thailand) trading community and to minimize the administrative problems of the colonial government. Currency was issued in order to facilitate trade and tax collections. In the British colonies, currency boards issued a local currency tied to sterling and backed by reserves in sterling. Price stability was facilitated since a balance of payments surplus was required in order to increase the currency issue. Banking services were provided mainly by banks owned by the colonizers that had offices only in major trading centers and were primarily concerned with the business of the foreign trading community.

As countries became independent after World War II, economic development became a central objective and with it the need to mobilize financial resources. Governments of newly independent countries thus had strong incentives to replace the currency boards with new central banks and to nationalize the colonial commercial banks. They could then use the new banking system to direct financing to the investment projects required by their development plans.

A further justification for the move to establish government control over the financial system was the widespread distrust of market processes in general and of market-oriented financial systems in particular. That distrust had ideological origins but was reinforced by the belief that private financial systems were subject to concentration of wealth and power, destabilizing speculation, and frequent failures of banking institutions. The financial disasters of the Great Depression were still fresh in memory.

The newly independent governments in Asia quickly replaced the colonial monetary authorities with central banks that were formally modeled after North American or European central banks and that had all the powers usually given to central banks. In particular, they had the power to issue currency without any direct link to inflows of foreign exchange.

In many cases the governments of the newly independent Asian states nationalized the existing commercial banks or acquired a controlling interest in them. In a number of cases the nationalized commercial banks were reorganized into a set of banks that, following both socialist and Japanese models, were to specialize in serving a particular sector, such as agriculture, industry, or foreign trade. But whether nationalized or not, banks were closely controlled by governments. The central bank established upper and lower limits for interest rates on various kinds of loans and deposits, and in many cases banks were required to invest certain proportions of their funds in particular categories of loans. The central bank also used "refinancing loans" to ensure that priority sectors received credit at low interest rates. In general, interest rates were kept low, partly for political reasons but also in response to a mistaken interpretation of Keynesian theory that was more applicable to depression circumstances in developed countries than to capital-poor LDCs.

African countries became independent some years later than the former colonies in Asia, and the former British colonies followed a pattern very similar to that of Asia. The former French colonies also followed much the same model at the microeconomic level, subjecting commercial banks to close control, regulating interest rates, and allocating credit to priority sectors at preferential interest rates. But their approach to central banking was quite different. Monetary unions, each with its own central bank, were established for French West Africa and for Central Africa. Each central bank issued a currency for the union. The exchange rate between the two CFA francs and the French franc was set and has remained at fifty to one since 1950.[1] Moreover, the policies of the two central banks were not autonomous; they were subject to some degree of control by the French Ministry of Finance.

In many respects the subsequent outcome of the financial policies of the developing countries in Africa were similar to those experienced previously by the Asian countries. The use of interest rate controls tended to "repress" banking systems in both areas of the world. Low interest rates on deposits led to the widespread use of alternatives to bank deposits as a means of holding wealth. Some people evaded exchange controls to shift funds abroad, others made use of local informal lending markets, and still others invested in gold and jewelry or bid up real estate prices. Total saving may have been reduced because of those financial policies, though the evidence on that point is not clear.

Low interest rates and credit allocation for special sectors caused inefficient allocation of the limited amounts of capital available to developing African countries. Moreover, the availability of low-cost credit led to widespread corruption. Finally, the allocation of credit on the basis of political rather than economic criteria resulted in numerous defaults on bank loans. Those defaults caused bank failures in many of the developing countries in Africa. They were not, of course, the only cause of bank failures; many LDCs were subjected to shocks from changing terms of trade and variations in the growth of demand in their developed country trading partners. But the politicization of banking systems made banks much more vulnerable to adverse economic events.

Asian countries generally achieved independence and created independent financial systems one or two decades earlier than the African countries. They also became disenchanted with politicized and repressed financial systems somewhat earlier than most African countries and accordingly undertook reforms or restructuring of their systems sooner.

A simple comparison of the ratios of broad money (M2) to GDP for the main countries of Asia and of Africa that we focus on in the subsequent discussion provides a crude indication of how the financial growth of the Asian countries preceded that of the African countries by roughly two decades (see Table 9.1). The average M2/GDP ratio for the African countries in 1980 was almost identical with that of the limited group of Asian countries in 1960.

What is remarkably different about the two groups of countries is that the Asian countries achieved steady increases in their M2/GDP ratios in the 1960s and 1970s and spectacular increases in the 1980s, whereas the African countries, both individually and as a group, experienced declining ratios in the 1980s. The rapid expansion of banking services and the role of the financial system in Asia during the 1980s coincide with the general, but not universal, trend toward greater freeing up of financial markets from direct controls and government manipulation. The decline in Africa's financial ratios reflects probably a combination of the generally worsening economic

TABLE 9.1
Financial Ratios of Asian and African Countries, 1960–1990 (M2/GDP)

Country	1960	1970	1980	1990
Asia				
Singapore	53.2[a]	66.3	64.0	98.6
Hong Kong			69.0	173.9[b]
Taiwan			59.3	151.4
Korea	11.5	33.0	32.9	41.1
Malaysia	24.2	33.9	53.0	66.9
Thailand	23.0	28.3	38.2	74.5
China			45.3	102.7
Indonesia		9.9	19.0	42.8
Philippines	18.9	21.2	21.0	34.4
Average	26.2	31.9	40.2	78.6
Africa				
Botswana			30.7	25.6
Zimbabwe			35.2	32.5
Cameroon		15.1	22.4	19.2[b]
Côte d'Ivoire		25.7	27.1	31.3
Senegal	21.4[a]	15.5	28.3	22.1
Nigeria	12.3	17.4	28.9	22.1
Kenya	22.9[a]	30.5	30.6	29.0
Zambia	15.2[a]	29.2	29.6	22.6
Malawi	14.0[a]	23.1	21.8	20.4
Ghana	16.7	18.9	18.5	13.4
Uganda	21.5	17.6	13.7	10.0[c]
Average	17.7	21.4	26.1	22.6

NOTE: The regional averages are simple averages for the countries included in the table.
a. Signifies initial dates after 1960. b. Data for 1988. c. Estimate.
SOURCES: World Bank, *World Tables 1992* (Washington, D.C., 1992); International Monetary Fund, *International Financial Statistics Yearbook 1992* (Washington, D.C., 1992).

conditions in Africa as well as the continuation of extensive governmental controls over financial institutions.

In the following sections, we attempt to describe the principal financial policies in the Asian and the African countries and suggest how these have influenced the divergent patterns of financial and, ultimately, economic development in the two regions.

Financial Reform in Asia

At the most general level, the redirection of financial systems in East and Southeast Asia away from interventionist, credit-allocation mechanisms to more market-oriented, multiservice systems has not occurred quickly, or completely, or universally. It has proceeded farthest in the most developed city-states of Singapore and Hong Kong. It has lagged in the now least developed and politically most unstable country, the Philippines, and also in Indochina and Burma (which are not covered in this review). Even this generalization needs to be qualified, because Korea and Taiwan have maintained substantial levels of intervention, especially over their banking systems, and rapidly developing China still has a highly controlled system.

Only in Singapore and Hong Kong, where per capita incomes are now approximately U.S.$10,000 and which are important trading and service centers, does it seem reasonable to say that the financial sector has become a significant growth-promoting industry. In most other countries of the region, it is more appropriate to claim that the financial sector and financial policies have changed to accommodate the needs of the economies and the changing orientation of national development policies. In no case can it be said that reform of the financial sector preceded or substantially contributed to accelerated development of the real economy.

Underlying the financial progress of most East and Southeast Asian countries are the following critical characteristics: they have avoided large budgetary deficits and their inflationary consequences most of the time;[2] they have kept exchange rates, whether pegged or floating, at realistic or equilibrium levels to promote export growth; and they have achieved relatively high rates of economic growth.[3] These basic tendencies of fiscal prudence and export-oriented exchange rates have had significant implications for financial policy. The financial systems have not been called upon to fund fiscal deficits but, more frequently, to absorb and allocate foreign exchange surpluses. In the countries with the most open foreign exchange systems, monetary policy has had, on occasion, to protect foreign exchange reserves, but this has not generally been a chronic problem. Thus, the main responsibility of the financial systems has been to mobilize and allocate savings to enterprises rather than to government, and to operate the payments system.

Although most countries of East and Southeast Asia have considered and even professed to adopt significant reforms at various times, the reality is that many countries have retained substantial direct controls or have reinstated direct controls after having relaxed them. In the following discussion we trace the extent of financial reform and the retention or reimposition of direct controls in these major areas of financial policy: allocating bank credit, setting interest rates, competition, dealing with bank insolvencies, instruments of monetary policy, management of the capital markets, and controlling foreign capital movements.

Credit Allocation

Until financial systems become highly developed and able to provide a wide range of financial services to all sectors of the economy, there is an understandable concern that some groups in the economy do not have sufficient access to financial services and that this will limit overall growth and deprive the disadvantaged groups of equitable treatment. Generally the concern focuses on access to credit rather than to savings or payment facilities, although there is evidence from a number of countries that these last two are the most needed services.

Practically all countries in East and Southeast Asia still have mechanisms for controlling or influencing the allocation of bank credit. The differences among countries are matters of form and degree rather than of substance. At one extreme are systems in which the central bank or the ministry of finance has a direct involvement in all the major lending decisions of the banks, both private and government owned. At the other extreme, the government may own or control one or two banks that specialize in lending to particular sectors, such as agriculture, or to certain industries or to particular groups, such as home buyers. Alternatively, the government may give guidelines to banks on the proportions of their loans that should go to particular purposes and may include in their standards for performance evaluation of the banks the extent to which they comply with these guidelines.

Singapore and Hong Kong are probably the only countries in the region that do not have any significant government involvement in the allocation of bank credit. Singapore did set up The Development Bank of Singapore in 1968 to do term lending to the industrial sector, but it has evolved over time into a general bank that is often used by the government to pioneer new areas of financial activity. The bank is government owned but is a profit-making institution run on commercial principles.

China is at the other end of the spectrum, with strong government involvement in the allocation of credit. Korea has always been much closer to the government-dominated end of the credit allocation spectrum. Despite the sale of some government-owned banks to private owners in the early

1980s, the Office of Bank Supervision has continued to be actively involved in bank credit allocation. The main instrument for this policy is the "lead bank" system, whereby one bank is designated to supervise all bank lending to major borrowing firms or groups. That bank must keep the Office of Bank Supervision fully informed on the loans granted and outstanding to that firm or group, and it frequently receives guidance on shifts in loan allocation or restrictions on granting further loans to specific borrowers.

The concerns about bank credit are commonly that not enough credit is going to medium-size and small businesses or to agricultural producers, that there is a deficiency of medium- and long-term credit, and that interest rates on all these kinds of credit are too high. Most Asian countries still have some credit programs that are intended to overcome these various credit "problems," but in recent years these special credit programs have received less emphasis because of the growing awareness that the perceptions of the basic problems were often wrong, or they were not readily solvable by additional amounts of subsidized credit.

The notion that there was a shortage of term financing has been counterbalanced by the growing recognition that most bank loans in Asia, especially to larger borrowers, although technically defined as short-term credits that mature in one year or less, are in fact rolled over and over and become long-term credit lines that are closer to permanent equity than to short-term credits. Interest rates on such credits may move up and down with prevailing market rates, but in many cases even the interest rate is not very onerous if it can be financed by an increase in the line of credit.

Medium-size and small businesses, on the other hand, often receive credit indirectly through their suppliers or from the buyers of their products. Even farmers are frequently able to obtain needed supplies such as fertilizer and seed on a credit basis from local merchants, who in turn may receive credit from banks. These multiple-stage credit arrangements, so common in Asia and in Africa, are important mechanisms for disseminating credit throughout the economy, at market interest rates, without direct banking relationships. In assessing the need for special credit programs for supposedly disadvantaged groups in the economy, it is important to determine whether these informal, multilayered, private credit arrangements are already meeting the needs reasonably effectively.

On the other hand, there is experience from some Asian countries, especially Indonesia, that it is possible for banking institutions to provide small-scale deposit and credit services to millions of customers in rural areas on a profit-making basis. The essential elements of this successful example are reasonable lending rates, strong repayment incentives, effective organization and supervision, and easy withdrawal of deposits.[4]

The almost universal experience of Asia, and Africa, is that highly subsidized credit intended for poor rural producers more often ends up benefiting the better-off inhabitants and those who control the distribution of the credit. These groups are likely to become strong advocates for the credit programs and to resist their discontinuation.

Nevertheless, despite the limitations of government-directed allocation of subsidized credit, most governments in Asia and Africa have at some time adopted such programs. The positive lessons in this regard from Asian experience are that such programs should be limited in size; they should be focused on clearly distinguishable target groups with potentially profitable production prospects whose use of funds can be monitored; they should have strong repayment incentives; and they should have minimal interest rate subsidization.

Setting Interest Rates

All countries in the region have at some time had systems of directly controlled bank interest rates on deposits and loans that were set by the monetary authorities below market-clearing levels. Taiwan was the first country to raise the level of controlled interest rates to approximate market-clearing levels. Beginning in 1953, bank deposit rates were set by the Central Bank at levels well above the inflation rate, and this led to significant growth of the banking system over the next two decades (McKinnon 1973, 114–15). In the mid-1960s, both South Korea and Indonesia followed this example and experienced similar growth of their banking systems. In all three of these countries, although the monetary authorities decided to raise deposit rates to near market-clearing levels and permitted some increase in bank lending rates, they also retained low, subsidized lending rates based on central bank credit for various priority categories of bank lending. When inflation accelerated in the 1970s, the authorities in both Korea and Indonesia were reluctant to increase the controlled deposit and loan rates sufficiently to correct for the inflation and the real rates again became negative.

Other countries in East and Southeast Asia have subsequently raised controlled bank interest rates above the prevailing inflation rates for varying periods of time and generally have experienced similar positive effects on the growth of the financial system. Few governments have given their banks total discretion over the setting of interest rates. In some countries where such discretion has been given, there was a "bankers club" or a bank cartel that could be counted on to listen to the monetary authorities' suggestions. In Indonesia the banks were given the authority to set their own interest rates on most types of deposits and loans in 1983. Government-owned banks, which accounted for 70 to 80 percent of total bank assets at that time, could be counted on to follow guidance from the Central Bank and Ministry of Finance, and recently these authorities have given strong guidance to the whole banking system on the appropriate level of interest rates. Much the same situation holds in Malaysia, Thailand, and Taiwan. In Singapore, the four dominant private banks can be counted on to follow the suggestions of the Monetary Authority of Singapore. In Hong Kong the bankers cartel sets rates. In China the banks are all government owned and the central bank determines interest rates. Thus, in no country in the region at present are bank interest rates really free from either direct control or strong government guidance.

Competition

Most countries of the East and Southeast Asian region have limited the entry of new banks and the opening of new branches by existing banks. Hong Kong has been the most permissive in allowing entry and encouraging competition in its relatively small territory. As a consequence, there are many foreign and domestic banks in Hong Kong and they use it as a base for serving all parts of the region. Singapore has allowed foreign banks to set up special entities, called Asian Currency Units, that serve the international market, but their activities are limited within Singapore. Even for the banks that are licensed to operate in Singapore, there are two categories of institutions, those with full licenses and those with restricted licenses. These limitations are designed to protect the domestic market for the fully licensed banks.

Most other countries of the region have been much more restrictive than Hong Kong or Singapore. Most other countries also have a higher proportion of, and a larger role for, government-owned banks, which are often given special protection or privilege relative to privately owned or foreign-owned banks.

In 1988 Indonesia opened entry for new domestic and foreign joint-venture banks in addition to the handful that had been authorized in 1967–1968 but still prohibited any fully foreign-owned branches. Within four years the number of commercial banks in Indonesia increased from 112 to

196, and the number of branch offices of banks throughout the country rose from 1,640 to 4,286 (Bank Indonesia, *Indonesian Financial Statistics,* May 1992). This sudden expansion in banking services in Indonesia may have been excessive and could be followed by bank failures and mergers. It may also reflect the concern that easy entry of new banks would not be continued indefinitely, so it was best to get established when the opportunity presented itself. There was also undoubtedly an insufficiency of banking services, and lack of competition contributed to poor quality of service. Opening up entry has revitalized the banking industry in Indonesia and made it much more responsive to customer demands and to new market opportunities.

Taiwan has also been reducing the barriers to entry of new banks in recent years, but on a less ambitious scale than in Indonesia. The cartel of the old mainland banks that transferred to Taiwan in 1949 has finally been broken, but the new banks still account for a limited share of total bank assets.

Most of the other countries, including Korea, China, Thailand, Malaysia, and Philippines, have kept fairly strong restrictions on new entry and have preserved the dominant role of government-owned or government-controlled banking institutions. These restrictions have often led to rapid growth of finance companies and other nonbank financial institutions, including informal curb-market operations, to make up for either the deficiency or the unrealistic prices of financial services. The protected banks generally have been inefficient and have frequently been used by government as sources of political funds or personal wealth.

The main reason given for restricting entry of new banks has been to prevent "excessive" competition leading to small, weak banks that could collapse and cause a financial crisis in times of adversity. Hong Kong has the largest number of banks, both absolutely and relative to the size of the economy, and has no bank deposit insurance system. It has experienced some financial crises and some bank failures, but the bank failures have not caused or seriously contributed to the worsening of the crises.

The more realistic explanations for restricting entry of banks are to preserve the advantages of existing bank cartels, to reduce the burdens of bank supervision, and to maintain the comfortable relationship between the banks and the regulators. When bank entry has been liberalized, it has generally led to reduced interest rate spreads and greatly improved services. It has also increased the demands on the regulators for effective supervision and in some cases raised demands for some form of deposit insurance to help guarantee the safety of the smaller private banks. Only a few countries in the region have gone very far down this path.

Dealing with Insolvent Banks

Most of the countries of the region do not have deposit insurance systems as protection against bank insolvency. Depositors therefore have to make their own assessments of the riskiness of individual institutions. In many countries this leads to differential deposit rates. The rates may be lower in government-owned banks, which are generally considered safe, as are foreign-owned banks, although the recent experience with BCCI may change the latter assumption. Private banks tend to be judged in terms of their political connections as well as the soundness of their management. Small, politically unconnected institutions are often considered risky and must offer inducements to attract depositors.

Generally speaking, government-owned banks and politically powerful private banks have not been allowed to fail in the region. Central banks have had the main responsibility for alleviating the short-run pressures on such banks. Many different schemes have been devised for sharing the ultimate burden of insolvency among the central bank, the budget, other banks, and the private owners, but seldom has any burden fallen on the depositors.

The common practice in most Asian countries for dealing with smaller private banks that become insolvent is to arrange mergers with stronger private or government-owned banks. The central bank often acts as the "marriage broker" and also may either take over some of the bad assets or make a contribution to the capital of the acquiring bank. The Indonesian policy of holding bank owners collectively and personally responsible for their bank's liabilities is a new approach that may still be challenged in the courts.

Over the past quarter-century, none of the countries of the region has experienced a serious banking crisis in which there has been a massive withdrawal of deposits and impending collapse of many banking institutions.[5] It would seem that the prevailing approach to bank failures in East and Southeast Asia, while it is not clearly defined or prescribed in statutes, has worked reasonably well to maintain confidence in the solvency of the whole banking system, if not always in the individual institutions.

Indirect Monetary Controls

The money markets of most Asian countries developed much earlier than those in African countries, so that most Asian central banks have the means to exercise indirect control of reserve money and short-term interest rates much more readily than their African counterparts.

Nevertheless, most Asian countries combine indirect control of reserve money with some direct allocation of credit. In managing the monetary base, the Asian central banks have used a variety of techniques. Some are variants on open market operations; others involve significant departures from market-oriented procedures. Several countries use Treasury bills for open market operations, but others such as Indonesia and Korea use central bank bills for this purpose.

When Korea, Taiwan, and Singapore experienced large balance of payments surpluses, the central banks moved to sterilize a large part of the inflow of reserves in order to control domestic demand. To do so they used special security issues and persuaded the banks to buy them. The government of Singapore has deposited funds from its budget surplus with the Monetary Authority of Singapore in order to absorb bank reserves. Taiwan has absorbed reserves by accepting deposits from the postal savings system. The Bank of Korea has required banks to buy stabilization bonds issued for the purpose.

At other times, the central banks of the Asian countries have needed to inject reserves into the banking system. They have done so by reversing their open market operations and also by using the discount window. Some countries are still providing credit to special sectors of the economy through the discount window and also by permitting banks to obtain funds from the discount window when they have liquidity problems. In most cases the central bank rations the amount of credit available through the discount window.

The short-run targets for monetary policy change with circumstances. When the balance of payments and exchange rate positions are satisfactory, the central banks' major concern is usually inflation control. A monetary aggregates approach is often the basis of policy, but there are frequent ad hoc shifts in policy in response to changes in the terms of trade or other cost-push factors.

Interest rate targets are also used, especially when interest rates have to be adjusted in response to factors affecting short-term international capital flows. Indonesia's monetary target has often been an interest rate rather than a quantity of reserves. Moreover, Bank Indonesia has found it necessary on a number of occasions to change the rules of the game in order to deal with the large movements of reserves related to foreign exchange transactions, for example, by shifting large amounts of government enterprise deposits out of the state banks into the central bank in order to remove reserves from the banking system.

In Malaysia the central bank used open market operations for a number of years and also influenced the market by lending to discount houses. Bank Negara Malaysia has also increased reserve requirements to offset large inflows of foreign capital.

The experience of Asian countries indicates the difficulties that African central banks will face as they shift to indirect monetary control. It takes some time to develop short-term securities markets with sufficient depth to permit their use for reserve control. Even when those markets work well in ordinary circumstances, they may not be able to absorb the shocks arising from large capital flows. The central bank will then have to take unusual measures, as has been done in a number of Asian countries. Central banks must not only be able to handle the mechanics of special deposit requirements or the sale of stabilization bonds; they must also retain the confidence of the banking system and other market participants in their intention to return to normal procedures as soon as possible.

In a regime of direct credit controls, the aggregate supply of credit can be controlled by the processes that govern its detailed allocation. When governments switch to market-based credit allocation, they can, with some difficulty, attempt to blend a system of aggregate credit ceilings with a market-based system of allocation. However, the international agencies that have pushed for market-based credit allocation have sometimes encouraged central banks to rely only on indirect controls and to use their money market operations as the primary means to influence the money supply, bank credit, and money market interest rates. This seems premature for most African countries.

Money Market Development

Money markets have been developed most fully in the large international financial centers of East and Southeast Asia, but they have also achieved considerable importance in Malaysia. Money markets are important for the purposes of liquidity management by the central bank, all financial institutions, and larger nonfinancial enterprises. They also provide the channel for implementation of indirect monetary policy instruments by the monetary authorities and, in the process, establish reference interest rates that serve as the basis for pricing most other types of financial instruments. Money markets consist of short-term claims, usually less than one-year maturity, and they may be denominated in domestic or foreign currencies.

As the authorities of the East and Southeast Asian countries have sought to promote the development of their money markets, they have often faced the dilemma of whether to let interest rates on money market instruments fluctuate freely in response to changing market conditions or to try to control or limit the movements of rates in an effort to impart a sense of stability. If rates on such instruments are controlled, there is usually an accompanying requirement for financial institutions to hold the instruments as part of their liquidity or legal reserves. When this happens, the money market instruments tend to lose their usefulness for liquidity management or generating realistic reference interest rates.

Malaysia, Thailand, Korea, Indonesia, and the Philippines have all at times taken steps to control money market interest rates and require financial institutions, especially banks, to hold certain amounts or proportions of the money market instruments. Sometimes these controlled rates and purchases have been for purposes of financing government deficits at low interest rates. More often it has been done to curtail domestic credit and monetary expansion while holding down the costs to the central bank of doing so.

Neither Singapore nor Hong Kong could engage in such controlled interest rates and forced purchases without jeopardizing their roles as international financial centers. Malaysia has also eliminated such controls, which has contributed to the growth of its money markets. Indonesia, Korea, the Philippines, Taiwan, and Thailand have all maintained or reinstated controls and have thus impaired the growth of their money markets.

Capital Market Development

Despite the efforts of many Asian countries to promote the early development of their capital markets, the evidence suggests that capital markets did not become significant and useful features of the financial system until the countries had achieved substantial economic development, including an important industrial sector that accounts for 20 to 25 percent of GDP. Before that, the banking system, if not too repressed, carried the main burden of financial intermediation, and the capital markets, if they existed, were artificially sustained through tax exemptions and subsidies.

It is also a common experience that, at some point, the capital markets would suddenly "come alive," usually reflecting a combination of domestic promotion and foreign interest. When that happened, the existing rules and regulatory structure, which were aimed more at promotion than at investor protection, often contributed to an expansionary bubble that sooner or later burst and left both foreign and domestic investors disappointed and disillusioned. Most countries of Asia, after going through this cycle, have then introduced new regulations and institutions that have helped to create more orderly and useful capital markets.

Capital markets have become one of the important symbols of modernity, and most countries of the region endeavored to promote capital markets before there was much demand for their services. Singapore and Hong Kong again provide the exceptions: they have allowed their markets to grow and to serve international customers without much promotion from government.

The two countries have been quite different in their approaches to regulation, however. Hong Kong had practically no governmental regulation until the Hong Kong stock market crisis in 1987, whereas Singapore has had fairly strict regulation at least since the early 1970s. This regulation did not, however, prevent a serious panic in the Singapore market over the Pan Electric Crisis in 1985, which led to a further strengthening of regulations.

Korea and Taiwan have the largest capital markets in East Asia, excluding Japan. Both countries have severely limited direct foreign participation in their markets. The Korean market is subject to both strong regulation and manipulation by the Ministry of Finance. In the early days of promoting the Korean capital market during the 1960s and 1970s, the government offered many incentives, including reduced income taxes for companies that would list their shares. When these incentives proved ineffective, the Ministry of Finance began to publish annual lists of companies that would be required to "go public" during the coming year. In most cases these companies would reluctantly "come to market" during the closing days of the year.

Korea has also restricted the number of securities companies operating in the market and has excluded foreign holdings of shares, except through a few highly controlled investment funds. The government has often had to bail out securities companies that had become insolvent and has not hesitated to call upon securities companies to support the prices of shares in the market. Frequently the government has had to ensure financing from the banks or other financial institutions to carry out these market support operations. Korea is now finally opening up its capital market to foreign investors, but the government is still heavily involved in controlling and manipulating all the participants.

The Taiwan market has been much less regulated than that of Korea and has been characterized by much speculation and instability. It has not been an important channel for raising new capital for local enterprises. Malaysia has achieved significant steady development of its capital market, especially since the termination of cross listing of companies with the Singapore markets.

Most of the other countries of the region have sought to develop their capital markets through incentives or direct intervention to encourage companies to issue or to guarantee a market for their shares. China, on the other hand, has been slow to permit capital markets but has recently authorized their operation in Shanghai and Shenzan. Most of the markets of the region have gone through at least one crisis of confidence that has seen the prices of shares tumble to a fraction of their previous levels. Taiwan and Malaysia have probably achieved the most developed and effective markets outside of Singapore and Hong Kong. The contribution of the capital markets to mobilizing finance for investment in Taiwan and Malaysia has reached roughly the level of the banking systems.

The basic lessons on capital markets for the African countries would seem to be not to push prematurely for capital market development, especially through subsidies and tax exemptions; and when the economy does achieve a sufficient level of industrialization and development, to prepare both the institutional structure and a legal framework that requires reasonable transparency and integrity of capital market participants to provide suitable investor protection, along with any promotional efforts.

Control of Foreign Capital Movements

Removal of controls over foreign capital movements has been a gradual process in most countries of the region. There are, however, a few exceptions. Indonesia moved to a totally open capital account system in 1971, largely because the authorities believed that, given the geographic nature of the country, it was impossible, and a waste of scarce resources, to try to enforce capital controls. Hong Kong and Singapore have maintained open foreign capital systems for many years, which is consistent with their traditional roles as *entrepots* for the trade and financing of their large neighbors.

Thailand, Malaysia, and Taiwan have retained some limited restrictions on foreign capital movements despite their rapid development and very large foreign exchange reserves. Korea, like Japan before it, has maintained extensive foreign exchange controls. The ostensible reason for these controls is to restrict capital flight in times of instability. But there is also concern about the inflows of foreign investment that may lead to foreign takeovers of domestic industries. China has retained controls over capital movements but has announced intentions to relax them substantially in the near future.

The open capital accounts in Indonesia, Singapore, and Hong Kong have put pressures on economic managers not to permit monetary and fiscal expansion that could lead to large outflows of foreign exchange reserves. Some writers, such as Dornbusch and McKinnon, based mainly upon Latin American experience, have warned against premature removal of foreign controls, which can lead to instability in the foreign capital account. The experience of Indonesia and Singapore suggests, however, that the open capital account, by imposing a powerful restraint on fiscal and monetary policy, can have a beneficial effect.

Financial Development in Africa

Macroeconomic Context

Since the mid-1970s, the systems of monetary management used throughout Sub-Saharan Africa (SSA) have been associated with serious economic imbalances, discussed in Chapter 4. These are reflected in high rates of inflation, capital flight, currency substitution, foreign debts that cannot be serviced, large public sector deficits, and insolvent financial institutions.

Numerous factors have produced this situation, including inappropriate domestic policies, external events, bad luck, and misguided donor initiatives. It must be said, however, that overambitious development programs financed through domestic credit and foreign loans played a major role in causing inflation and balance of payments difficulties. Unwillingness to make the adjustments in fiscal and monetary policy required by changes in terms of trade and by adverse weather conditions compounded these difficulties. Attempts to support unrealistic exchange rates by exchange controls adversely affected the capacity to export and led to capital flight. The effort to maintain low, often negative, real interest rates raised the incentives to move capital abroad.

At home the use of interest rate controls discouraged savings and caused those who did save to invest in inflation hedges rather than use the banking system. Ceilings on loan rates and the allocation of a large proportion of bank credit to state enterprises and to favored borrowers in favored sectors resulted in an inefficient allocation of capital and, in many countries, in defaults on a high proportion of bank loans. That in turn led to insolvency of many banks, especially among those owned or controlled by the government.

Although some countries have fared better than others, nearly all the countries of SSA face the need for a major overhaul of their banking systems and a rationalization of their policies and procedures for controlling the total volume of credit and the allocation of available credit between government and the private sector.

In general there is some indication that since the mid-1980s, countries such as The Gambia, Ghana, and Uganda have moved toward stability. That progress reflects a greater willingness on the part of governments to face the need for a serious stabilization effort. It also reflects the relative stability in the external conditions facing Africa during the last half of the 1980s.

Donor Pressure for Financial Reform

The IMF, the World Bank, and other aid donors have frequently made their grants and loans contingent on adoption of a financial reform package. Several elements are common to those packages. All of the countries engaged in adjustment and reform have been simultaneously involved in efforts to improve fiscal policy and monetary management. Most of the donor-sponsored programs include limits on the overall supply of bank credit and often specify the maximum amount of credit to be used by the government and state enterprises.

The donor-sponsored packages have also emphasized the need to deregulate deposit and loan interest rates and to reduce or eliminate special low-interest credit programs for particular sectors, along with the requirements that banks allocate certain proportions of their loans to those sectors. Those programs have also supported efforts to complete the rehabilitation or orderly liquidation of insolvent banks and to improve bank management and supervision.

The general thrust of these reforms has been to move the financial systems in SSA toward more market-oriented operations. In the interest of completing that process some recent donor-sponsored packages have encouraged or even required central banks to take some of the measures that could provide the basis for a system of indirect control of the volume of credit. As a preliminary to the control of monetary aggregates by open market operations, central banks have been encouraged to develop markets for short-term securities while at the same time improving their own capabilities to manage the monetary base.

The case for a shift to a market-based financial system rests on three considerations: first, the general case for the efficacy of market processes, which has come to be widely and often uncritically accepted; second, a general recognition of the poor performance of the directed credit regimes that have been used in Sub-Saharan Africa; and third, the pressure on SSA governments and central banks exerted by the increasing internationalization of financial markets. Many SSA countries have already suffered from capital flight. Moreover, the loss of confidence in the monetary and fiscal policies of many SSA countries has made them vulnerable to further losses of capital. In countries where capital controls have become ineffective or have been removed, it appears necessary to offset lack of confidence by maintaining real interest rates substantially above those in developed countries.

As their difficulties became more severe, many of the governments of African countries acceded to the pressures for financial reform from the IMF, the World Bank, and the AID donors. The reforms are discussed in the following sections.

Credit Allocation

Although direct credit allocation programs have not been eliminated, they have been scaled back as part of the general shift toward greater reliance on market processes. The privatization of some state enterprises and efforts to control the deficits of others have reduced the need to make special credit allocations for them. The poor condition of many state-sponsored development banks, together with the reduction in World Bank support, has forced them to limit their lending. In a number of countries the special credit arrangements for crop financing have been abandoned or rationalized.

More generally, development banks are no longer regarded as central to the development process. In most countries there is a continuing interest in improving the arrangements for financing small business and for providing term lending to small and medium-sized enterprises. But the failures of special credit arrangements in the past have dampened enthusiasm for large-scale expansions or new versions of those programs.

Interest Rate Liberalization

The wisdom of the whole apparatus of interest rate regulation and credit allocation has been questioned by economists at least since the early 1970s. The change of attitude reflected the observations of economists who were directly involved in development programs as well as the more general shift of opinion away from *dirigisme* in favor of market-oriented policies. The work of Shaw (1973) and McKinnon (1973) played an important role in directing attention to the problems posed by directed credit regimes.

In the past five or six years a number of African countries have liberalized or eliminated their controls over deposit and lending rates at commercial banks. Special credit allocation programs have been reduced in scope and a few countries have removed their overall credit ceilings. The intention of those changes was to permit market forces to play an increasing role in determining interest rates and the allocation of credit. But market forces seem to be rather weak in some of the countries that liberalized rates. In most countries lending rates have risen following liberalization but have followed the inflation rate with some lag, so that real interest rates have tended to vary inversely with the inflation rate. Although loan rates may be following the market-clearing level, that is not generally true for deposit rates.

Especially in the small to medium-sized countries such as The Gambia, Ghana, and Malawi, the banking sector is very concentrated and nonbank competition in the formal markets is limited. In Ghana and The Gambia competition has been further restricted because some banks have been under supervisory restraint pending their recapitalization. In those and other countries the very few banks have well-established relations with their customers and each other, making it possible for banks to earn very wide spreads between deposit and loan rates. If all deposit rates were increased, the marginal cost of funds attracted from the general public would be far above the average cost. Banks that need additional funds can, of course, make separate offers for large term deposits without raising rates generally. In many cases, however, banks have had little incentive to bid for deposits because central banks have imposed credit ceilings while permitting excess reserves to accumulate.

In The Gambia rates were liberalized as part of a general economic recovery program. One objective was to raise nominal interest rates to make real rates positive. The inflation rate fell sharply while bank loan rates remained virtually unchanged at about 25 percent and real lending rates rose sharply to 15 percent. The bank loan rates in The Gambia may be close to market-clearing rates given the credit ceilings and excess reserves, but the rates are set in an oligopolistic market. Deposit rates actually fell a little, providing a 2 to 3 percent real return to depositors, while banks earned a 13 percent spread between loan and deposit rates.

In Malawi, where there are only two commercial banks, interest rate spreads increased from an already wide 7 percent in 1985 to 9.5 percent in 1991, as the lending rate rose to 20 percent while deposit rates remained at

11.5 percent. With inflation running at over 10 percent, real deposit rates were virtually zero.

In some larger countries the resort to market forces may be working much more effectively. Nigeria has many commercial banks and an active nonbank financial sector. After removal of interest rate regulation, deposit and loan rates increased together while the spread between deposit and loan rates remained very low. Both rates rose during the rapid inflation of 1988–89 with deposit rates lagging, as often happens. By 1991, when inflation had slowed to about 12 percent, deposit rates were around 15 percent while loan rates averaged 20 percent.

In Kenya loan rates rose faster than deposit rates after deregulation. The spread between deposit and lending rates seems to have settled at around 5 percent. That figure would be considered high in a developed country, but given the higher reserve requirement and the loan losses suffered by banks in most LDCs, it does not seem unreasonable.

Bank Failures

Bank failures have been widespread in SSA, especially among the banks owned or controlled by governments. Some of the losses can be attributed to inadequate diversification in economies subject to severe shocks from weather, terms of trade, and economic policy. They can also be blamed on inexperienced management and political influence on lending decisions.

Some failing banks had lent heavily to government corporations that sustained losses. Banks in The Gambia and Senegal lent heavily to government-sponsored organizations involved in crop financing and processing of agricultural products. Government-sponsored banks also lent to development projects that failed.

In addition to the banks that have been formally declared insolvent, a considerable number of banks have portfolios with substantial amounts of nonperforming loans. In Nigeria, for example, there have been only two important bank failures (both banks owned by state governments), but the reports of bank supervisors indicate that many banks have been seriously compromised by assets that include nonperforming loans but no provision for losses. Similar problems are likely to exist in other countries that have not had large-scale insolvencies.

Approaches to Bank Rehabilitation

Three different approaches have been used to deal with the problem of loan losses. In some cases banks have been liquidated and depositors forced to wait for whatever recoveries can be made from the portfolios of the failed banks. In Senegal depositors of several banks will be paid off only as recoveries proceed, preference being given to small depositors. Some of the loss will be borne by the government, whose corporations were major depositors in some of the failed state banks.

More commonly a procedure called "open bank assistance" has been followed. The bank's nonperforming assets are taken over by a government corporation. The government then recapitalizes the bank by providing enough assets in the form of government securities to give it a positive capital base. At the same time a new management is put in place together with a staff training program. The depositors' position remains unchanged throughout while the government ultimately sustains a loss equal to the excess of the value of the assets provided to the bank over the value of recoveries from the loans taken over. The cost to the government is essentially a recognition of losses it sustained in the past by implicitly guaranteeing the obligations of banking institutions. The issue of government securities in the recapitalization process has no immediate impact on expenditures for goods and services. Neither the government nor the bank buys anything and the depositors are no wealthier then before. However, the government is saddled with a future interest burden whose capital value is related to the amount of the recapitalization.

In some cases open bank assistance is linked to efforts to find another bank that will put in new capital. Usually the government must provide funds to replace doubtful assets. In Senegal, for example, the Credit Lyonnaise became the majority shareholder in Union Senegalais de Banques.

If the open bank assistance process could be completed speedily it would be a way of minimizing the financial disruption associated with bank failures. But in practice the process has been a tortuous one. In both The Gambia and Ghana the process of loan evaluation and recapitalization took a long time. In the meantime bank lending was inhibited by supervisory restraints on the undercapitalized banks. Moreover, in Ghana banks felt constrained to give preference to loans to indebted customers in order to avoid forcing them into bankruptcy and generating further losses.

The third approach is to permit banks with doubtful loans on their books to continue operating normally in the expectation that an improvement in general economic conditions will enable borrowers to pay off their debts and restore the banks to solvency. Under the right macroeconomic circumstances, together with improved supervision to reduce the number of new loans to weak borrowers, that approach may succeed with those banks whose position before reform is not too bad.

Supervision and Deposit Insurance

African banking debacles have caused a number of governments to overhaul their agencies for bank examination and supervision. The largest scale reorganization of bank supervision is underway in the West African Monetary Union. There the BCEAO, which serves as central bank for the Union, has established a new supervisory commission that will supersede the bank supervisors of the individual member countries. The new commission is expected to conduct frequent audits. It is hoped that the supranational authority will be able to take effective action to improve bank lending procedures.

The central banks in other countries are developing new supervisory standards and stepping up their staff training programs while the bank rehabilitation process is still underway. Nigeria and Kenya have established formal deposit insurance. In Nigeria the new Nigerian Deposit Insurance Corporation (NDIC) will also be largely responsible for bank supervision. The new corporation begins its work at a time when the portfolios of insured banks include a substantial proportion of nonperforming loans. At first, the insuring agency will not liquidate the failed banks. In effect the insurance program reinforces the government's commitment to the depositors (at least up to the amount covered) so that the danger of runs on the bank may be reduced. It is hoped that, in time, improved banking practice and continuing inflation may bring some banks back to solvency.

Bank failures in Africa and elsewhere serve to highlight the potential costs of a formal deposit insurance program. That concern is reinforced by the limited effectiveness of bank supervision in many African countries. Nonetheless, it is not possible for African governments to simply ignore the problems that are addressed by deposit insurance. In most SSA countries governments have an implicit commitment to protect depositors. In the event of bank failures there are strong pressures on the government to honor that commitment.

The most important thing is for each government to do what it can to limit the risk of failure. They can begin by resisting any tendency to pressure banks to lend to poorly managed government corporations or to participate in subsidized loan programs for politically favored groups. They can improve bank supervision and take prompt action to enforce their prudential regulations effectively.

Nonetheless, there will be insolvencies, and governments must have some policy for dealing with them. They have to decide whether to insure all deposits, only small ones, or none at all. They also must decide how to deal with banks that fail or are about to do so. They can force banks to liquidate or arrange a merger that will usually require an infusion of cash by the government. Finally, they can provide open bank assistance, covering the bank's losses, providing cash as needed, and ultimately recapitalizing the bank.

Any disposal procedure can be used with any insurance arrangement. In practice the insurance system is bound to affect the way in which the authorities deal with a failing bank. If all depositors are covered, the government can choose what appears to be the cheapest method of dealing with the bank. Uninsured depositors will be protected if the bank is kept open or sold to another bank that assumes its liabilities. In a liquidation, uninsured depositors will have to share the losses with the government.

In considering its options governments will have to judge whether there are realistic possibilities for selling failed banks, especially when the number of banks is very small, and they will have to recognize that a liquidation will impose considerable costs on borrowers who will have to establish new connections with other banks. In many cases it will appear that the only feasible option is open bank assistance. In that case, of course, it will make little difference after a failure whether depositors are insured or not.

It may make a difference beforehand if there is some uncertainty about the fate of failed banks so that surveillance by large uninsured depositors may exert some influence on the banks' risk-taking choices. In general, depositor surveillance has not been effective in preventing banks from getting into trouble. On the other hand, uninsured depositors will leave a bank that is known to be weak. Their action is likely to force the supervisors to take action and will prevent the bank management from continuing to raise funds in the hope of gambling its way to survival. In view of the political links between banks and government, the flight of uninsured depositors may be needed to induce regulators to act. Note, however, that the role of the uninsured depositors depends on their expectations about the supervisors' actions. If banks are deemed too big to fail, everyone is insured anyway.

Although circumstances vary from country to country, a case can be made for insuring the small depositors and not insuring large depositors. Resolution of failures by the cheapest means should then be the preferred procedure.

The no-insurance alternative leaves all the options open but also leaves the government exposed to pressures to avoid liquidations. Those pressures can be reduced by offering risk-free options such as savings bonds or postal savings accounts to depositors who are especially interested in safety. Another alternative would be a two-tiered banking system with tightly regulated full service commercial banks, together with less regulated "merchant banks" taking only large deposits.

Money Market Development

A number of African countries are working to develop short-term security markets. The central banks of Ghana, The Gambia, Nigeria, and Zambia have been holding auctions for Treasury bills. These auctions have a dual purpose. They can provide a means for indirect control of the monetary base. It is also hoped that when the auction is well established, nonbank buyers may be induced to hold bills and a secondary market will gradually develop.

The bill auctions are conducted in very thin markets with only a few banks participating. There is reason for concern about excess volatility or that banks will collude in making bids. However, the main difficulty in developing these auction markets appears to be the reluctance of the governments to pay the interest rate required to sell the amount of bills originally scheduled for auction. The central bank can, if it wishes, choose the amount to be sold after examining the bids and can therefore set the price by adjusting the volume. Moreover, it can let the banks know what range of bids will be considered acceptable.

Nonetheless, it does appear that, with some experience and a desire on the part of the government and central bank to make the auction succeed, a real market for bills can be developed. In The Gambia, where the central bank had offered bills on tap for several years, the central bank has been able to sell the targeted amount of bills. Some nonbank government enterprises have participated in the auctions, although private bids have been negligible. The prices at the auction have been relatively stable, but this may reflect the recognition by the parties involved of the need for stability.

In Ghana the central bank was for a time unable to sell the targeted amount of bills because it did not wish to entertain bids at rates high enough to clear the market. More recently the auction has been more successful and now plays a significant role in the reserve control process. Ghana has tried to foster the secondary market by establishing a discount house following the British pattern. The market has remained thin because of difficulties in launching the bill auction and such complications as variations in the eligibility of different government security issues for rediscount at the central bank.

Indirect Control of Money Supply

The establishment of short-term security markets is a useful step in building a market-based credit allocation system since the yields on a standard, low-risk, short-term security can establish a uniform cost of funds to all lending institutions as well as a minimum opportunity cost for lenders. It also provides a basis for the development of longer-term security markets.

However, the security markets cannot accomplish a rational allocation of available capital resources unless the determination of the aggregate supply of bank credit is consistent with national economic objectives. Central banks may choose to control some monetary or credit aggregate or they may choose to control a central interest rate. In either case their decisions must be consistent with the constraints imposed by international capital flows.

As we noted in the last section, a number of central banks in SSA have been working to develop their short-term security markets and may soon be able to exercise some control by means of Treasury bill auctions. None of the short-term markets is sufficiently developed. Nor are the central banks themselves ready to undertake open market operations. While they await further development of money markets, central banks will need to develop procedures for indirect control that do not depend on the existence of well-developed secondary markets for government securities. The Gambia, Ghana, and Nigeria have had some success in using the Treasury bill auction method to withdraw funds from the market. At some point they will wish to inject funds into the market. That can be done for a time by letting maturing bills run off, but sooner or later they will need to find new methods for increasing the supply of reserve money without lending directly to the government. They will also need to develop procedures for establishing interest rate and monetary aggregate targets as they move from direct credit control to indirect control regimes.

Long-Term Markets

The banking systems of many African countries are being restored to solvency; management and supervision are improving, and central banks are moving toward indirect control of the supply of money and credit. But even with complete success in those areas, African banking systems will still affect only a limited part of the economies in which they operate. When working well, they have provided a safe haven for the part of the population that can save and wishes to do so in financial form rather than invest in their businesses or those of relatives. However, banks offer very limited service to the rural areas where most Africans live. A large part of the savings flowing into banks has been used to finance government deficits or the investments of government enterprises. The remainder of bank assets consists mainly of loans to traders or loans secured by urban real estate.

Critics of African financial systems frequently complain about the lack of formal finance for agriculture and smaller firms and the lack of longer-term lending. Critics are basically correct in asserting that commercial banks do not serve those markets. Funds disbursed as mortgage loans may, of course, be used for other purposes, and although term loans may be uncommon, banks may regularly roll over short-term loans for established customers. Nonetheless, commercial banks give the impression of concentrating on short-term commercial credit.

In a few countries other private institutions provide other types of credit. "Merchant banks" or "finance companies," taking only large deposits and being subject to less restrictive supervision, are capable of providing term loans and of making loans to relatively new or small businesses. Leasing companies can also provide term loans with a different type of security. It is important to recognize that, to make small business loans or lend to new businesses, evaluating borrowers and monitoring their performance may make the cost of lending quite high compared with rates charged to well-established customers.

In all developing countries informal markets supply much of the credit to small and medium-sized businesses and to new ventures. In those markets lenders and borrowers usually have personal connections of some sort that reduce the risks of lending and the need for evaluation and monitoring. Up to a point, then, the need for additional formal channels may be exaggerated. However, the existing arrangements have certain limitations. To the extent that they rely on established connections they do not serve any individuals who do not have banking connections or links to the sources of informal finance.

In many parts of Africa women play an important independent role in agriculture and some types of marketing. The available credit sources are usually inadequate for their activities. Some women in urban areas need additional credit for trading or artisan activities, but a much larger number of the women who can usefully employ additional credit are to be found in rural areas. There are a number of special women's credit programs, mostly sponsored by nongovernmental organizations (NGOs). Experience gained in those programs should be used to broaden their application and to find some way to channel funds to women from the formal financial system.

Although women have special credit problems, the arrangements for providing rural credit are generally unsatisfactory. Finance through marketing boards and government-sponsored cooperatives has often resulted in heavy losses that were ultimately borne by the government. In the past, private traders in cash crops provided some rural credit. Rural traders and shop-keepers also provided credit, using bank loans to supplement their own funds. Much of that activity was undermined by the low-cost credit supplied by government agencies.

Much can be learned from some of the relatively large experiments, such as the ones in Indonesia (Robinson 1992), although there is certainly no general formula for supplying rural credit in all the varying situations to be found in developing countries. It can be said that no credit program is likely to succeed that does not charge borrowers the full cost of loan funds plus the cost of evaluation and monitoring required to operate the program. Obviously, sanctions against defaulters must be enforced.

Capital Markets

In much of Africa the largest-scale enterprises have been those sponsored by the state. Many of those enterprises are being privatized and it is unlikely that many new state enterprises will appear in the near future. It will be necessary for banks, often also newly privatized, to develop their capacity to deal at arm's length with those enterprises and to adapt their lending arrangements to new circumstances. These considerations raise the question about the potential role of debt and equity capital markets in African countries.

Although there has been considerable interest in establishing equity and long-term debt markets, it is doubtful whether any substantial effort to develop formal capital markets can or should be undertaken in most countries of Africa at this time.

Before capital markets can develop there must be a legal framework that provides the basis for issuance of securities to be held by persons or organizations not participating in the management. Shareholders and debtholders must have access to reliable reports of the condition and performance of any companies whose securities they might hold. They can do so only if there are legal requirements for audited reporting of the relevant facts and some arrangements to ensure enforcement of those requirements. The legal framework should be put in place before there is any substantial public trading of securities. Once a legal framework exists, securities can be issued and traded without direct intervention by the government, although with careful government supervision of the market participants to ensure that they comply with the prudential rules.

It seems unlikely that public debt issues will have much success in any country that has not achieved a reasonable degree of price and exchange rate stability. If these preconditions do not exist then such debt issues are likely to be taken up by the banking system, including the central bank, adding to the instability.

Conclusion

The most general conclusion from this comparison of Asian and African financial systems and policies is that most African countries still lack many of the critical preconditions for so-called "modern" financial institutions and markets. For this reason they should concentrate on fairly simple and basic aspects of financial development rather than push for new instruments and markets that require sophisticated communications, a well-developed legal infrastructure, and efficient supervision and regulation for their success.

Fancy new financial gadgets will not solve the underlying macroeconomic problems or promote rapid industrial development. The important objectives are to improve the basic financial instruments and markets so that (1) the payments system works reasonably well, (2) potential savers have access to instruments and institutions that will provide liquidity as well as maintenance of value, and (3) potential investors with sound projects can obtain part of their financial needs from the financial system on terms that are reasonable and reliable. Once those objectives have been attained, it is time to begin preparation of the legal, human, and institutional infrastructure for more complicated financial activities.

NOTES

1. The CFA franc was finally devalued by 50 percent in January 1994.
2. The exceptions include the Philippines on several occasions, Thailand, and Malaysia in the early 1980s.
3. The Philippines is, again, an exception.

4. See Patten and Rosengard (1991) and Robinson (1992) for a detailed discussion of these programs.

5. See Sundararajan and Balino (1991), who describe banking crises in Thailand and the Philippines as well as in several Latin American countries. In Thailand the problems arose in the finance companies and had little impact on the banking system. In the Philippines there was general loss of confidence in the government in the early 1980s that resulted in a shift away from bank deposits. But the government managed to rescue enough of the big banks so that there was not a major flight from the peso.

BIBLIOGRAPHY

Callier, Philippe, ed. 1991. *Financial Systems and Development in Africa.* Washington, D.C.: World Bank, Economic Development Institute.

Caprio, Gerard Jr., and Patrick Honahan, eds. 1991. *Monetary Policy Instruments for Developing Countries.* Washington, D.C.: World Bank.

Cheng, H. S., ed. 1986. *Financial Policy and Reform in Pacific Basin Countries.* Lexington, Mass.: Lexington Books.

Cole, David C. 1988. "Financial Development in Asia." *Asian-Pacific Economic Literature,* Volume 2, Number 2: 26–47. Canberra, Australia: National Center for Development Studies, Australian National University.

———. 1993. "Financial Reforms in Four Southeast Asian Countries: Indonesia, Malaysia, Philippines and Thailand." Conference on Financial Sector Development in Asia, September. Asian Development Bank, Manila.

Cole, David C., and Hugh T. Patrick. 1986. "Financial Development in the Pacific Basin Market Economies." In *Pacific Growth and Financial Interdependence,* ed. Augustine H. H. Tan and Basant Kapur. Sydney: Allen and Unwin.

Cole, David C., Hal S. Scott, and Phillip Wellons. 1994. "The Asian Money Markets: An Overview." In *Asian Money Markets: Focus of Financial Policy,* ed. David C. Cole, Hal S. Scott, and Phillip Wellons. New York: Oxford University Press.

Cole, David C., and Betty F. Slade. 1991. "Reform of Financial Systems." In *Reforming Economic Systems in Developing Countries,* ed. Dwight H. Perkins and Michael Roemer. Cambridge, Mass.: Harvard University Press.

Davies, Gethyn. 1960. *Central Banking in South and East Asia.* Hong Kong: Hong Kong University Press.

Duesenberry, James S., and Malcolm McPherson. 1991. "Monetary Management in Sub-Saharan Africa: A Comparative Analysis." Harvard Institute for International Development, CAER Discussion Paper Number 7, June.

Effros, Robert C., ed. 1982. *Emerging Financial Centers, Legal and Institutional Framework.* Washington, D.C.: International Monetary Fund.

Emery, Robert F. 1970. *The Financial Institutions of Southeast Asia.* New York: Praeger.

———. 1991. *The Money Markets of Developing East Asia.* New York: Praeger.

Fry, Maxwell. 1988. *Money, Interest, and Banking in Economic Development.* Baltimore: Johns Hopkins University Press.

Goldstein, Morris, David Folkerts-Landau, Mohamed El-Erian, Steven Fries, and Liliana Rojas-Suarez. 1992. *International Capital Markets: Developments, Prospects, and Policy Issues.* Washington, D.C.: International Monetary Fund.

International Monetary Fund. 1992. *International Financial Statistics Yearbook 1992.* Washington, D.C.

Lin, See-Yan, Chung Tin-Fah, Lim Chee-Sing, and Wan Hamdan. 1990. *Money Markets in Malaysia.* Kuala Lumpur: Bank Negara Malaysia.

McKinnon, Ronald I. 1973. *Money and Capital in International Development.* Washington, D.C.: Brookings Institution.

Nascimento, Jean-Claude. 1991. "Crisis in the Financial Sector and the Authorities' Reaction: The Philippines." In *Banking Crises: Cases and Issues,* ed. V. Sundararajan and T. J. T. Balino. Washington, D.C.: IMF.

Patten, R. H., and Rosengard, J. 1991. *Progress With Profits: The Development of Rural Banking in Indonesia.* San Francisco: ICS Press.

Rhee, S. G. 1992. *Securities Markets and Systemic Risks in Dynamic Asian Economies.* Paris: OECD.

Robinson, Marguerite S. 1992. "Rural Financial Intermediation: Lessons from Indonesia: Part One. The Bank Rakyat Indonesia: Rural Banking, 1970–91." Harvard Institute for International Development, Development Discussion Paper Working Series, October.

Scott, R. H., K. A. Wong, and Y. K. Ho, eds. 1986. *Hong Kong's Financial Institutions and Markets.* Hong Kong: Oxford University Press.

Shaw, Edward. 1973. *Financial Deepening and Economic Development.* New York: Oxford University Press.

Skully, Michael T., ed. 1982. *Financial Institutions and Markets in the Far East.* New York: St. Martin's Press.

———, ed. 1984. *Financial Institutions and Markets in Southeast Asia.* New York: St. Martin's Press.

Sundararajan, V. and T. J. T. Balino, eds. 1991. *Banking Crises: Cases and Issues.* Washington, D.C.: IMF.

Tan, A. H. H., and Basant Kapur, eds. 1986. *Pacific Growth and Financial Interdependence.* Sydney: Allen & Unwin.

Tseng, Wanda, and Corker, Robert. 1991. *Financial Liberalization, Money Demand, and Monetary Policy in Asian Countries.* Occasional Paper 84. Washington, D.C.: International Monetary Fund.

World Bank. 1992. *World Tables 1992.* Washington, D.C., 22.

CHAPTER 10

Foreign Direct Investment

Louis T. Wells, Jr.

Across Africa economic reform programs place high hopes on foreign direct investment (FDI). In the past the policies of most African countries toward FDI reflected a skeptical view of such investment. With reform, new legislation reflects the expectations that foreign investment will make up substantial parts of the shortfall in capital needed for investment and will provide technology, management skills, and access to foreign markets. By the late 1980s change was visible in many African countries. By 1988, according to the Annual Report of the International Finance Corporation, revised or new foreign investment laws were being introduced in more than twenty Sub-Saharan African countries (Bennel 1990, 155).

On occasion, the experience of Asian developing countries is cited when African countries seek foreign investment. Yet Asian experiences offer complex lessons. They suggest that some of the hopes with respect to foreign investment are probably too high; that the new legislation in Africa favoring foreign investment must be accompanied by more difficult macroeconomic reforms to generate significant inflows of FDI; and that certain of the successes of Asia cannot be repeated because of changes in the structures of the world industries involved.

Today, the amounts of foreign direct investment in some Asian countries stand in sharp contrast to figures for Africa. In 1990 the ASEAN countries received five times the amount of foreign investment that went to all of Africa (Table 10.1). Although FDI accounted for more than 25 percent of domestic capital formation in Botswana and Swaziland, it was important

TABLE 10.1
Foreign Direct Investment Inflows by Region (millions of dollars)

Host region	Annual average, 1980–85	1990
African countries	1,411	2,196
Oil exporting	1,044	1,633
Other	367	563
ASEAN countries	2,913	11,579
Brunei	−1	−1
Indonesia	227	964
Malaysia	1,058	2,902
Philippines	35	530
Singapore	1,330	4,808
Thailand	264	2,376
East Asian countries	825	2,828
Korea	98	715
Hong Kong	542	783
Taiwan	185	1,330

SOURCE: United Nations, *World Investment Report 1992* (New York), Annex Table 1.

otherwise only in Côte d'Ivoire and the mining and oil countries of Africa (see Table 10.2). In fact, a large part of the investment that has come to Africa from abroad has been concentrated in natural resource industries rather than in manufacturing. Further, when foreign manufacturing firms have invested in Africa, their markets have almost always been local; there has been virtually no parallel to the large investment in Asia to manufacture for overseas exports. (Table 10.3 shows the strikingly high role of FDI in the exports of several Asian countries; no comparable data are available for Africa.)

New development strategies in Africa are leading countries to turn more to foreign investment; nonetheless, Africa's share of all FDI to developing countries has steadily declined since the early 1960s, from about 17 percent in 1960 to less than 6 percent in 1987 (Brewer 1991; Cockcroft and Riddell 1991). In contrast, Asia's share grew steadily to more than half of all FDI to developing countries.

The overall figures mask dramatic differences in the roles of FDI, even among the Asian countries. For 1986 to 1989, inflows of FDI have repre-

TABLE 10.2
Ratio of Foreign Direct Investment Inflows
to Gross Domestic Capital Formation

Host country	1971–75, %	1986–89, %
ASEAN countries		
Indonesia	4.6	2.3
Malaysia	15.2	9.6
Philippines	1.0	8.5
Singapore	15.0	35.2
Thailand	3.0	4.9
East Asian countries		
Korea	1.9	1.6
Hong Kong	5.9	19.1
Taiwan	1.4	3.6
African countries		
Botswana	−24.3	25.7
Congo	31.6	5.2
Côte d'Ivoire	5.4	5.9
Gabon	10.8	9.3
Ghana	9.7	0.9
Kenya	2.9	1.4
Liberia	37.3	8.6
Nigeria	4.9	11.8
Senegal	5.1	−0.7
Sierra Leone	8.6	−28.5
Swaziland	16.1	30.3
Togo	−5.3	2.2
Uganda	−0.8	0.9
Zimbabwe	—	−1.5

SOURCE: United Nations, *World Investment Report 1992* (New York), Annex Table 7.

sented 35 percent of domestic capital formation in Singapore; in Korea, only 1.6 percent. The other East and Southeast Asian countries are scattered between these two extremes (Table 10.2).[1]

By the 1970s foreign investment was no longer a pressing ideological issue in most of Asia. Almost absent was the anti–foreign investment rhetoric that

TABLE 10.3
Shares of Foreign Affiliates' Exports in Total Exports

Host country	Share, %	Year
Korea	29.0	1986
Malaysia	45.7	1988
Philippines	34.7	1987
Singapore	86.1	1988

SOURCE: United Nations, *World Investment Report 1992* (New York), Annex Table 8.

was so popular in Latin America through the 1960s and 1970s and persisted longer in much of Africa. Indonesia was eagerly courting foreign investment in the early 1970s, although its enthusiasm varied over time. Today, Korea and Taiwan, which have long been hesitant, are more open to foreign investment.

Costs and Benefits of FDI

Evaluating foreign direct investment has proved to be a difficult task. Few doubt that it brings capital, technology, management skills, and access to foreign markets. Placing values on these is difficult enough. On the other hand, foreign investment has on occasion been charged with a wide range of evils: importing technology that is too capital intensive; bringing in outdated technology; exploiting local labor; paying local labor too much and thus driving up wages; favoring imported sources of components and materials over local ones; using transfer prices to escape local taxes and to avoid sharing returns with local partners; encouraging corruption; polluting the environment; and so on. Many of the questions that must be resolved are economic, but political and sociological issues loom large as well.

Available studies suggest several conclusions. *First,* under conditions that are common in developing countries some foreign investment is likely to be beneficial and some harmful, the balance depending to a great extent on the economic policies that are in place. *Second,* some of the harmful impacts that critics attribute to foreign direct investment are in fact results of industrialization, whether the means of industrialization are domestic or foreign. The risks of harm in these cases are probably best managed with general policies, such as environmental regulations, antimonopoly laws, and so on, rather than by specifically targeting foreign investors. *Third,* some of the impacts of foreign investment are so complex that they are likely never to be understood fully. The demonstrated beneficial first-round impacts of certain kinds of FDI under liberal economic policies seem great enough that better measurements of the complex subsequent impacts are unlikely to reverse the positive first-round effects.

Dozens of studies have examined the behavior of the foreign investor.[2] They address such issues as whether the foreign firm is more likely to import its inputs than is the local firm and whether its technology choices differ systematically from those of a local firm. They try to measure the employment associated with foreign investment and the impact of such investment on host countries' balance of payments. Such studies have limited usefulness to the policy maker. Frequently, the choice is between foreign investor or no investor for a particular activity; rather than knowing that a domestic investor might be better if he or she were available, the policy maker usually needs to know whether the net impact of the interested foreign investor would be positive or not.

There are now a few studies that have attempted to measure the net benefits and costs in narrow economic terms of foreign direct investment, using various sorts of cost/benefit frameworks. Although the methodologies differ from study to study, the conclusions are strikingly consistent: on the order of 60 percent to 70 percent of the projects that foreign investors propose are beneficial to the host country. In the remainder of them, the costs exceed the benefits.[3] In the best of the studies, the conclusions come after researchers have made a number of adjustments to the measures that companies use to determine their results. Values of the output of plants, for example, are changed to reflect costs to the host country of obtaining equivalent goods from alternative sources (usually assumed to be imports). Shadow prices are assigned to inputs where actual prices do not reflect scarcity values.[4] However carefully done, these studies do not purport to take into account externalities associated with the investments studied. Thus, they ignore benefits such as the training of workers or managers who eventually take their skills elsewhere in the economy, the impact of an investment on other firms by demonstrating good management techniques, and so on. But they also ignore negative externalities, such as pollution and displacement of local savings. Nevertheless, the net benefits from the majority of projects are sufficiently large that it is difficult to believe that the unmeasured negative impacts would offset the measured gains.

Even more important is what these studies have to say about the relation between a host country's policies and the economic effects of foreign investment. The likelihood that a particular project will be economically harmful is closely associated with how much protection from competition the host country grants to the industry. The higher the protection from competing imports, the greater the likelihood that the project will be economically harmful. More open economies have less to fear from foreign investment, at least in economic terms, than do more closed economies. With international competition, the foreign investor is likely to profit only from investments that also benefit the country.

Of course, such research has nothing to say about the political issues involved. Latin American countries have long feared that heavy reliance on foreign investment would increase their dependence on countries that were homes to investors. At the extreme, home countries might intervene if hosts took actions that were not in the interest of foreign investors. Indeed, there was a time when "gunboat diplomacy" might have justified such fears. Recently, however, such intervention has been rare, or at least more subtle. Although the United States has laws that restrict foreign aid to countries that expropriate U.S. foreign investment, and that instruct U.S. delegates to international institutions to vote against loans to such countries, the laws have been used only rarely. It has not been easy to identify many recent cases of strong home country intervention on behalf of foreign investors.

The charges that foreign investors contribute disproportionally to corruption, pollution, and safety problems in developing countries is especially difficult to evaluate. Studies have not shown foreign firms to be more guilty than local firms in these areas. In fact, the foreign firms often come out better. These are largely problems associated with industrialization and should be managed as such, whether the investors are foreign firms or local firms.

Perhaps more serious, foreign investors are charged with creating tastes for expensive, well-advertised consumer goods. They encourage customers to purchase items that cost more than local brands. But with the ease of international communications today, such tastes are easily stimulated even without the physical presence of the foreign firm. Even in Vietnam, where the U.S. embargo prohibits investment and trade by U.S. firms, American consumer products such as Coca-Cola are widely available. If tastes for foreign products are to be stimulated anyway, it may be better to allow local manufacture. In fact, several foreign firms may be better than just one or two, since they may compete away at least substantial amounts of the excess profits that might be associated with marketing skills. Asian experience, moreover, has shown that local firms are not helpless against international marketing giants. They have, on occasion, mastered marketing skills that enabled them to compete successfully with foreign firms. For example, local flashlight battery firms have driven out a major American competitor in Indonesia. Although empirical research has not answered all questions about foreign investment, the evidence is rather convincing that the bulk of such investment is helpful to development and, most important, that the net benefits increase with economic liberalization.

Nevertheless, FDI has played quite different roles at different times and in different countries in Asia, even in the very successful ones. Moreover, the prospects for capturing the potential gains from foreign investment differ according to the sector of foreign investment. Accordingly, this chapter deals first with investment in import-substituting manufacturing and then with manufacturing for export.

Import-Substituting Manufacturing

In Asia foreign manufacturing investment has typically come first for the domestic market, and later for exports. Moreover, the kinds of policies that appear to attract the two kinds of investment in manufacturing have been different.

Some foreign direct investment in manufacturing in Southeast Asia pre-dates independence, but most such investment was made more recently. Malaysia and Indonesia, as well as Thailand, all attracted considerable investment in manufacturing for their domestic markets during the periods in which they emphasized industrialization through import substitution. For example, foreigners owned as much as 56 percent of Malaysian manufacturing in 1974; in Indonesia, foreigners held about 23 percent (Hill and Jones 1984, Table 7). Particularly important, foreign firms brought the technology that was needed for local manufacture. More recently, with shifts in national development strategies, foreign investment has grown dramatically in plants designed to manufacture for export markets. Singapore and Hong Kong have been the principal exceptions to the usual pattern of a rather extensive period of import substitution preceding significant foreign investment for manufactured exports. In both of these sites, extremely small home markets led to an early emphasis on exports.

Asia

Foreign investment has captured quite different shares of the domestic market in different Asian countries. Some countries, particularly Korea and

Taiwan (and Japan), severely restricted foreign investment that was to produce for the domestic market.[5] In 1979 foreigners owned only 13 percent of
Korean manufacturing, a little more than half the share that foreigners
owned in Indonesia and almost a quarter of the share in Malaysia (Hill and
Jones 1984, Table 7, 1974 data for Indonesia and Malaysia).

High savings rates in Korea and Taiwan, and the availability of other
forms of foreign capital in Korea, obviated the need for FDI. The populations of both countries were comparatively highly educated. Korea inherited
at least some industrial base from the Japanese occupation; Taiwan attracted
many entrepreneurs from mainland China as the Communists took over
there. Both countries were determined and seemed able to build their own
technical and managerial skills on these starting bases. When foreign technologies were needed, Korea in particular seemed able to induce Japanese
firms to sell know-how without equity investment. In contrast, by the early
1970s the larger developing countries of Southeast Asia were eagerly trying
to attract foreign manufacturing investment to serve the local market.[6]
Throughout the region Japanese firms dominated import-substituting foreign investment. As the companies that had been supplying the markets
through trade, they were most familiar with the opportunities. They were
supplemented by firms from Hong Kong, Taiwan, and India, along with
scattered investments by firms from the United States and, particularly, the
former colonial powers (Wells and Warren 1979).

Protection of markets through tariffs or quotas served as the principal
incentive for foreign firms. With sufficiently high tariffs or with bans on
imports, a profitable market could be guaranteed for almost any domestically
oriented project. Although Asian governments have frequently offered tax
holidays to such investors, study after study has shown that holidays have
had little impact on investment decisions for firms that serve the domestic
market (Guisinger 1985).[7]

Governments usually intended protection to be a short-term incentive;
with the maturing of infant industries, protection was to be lowered. Yet
once industries were in place, protection came to be regarded as permanent
by both company and government. Many industries established under protection had no hope of becoming efficient. Others failed to become efficient
because the rewards to management from lobbying government for continued or increasing protection were much greater than those that could be
obtained from attention to lowering costs. Labor in the new factories supported continuing protection, recognizing that high wages and job security
derived from the lack of pressure on firms to cut costs. Levels of economy-
wide nominal protection grew as industrialization moved toward upstream

industries. Downstream operations established earlier could not survive with the high-cost inputs that resulted as protection was offered to industries supplying them, unless final products received still more protection. The result was climbing import barriers.

In Asia, the impact of high levels of protection on the efficiency of foreign investment has been clear. In their study of Indonesia, Encarnation and Wells (1986) found that a third or more of proposed foreign import-substitution projects promised negative returns to the economy. A study of domestic manufacturing projects would probably have shown numbers that were not strikingly different, although perhaps slightly smaller as excess rents would have accrued to domestic investors rather than being remitted abroad. The higher the effective protection for an industry, the larger the percentage of projects that seemed to be harmful. Whatever the source of investment, high rates of import protection led to a disjuncture between private and economic profits. Protection distorted the economy so much that investment decisions could not be left to private firms without a substantial risk of many projects that would subtract from national income.

Intuitively recognizing the dangers of harmful investment, countries established screening organizations that were charged with saying "no" to foreign (and, in some cases, domestic) investments that would likely have negative effects on the economy. Indonesia had its Capital Investment Board (BKPM), and the Philippines and Thailand had their Boards of Investment (BOIs). Taiwan and Singapore also had screening organizations.

Most screening organizations in Southeast Asia failed to accomplish the tasks that were at least nominally assigned to them (Wells and Wint 1991). They are widely considered to have failed in singling out harmful investors.[8] Their tedious processes have discouraged foreign investment, much of which would have been beneficial. A study (Encarnation and Wells 1986) found that the screening organization in one Southeast Asian country was as likely to accept as to reject a project that would be economically harmful, as measured by standard economic techniques. Although the screening organization collected the data required for such an analysis, it did not actually do the calculations. In fact, no Southeast Asian country routinely performs serious calculations to determine the impact of a proposed investment on the host economy (Wells and Wint 1991). Such calculations seem to be done only when they are required for financing by an international organization, such as the World Bank. On occasion, some superficial (and misleading) calculations do accompany decisions on awarding investment incentives, but not for the basic approval decision.

As a result, economic analysis has rarely guided the decision process of screening organizations, as international institutions and other advisers expected when investment agencies were established. The decision process in some countries seemed, rather, to be a political one. The screening organization could delay approval in order to give local business (either domestic or foreign-owned firms) or other interests a chance to organize political opposition to the proposed investment. Sufficient political opposition would mean that the project would not be accepted. If strong opposition did not materialize, the project would be approved.

From country to country in Asia, screening organizations have differed in their authority. The Thai BOI could turn down a company for incentives, but the company was free to invest in Thailand without BOI approval if it was willing to forgo incentives. Since the BOI had considerable influence over tariffs, its approval was essential to the profitability of many projects. On the other hand, no foreign company was allowed to invest in Indonesia without BKPM endorsement, and most large domestic investments were also subject to approval. (Separate procedures governed a few industries, in particular oil and the financial sector.)

From a purely economic point of view, recent reforms in Asia have reduced the need for screening projects proposed for the domestic market. With lower levels of protection, the odds have increased that projects that are profitable to an investor will also be beneficial to a country. The reduced protection may mean that less investment is attracted to the local market, but what comes is likely to be beneficial. A number of Asian countries, implicitly recognizing this relationship and eager to rid themselves of the cumbersome decision processes that had failed to reject harmful projects and that discouraged would-be investors,[9] have streamlined the screening process. In Indonesia the time required for approval has been cut to a fraction of what it was.

Africa

Africa has also had some experience with foreign direct investment in import-substituting manufacturing. Even small African countries have their shoe plants (several started by Bata), breweries (often licensed from abroad), and umbrella assembly plants (sometimes owned by Chinese investors). In Africa, foreign investment, or at least foreign participation, has not been unusual in cement plants, textile factories, and factories in a few other industries where efficiency can be attained at small volumes or where high shipping costs and large amounts of protection have provided barriers to import competition. But overall, the level of foreign investment for import substitution in Africa has remained small, principally because of the small size of local markets, but also because of overvalued exchange rates, other discouraging economic policies, and ideological stances, many of which have turned away domestic as well as foreign private investment.

Nigeria has a substantially larger market than most other African countries. Yet even in Nigeria there has been nothing like the foreign manufacturing investment that has characterized the successful Southeast Asian countries. The oil boom of the 1970s and early 1980s supported an overvalued exchange rate and other macroeconomic policy imbalances that tended to make local manufacture uncompetitive, whether by foreign or domestic firms.

What lessons can Africa learn from Asia? Korea and Taiwan do not appear to be useful models for import substitution in most of Africa. African countries do not have especially high savings rates; with declining foreign aid, there is little hope of their receiving much capital from this source; and foreign loans are unlikely to provide further capital. No African country has inherited even the small industrial base that Korea did; nor do African countries have the levels of education that characterized Taiwan and Korea. None has the inflow of experienced industrialists that came to Taiwan after World War II, and there is no equivalent of the Japanese–Korean relationship to enable an African country to import technology without foreign equity.

The experiences of the larger Southeast Asian countries, all of which turned to foreign investment for some of their technology and capital, are more relevant. In no case did foreign investment dominate; domestic savings and technology from other sources were of overwhelming importance. Yet the role of FDI was significant and even very large in Malaysia and Singapore.

The countries that attracted foreign investment followed policies supporting that goal. Import protection was the most important; if high enough, it could lead to foreign investment almost regardless of other policies. But high import protection led to applications from foreign firms for projects that were economically harmful to the host country. Screening organizations were generally unsuccessful in rejecting such projects. There is no reason to think that African countries will screen any better. Thus, they would do well not to emulate the high protection that was granted by some of the Southeast Asian countries early in their industrialization.

As Southeast Asian countries have undergone economic reform and lowered rates of protection, foreign investment has continued for the local market. But investment inflows became more sensitive to other policies once protection declined. If African countries accept that protection should be limited, they will also need to make their investment climate more attractive. Indonesia has shown that tax incentives are not necessary. With economic liberalization, however, convertible currencies, freedom from bureaucratic intervention, and perhaps few restrictions on equity ownership may be required to attract foreign firms to produce for the local market.

Export Manufacturing

A particularly striking difference between Africa and Asia lies in the role of foreign direct investment in export manufacturing. In Singapore, Malaysia, Thailand, and Indonesia foreign investors account for significant and growing exports of manufactured goods. The result has been diversification of exports and greater opportunities for domestic firms to enter the export market. In Africa, it seems, there are only a few parallels: one is Mauritius and perhaps some countries on the rim of South Africa, largely within the Rand bloc, producing for the South African market.

It is in export manufacturing that experiences from certain Asian countries are likely to be particularly useful for a number of African countries. The first lesson is that there is no single "Asian story." Korea (and Japan) relied heavily on the production of locally owned enterprises for export as well as domestic markets. Nevertheless, foreign affiliates accounted for 29 percent of Korean exports in 1986 (see Table 10.3). But nonequity ties were particularly important. Technology was imported through licensing agreements. Initial production may have been for the local market, but exports were soon to follow. Samsung, Lucky Gold Star, and other large Korean conglomerates (*chaebols*) remained Korean owned, although they bought foreign know-how. At the same time, the marketing of labor-intensive exports by smaller Korean firms was frequently handled by foreign buyers; overseas firms contracted production to local companies rather than investing in their own factories. Nike, Reebok, and Adidas entered contractual arrangements with Korean shoe makers to supply sports shoes for their overseas markets rather than building their own factories in Korea.

The overall role of foreign ownership has been somewhat greater in Taiwan, where 20 to 25 percent of manufactured exports originated with foreign firms in the 1970s (Wade 1990, 149).[10] Foreign-owned firms have manufactured locally some major inputs for export industries and a number of foreign firms have operated export-oriented plants in export processing zones. As in Korea, there were many contractual arrangements between foreign buyers and local manufacturers. In the 1970s over half of foreign firms' exports were in electronics and electrical appliances, a sector dominated at the time by foreign enterprises. Access to the domestic market was often conditional on exports. Proposals for foreign-owned projects were considered by an agency that had considerable discretion and that regularly imposed performance requirements, usually in the form of export demands.

Taiwan had an unusually large supply of entrepreneurs and managers because many fled to Taiwan from mainland China during the 1940s. Domestic firms were long protected from foreign investors that might compete with them, particularly in labor-intensive activities. But local firms were closely monitored by government, and protection would decline if their performance indicated that they were not becoming efficient (Wade 1990). Taiwan's bureaucracy was unusually able to check firms' activities against world efficiency standards and to enforce performance requirements. Thus the foreign investor was essential, providing management skills and competition.

Singapore lies at the opposite end of the spectrum from Korea. Few local manufacturers existed, because entrepreneurs were unwilling to build plants to serve such a small market and even less likely to invest entirely for export markets, considered by local entrepreneurs to be exceedingly risky. There were some exceptions: a few local firms were built when contracts with foreign firms moderated the risk, particularly in textiles. But this was not to be the major model for Singapore's ties to foreign firms. Much of the investment for manufactured exports in Singapore was undertaken directly by foreign firms that knew and had access to markets abroad. The result was a heavy reliance on foreign investment, which, according to one source, has accounted for 80 to 90 percent of Singapore's manufactured exports since 1970 (Lim and Fong 1991, 92).[11]

Indonesia offers a third pattern. Richly endowed with mineral and other natural resources, the country long ignored manufactured exports. To some extent, foreign investors participated along with state-owned and private domestic firms to supply the domestic market with manufactured goods. Yet in light of the huge population, total foreign investment was small, only $5 billion from 1980 to 1991 (*The Economist,* March 20, 1993). Recently, however, Indonesia turned to foreign investment in a dramatic and successful effort to develop manufactured exports.

Indonesia was superficially like Korea and might have been expected to behave similarly. It had a potentially attractive domestic market that led to many locally owned, or at least joint venture, manufacturing firms. But the government did not have the tools or the bureaucracy to demand exports of domestic firms as did Korea. A convertible currency, the proximity of Singapore, and the availability of overseas Chinese finance meant that credit allocation (even with state-owned banks) and exchange controls were not useful tools for the Indonesian government to impose its will on local business. Most imports were not subject to license and tariffs and often controls were easily evaded because of a corrupt customs service and borders that are difficult to police. Social contracts that would generate obligations on the part of business were not easy to develop in a country of diverse cultures, especially when the bulk of private domestically owned manufacturing was in the hands of ethnic Chinese. Thus the bureaucracy had neither the tools nor the inclination to move business toward efficiency and export markets. A Korea-like option probably would never have been feasible in Indonesia; it was certainly not the route chosen.

When oil prices fell in the 1980s and manufactured exports were needed to bolster foreign exchange earnings, Indonesia turned mainly to foreign-owned firms' plants to supply foreign markets. Foreign investment approvals more than doubled between 1988 and 1992 and a large portion of these projects aimed to produce for export markets.[12] Manufactured exports grew during this period from $11.5 billion to an estimated $22.3 billion; much of the growth is accounted for directly or indirectly by FDI.

New foreign investment for export was supplemented by some conversions of existing plants established to supply the domestic market. A few foreign-owned manufacturing plants began to export when government desires became clear. Bata, for example, whose local manager had claimed that Indonesia could not export shoes, began to export from its Indonesian shoe factory after the feasibility had been demonstrated by foreign investors. In addition, some large local business groups have responded to the new policy directions.

Malaysia and Thailand had smaller populations than Indonesia, and thus more limited domestic markets, but the constraints of size were not nearly as tight as those of Singapore. Thus, especially in the case of Thailand, considerable manufacturing investment was made by local firms to supply the domestic market. As in Indonesia, relatively free currencies, somewhat open borders, ethnic diversity, and perhaps the limited capabilities of the bureaucracies meant that a Korea-like approach was unlikely to succeed. The tools to force local firms to turn to export markets were largely absent. The early development of export markets for manufacturers was left to foreign investors.

From 1980 to 1991, Malaysia accumulated some $15 billion in foreign investment; Thailand, nearly $10 billion (*The Economist,* March 20, 1993). Western firms built an important export-oriented electronics industry in Malaysia, before the dramatic shift in development strategy occurred in Indonesia. By 1988 foreign affiliates accounted for more than 45 percent of Malaysia's exports (Table 10.3). Like those of Indonesia, Thailand's manufactured exports began to grow recently, and they have involved many of the same types of firms that have been responsible for Indonesia's growing nontraditional exports.

For Southeast Asia, the home countries of foreign investors for export manufacture differed at different times. The shifts are important, since the likely sources of such investment should influence policies in Africa. American, and to a much lesser extent European and Japanese, investors built the early foreign-owned export factories in Southeast Asia. U.S. manufacturers accounted for close to 20 percent of Singapore's manufactured exports in 1977 (Blomstrom, Kravis, and Lipsey 1988), and most of the electronics firms in Malaysia were also American. By 1974 about three-quarters of the sales of U.S. affiliates in Malaysia and Singapore were for exports.

Japanese investors also built some export-oriented manufacturing plants in the region, but their manufacturing investments have, until very recently, remained focused largely on local markets. For Japanese affiliates, export sales were only 13 percent of total sales in Malaysia and 37 percent in Singapore (Hill and Jones 1984, Table 4). In 1983 manufactured exports of Japanese affiliates from developing Asia were only 4 percent of those by U.S. affiliates (Blomstrom, Kravis, and Lipsey 1988). More important has been the increasing export from plants built earlier by the Japanese for the host market. Indonesia's Astra, for example, partly owned by Toyota, had long sold automobiles and auto parts almost entirely on the Indonesian market; eventually it began to supply engines from its new Indonesian engine plant to Japan and Taiwan. The rising value of the yen against the currencies of its major markets has been pushing Japanese firms to look for lower-cost manufacturing bases. Often that has meant the use for exports of plant already established for the local market. Recently, Japanese firms have taken to building more new plants designed principally to serve export markets.[13]

But the story of recent investment for export manufacturing in Southeast Asia has been strikingly different from the past. Throughout the region, the most important sources of such investment have been Taiwan, Hong Kong, and Korea, whose investors seek export platforms particularly in Indonesia and Thailand. The East Asian NICs even have been the largest source of export-oriented foreign investors as far afield as Sri Lanka and Mauritius. East Asian developing countries have been investing in Southeast Asia since the early 1970s, but primarily to serve local markets (Wells and Warren 1979). Many of these investors were ethnic Chinese; often the investment opportunities had been identified by overseas Chinese in the host countries who were related in some way to the foreign owners and familiar with the local market. But even the early wave of East Asian investors included some firms seeking export quotas for markets in the industrialized countries. Hong Kong firms, for example, established affiliates in Southeast Asia to take advantage of textile quotas, when exports from Hong Kong were constrained (Wells, Jr. 1983, 54–57). Although some recent investors from Korea, Taiwan, and Hong Kong have also sought quotas, most have not. They are a new breed.

By the early 1990s firms in Korea, Taiwan, and Hong Kong had a substantial history of exporting to the industrialized countries. They had built valuable reputations with their buyers abroad for reliable quality and punctual delivery. But some of these exports were threatened in the late 1980s as the Korean won and the Taiwan dollar were revalued,[14] and as both countries lost their preferential access (under the Generalized System of Preferences [GSP]) to the United States and other industrialized markets. Moreover, wage rates increased in Hong Kong, Korea, and Taiwan as development progressed; workers were often scarce, even at the going wage, for low-prestige labor-intensive jobs. Hong Kong investors began to diversify their risks in the face of the 1997 takeover of Hong Kong by the People's Republic of China. Consequently, firms from all these countries sought new sites for manufacture, bringing with them the reputations that they had built with buyers from the industrialized countries. Southeast Asia offered low wages and GSP and was nearby. By one account, Taiwan, Korea, Hong Kong, and Singapore firms made up about one-third of all FDI in Thailand, the Philippines, Indonesia, and Malaysia from 1985 to 1991 (*The Economist* 1993).

The recent wave of export-oriented investors from East Asia has been especially beneficial, because the firms have served as catalysts to induce local firms to export. These exporters have attracted unaffiliated foreign buyers, whereas American and Japanese firms usually produce for their own use. Mauritius recruited Hong Kong textile firms, which then attracted foreign buyers who began to visit local Mauritian firms and to place trial orders. Foreign investors have served as catalysts in this and other ways for garment makers in Bangladesh and for shoe and plywood firms in Indonesia (Rhee and Belot 1989). Sometimes the "demonstration effect" of one successful exporter is enough to convince a local firm that it should reach out for more distant markets.

In recent years the increasing importance of exporters among foreign investors has encouraged policy change in Southeast Asia. The screening processes established to approve or reject foreign investment soon proved particularly inappropriate to export manufacturers. Without protection for their output, export manufacturers are unlikely to have harmful economic effects. The risks are significant only if firms produce with subsidized inputs. On the other hand, these foreign investors can be fickle; almost any discouraging policy leads them to choose another of the many low-wage countries that are eager to attract investors. A cumbersome approval process frightens them off.

In response to these factors and the effects of lowered import barriers, Southeast Asian countries began to revise their screening processes. In Singapore, no change was needed; export manufacturers had been the rule from the outset, and the Economic Development Board, Singapore's foreign investment agency, had been designed to attract them, not to reject particular investors. But elsewhere foreign investment agencies began to be viewed as a hindrance. In some cases, efforts were made to streamline the general approvals process; in other cases, the approach was to bypass the old screening agency, especially for export firms.

Policies for Africa

A number of African countries are now looking to foreign markets to sell manufactured goods. Because the countries of Southeast Asia have succeeded in tapping foreign markets for manufacturers, their experiences can be useful for African countries that attempt to follow this route.

A basic lesson from Southeast Asia is that foreign investors can play major roles—and may be essential—in manufacturing for export. They will be needed for their technology and management skills, but especially for access to overseas markets and for their role as catalysts.

Where will those investors come from? Geography and old colonial ties often matter when it comes to attracting foreign firms for export. But neither promises much help to Africa.[15] Mexico and the countries of the Caribbean benefited from their proximity to the U.S. market when they began to emphasize manufactured exports. Similarly, Ireland, Spain, Portugal, and Greece drew advantages from their location on the edge of Europe. In general, African countries do not have similar nearby markets; the exceptions are a few countries on South Africa's borders. Further, unlike Mexico, Ireland, Greece, Spain, and Portugal, many African countries have little prospect of being included in free trade arrangements (except for the limited provisions under the Lomé Treaty) with their major markets.

In recent years, Southeast Asian countries have drawn many of their export investors from nearby East Asian countries. Africa is farther afield from these important home countries. Moreover, as wages rise in the low-wage countries that have benefited from the European Community, Africa does not provide the same obvious attraction for export firms as has Southeast Asia for East Asians. Many such companies are likely to view Eastern Europe, not Africa, as an obvious place to manufacture for the European Community.

East Asian firms have proved willing to locate far from their home countries. Korean firms have recently gone to Costa Rica and are showing increasing interest in Colombia and Mexico. Taiwan firms have already located plants in Africa, although primarily for the local market. Hong Kong firms flocked to Mauritius to gain textile quotas. The evidence suggests that Africa can attract such firms, with proper policies, in spite of its distance.

In Asia and elsewhere, however, export-oriented manufacturers have proved especially sensitive to host country politics. Not interested in the domestic market where they locate, they are free to build their plants in a wide range of countries, so long as their hosts offer low-cost labor and meet certain other needs. They must find an attractive investment climate or they will go to a competing site.

Few African countries offer policies approaching those of the Southeast Asian countries that have attracted large amounts of FDI for export. Those policies have included (1) an appropriate set of macro policies, including a convertible currency, an exchange rate that makes manufacturing profitable, and a corporate tax rate that is "reasonable"; (2) a method under which firms can import, without duty or bureaucratic impediments, components and materials needed for export manufacture (through duty exemptions as in Indonesia, through export processing zones as in Malaysia, or through very low tariffs generally in Singapore and Hong Kong); (3) a foreign investment authority that does not hinder investment (typically the result of administrative reform of a general screening agency or the establishment of a separate body for export firms); (4) successful efforts to reduce or to hold down regulation and bureaucratic hassle (for all firms, as in Indonesia, or through the establishment of less bureaucratic export processing zones as in Sri Lanka); and (5) for countries not well known to potential investors, an effective investment promotion program (as in Singapore and Taiwan). The following sections will explore each of these areas in turn.

Macro Policies

The macro policies that attract foreign firms to manufacture for export markets are similar to those recommended elsewhere in this volume, especially in Chapter 4.

For a country to be a competitive site for exports, it must have an exchange rate policy that leads to costs low enough to enable a manufacturer to profit while selling at world market prices. Even in the absence of exchange controls, Indonesia for some years maintained an overvalued exchange rate that made it rather unattractive to manufacture for exports. It was only after the government devalued its exchange rate and maintained a flexible rate that nontraditional manufactured exports took off. Overvalued exchange rates have been common in Africa, along with exchange controls and import restrictions. Recently a number of African countries, such as Nigeria and Ghana, have moved toward more realistic exchange rates.

Because there are many low-wage countries that have no exchange controls, foreign firms that manufacture for export are unlikely to locate in a country with exchange controls, because of their fear that they will face problems with needed imports and with remission of earnings (with the exception of firms that are seeking textile export quotas, which are scarce and thus have a value that can induce a firm to accept problems that it would otherwise avoid). Exchange controls are almost totally absent in the market economies of Southeast Asia. But not all African countries have abolished exchange regulations that have been major deterrents to foreign investors for export manufacturing.

Investors with a choice of location are reluctant to pay exorbitant taxes, and plenty of potential host countries do not charge high income taxes. On the other hand, numerous studies have shown that taxes, once they fall into a reasonable range, are rarely the decisive factor in investment decisions, except for location decisions *within* a market (Guisinger 1985). The Southeast Asian experience suggests that a reasonable corporate income tax rate is something on the order of 25 to 35 percent, the band to which corporate tax rates in the successful countries have gravitated. The Indonesian experience also shows that tax holidays are not necessary once corporate tax rates are lowered to this range. In the mid-1980s Indonesia's tax reform abolished all tax holidays; yet foreign investors flocked to the country soon thereafter.

Tax holidays have also proved to be a poor substitute for a low general tax rate. If tax exemptions are granted on a permanent basis, the government never collects any taxes and thus loses one of the principal sources of gain from export manufacture. If tax holidays are temporary, the firm receiving them recognizes that it will eventually have to pay the high corporate tax rate and is likely to go elsewhere. When the corporate rate is particularly high, as it has been in Sri Lanka, temporary tax holidays have a way of becoming permanent.

The implication for Africa is that general tax reform is a prerequisite for attracting and obtaining satisfactory benefits from foreign investment for export manufacture. That reform should be accompanied by an end to tax holidays and other exemptions. Such tax reforms are underway in The Gambia, Ghana, Kenya, Lesotho, Malawi, and Zambia.

Imports of Materials and Components

All the Southeast Asian countries that have developed manufactured exports have made provisions for manufacturers to obtain materials and components from abroad without duties.[16] Some such arrangement appears essential if foreign firms are to manufacture for export. There have been different approaches, however (see Chapter 11 for a fuller discussion).

Singapore and Hong Kong imposed virtually no import controls—quantitative or tariff—for the whole economy. The Philippines, Malaysia, and Taiwan created export processing zones, into which investors could import without constraints. Indonesia and Malaysia provided for "bonded factories," which could be located anywhere in the country. Although they were subject to strict accounting requirements and, at the outset, to providing bonds against duties, qualifying firms could import without paying duty. (Indonesia had reduced the bureaucratic problems associated with importing by contracting major customs tasks to a foreign enterprise and dismantling part of its licensing requirements and import monopolies.)

While general tariff reduction, export processing zones, and duty exemption arrangements have all worked, rebate (or drawback) systems have more often failed, although Indonesia offered a successful case for a while. Potential investors have, with reason, doubted that they would receive duty refunds quickly. As a result, they have gone to countries that offered more secure arrangements. Many African countries still promise duty rebates rather than instituting exemption programs or building export processing zones. Rebates are unlikely to prove more attractive to foreign firms in Africa than they have in Asia.

Export processing zones can serve a special role as safe havens for investors who fear domestic turmoil, if the government provides convincing security for the zones. The civil war in Sri Lanka, for example, has been well known to investors. Yet the country has successfully attracted quite a few export manufacturers to locate in its free trade zones, with the promise of security. Some of the African countries with security problems might find this approach useful.

On the other hand, export processing zones tend to be expensive and risky to develop. Thus, one of the alternative approaches to export processing zones—duty exemptions or sharp overall reductions in import restrictions—is likely to be suitable for a number of African countries. African countries can learn a great deal from the original, successful, Indonesian exemption program as an alternative to investing in export processing zones.

Creating an Appropriate Screening Organization

With the shift in emphasis to export manufacturing in countries such as Indonesia, screening organizations have been reformed. The first steps have usually been to accelerate the decision process and to simplify the application process. In Indonesia, the time allowed for the BKPM to make a decision was dramatically shortened to encourage investors. In practice, it became very rare for a proposal to be rejected. Vietnam has similarly tried to legislate shorter approval times.

In the Philippines and Vietnam an additional approach was used. Although the Philippine Board of Investment (BOI) was reformed, with objectives similar to those for the BKPM, a separate, parallel process was established for firms that would locate in an export processing zone. Decisions by this alternative agency were to be quick and virtually automatic. Vietnam has similarly delegated approvals for investments in an export processing zone to the zone administration, which includes a representative of the foreign investment agency (SCCI). Where the general agency is difficult to reform, or where a strong case remains for careful review of other proposed projects, delegation to a separate organization has proved a useful vehicle for handling export manufacturers, whose projects are particularly unlikely to be harmful for the economy.

Reform of the approval process in Southeast Asia has often gone further than cutting the time for review of proposals or delegating decisions on export projects. Other efforts have included shifting from a "positive list" to a "negative list" for foreign investment. Indonesia once had a positive list of sectors that were open to foreign investors. Negotiations often took place about entry into sectors that were not listed. The new welcoming attitude toward foreign investors in the mid-1980s was accompanied by a list of industries that were closed to foreign investors; the positive list was dropped, and industries not on the negative list were open. The goal was to make the negative list as short as possible and to make the outcome of screening predictable to prospective investors.

Other efforts at "transparency," to make the criteria for acceptance clear to would-be investors, have been less successful. Lists of criteria, such as were published in Sri Lanka, have not given weights that were to be attached to sometimes conflicting criteria and the criteria seemed rarely to reflect the actual decision process. Where rejections are frequent, political interests probably dominate economic interests; complete transparency is then a difficult goal to achieve.

In a number of African countries, investment agencies survive that were designed as a safeguard against bad projects under import-substituting strategies and are leftovers from days of a different ideology. They have rarely provided much of a safeguard, if the Asian experience is any guide, but they have almost certainly discouraged foreign investment. With economic liberalization and new ideologies, the agencies are unnecessary relics. If export manufacturing is to be encouraged, these screening organizations should be reformed, as in Indonesia, or bypassed, as in the Philippines and Vietnam. An alternative, under consideration in Ghana in 1993, is the total elimination of the screening function. Ghana would then be like Hong Kong, which does not screen incoming investors; it would also be somewhat similar to Thailand, which does not screen investors who do not seek incentives.

Freedom from Bureaucratic Hassle

Some of the economies of Southeast Asia were heavily regulated in the past. In Indonesia, large numbers of permits were required for almost any business activity, industrial capacity was licensed by volume and by product, and extensive documentation was required for exports. Red tape has been a strong deterrent to mobile export-oriented firms.

Efforts to lessen bureaucratic barriers to business have proved strikingly difficult. Bureaucrats resist attempts to reduce their power (and, sometimes, unofficial incomes). Moreover, some existing businesses have gained from the protection against competition afforded by bureaucratic barriers. None-theless, Indonesia has had some success in deregulation (Bresnan 1993). The key to success seems to have been promotion of the concept of a "deregu-lation policy" and the maintenance of momentum in the form of regular, seemingly significant, steps ("packages") to implement the policy. In many African countries, similar reforms will be required if private investment, foreign or domestic, is to grow.

Promotion Efforts

Investment promotion—marketing efforts to attract foreign firms to a par-ticular country—has become a professional activity. Many countries spend large sums of money on investment promotion; much is wasted. In fact, some of the countries of Southeast Asia that have recently attracted large amounts of export-oriented foreign investment spend very little on invest-ment promotion.

Thailand and Indonesia have recently been in a peculiarly advantageous position with respect to East Asian investment. The Philippines and China, potential competitors, appeared politically risky; the countries of the former Indochina had not yet implemented attractive investment policies; most of South Asia was still mired in bureaucratic problems; and comparatively high wage rates were the rule in Singapore. As a result, Thailand and Indonesia (and, to some extent, in spite of higher wage rates, Malaysia) were in a special position when the currencies of Korea and Taiwan were revalued, GSP status was withdrawn, and China's takeover of Hong Kong was approaching. Moreover, both host countries had significant Chinese populations, and were thus well known to Chinese investors from Taiwan and Hong Kong. As a result, investors from Korea, Taiwan, and Hong Kong came to Indo-nesia and Thailand without the need for investment promotion; there was little competition.

Taiwan and Singapore were in a different position when they began to seek FDI in the 1950s and 1960s. They were relatively unknown to the investors they were seeking from Europe and the United States, and they seemed rather risky. Singapore had racial problems and, for a while, military tension with Indonesia; Taiwan faced the possibility of invasion from main-land China. Both countries mounted investment promotion programs that proved extremely effective in making the countries known to would-be investors and in overcoming their image problems. Moreover, promotion agencies in both countries went beyond efforts to obtain attention and change images; they took steps that would actually generate investment.

Both emphasized personal selling (as have the other well-received promotion programs, such as those of Ireland and Costa Rica). Wade (1990) describes the approaches used by Taiwan to woo wanted investors. These included efforts such as tracking down U.S. managers or their spouses who had had contacts with Taiwanese in their college days. The goal was to provide a personal basis for calling on decision makers in companies to sell them on investment in Taiwan. Singapore's effort, better documented, has been equally aggressive in approaching the management of firms that it wanted. The story of how the Economic Development Board approached and captured Apple computer, for example, has been told elsewhere (Wells and Wint 1990).

Other countries that have not been successful in their promotion efforts have tried to inform and change images by running advertising campaigns, sponsoring investment missions, and developing project proposals, but they have not undertaken the personal selling effort that actually generates investment. They have failed to get their officials to call on managers of prospective firms in their home countries (Wells and Wint 1990).

In investment promotion, organizational issues have proved to be important. Several Asian countries have attempted to convert screening organizations to effective promotion organizations, but the efforts have not been successful. Indonesia's BKPM, which was created as a screening organization, has made virtually no effort at personal selling, although it is now charged with promotion and its screening function has largely disappeared. Although BKPM sponsors investment missions, supports advertising, and prepares project proposals, it has failed to call on prospective investors abroad. The BOI of Thailand has also been charged with promotion. Although perhaps somewhat more successful than BKPM, it has still not done much on the investment-generating side. Much of its promotion effort has been subcontracted to others.

In an effort to dismantle screening and to encourage investment, Asian countries and others have renamed old screening organizations as "one-stop shops." The newly named organization is to provide services for would-be investors, so that they do not have to deal with more government agencies. But the change has rarely accomplished much. The problems of "one-stop shops" have been so great that many investors have called them "one-*more*-stop shops" (Wells and Wint 1991).

Effective investment promotion requires careful targeting. No promotion program has sufficient budget (and sufficient numbers of skilled salespeople) to cover all potential home countries and all potential industries. Targeting must be realistic, aiming at firms with a real reason to consider the country. Usually it is better to build on what is already coming to the country than to try to promote in countries and industries from which investment has not materialized. Some Southeast Asian countries have established overseas offices in countries that have generated little investment, drawing away officials who might have been effective elsewhere. Choices were made based on where officials preferred to live or on funding offered by donor countries.

Experience suggests that export-oriented investors from Europe and the United States tend to move most easily to countries very near the target market. For the United States, this means Mexico and the Caribbean; for Europe, it means Portugal, Ireland, Eastern Europe, and the countries around the Mediterranean (Wells 1992). Historically, the electronics industry has been a major exception, but firms from this industry are now particularly difficult to attract. Wage rates are of declining importance in the manufacturing process, and the externalities, in terms of technicians and proximity to suppliers and consumers, now available in Malaysia and Singapore are too attractive for most other countries to overcome.

The export investors that have come to Southeast Asia from the nearby NICs of Asia have been willing to go farther afield, even to Latin America. Appropriate promotion policies may attract some of them to Africa. These investors may make better promotion targets than firms in the United States, Europe, and Japan. Textile firms from the East Asian NICs may be the most appropriate first targets for African countries because they have been the leading investors in Southeast Asia and still seek sites with unfilled export quotas.

Conclusion

Experiences in Asia offer useful lessons for a number of African countries, but they do not offer solutions to problems that are uniquely, or especially, African. Recent experience in Asia says little about attracting investors to countries with inadequate infrastructure, or to landlocked countries with expensive access to industrialized markets. Although mining and petroleum activities have been developed by foreign firms in remote parts of Indonesia and other countries with little or no infrastructure in place, manufacturing investment in Asia has gone to sites with developed ports, roads, power, and telecommunications.

Moreover, recent experience in Asia has little to say about attracting foreign firms where very low levels of education and literacy prevail, as is the case in many parts of Africa. As the appendix to Chapter 2 shows, Africa today is behind Asia of 1965 on both of these counts, though closer to Southeast Asia than to East Asia.

In spite of the special problems of some African countries, however, there is much for Africa to learn from Asian experience. Obviously, successful policies are not to be copied slavishly. Adaptation will often be required. But it should not be necessary for African countries to repeat all the mistakes made in Asia.

A few warnings are in order: most developing and East European countries that have turned to foreign investment have done so with unrealistically high expectations. Western firms did not flock to Indonesia when it liberalized its investment policies in the late 1960s. Singapore had to work hard to woo foreign firms. There is no large pool of investors waiting for a particular country to institute new policies, as politicians often seem to believe. Countries that have attempted radical reforms, such as Ghana and Nigeria, have not yet seen an upsurge in foreign investment.[17]

Foreign investors tend to be fickle. They follow other firms and succumb to fashions in investment locations. The available data for Africa show declining foreign investment over the 1980s. Starting a new trend is difficult; riding an existing trend is easier.

Further, when policies change, the parties that show early interest typically include an unhealthy share of borderline characters. A number are likely to be promoters rather than investors themselves. Some are simply swindlers. Others bring little money. In the early arrivals are typically groups that want to build hotels and similar travel facilities with others' money, or establish consulting firms to guide other investors who might appear. This can be discouraging to policy reformers.

Moreover, for few countries has foreign investment served as the major engine of growth. Only in Singapore, Hong Kong, and Malaysia has foreign investment accounted for more than 10 percent of domestic capital formation. Foreign direct investment is not likely to serve as the solution to shortfalls in capital needed for investment; it will contribute, but other sources must be tapped. Singapore, with the largest amount of foreign investment in Asia (as a percentage of total capital), also has one of the highest savings rates in the world. FDI is unlikely to displace the need for domestic savings.

Foreign investment also has political consequences that must be managed. Foreign investors may at first be looked on favorably by the local business community, because they provide markets and joint venture partners. Nevertheless, views of local business leaders often change. Eventually, foreign firms may well be seen as competitors with unfair advantages.

In sum, foreign investment can contribute to Africa's development process, but it is no panacea. It can make its potential contribution to African countries whose governments create an attractive environment and aggressively seek foreign investors.

NOTES

1. For other data sources, see Brewer (1991, Table 4–1) and Lim and Fong (1991, 34).

2. For an excellent summary of the literature, see Grieco (1986).

3. Lal and Streeten (1977); Reuber (1973); Encarnation and Wells (1986).

4. The origin of most of the methodologies lies in Little and Mirrlees (1969).

5. Taiwan's domestic savings rate (28.7 percent) was slightly higher than its investment rate from 1965 to 1981. Korea financed around one-third of its investment from abroad, but one-third of its capital imports came from aid and almost two-thirds from loans; FDI was negligible (Scitovsky 1985).

6. The story of foreign investment in Indonesia is particularly carefully related in Hill (1988).

7. For a summary of this and other research, see Wells (1986, 58–60) and Rolfe et al. (1993, 335–356).

8. The agencies in Taiwan and Korea have been less studied. There is some evidence that Taiwan's screening agency was more effective than those in ASEAN in accomplishing some kind of explicit national policy. See Wade (1990).

9. As will be noted later, the desire for export-oriented investment was especially important in driving reform.

10. Lim and Fong (1991, 94) suggest a declining percentage since 1982.

11. See Table 3 for 1988 data.

12. More than 70 percent of the output of plants owned by East Asian investors was to be exported. (Data are from BKPM approvals, January 1, 1990, to July 31, 1991.) For more information, see Wells (1993).

13. According to a recent survey of Japanese subsidiaries in ASEAN countries, 64 percent of those already existing target the domestic market; for planned subsidiaries, the number was slightly less, at 56 percent (*The Economist,* June 12, 1993, 77).

14. From 1985 to 1992, for example, the Taiwan dollar increased by 50 percent against the U.S. dollar.

15. See Bennel (1990) for UK firms. Little new French investment has recently entered Francophone Africa except for oil (Cockcroft and Riddell 1991).

16. The importance of access to imports was pointed out early by David Morawetz (1981).

17. Nigeria's reforms are described in Brewer (1991) and Ghana's in Leith and Lofchie (1993).

BIBLIOGRAPHY

Bennel, Paul. 1990. "British Industrial Investment in Sub-Saharan Africa: Corporate Responses to Economic Crisis in the 1980s." *Development Policy Review* 8(2): 155.

Blomstrom, Magnus, Irving B. Kravis, and Robert E. Lipsey. 1988. "Multinational Firms and Manufactured Exports from Developing Countries." NBER Working Paper.

Bresnan, John. 1993. *Managing Indonesia.* New York: Columbia University Press.

Brewer, Thomas L. 1991. "Foreign Direct Investment in Developing Countries: Patterns, Policies, and Prospects," *Policy, Research, and External Affairs Working Papers.* Washington, D.C.: The World Bank, International Economics Department, June.

Cockcroft, Laurence, and Roger C. Riddell. 1991. "Foreign Direct Investment in Sub-Saharan Africa," *Policy, Research, and External Affairs Working Papers.* Washington, D.C.: The World Bank, International Economics Department, March.

The Economist, March 20, June 12, 1993.

Encarnation, Dennis J., and Louis T. Wells, Jr. 1986. "Evaluating Foreign Investment." In *Investing in Development: New Roles for Private Capital,* ed. Theodore H. Moran. New Brunswick: Transaction Books.

Grieco, Joseph M. 1986. "Foreign Investment and Development: Theories and Evidence." In *Investing in Development: New Roles for Private Capital,* ed. Theodore H. Moran. New Brunswick, N.J.: Transaction Books.

Guisinger, Steve. 1985. *Investment Incentives and Performance Requirements.* New York: Praeger.

Hill, Hal. 1988. *Foreign Investment and Industrialization in Indonesia.* Singapore: Oxford University Press.

Hill, Hal, and Brian Jones. 1984. "The Role of Direct Foreign Investment in Developing East Asian Countries." Mimeo.

Lal, Sanjaya, and Paul Streeten. 1977. *Foreign Investment, Transnationals and Developing Countries.* Boulder, Colo.: Westview Press.

Leith, Clark J., and Michael F. Lofchie. 1993. "The Political Economy of Structural

Adjustment in Ghana." In *Political and Economic Interactions in Economic Policy Reforms: Evidence from Eight Countries,* ed. Robert H. Bates and Anne O. Krueger. Oxford: Blackwell.

Lim, Linda Y. C., and Pang Eng Fong. 1991. *Foreign Direct Investment and Industrialization in Malaysia, Singapore, Taiwan and Thailand.* Paris: OECD Development Centre.

Little, Ian M. D., and James A. Mirrlees. 1969. *Manual of Industrial Project Analysis in Developing Countries,* Volumes 1 and 2. Paris: OECD.

Morawetz, David. 1981. *Why The Emperor's New Clothes Are Not Made in Colombia.* New York: Oxford University Press for the World Bank.

Reuber, Grant. 1973. *Private Foreign Investment in Development.* Oxford: Clarendon Press.

Rhee, Yung Whee, and Therese Belot. 1989. *Export Catalysts in Low-Income Countries: Preliminary Findings from a Review of Export Success Stories in Eleven Countries.* Industry Series Paper Number 5. Washington, D.C.: The World Bank, Industry and Energy Department.

Rolfe, Robert, et al. 1993. "Determinants of FDI Incentive Preferences of MNEs." *Journal of International Business Studies* 24(2): 335–56.

Scitovsky, Tibor. 1985. "Economic Development in Taiwan and South Korea: 1965–1981." *Food Research Institute Studies* XIX(3): 215–64.

Wade, Robert. 1990. *Governing the Market.* Princeton, N.J.: Princeton University Press.

Wells, Louis T., Jr. 1983. *Third World Multinationals.* Cambridge, Mass.: MIT Press.

———. 1986. "Investment Incentives: An Unnecessary Debate." *The CTC Reporter* 22: 58–60.

———. 1992. "Conflict or Indifference: U.S. Multinationals in a World of Regional Trade Blocs." *Technical Papers,* Number 57. Paris: OECD Development Centre.

———. 1993. "Mobile Exporters: New Foreign Investors in East Asia." In *Foreign Direct Investment,* ed. Kenneth A. Froot. Chicago: University of Chicago.

Wells, Louis T., Jr., and V'Ella Warren. 1979. "Developing Country Investors in Indonesia." *Bulletin of Indonesian Economic Studies* 15(1): 69–84.

Wells, Louis T., Jr., and Alvin Wint. 1990. *Marketing a Country: Promotion as a Tool for Attracting Foreign Investment.* Occasional Paper 1, Foreign Investment Advisory Service. Washington, D.C.: IFC/MIGA.

———. 1991. *Facilitating Foreign Investment: Government Institutions to Screen, Monitor, and Service Investment from Abroad,* Occasional Paper 2, Foreign Investment Advisory Service. Washington, D.C.: IFC/MIGA.

CHAPTER 11

Trade Policies and the Promotion of Manufactured Exports

Catharine Hill

It is generally believed that expanding exports, particularly of manufactured goods, contributes to growth and development. Given the experience of the Asian economies, what types of policies can the African economies pursue to encourage exports in general, and the export of manufactured goods in particular? From the 1950s and 1960s onward, Asian countries employed export processing zones, tariff and licensing rules guaranteeing exporters access to imports at world market prices, and policies to facilitate the marketing of exports on world markets. But were these approaches intended to offset disincentives created by the macroeconomic environment and other policy interventions, or to resolve some specific microeconomic market failures? This chapter examines Asia's experience to discover how successful their export promotion policies have been, and how they might be applied in Africa.

Theoretical Justifications for Promoting Exports

Two types of argument can be made for export promotion policies. Export promotion policies may be used to offset the antiexport bias in the economy from other policy interventions, resulting in more neutral incentives across sectors. Alternatively, exports may be promoted in the belief that externalities are inherent in growing exports, in which case policy makers would want to encourage exports further, not just offset disincentives from other policies (Milner 1990b; Falvey and Gemmell 1990). In both cases, export promotion policies are justified on the grounds that export levels are less than optimal. Increasing exports may contribute to increased welfare through either static resource reallocation effects or increased growth.

Antiexport bias can result from a variety of policy interventions. Import restrictions, including tariffs and quantitative restrictions, are a major cause of such bias. Consider an economy with three sectors: exportables, importables, and nontradable goods. Assume the country is small, so that the world prices of traded goods are given. A tariff or quantitative restriction will increase the domestic currency price of imports relative to exports. If the export sector uses imports as inputs, the export sector will be further discouraged. This is the "input tax" source of antiexport bias (Milner 1990b, 91).

The real exchange rate, which measures the relative price of tradable goods to nontradable goods in the economy, also affects the profitability of both exports and imports relative to nontradable goods. An overvalued exchange rate is often defined as one where the price of nontradable goods in the economy is too high relative to the price of tradable goods. This results in more production of nontradables and in less production and more consumption of tradables than would otherwise occur or is considered optimal.

Removing distortions discouraging exports contributes to the textbook static benefits of moving toward free trade. Removing antiexport biases can also be associated with increased competition and the possibility of exploiting economies of scale. Increased competition could result in both static gains, by reducing monopoly losses, and dynamic benefits from increased growth. Through these channels, exports may contribute to or be associated with improved economic performance (Dornbusch 1992).

If exports are discouraged by some set of policies, the first-best solution is to change those policies: liberalize imports or change the exchange rate. If for some reason this is not an option, export promotion policies such as subsidies may be a second-best solution. A set of commercial policies could be designed that removed all antiexport bias but would still be second best to the nonintervention case, because of the administrative costs of these policies, which can be high.

In thinking about using export promotion policies as second-best solutions to remove antiexport bias, it is very important to keep in mind the reasons why the first-best options are not available. Policy makers should question whether the same constraints affect the likelihood of second-best policies being successfully adopted. For example, if a government is unwilling to remove tariffs on imports because it both wants to protect the import sector and needs the tariff revenue, a second-best export subsidy is going to be no more acceptable to the government than the first-best solution of removing the tariff. Export subsidies use government revenue and shift incentives away from the protected import substitutes. As an example, when Thailand adopted trade reforms in 1982, tariff reductions were constrained by the government's reliance on tariffs as a source of revenue (Bhattacharya and Linn 1987). This constraint on reducing tariff protection clearly also constrained the second-best policy of offsetting the incentive effects of tariffs with export subsidies.

In some cases, the first-best policy may not be an option because of institutional constraints. For example, nominal exchange rate changes are not an option in the African CFA zone countries. In this case, second-best policies may have to be used, and the inability to use the first-best policy need not imply anything about the likelihood of success of second-best policies.

It has also been argued that, in some cases, export promotion policies may be first-best policies. If there are external economies to exports, promotion of exports beyond just offsetting existing disincentives would be justified (Findlay 1984). For example, exporting may be an effective method of learning or of importing technologies or foreign know-how. If some of this knowledge spills over and benefits firms or individuals other than just the exporter, then there are positive externalities to exports and specific export promotion would be justified. For export promotion to be first-best, these externalities would have to exist for export production and not tradable goods production more generally. If the externalities result from the traded goods sector as a whole, not just exports, then a preferred policy would affect both the import and export sectors relative to nontradables.

Before specific examples of export promotion policies are examined, the relationship between these policies and the macroeconomic environment needs to be addressed in more detail. Specific trade policies cannot easily substitute or compensate for an overvalued exchange rate or an unstable macroeconomic environment. In theory, a set of export incentives and import restrictions could be devised that offset any disincentives from the macro-economy, but the degree of precision and responsiveness implied for government policy is unrealistic. These policies have proven to be relatively difficult to "fine-tune" and adjust often, in part because special interest groups arise. The pressures on the economy leading to an overvalued exchange rate and macroeconomic instability would also operate to make the adoption of such a set of policies extremely difficult. As an example, if macroeconomic instability results from large government deficits, export subsidies are probably not an option for the government because of effects on the deficit. Similarly, government deficit concerns will make investment in export-oriented infrastructure or duty-free access to imports more difficult.

The credibility and sustainability of policies are also important if they are to be effective. Trade and microeconomic policies to encourage exports will not be viewed as either credible or sustainable in an environment of macroeconomic instability and macroeconomic disincentives to exports. The desired allocation of resources to exports is unlikely to be forthcoming under these conditions.

Exports and Economic Growth: Empirical Evidence

The relationship between growing exports and growing national income would seem to command as great a consensus among economists and policy makers as any proposition about economic growth. A glance at the data of nine East and Southeast Asian countries and a sample of African countries, arrayed in Figure 11.1, confirms expectations. The Asian countries lie almost entirely in the northeast corner of the scatterplot, with higher export growth and higher GDP growth. African countries lie mostly to the southwest, with lower growth rates for both variables. The major exceptions are Botswana and Mauritius, African success stories, and the Philippines, Asia's laggard.

Much work has been done on the relationship between trade and growth. Early evidence for a larger group of countries is reviewed in Balassa (1989) and Pack (1989). The 1987 *World Development Report* discusses at length the benefits of an outward-oriented trade strategy. There is a large recent literature on the empirical relationship between outward-oriented policies and economic growth, including Harrison (1991), Matin (1992), and Dollar (1992). The 1991 *World Development Report*, surveying the empirical evidence, concludes that most studies find a positive relationship between GDP growth and openness, using a variety of measures of openness and controlling for a variety of other variables. In particular, if factor input use is controlled for, the empirical evidence supports a positive relationship between productivity growth and openness or exports. The more recent evidence is also reviewed in Dornbusch (1992), who quotes Edwards (1991):

> The sum of the evidence (though few individual pieces) amounts to persuasive evidence of the beneficial effects of an outward trade orientation. The conventional wisdom has become that increasing exports successfully contributes to economic growth.

Some caution is warranted. The 1991 *World Development Report* discusses the problems of using actual trade flows as a proxy for trade policies and the problems with measuring trade policies more directly. The empirical evi-

FIGURE 11.1
Exports and GDP Growth

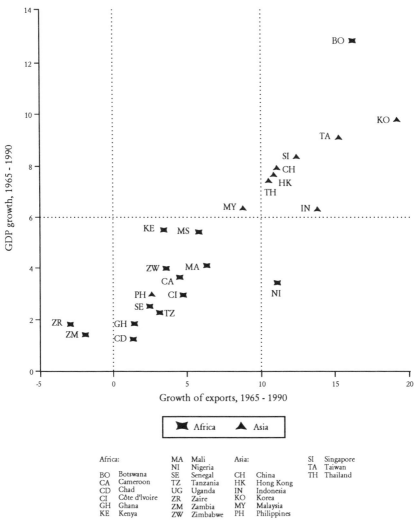

SOURCE: World Bank, *World Development Report 1992* (Washington, D.C., 1992).

dence is also problematic because of the need to control for all the other variables that affect growth. It is possible that some other set of policies explains both trade performance and economic growth. There are questions about whether cross-section data alone are adequate for the empirical work. Finally, there are still unresolved issues relating to causality and robustness.

Levine and Renelt (1992) examine the results of recent cross-country growth regressions that look at the statistical relationship between growth and a variety of variables. They stress that these regressions are not structural models and cannot establish causal relationships. They also conclude that the results are very sensitive to small changes in the variables on the right hand side. Levine and Renelt do find a positive and robust correlation between growth and the share of investment in GDP and between the ratio of trade to output and the investment share.

The empirical evidence on the links between exports or trade policies and growth, therefore, is quite suggestive but far from simple and conclusive. Given the nature of the theoretical relationships between exports and economic performance and the theoretical explanations for growth more generally, we should not be surprised that there is not a simple and clear empirical relationship. Nonetheless, the theoretical arguments and the existing empirical evidence have been considered adequate foundations for the profession, if not always the countries concerned, for policy advice recommending increased outward orientation.

The data of Figure 11.1, showing that Africa's export growth and GDP growth have both been significantly slower on average than East and Southeast Asia's, suggest there may be a role for export promotion policies in promoting growth in Africa.

International Constraints on Export Promotion Policies

The external environment facing the African economies in the 1990s is significantly different from that facing the Asian economies as they turned toward outward-looking strategies in the 1960s and 1970s. This may affect some of the policy choices that the African economies make and the subsequent impact these policy choices have on their economies. There is much evidence, however, that even in the world economy of the 1990s there will be net benefits from increased outward orientation.

Real GNP in the industrial countries and world trade have grown over the last three decades, which improves the prospects for exports. Despite significant slowdowns in the 1980s, the industrial countries are increasingly affluent. East and Southeast Asia, including China, are themselves new potential markets. Tariff rates have fallen significantly as a result of the GATT:

the average tariff rate on products in industrial countries in 1988 was about 5 to 6 percent, down from about 40 percent in the late 1940s.

Offsetting these positive developments, protectionist pressures in industrial countries increased significantly in the 1980s, resulting in increased nontariff barriers to trade. The IMF (Kelly et al. 1988) reports that the share of industrial country nonfuel imports subject to nontariff protection increased from 19 percent in 1981 to 23 percent in 1987, and to 25 percent on imports from developing countries. The number of voluntary export restraint arrangements (VERs) increased from 135 in September 1987 to 261 by mid-1988 (Kelly et al. 1988, 1). Much of the protection is against sectors in which developing countries, especially those in the upper middle income range, have comparative advantage. The NICs have been most often subject to antisubsidy responses in the industrial countries in the 1980s (Thomas and Nash 1991, 185).

The increase in nontariff barriers, including VERs, has contributed to discrimination in the treatment of exports from developing countries. The Multifibre Arrangement (MFA), which restricts exports of textiles and clothing, is the major example and has become increasingly restrictive. This removes from free international competition a large sector in which many developing countries have comparative advantage. The MFA has affected export processing zones (EPZs) in particular, because much production in EPZs is textiles. Many investors in EPZs in Southeast Asia and elsewhere are from textile-exporting East Asian countries that face binding quota restrictions in their home countries. In 1980 about half of the investment in Sri Lanka's EPZ was by textile-exporting countries facing quotas. Although the MFA works against East Asian exporters (and increasingly against Southeast Asia exports, too), it could represent an opportunity for African countries that, like Mauritius, can attract investment from East Asia.

Export pessimism is not new, as Tomich et al. remind us in Chapter 5. The version expounded by Nurkse and Prebisch in the 1950s has been discredited by the experiences of those developing countries that have successfully exported, as well as by a large empirical literature that does not support the secular decline of the terms of trade for developing countries. More recent export pessimism is based on the new protectionism of the last fifteen years in the industrial countries. Cline (1982) and Ghosh (1992) warn other developing countries against trying to follow the development strategy of the successful East Asian exporters, particularly in the industrial countries' markets. They question whether the world can continue to import sufficiently from the developing countries to make this strategy work.

It is unclear whether the international economy is more or less conducive to exports from developing countries today than it was twenty years ago. For the African economies, the answer may be irrelevant. Even if the world economy were less open than in the past, and if the means to promote exports are more limited, African countries can improve economic performance by increasing their exports. GATT rules clearly constrain developing country choices of export promotion policies (Falvey and Gemmell 1990). They distinguish between export and other subsidies, between export subsidies on primary and nonprimary products, and between export subsidies by developed and developing countries. In general, export subsidies seem to be more available to developing countries but nonetheless subject to trading partner complaints of domestic harm and imposition of countervailing duties. The GATT rules on subsidies are complicated and ambiguous. The GATT does not include a comprehensive definition of subsidy. It does include an illustrative list of export subsidies. The rebate or exemption of indirect taxes is not considered a subsidy, whereas the rebate or exemption of direct taxes is. EPZs, duty rebates or exemptions, and subsidies to export marketing services are all acceptable under GATT. If the goal of policy is the general promotion of exports, however, these are all no better than second-best. The most neutral policies would be the exchange rate and import liberalization policies that are not constrained by the international community.

Specific Export Promotion Policies

The Asian economies have used a variety of export promotion policies. Falvey and Gemmell (1990) divide them into *input-related* incentives, *output-related* incentives, and *externality-related* incentives. Input-related incentives include such policies as tariff and tax rebates and exemptions for exporters and their suppliers on imported inputs, wastage allowances, subsidies on public utility services, special depreciation rules on capital inputs, and preferential credit arrangements. Output-related policies include special tax exemptions, preferential export credits, direct export subsidies, the provision of infrastructure, and government help with overseas marketing. Externality-related incentives include such policies as export quality interventions. These policies have been used by one or more of the East and Southeast Asian countries at various times.

Three widely used export promotion policies in Asia will be examined in more detail here: export processing zones (EPZs), duty rebates or exemptions, and government support for marketing. EPZs combine input-related, output-related, and externality-related incentives. Duty rebates or exemptions are input-related incentives. Falvey and Gemmell (1990) classify marketing support as output related, but it could also be considered an externality-related incentive. The purpose of each policy, the lessons from Asia, and the experience in Africa with use of these policies, both successful and unsuccessful, are examined below.

Reliable Access for Exporters to Imports at World Market Prices

If tariffs or quotas are increasing the domestic price of imports in the economy, the price of importables relative to exportables increases in the domestic market. This discourages the production of exports relative to importables. If all goods are final consumption goods, the production of import substitutes will be more profitable relative to production for export. This will also be the case if some imports are inputs. Exporters face world market prices for their goods but pay higher prices than on world markets for imported inputs, reducing their profitability relative to other sectors.

The purpose of duty-free access for exporters to imports is to offset the disincentive created by higher import prices resulting from tariffs and quotas. A duty exemption system exempts exporters from paying taxes on imported inputs used on export production. Under a duty drawback (or rebate) system (or facility), exporters get reimbursed for duties paid on imported inputs. This can be done on a case-by-case basis with actual duties paid rebated or according to a fixed input-output schedule. The former system reduces distortions more but is more costly administratively. Bonded manufacturing warehouses and EPZs are alternative methods of supplying particular exporters with duty-free access to imported inputs.

It has been argued by Wade (1988b, 1) that duty-free access to imported inputs for exporters is *necessary* for manufactured exports. However, ability to compete will also depend on nontraded factor prices. If these prices are lower than competitors', this can offset the effects on profitability of exporters on world markets of higher imported input costs. A devaluation can, for example, increase the profitability of exporters in world markets. It is therefore not clear that removal of tariffs on inputs is a necessary condition for successful manufacturing exporters, although it is one way to increase incentives if alternatives such as removal of tariffs and quotas throughout the economy or devaluation are not options.

Reliable access to imported inputs is as important as the price (Keesing and Lall 1992, 179). If imported inputs are not readily available, the production of exports will be unreliable, making marketing more difficult.

Duty-free access for exporters offsets the disincentive created by distorted input prices, but it creates other problems. First, the price of imports will differ for different producers. Export producers will have an incentive to use more imported inputs than other producers. This also creates an incentive to sell the imported inputs in the domestic market at the higher protected price, presenting opportunities for rents and, hence, abuse. Second, administrative costs can also be high. Third, government revenue declines.

Experience in Asia

Many of the Asian economies have had programs to provide exporters with access to imported inputs at world market prices. Hong Kong and Singapore, with no tariffs or quantitative restrictions, are examples of the best solutions. Korea and Taiwan, in contrast, with protection for imports in place, have had programs for exempting exporters from paying tariffs on imported inputs (Rhee 1985; Wade 1988a, 1988b). Indonesia also has a policy of duty-free access to imported inputs used in the export sector.

In Taiwan major established exporters do not pay duties. Instead, any duties owed are canceled if proof of exports is shown within a year and a half. Exporters have to supply a bank guarantee for the duty plus penalties. Other exporters get reimbursed for duties paid once exports actually take place. Rebates are based on input coefficients that are established independently by the government to discourage exporters' importing more than necessary and selling in the domestic market at protected prices. For established products, predetermined input-output coefficients are used and published annually by the government. Exporters get rebates up to the published input requirement, based on actual imports. For new products, coefficients are determined individually. Final exporters may claim the rebate if they import directly while suppliers to exporters who import may claim the rebate as well. Financial arrangements have arisen to protect the supplier if the exporter fails to export.[1]

Administrative requirements of rebate programs include determining, revising, and publishing the input coefficients in a timely manner; collecting tariffs; and rebating tariffs upon determination that exports have occurred. The administrative requirements needed to support a system of free trade for exporters but not for the domestic market are significant (Rhee 1985; Wade 1988a, 1988b).

Indonesia introduced a duty rebate system and an exemption system in

May 1986. The decline in fuel prices in the early 1980s threatened to reduce Indonesia's growth and worsen its balance of payments. In response, the government adopted a set of conventional reforms, both macroeconomic and microeconomic, to encourage in particular non-oil or gas exports (Hill 1990; Bank Indonesia, various years). The duty rebate and exemption systems replaced an earlier export credit program, which was dropped in 1985, in part because it was considered a subsidy under GATT rules. Firms that export at least 85 percent of their production are exempted from both import licensing and import duties. Other exporters have access to a drawback facility. By mid-1987 the system was available to all qualified exporters. In December 1987 the exemption from import licensing and duties was extended to firms exporting 65 percent of their production. Its success was supported by reform of the customs service in 1985, under which a Swiss company (Société Générale de Surveillance SA) became responsible for establishing import values and duty rates, among other reforms. This seems to have eliminated corruption and bureaucratic delays for both imports and exports.

The duty rebate and exemption scheme was only one part of a reform package aimed at encouraging exports. The rupiah was devalued twice, in April 1983 and September 1986. Supported by tight macroeconomic policies, this resulted in sustained real devaluation from 1986 on. There has also been some liberalization on the import side. In 1984 the average nominal tariff rate in Indonesia was 33 percent, with a range from 0 percent to 225 percent. Nontariff barriers applied to 20 percent of import categories. In 1985 the highest tariff was reduced to 60 percent and the average to 23 percent (Bhattacharya and Linn 1987, 50–51), and further reductions have been undertaken in recent years. Nontariff restrictions, including licensing and quotas, are being replaced with tariffs. Bonded zones were established and import licensing for exports was liberalized (Bank Indonesia 1986/87). The share of imports subject to licensing was reduced from 30 percent to 15 percent as a result of reforms in 1986 and 1987 (Bhattacharya and Linn 1987). As a result of the entire package, manufactured exports have increased significantly since 1983. Although three products account for most of manufactured exports, there has also been some increased diversification since 1986.

Thailand, the Philippines, and Malaysia also have duty rebate and exemption programs. The World Bank (Bhattacharya and Linn 1987) reports that

the experience with administering these systems of tax exemptions or duty drawbacks has been unsatisfactory, because of limited access (especially by small and indirect exporters) and slow and cumbersome procedures. In none of these countries have these systems been as comprehensive in coverage, automatic in access, and effective in administration, as has been the case in Korea.

Both the Philippines and Malaysia have limited the effectiveness of the programs by having "domestic availability tests," which favor domestic inputs. In Thailand the effect of the program on government revenue has been a concern. This is an example of how second-best policies may face the same constraints as the first-best alternatives. In Malaysia, there have been concerns about abuse of the system, as a result of inadequate monitoring (Bhattacharya and Linn 1987). In discussing Thai textile exports, Suphachalasai (1992) concludes that the duty drawback system has been of some help, but not costless. And the major explanation for growing textile exports has been the country's macroeconomic policies, including a competitive real exchange rate. In the Philippines the duty drawback system is used by only 20 percent of exporters (Noland 1990). Its effectiveness has been limited by not being generally and automatically available to all exporters. In addition, Philippine macroeconomic policies contributed to increasing overvaluation in the 1970s, and export promotion policies could not offset their negative effects on exports (Tecson 1992).

The experience from several Asian economies suggests that policy makers were able to design a variety of programs to make imported inputs available to exporters at world market prices while maintaining some protection of the import sector. This increased incentives to exporters from what they would otherwise have been. In other Asian economies, the policies have been less successful. Exactly how much of the successful Asian exporters' performance can be attributed to these policies has not been determined. Given this, it is difficult to compare costs with benefits. In thinking about policy options for Africa, perhaps a useful strategy is to consider whether the conditions in Africa suggest that likely benefits of such a program would be more or less than in Asia, and whether likely costs would be higher or lower.

Experience in Africa

Two countries' experiences will be discussed, Kenya and Botswana, followed by possible lessons for Africa more generally. Kenya currently has several programs—the Export Compensation Scheme, Manufacturing Under Bond, and import duty and VAT remission schemes—that are intended to give exporters access to imported inputs at close to world prices.

The Export Compensation Scheme (ECS) is supposed to compensate exporters for government taxes on inputs after export. The ECS was introduced in 1974. Originally, exporters of manufactured goods were given a 10 percent payment of the value of exports to compensate for higher costs of imported inputs resulting from tariffs and other government policies. At this time, an earlier duty drawback and rebate system for imported inputs was eliminated. In 1982 an incremental scheme was instituted, to be replaced in 1984 by an increase in the basic rate to 20 percent. (Rebating a flat percentage is administratively much easier than rebating import duties actually paid.)

Analysis of the export compensation and import duty remission programs identifies a variety of problems with the Export Compensation Scheme (Bellhouse Mwangi Ernst & Young 1992). Different exporters receive too much or too little relative to import duties actually paid. In addition, exporters bear the costs that result from the time lag between paying import taxes and receiving compensation. When exporters are uncertain about when, if ever, they will receive subsidy payments or tax rebates, they discount the incentive, which lowers its impact on expected profitability. Lewis and Sharpley (1988) note that in 1984 there were lags in payment up to forty weeks and that few exporters benefited from the program. Total payments equaled only 4 percent of the value of manufactured exports. This could not offset the disincentives of rising tariff rates on imported inputs. In 1990 compensation took over twelve months (USAID 1991, 60). Other analyses of the ECS report that it is difficult to qualify for export compensation and only some exporters benefit from it (USAID 1991, 74).

The Manufacturing Under Bond (MUB) program, instituted in 1984, has not worked. Under this program, all inputs can be imported duty free and all output exported duty free. In 1990 only four producers used the MUB program, and they faced long delays in getting duty-free imports.

Why didn't these policies work in Kenya? One answer is that the overall environment toward exports was too negative. The obstacles to exporting could not be overcome by these policies alone. Lewis and Sharpley (1988) discuss Kenya's policy environment from 1964 to 1984, noting a host of policies discouraging exports:

1. One example is domestic price controls. If a domestic firm could export at a price above marginal cost but below average cost, the government would reduce domestic market prices, eliminating incentives to export (Lewis and Sharpley 1988, 38–39).

2. As discussed in Chapter 4, there is little evidence of an appreciation of

the real exchange rate from 1964 to 1984 in Kenya. Lewis and Sharpley, however, caution that at the prevailing real exchange rate, there was excess demand for foreign exchange that was dampened by other policies, including tariffs, quantitative restrictions, and in some periods contractionary aggregate demand management policies. This suggests that the prevailing real exchange rate was overvalued and discouraged exports, even though little real appreciation had occurred. Kenya's deteriorating terms of trade over this time period contributed to the real exchange rate problem. Kenya's terms of trade index fell from 161 in 1964 to 74 in 1989 (USAID 1991, 8). If Kenya's real export prices had not declined, the prevailing real exchange rate might have been consistent with an acceptable balance of payments. With declining terms of trade, there was instead an excess demand for foreign exchange. The ratio of exports, including nonfactor services, to GDP fell from 31 percent in 1985 to 25 percent in 1989.

3. Increasing tariff protection from 1970 to 1984 implied increased discrimination against exports. Lewis and Sharpley (1988, 60) report doubling of effective protection of import-substitution sectors in Kenya. USAID (1991, 9) reports effective rates of protection for the manufacturing sector of about 90 percent, with some sectors as high as 1,000 percent. This import-substitution strategy has led to a highly inefficient manufacturing sector that is incapable of exporting.

4. From 1971 through the early 1980s import licensing became increasingly important. Starting in 1982, attempts were made to liberalize the system. Quantitative restrictions hurt exporters, not only by further increasing the domestic price of imported inputs, but by making some goods unavailable. Lewis and Sharpley (1988, 60, 64–65) report that before import licensing, firms wanting to import certain types of packaging could do so at higher prices including tariffs, although these were eventually rebated. But with licensing, they in some cases could not import packaging at any price. Some manufacturers trying to export reported that they could not compete on world markets because packaging did not meet world standards. Exporters also need licenses, as well as Customs and Excise Department approvals and approval for transport through the Kenya Ports Authority or the Kenya Air Handling Limited facilities. All of these interventions increase the cost of exporting.

5. Lewis and Sharpley suggest that administration of the sales tax up to 1984 also worked against exports. Exporters paid the tax on imported inputs, to be compensated after exporting. The tax was charged on imports and domestic goods, implying neutral incentives. There was concern, however,

that producers for the domestic market underpaid the tax, increasing their protection relative to exporters.

6. Problems of administration—including the uncertainty of payments, need for payoffs, lack of clear direction from above, and lack of transparent rules—helped to reduce the incentive value of export promotion devices.

Kenya's experience from 1964 to 1984 demonstrates that if the overall thrust of policy is to protect import-substituting sectors, it is unlikely that effective policies will be implemented to offset disincentives to export. The Export Compensation Scheme was intended to do this, but it had very little effect.

New programs, instituted by Kenya since 1990, have tried to revive and reform the duty drawback and exemption programs (USAID 1991, 77). These have been plagued with similar problems, however. Could these programs have been structured to achieve their objectives? It would depend on the government's willingness to forgo tariff revenue and subject domestic producers of intermediates to international competition. The direction of policy over almost three decades suggests the government has not been willing to take these steps.

Botswana is an African economy that has avoided an antiexport bias in its policies, despite its dependence on diamond exports. As a result, manufacturing and manufactured exports have grown rapidly. It is an example of an African economy that has maintained incentives and an orientation more similar to the Asian economies than its neighbors.

Botswana's reliance on diamond exports made it a likely candidate for Dutch disease. But Botswana has employed macroeconomic policies that avoided many of the difficulties other countries have experienced managing commodity export booms. By all measures, no real exchange rate appreciation of any significant size or duration has taken place (Hill 1991), so that nontraditional export goods were not crowded out.

At the same time, Botswana has eschewed the use of protective trade policies. It is a member of the Southern African Customs Union (SACU) with South Africa, Lesotho, and Swaziland, which calls for free trade among the four member countries. South Africa is Botswana's major source of imports, with the customs union accounting for almost 80 percent of imports in 1989. Although this could be the result of trade diversion, with the external tariff being set by South Africa, location and transportation costs make South Africa the most likely competitive source of imports for Botswana.

Under the customs union, Botswana can protect infant industries from competition with tariffs for up to eight years. It has done so only twice, for beer and soap (Harvey and Lewis 1990). In 1982 the government instituted subsidies to some firms through the Financial Assistance Policy (FAP), which was limited to manufacturing and noncattle agriculture. The program therefore neutrally subsidizes nontraditional tradable goods, both importables and exportables.

Helped by these policies, manufacturing growth has been significant. Real manufacturing GDP grew on average over 7.5 percent annually during 1974–85, an indication that Dutch disease has not been a problem in Botswana. Although nontraditional exports (excluding meat, diamonds, and copper) are a small share of total exports, their share did not fall during the 1980s, suggesting that nonboom traded goods have not been crowded out.

The evidence from Asia and Africa suggests that avoidance of an overvalued exchange rate and high levels of protection for imports is the best way to avoid antiexport bias in the economy. If an economy is committed to moving toward outward orientation and more neutrality in incentives, duty rebate and exemption programs can offset moderate levels of protection to the import sector. They do involve administrative costs that can be high and can conflict with other government objectives. In the presence of high levels of import protection and little real commitment to liberalization, it is unlikely that these policies can work. Creating them under these conditions probably results mostly in administrative costs, opportunities for abuse and rent-seeking, and few benefits.

Export Processing Zones

EPZs are industrial estates with rental buildings, usually fenced in, that house manufacturing for export. EPZs provide exporters with duty-free imported inputs, infrastructure, utilities that are sometimes subsidized, usually a favorable regulatory environment, and often tax holidays. Normally the exports are produced for industrial country markets. Conditions in an EPZ are meant to increase the profitability of investment in the export sector, attracting both foreign and domestic investors.

The expected benefits of EPZs include employment, foreign exchange earnings, technology transfer, and demonstration effects. In economies with underemployed and unemployed labor, EPZs are meant to increase employment by attracting investment to the EPZ that it is assumed would not otherwise occur. Warr (1989) sees EPZs as primarily a way of "exporting" labor. EPZs can also lead to increased demand for domestic raw materials and intermediate inputs further contributing to value added. These benefits presume excessive unemployment and too little investment in the economy.

In economies with many distortions discouraging exports, EPZs are meant to increase exports of manufactured goods from what they would otherwise be by eliminating these distortions within the EPZ. It is thought that EPZs can be set up in an economy with lots of distortions more quickly than alternative policies to guarantee access of exporters to duty-free imports. Duty exemptions or rebate systems need information on input-output relationships, and obtaining these data requires a certain amount of technical and administrative capacity. There is potential for abuse of these systems as well, with duty-free inputs not being used for export. An EPZ is meant to avoid these costs, since use of duty-free imports is much more easily monitored in an EPZ. The cost is that EPZs benefit only firms inside the zone, excluding many actual or potential exporters. Among those excluded are existing or new firms that could export some but not all of their output. A duty-free import system that applied to the whole economy would potentially affect more producers for export, while reduction in tariffs and quantitative restrictions would reduce price distortions to an even greater extent. Nonetheless, an EPZ may be a useful step in the direction of trade liberalization. If successful, manufactured exports will increase. Note that much of the foreign exchange earnings belongs to foreign owners, but some will be earned by domestic factors of production.

A frequently cited benefit of EPZs is their "demonstration effect." In an economy that has followed inward-oriented policies, an EPZ may be useful in demonstrating the potential benefits of an outward-oriented set of policies. An EPZ is easier to institute than broad liberalization throughout the economy. If it results in increased exports and employment, the EPZ's success may contribute to further policy reforms toward a more open economy. Kenya is in the process of setting up EPZs. It is hoped, as stated in donor documents, that the EPZs will demonstrate to Kenyans that a trade liberalization does increase investment, exports, and employment. On the other hand, there is also the possibility that an EPZ can delay further trade reforms, either by being seen as a sufficient response alone or by relaxing the foreign exchange constraint on the margin. Other frequently mentioned benefits are the training of managers and other workers, and technology transfer.

Possible costs of EPZs offsetting expected benefits are varied. There is a frequently expressed concern that EPZs are environmentally unfriendly. According to the World Bank (1992, 20), there is no evidence that EPZs face different environmental regulations than other domestic firms. To the extent that firms in EPZs create environmental costs, there may in fact be economies of scale in dealing with them in EPZs, such as in the monitoring and disposal of waste. Warr (1989) emphasizes the mobility of foreign investment in EPZs. This is not really a cost, but it contributes to limiting benefits. This puts foreign firms in a strong position for negotiating special conditions and suggests few long-term relationships or linkages with the economy. Countries competing for foreign investment may grant tax holidays, which reduce government revenue.

In calculating net benefits, infrastructure and utility costs must be included. Utility rates are often subsidized, particularly to firms in EPZs, which often have high energy demands (Warr 1989, 69–70).

Some of the costs and benefits of EPZs are more easily quantified than others. Benefits that are difficult to quantify include learning by local firms and workers, technology transfer, increased information about the economy by foreign investors, or learning by the government about effective encouragement of exports.

Experience in Asia

In 1988 EPZs accounted for 4 to 5 percent of developing country manufactured exports. Eighty percent of these came from Malaysia, Korea, and Taiwan. The World Bank (1992, 3,29) reports on eighty-six fenced EPZs in twenty-seven developing countries in 1990. Of these, thirty-six were in Asia (twelve in Malaysia, three in Indonesia, four in the Philippines, three in Taiwan, three in Thailand, and two in Korea), forty-one in Latin America and the Caribbean (with nineteen in the Dominican Republic), and only four in Sub-Saharan Africa. Asia accounted for over 70 percent of the employment in EPZs and well over 80 percent of exports.

All Asian EPZs are public. In Latin America, EPZs are increasingly privately developed. Most investors in EPZs are foreign. Manufactured exports from EPZs are labor intensive, mostly textiles and electronics.

Taiwan started using EPZs as a policy tool in 1965. The Kaohsiung EPZ started exporting in 1966 and by 1973 employed 57,000 people (World Bank 1992, 26). Taiwan was already exporting manufactured goods when EPZs were initially created, having adopted economywide duty-free policies in 1955. The trade regime, however, was still highly distorted, and there were few foreign investors, who were the main target for EPZs. Taiwan went on to liberalize further in the 1970s and 1980s. EPZs may have played a specific role in a more general policy environment focused on exports.

TABLE 11.1
Comparison of Export Incentives Granted to EPZ Firms in Asian Countries

	Indonesia	Malaysia	Philippines	Thailand
Corporate income tax abatement	Variable reductions on 20–45% tax rates; accelerated depreciation	95% exemption for five years	35% tax on corporate income	100% exemption for three to eight years, reductions thereafter for five years; loss carryforward for five years
Capital/profits repatriation	Repatriation of capital subject to approval	Unrestricted	Subject to the availability of foreign currency	Unrestricted
Duty treatment for all imports and exports	100% exemption	100% exemption for new goods deemed essential and directly used for manufacturing	100% exemption	100% exemption
Number of days to receive approval	30–180	Not available	10–30	90
Tax on dividends	20% tax	10% tax	35% tax	100% exemption for five years
Restrictions on foreign or local ownership	Subject to controls	None	No foreign ownership of land permitted	Subject to controls
Sales to local market	Not allowed	20% of total output	2% of total output	20% of total output
Management of foreign currency	Controlled	Controlled	Priority in allocation of foreign exchange	Controlled during foreign exchange crisis

SOURCE: The Services Group, in association with Mwaniki Associates Ltd. and SRI International, "The Enabling Environment for Kenyan Export Processing Zones" (submitted to the Ministry of Finance of the Republic of Kenya, U.S. Agency for International Development, Document No. PNABH669, 1990, 20–21).

Korea created the Masan Free Export Zone in 1970 and the Iri Zone in 1974–75. Like Taiwan, Korea had already moved toward an export promotion policy in the 1960s. EPZs again were used to attract foreign investors to an economy already focused on exporting. In 1985 EPZ exports accounted for only 2.9 percent of manufactured exports. EPZs have been successful in Korea, but Korea's overall success in promoting manufactured exports relies little on them.

Malaysia and the Philippines created zones in 1972, Indonesia in 1973. By 1989 Malaysia had ten zones, directly employing 100,000 people, and accounting for annual exports of U.S.$1.6 billion. The Philippines had six zones, directly employing 30,000 people, and accounting for U.S.$200 million in annual exports. Indonesia had two zones employing 15,000 and exporting U.S.$25 million annually (The Services Group 1990, 13). Thailand started using EPZs in 1981. As of 1989 there were two, employing 20,000 workers. Table 11.1 compares the export incentives granted to EPZ firms in these four countries.

Warr (1989) summarizes several cost–benefit studies of EPZs in Indonesia, Korea, Malaysia, and the Philippines.[2] He concludes that some expected benefits have been quite small. EPZs purchase few inputs locally except labor. Indonesia is an exception, where local textiles are purchased by EPZ firms. Generally low demand for local inputs results from relatively high prices and low quality, as well as a desire or strategy on the part of EPZ firms to remain internationally mobile.

Little technology is transferred. If the technology is simple, as in textiles, then the technology is generally readily available to LDCs, both within and outside EPZs. If the technology is not readily available, as in electronics, then firms in EPZs are protective of the technology. In some countries, already relatively open and advanced, some technology transfer may occur as firms in EPZs come to rely on domestic suppliers. These backward linkages and technology transfers are not usual. Workers receive some basic industrial skills, but most workers are assembly workers. One skill that would be quite useful for developing countries is marketing in the industrial economies. But employees in EPZ firms often receive little training in marketing, because much EPZ production is made with buyers already committed (Sabre Foundation 1983, 9).

Warr (1989, 82) calculates internal rates of return for EPZs in Indonesia, Korea, Malaysia, and the Philippines of 26 percent, 15 percent, 28 percent, and −3 percent, respectively. Almost all the benefits in Korea, Malaysia, and the Philippines result from employment and foreign exchange earnings. The major costs in each case, contributing to a negative rate of return in the

Philippines, are for infrastructure and subsidies. In the Philippines, there is also a large cost from subsidizing domestic borrowing by EPZ firms. Warr concludes that the benefits of EPZs are limited, with EPZs being primarily a way to absorb unemployed labor. But even here, he warns that EPZs can only do a little. EPZs are not the solution to employment problems in developing countries.

EPZs have been an important export promotion policy in Malaysia. Firms receive a variety of the usual EPZ incentives—exemption from import duties, subsidized infrastructure, and fewer bureaucratic delays (Beng 1992). More than half of Malaysia's manufactured exports came from EPZs in 1982, and bonded zones accounted for an additional 10 percent. But the net present value of investments in EPZs was sensitive to assumptions about the discount rate and the shadow price of labor (Bhattacharya and Linn 1987, 99). There was little confidence that the net present value was positive. At the same time, evidence of few linkages with the domestic market and little technology transfer or labor training suggested that the hard-to-quantify benefits of EPZs do not appear to work in the direction of increasing net benefits in any significant way. Balasubramanyan (1988) reports that in both Malaysia and the Philippines, firms in EPZs used more capital-intensive means of production in industries such as garments and electronics than similar industries in Korea and Taiwan and than other domestic firms. This resulted from heavy subsidies to capital. Such policies clearly reduce the possible benefits from EPZs through employment creation.

The World Bank (1992, 3), in a study of EPZs, lacking information to do cost–benefit analysis, assesses success based on the number and type of investors, employment, exports, occupancy, and any unusual costs or problems. Of sixty zones analyzed, it concluded that 40 to 50 percent were successful, 20 to 30 percent were partly successful, and 20 percent were unsuccessful. Most of the successful EPZs were Asian, with some successful ones also in the Dominican Republic and Jamaica. Exports from EPZs, however, account for a relatively small share of total manufactured exports. Exports from firms with access to duty exemption or drawback systems account for a larger share of manufactured exports, as do exports produced under in-bond systems. Foreign exchange earnings by EPZs are low relative to exports, because value added is 25 percent or less. Wages and working conditions tend to be as good as or better than those for similar jobs outside EPZs. In EPZs producing electronics, firms do have two to three shifts, so that workers work unconventional hours. Most employees are young women sixteen to twenty-five years old. This again suggests that few long-term relationships are established (World Bank 1992, 15–20).

It is difficult to know what the demonstration effects of EPZs have been. The World Bank suggests that EPZ successes may have had a positive effect on trade policy reform in Malaysia, Sri Lanka, and Taiwan. In other Asian countries, including Korea, EPZs have accounted for such a small share of total exports that it is unlikely that they had much effect on policy. In some economies, including Korea, EPZs have been used to increase manufactured exports in specific sectors and therefore have not played a more general demonstration role.

Where EPZs have failed, there have been several reasons. If a zone is located in an area as a means of developing that area, for example, in rural, remote areas or small cities, the zone rarely is successful. EPZs also fail when the overall environment is not favorable because of political instability, poor infrastructure, or excessive business regulations. The incentives offered through EPZs may not be able to offset these other factors that discourage foreign and domestic investment.

Experience in Africa

EPZs are relatively scarce in Africa. Narrowly defined EPZs exist in Liberia, Senegal, and Togo. If the definition is extended to include factories with in-bond or duty-exemption arrangements, Ghana and Mauritius would be added to the list. An EPZ in Zaire never attracted any investors. A zone built in Liberia in 1975–1976 employed 700 people in 1986 and only 15 in 1989. Senegal constructed an EPZ in 1974–1976, fifteen miles from Dakar airport and eight miles from a port. In 1981 four firms employed 500 people (The Sabre Foundation 1983, CS3–1) and in 1990 employment was reported at 1,200 (World Bank 1992, 29). Employment was restricted by high wages, which are controlled by Collective Bargaining Agreements. In 1983 the Sabre Foundation (1983, CS3–2) reported wages in Senegal to be over five times wages in Sri Lanka.

Mauritius is often cited as an exception to the general failure of EPZs in Africa. The Export Processing Zone program was started in 1970. By 1988 annual EPZ exports totaled $520 million and employed about 100,000 people. In 1985 Mauritius's EPZ exports exceeded sugar exports, long the major export commodity. Textiles and apparel account for about three-quarters of EPZ output. In addition to industrial estates, individual firms can get EPZ status, so that in effect the whole country is an EPZ (The Services Group 1990; Bheenick and Schapiro 1989). During the 1970s the number of EPZ firms in Mauritius increased to 100. Employment increased by over

4 percent per year. In the late 1970s the success of EPZs appeared to slow. In response, the government adopted a set of policies to promote exports further. Importantly, the rupee was devalued 50 percent between 1979 and 1981.

Mauritius's success with EPZs may be explained by a variety of factors. The population is relatively well educated, with close to a 90 percent literacy rate, and there is an active entrepreneurial class. In contrast to other African economies, the government has maintained a macroeconomic environment that made production for export profitable. This was reinforced by the variety of incentives offered under the EPZ program, which is more generally available than in other countries. In addition, the island has a good road system.

The Mauritius EPZ experience demonstrates the potential of an export-oriented strategy while confirming some of the limitations of EPZs. Linkages with the rest of the economy have been slow to develop. EPZ exports are primarily textiles, and much EPZ investment is footloose. Nonetheless, EPZs contributed significantly to exports and employment.

What is the potential role of EPZs in Africa in promoting manufactured exports? The evidence from Asia suggests that they might play a limited role in a few countries, but they should not detract from more general trade and macroeconomic reforms of the economy. EPZs have not in general been used successfully in countries just starting to produce manufactured exports (World Bank 1992, 21), which suggests that the African economies should not place undue emphasis on them. When successful, EPZs can attract foreign investment, increase employment, and earn some foreign exchange for the home country. But even then they do not seem to be a dynamic source of economic development. The foreign investment tends not to be committed to the country in the long run, there are few linkages with the rest of the economy, and the employment relationships are short run. All this suggests that EPZs may be useful in limited ways, as long as not too much is expected of them. If African economies are committed to encouraging manufactured exports, continued tariff reform and avoidance of real appreciation seem the most promising policies. Then EPZs might be encouraged on a limited basis to help increase employment. Making them private might screen out EPZs with low net benefits.

Marketing

The world market does not have an address to which developing countries can ship manufactured exports at world market prices. Instead, foreign buyers have to be located. Is there a role for government intervention here? There may be economies of scale, externalities, or public goods characteristics to knowledge or information about foreign markets that justify government intervention. This sort of trade policy, rather than offsetting another policy distortion, could be justified on a longer-term basis as a first-best response to a market failure. For example, if too little is invested in obtaining information about foreign markets because knowledge cannot be captured for long by a single firm, then government investment in such knowledge may be justified.

Experience in Asia

Many governments have created public sector trade promotion organizations (TPOs) to help market manufactured exports. The four successful exporter economies—Korea, Singapore, Hong Kong, and Taiwan—all have supported export marketing through the public sector (Keesing 1988). The experience of these countries, however, must be used with caution to argue for TPOs in other developing countries trying to increase manufactured exports.

All four Asian economies support export marketing in a variety of ways, both in the private and public sector. All support private trading companies and a variety of private services to exporters. Three of the four public sector TPOs were set up after the countries' policies were generally supportive of exports. They were not substituting for or offsetting other disincentives, but contributing to an overall supportive environment. Hong Kong's Trade Development Council (HKTDC) was set up in 1966, and Singapore's Trade Development Board (STDB) in 1983. Both Hong Kong and Singapore had long been free ports and had been exporting manufactured goods for a decade or more (Keesing 1988, 8–9). Taiwan's China External Trade Development Council (CETDC) was set up in 1970. Korea's Trade Promotion Corporation (KOTRA) was created in 1962, before the overall environment in Korea was supportive of exports generally.

Data on expenditures, staff, and overseas offices as reported in Keesing (1988) are presented in Table 11.2. Keesing (1988, 19) divides the functions of these organizations into "1) trade-related information and inquiry services, 2) trade promotion (trade fairs, missions, publicity), 3) market analysis and market development, and 4) assistance to firms in product design, packaging, actual marketing and other practical needs (e.g. training)." HKTDC concentrates on the first two functions; the other three organizations undertake all four more broadly.

TABLE 11.2
Data on TPOs

	Expenditures	Staff	Overseas offices
KOTRA	$41 million[a]	748 (1986)	77 (1987)
STOB	$10 million[b]	353 (1986)	18
HKTDC	$30 million[c]	650 (1988)	20 (1985)
CETDC	$33 million[d]	600 (1988)	28

a. Preliminary budget, 1987.
b. 1986–87.
c. 1987–88 budget.
d. 1987.
SOURCE: Donald B. Keesing, *The Four Successful Exceptions* (UNDP-World Bank, Trade Expansion Program, Occasional Paper 2, 1988).

How does one tell that these marketing efforts have been productive? If the objective is to increase exports, then expenditures on these programs should at least increase exports above what they would have been otherwise and by more than a subsidy equal to the cost of these programs. Returning to an earlier example, if the justification for the government intervention is that knowledge is a public good, then too little would be invested by the private sector in obtaining knowledge and as a result exports would be less than otherwise. The success of the policies can be judged therefore by their effects on exports and their cost. This is very difficult to evaluate in practice. In the four Asian economies, exports have grown very fast and the cost of their marketing support programs has been kept at .05 to .10 percent of the value of manufactured exports (Keesing 1988, 6). But the quantitative impact of these policies on exports has not been determined. The evidence for their success is impressionistic. Keesing (1988, 33) concludes that

> the activities of the best of these organizations do appear well designed to overcome the information barriers encountered in trying to expand exports rapidly. Thus it is probable that they have indeed accelerated export growth substantially at low cost.

Experience in Africa

Many developing countries in Africa support TPOs within the public sector, including Ghana, Kenya, Malawi, Nigeria, Tanzania, the Congo, Senegal, Somalia, Uganda, Zaire, and Zambia (Hogan, Keesing, and Singer 1991). It is generally concluded that they have been ineffective across the board for a number of reasons.

- Many TPOs were created while the overall environment still protected the import sector and their services could not offset the macroeconomic disincentives to exports.
- Public sector TPOs often have multiple objectives that make the achievement of any one objective difficult, if not impossible. Regional dispersion and "indigenization" of business are two objectives, for example, that can result in a TPO being ineffective at promoting exports.
- TPOs are often created in the public sector as the only provider of services to the export sector. This prevents or hinders the private sector from providing these services in cases where it could do so more effectively. The private sector may be discouraged either by regulation or because the TPO supplies services, even if inadequate, for free.
- Generally, TPOs have been put in Ministries of Trade and are often ineffective with little claim on resources or influence over policy (Hogan, Keesing, and Singer 1991).
- Government employees are generally unsuited to the task and government procedures are too inflexible (Keesing and Singer 1991).

Kenya has supported a parastatal that, although not exactly a traditional TPO, has contributed to increasing nontraditional exports through marketing. The Horticultural Crops Development Authority (HCDA), created in 1967, concentrates on smallholder development, extension services, and information on international prices. It also issues "Export Certificates," which certify product quality and the reasonableness of prices, for a fee (USAID 1991, 33, 92). HCDA helps smallholders market their crops by maintaining contacts with traders and exporters. HCDA finances its activities by a direct tax on export produce and does not receive revenue from the government.

Horticultural exports have increased from 0.3 percent of total exports in 1968 to 3.3 percent in 1986. The private sector, foreign firms, and the government, as well as Kenya's comparative advantage, all contributed to the expansion of this sector. The sector consists of small-scale private enterprises, with the exception of pineapples and flowers, which are produced on a larger scale. Large producers are often joint ventures with foreign investors and rely on their established export markets. Small producers use export agents for marketing.

HCDA's role in marketing is limited but important, consisting primarily of quality control and information. Large producers have access to information about markets in other countries, but smaller exporters rely on the government. The HCDA is also responsible for preshipment inspection at the airport to maintain quality. This helps with any possible externality problems with substandard produce damaging Kenya's general quality reputation on world markets.

The actual quantitative effects of the HCDA on exports are difficult to determine. Clearly the expansion of horticultural production in Kenya was the result of the response of private producers and exporters to market opportunities. But the government policies appear to have reinforced these opportunities and intervened in ways to supplement the market rather than interfere with it (Schapiro and Wainaina 1989).

What are the lessons for African economies? Export marketing efforts may play a role in promoting exports in certain sectors in certain countries. But they, too, have a limited role to play. There is little evidence that official support for export marketing can be effective in economies in transition toward export promotion policies. They may even be of little benefit for countries just starting to export manufactured goods, which may be able to market products effectively through established channels.

Nonetheless, the Kenyan example suggests that in limited areas in some countries, support for export marketing may be cost effective. The HCDA seems to have complemented the private sector in important ways in promoting horticultural exports. It did so at a time when Kenya was not following a policy broadly supportive of exports, but in a sector in which Kenya had a strong comparative advantage. Quality control may be a particularly important area where the government can effectively intervene.

A recent example from Africa confirms the importance of quality control and suggests an important role for the government to avoid free rider problems. Nigeria abolished six federal commodity marketing boards in 1987, including the Cocoa Marketing Board. It was hoped that eliminating the marketing monopolies would lead to higher prices and increased output. An unintended side effect was a reduction on world local markets. The government has since reintroduced licenses for marketers of cocoa and instituted better inspection procedures (Hackett 1990).

Asia's experience also suggests that there may be an important role for the government to play in quality control. Korea instituted a system for inspecting export goods for quality in the early 1960s. The purpose was to help create a reputation for good quality for Korean exports, considered important to successful exporting (Rhee, Ross-Larson, and Pursell 1984). Taiwan also has a quality control system. Starting in the 1950s, certain exports had to be inspected for quality. By 1976, 60 percent of the value of exports was subject to inspection. This proved costly and the system was reformed. Now firms who want to export must have their quality control methods graded periodically. Depending on the results, some firms may not export, some can with inspection of their goods, and others are free from inspection. The system is set up to minimize the administrative costs for exporters. For example, if inspection delays exceed five days, the inspectors take samples to inspect later and the shipment can proceed. Penalties are imposed if the goods do not meet quality standards. Since the mid-1980s the number of export goods subject to inspections has been significantly reduced (Wade 1990, 144–5).

Keesing and Singer (1991) argue in favor of moving toward increased support for the private sector and less use of TPOs to supply marketing and other services to exporters. Exporters should have access to commercial support services, domestic and foreign.[3] Given constraints on government expenditures and capacity, it may make sense in Africa to achieve what benefits are possible through the private sector and foreign firms. In the four Asian economies, the private sector was encouraged at the same time the public sector supplied marketing services. In Kenya foreign firms played an important role in the marketing of horticultural exports along with the HCDA. The information and marketing skills needed may in some cases be supplied more effectively by the private sector or through imports rather than through the public sector. If there are externalities or public goods problems in establishing marketing services to manufactured exports, a subsidy to the private sector would be justified. But given the difficulties of quantifying the benefits of marketing programs and the constraints on government expenditures in Africa, subsidies should be modest at best. Whatever government's role in marketing, it should not prevent the private sector from supplying the services or the export sector could be harmed by ineffective government intervention.

Conclusions

Duty rebates and exemptions are a policy tool to offset the antiexport bias resulting from import protection. EPZs serve a similar function while also, in principle, taking advantage of economies of scale in providing infrastructure to exporters. Government support for marketing of exports is meant to capture externalities or compensate for the public goods nature of investment in knowledge. The Asian economies have used many of these and other export promotion policies at various times over the last three decades.

The experience of Asia and Africa, however, does not suggest that these policies can be used successfully as substitutes for other adjustments. Export promotion policies involve administrative costs and create rents, while policies that minimize administrative costs and rent-seeking should be preferred in Africa. In addition, subsidies to exports are increasingly being met with countervailing duties by industrial countries. Although it is not clear that this will happen to the African economies until they are much more of a threat on world markets, it still creates a preference for alternative policies. These policies were used in Asia to offset lower levels of import protection than exist in many African economies. The use of export promotion policies to offset higher levels of protection increases their costs and intensifies conflict with other objectives, especially fiscal restraint. Asian experience does not suggest that these policies can substitute for responsible macroeconomic policies or a properly valued exchange rate. The potential of export promotion to encourage exports can be realized only as a complement to sound macroeconomic policies.

NOTES

1. Korea's system is similar to Taiwan's but relies on export orders rather than proof of exports (Rhee 1985; Wade 1988a, 1988b).

2. The EPZs studied are as follows: in Indonesia, the Jakarta Export Processing Zone; in Korea, the Masan Free Export Zone; in Malaysia, the Penang Free Trade Zone; and in the Philippines, the Bataan Export Processing Zone.

3. They in fact argue in favor of subsidizing the cost of such services to exporters on the grounds that manufacturing exports have positive externalities in the form of technology acquisition, learning, and training. Since subsidizing manufactured exports directly is against international trade rules, while subsidizing services to exporters is not, this is a second-best way of capturing externalities. This justification for subsidizing the private market provision of marketing differs from the public

good nature of knowledge about markets more specifically. Using marketing subsidies to encourage manufacturing exports more generally is a second-best response.

BIBLIOGRAPHY

Balassa, Bela. 1989. "Outward Orientation." In *Handbook of Development Economics,* Volume 2, ed. H. Chenery and T.N Srinivasan. Amsterdam and New York: North-Holland.

Balasubramanyan, V. N. 1988. "Export Processing Zones in Developing Countries: Theory and Empirical Guidance." In *Economic Development and International Trade,* ed. David Greenway. New York: St. Martin's Press.

Bank Indonesia. Various years. *Annual Report.*

Bellhouse Mwangi Ernst & Young. 1992. "Draft Final Report, Export Compensation and Import Duty Remission Study and Indirect and Small Exporter Study." Volume 1, Main Report, 17-7-92.

Beng, Gan Wee. 1992. "Industrialization and the Export of Malaysian Manufactures." In *The Dangers of Export Pessimism,* ed. Helen Hughes. San Francisco: ICS Press.

Bhattacharya, Amarendara, and Johannes F. Linn. 1987. "Trade and Industrial Policies in the Development Countries of East Asia." World Bank, Report No. 6952.

Bheenick, Rundheersing, and Morton Owen Schapiro. 1989. "Mauritius: A Case Study of the Export Processing Zone." In *Successful Development in Africa,* ed. Earl McFarland. Economic Development Institute of the World Bank.

Byrne, J. J. 1985. "Zimbabwe Export Development Project, Proposed Zimbabwe Export Promotion Authority." Dublin, Ireland: CTT Technical Assistance Programme.

Cline, William R. 1982. "Can the East Asian Model of Development Be Generalized?" *World Development* 10 (2).

Dollar, David. 1992. "Outward-Oriented Developing Economies Really Do Grow More Rapidly: Evidence from 95 LCDs, 1976–1985." *Economic Development and Cultural Change.* 40 (3): 523–44.

Dornbusch, Rudiger. 1992. "The Case for Trade Liberalization in Developing Countries." *Journal of Economic Perspectives* 6 (1): 69–85.

Edwards, S. 1991. "Trade Orientation, Distortions, and Growth in Developing Countries." Los Angeles: University of California. Mimeo.

Falvey, Rodney E, and Norman Gemmell. 1990. "Compensatory Financial and Fiscal Incentives to Exports." In *Export Promotion Strategies, Theory and Evidence from Developing Countries,* ed. Chris Milner. New York: New York University Press.

Findlay, R. 1984. "Growth and Development in Trade Models." In *Handbook of*

International Economics, ed. R. W. Jones and P. B. Kenen. Amsterdam and New York: North-Holland.

Fitzgerald, Bruce, and Terry Munson. 1989. "Preferential Credit and Insurance as Means to Promote Exports." *World Bank Research Observer* 4 (January).

Geiger, Theodore. 1973. *Tales of Two City-States: The Development Progress of Hong Kong and Singapore.* National Planning Association. Studies in Development Progress, No. 3.

Ghosh, Jayati. 1992. "Can World Markets Continue to Absorb Export-Led Strategies of Developing Countries? The Export Pessimist's Case." In *The Dangers of Export Pessimism,* ed. Helen Hughes. San Francisco: ICS Press.

Greenway, David. 1990. "Export Promotion in Sub-Saharan Africa." In *Export Promotion Strategies, Theory and Evidence from Developing Countries,* ed. Chris Milner. New York: New York University Press.

Hackett, Paul. 1990. "Nigeria: Economy." In *Africa South of the Sahara: 1990.* London: Europa Publications Limited, 775–83.

Harrison, Ann. 1991. "Openness and Growth: A Time Series, Cross-Country Analysis for Developing Countries." Background paper for the 1991 World Development Report. The World Bank.

Harvey, Charles, and Stephen F. Lewis. 1990. *Policy Choice and Development Performance in Botswana.* New York: Macmillan in association with OECD Development Centre.

Helleiner, Gerald K., ed. 1992. *Trade Policy, Industrialization, and Development: New Perspectives.* New York: Oxford University Press.

Hill, Catharine B. 1991. "Managing Commodity Booms in Botswana." *World Development* 19 (9): 1185–96.

Hill, Catharine B., and D. Nelson Mokgethi. 1989. "Botswana: Macroeconomic Management of Commodity Booms, 1975–86." In *Successful Development in Africa,* ed. Earl L. McFarland, Jr. Economic Development Institute of the World Bank.

Hill, Hal. 1990. "Indonesia: Export Promotion After the Oil Boom." In *Export Promotion Strategies, Theory and Evidence from Developing Countries,* ed. Chris Milner. New York: New York University Press.

Hogan, Paul, Donald B. Keesing, and Andrew Singer. 1991. *The Role of Support Services in Expanding Manufactured Exports in Developing Countries.* EDI Seminar Series.

Hughes, Helen, ed. 1992. *The Dangers of Export Pessimism.* San Francisco: ICS Press.

Investment Promotion Centre. *Kenya: Export Processing Zones.* Standard Chartered, Financial Services Limited. Promotional brochure.

Keesing, Donald B. 1988. *The Four Successful Exceptions: Official Export Promotion and Support for Export Marketing in Korea, Hong Kong, Singapore, and Taiwan, China.* UNDP-World Bank, Trade Expansion Program, Occasional Paper 2.

Keesing, Donald B., and Sanjaya Lall. 1992. "Marketing Manufactured Exports from Developing Countries: Learning Sequences and Public Support." In *Trade Policy, Industrialization, and Development: New Perspectives,* ed. Gerald K. Helleiner. New York: Oxford University Press.

Keesing, Donald B., and Andrew Singer. 1991. "How Support Services Can Expand Manufactured Exports: New Methods of Assistance." Policy, Research, and External Affairs, Country Economics Department, The World Bank, WPS 544.

Kelly, Margaret, Naheed Kirmani, Mirand Xafa, Clemens Boonekamp, and Peter Winglee. 1988. *Issues and Development in International Trade Policy.* IMF Occasional Paper No. 63.

Koskella, Richard T. 1992. "Study of Export Trading Houses." IMCC, prepared for the Ministry of Industries, Science and Technology. Government of Sri Lanka.

Kumar, Rajiv. 1987. "Performance of Foreign and Domestic Firms in Export Processing Zones." *World Development* 15 (10/11): 1309–19.

Lazard Frères et Cie, Lehman Brothers, S.C. Warburg & Co. Ltd. 1992. "The Republic of Indonesia." Memorandum.

Levine, Ross, and David Renelt. 1992. "A Sensitivity Analysis of Cross-Country Growth Regressions." *The American Economic Review* 82 (4): 942–63.

Lewis, Stephen, and Jennifer Sharpley. 1988. "Kenya's Industrialization, 1964–1984." Institute of Development Studies Discussion Paper No. 242.

Matin, Kazi M. 1992. "Openness and Economic Performance in Sub-Saharan Africa: Evidence from Time-Series Cross-Country Analysis." Country Economics Department, The World Bank, WPS 102S.

Milner, Chris. ed. 1990a. *Export Promotion Strategies, Theory and Evidence from Developing Countries.* New York: New York University Press.

Milner, Chris. 1990b. "The Role of Import Liberalization in Export Promotion." In *Export Promotion Strategies, Theory and Evidence from Developing Countries.* New York: New York University Press.

Nam, Chong-Hyun. 1990. "Export Promotion Strategy and Economic Development in Korea." In *Export Promotion Strategies, Theory and Evidence from Developing Countries,* ed. Chris Milner. New York: New York University Press.

Noland, Marcus. 1990. *Pacific Basin Developing Countries: Prospects for the Future.* Washington, D.C.: Institute for International Economics.

Pack, Howard. 1989. "Industrialization and Trade." In *Handbook of Development Economics,* ed. H. Chenery and T. N. Srinivasan. Amsterdam and New York: North-Holland.

———. 1993. "Productivity and Industrial Development in Sub-Saharan Africa." *World Development* 21 (1).

Pangestu, Mari. 1993. "Indonesia: Toward Non-Oil Exports." In *The Dangers of Export Pessimism,* ed. Helen Hughes. San Francisco: ICS Press.

Rhee, Y. W. 1985. "Instruments for Export Policy and Administration: Lessons from the East Asian Experience." World Bank Staff Working Paper No. 725.

Rhee, Yung Whee, Bruce Ross-Larson, and Garry Pursell. 1984. *Korea's Competitive Edge: Managing the Entry into World Markets.* Baltimore, Md.: Johns Hopkins University Press.

Rondinelli, Dennis A. 1987. "Export Processing Zones and Economic Development in Asia: A Review and Reassessment of a Means of Promoting Growth and Jobs." *American Journal of Economics and Sociology* 46 (1).

Sabre Foundation. 1983. "Free Zones in Developing Countries: Expanding Opportunities for the Private Sector." Final Report, Bureau for Program and Policy Coordination. U.S. Agency for International Development.

Schapiro, Morton Owen, and Stephen Wainaina. 1989. "Kenya: A Case Study of the Production and Export of Horticultural Commodities." In *Successful Development in Africa*, ed. Earl McFarland. Economic Development Institute of the World Bank.

The Services Group, in association with Mwaniki Associates Ltd. and SRI International. 1990. "The Enabling Environment for Kenyan Export Processing Zones." Submitted to the Ministry of Finance of the Republic of Kenya. U.S. Agency for International Development, Document No. PNABH669.

Shepherd, Geoffrey, and Carlos Geraldo Langoni, eds. 1991. *Trade Reform: Lessons from Eight Countries.* San Francisco: ICS Press.

Spinanger, Dean. 1984. "Objectives and Impact of Economic Activity Zones—Some Evidence from Asia." *Weltwirtschaftliches Archiv* 120:64–89.

Suphachalasai, Suphat. 1992. "Thai Textile Exports." In *The Dangers of Export Pessimism,* ed. Helen Hughes. San Francisco: ICS Press.

Svedberg, Peter. 1988. *The Export Performance of Sub-Saharan Africa 1970–1985.* Seminar Paper No. 409. Stockholm: Institute for International Studies.

Trade Development Institute of Ireland (TDI). 1988. "Institutional Development for Export Promotion in Zimbabwe." Harare, Zimbabwe: Ministry of Trade and Commerce.

Tecson, Gwendolyn R. 1992. "Markets for Philippine Manufactured Exports." In *The Dangers of Export Pessimism,* ed. Helen Hughes. San Francisco: ICS Press.

Thomas, V., and J. Nash. 1991. *Best Practices in Trade Policy Reform.* New York: Oxford University Press.

Toh, K. 1992. "Export and Investment Services in Thailand." USAID (AFR/EA). Mimeo.

USAID. 1991. "Kenya Export Development Support (KEDS) Project Paper." PD-BCB71.

Wade, Robert. 1988a. "Taiwan, China's Duty Rebate System." Trade Policy Division, Country Economics Department, The World Bank.

———. 1988b. "How to Organize a Duty Rebate Scheme—A Successful Non-

Korean Example." Trade Policy Division, Country Economics Department, The World Bank.

———. 1990. *Governing the Market.* Princeton, N.J.: Princeton University Press.

Warr, Peter G. 1989. "Export Processing Zones: The Economics of Enclave Manufacturing." *World Bank Research Observer* 4 (1).

World Bank. 1987. *World Development Report 1987.* Washington, D.C.

———. 1988. "Road Deterioration in Developing Countries: Causes and Remedies." World Bank Policy Study. Unpublished.

———. 1991. *World Development Report 1991.* Washington, D.C.

———. 1992. *Export Processing Zones.* Policy and Research Series No. 20. Country Economics Department.

———. 1992. *World Development Report 1992.* Washington, D.C.

About the Authors

David L. Lindauer is professor of economics at Wellesley College and a faculty associate with HIID. In his work with HIID and as a frequent consultant to the World Bank, Dr. Lindauer has conducted research or provided advice on economic development in Kenya, Malawi, Sierra Leone, Sudan, Zambia, Korea, Malaysia, Vietnam, and the Philippines. He has published articles in numerous journals of economics and development, and he is one of the contributors to *Markets in Developing Countries: Parallel, Fragmented, and Black,* published by ICS Press in 1991.

Michael Roemer is an institute fellow of HIID, coordinator of HIID research, and project manager of the HIID-led Consulting Assistance on Economic Reform project. He is a member of the faculty of the Department of Economics and the John F. Kennedy School of Government at Harvard University. Dr. Roemer has served as a consultant to the governments of a number of developing countries, among them Indonesia, Ghana, Kenya, and Tanzania. He has written or edited several books, among them the ICS Press title *Markets in Developing Countries: Parallel, Fragmented, and Black* (edited with Christine Jones).

David C. Cole is an economist at HIID and a lecturer on economics at Harvard University. He is also resident adviser to the Ministry of Finance in Indonesia. Dr. Cole's research and practical development experience in Asia and Africa spans nearly five decades and has involved, in addition to his advisory service in Indonesia, work in China, Korea, Nepal, the Philippines, Sri Lanka, Thailand, Vietnam, Egypt, Mali, and Sudan. He has published widely and is volume editor (with Hal S. Scott and Philip Wellons) of the forthcoming book *Asian Money Markets: Focus of Financial Policy.*

James S. Duesenberry is William Joseph Maier Professor of Money and Banking, Emeritus, and former chairman of the Department of Economics at Harvard University. In recent years he has been a consultant to HIID in Indonesia, Sri Lanka, and The Gambia. In his long career, he has also been a member of the President's Council of Economic Advisers and chairman of the board of directors of the Federal Reserve Bank of Boston. Dr. Duesenberry has published many articles and books, including the classic *Money, Banking and the Economy* (with Thomas Mayer and Robert Z. Aliber).

Richard H. Goldman is a fellow of HIID and lecturer in the Harvard University Department of Economics and John F. Kennedy School of Government. He is the coordinator of HIID's summer executive program on Macroeconomic Adjustment and Food/Agricultural Analysis. Dr. Goldman has had extended periods of residence in Malaysia, Pakistan, and Kenya, where he has served as a policy adviser. He has also participated in policy analysis in Indonesia, Sri Lanka, and Malawi. His recent research has focused on comparing food systems development in various parts of the world.

Catharine Hill is professor of economics at Williams College and chairman of the Center for Development Economics at Williams. Dr. Hill has served as a consultant to the World Bank and to the Committee on Banking, Finance, and Urban Affairs of the United States House of Representatives. She has published numerous articles, working papers, and reviews in development economics and has contributed to several multiauthor volumes.

Jeffrey D. Lewis is an economist at the World Bank, where he works in the Country Operations Division for Indonesia. Before joining the Bank, he was an institute associate at HIID for nine years, including five years as a resident adviser in the Indonesian Ministry of Finance. Dr. Lewis has also served as a consultant in Colombia, Venezuela, Bangladesh, Turkey, Uganda, and Zambia. His areas of research include economic modeling, exchange rates and trade policy, and stabilization and structural adjustment in developing economies.

Malcolm F. McPherson is a research associate at HIID. He has had extensive experience in African economic affairs, acting as adviser to the minister of finance and trade in The Gambia, serving as director of the Economic and Financial Policy Analyses Project in the Gambian Ministry of Finance and Trade, and lecturing on macroeconomic policy, budgeting, and financial management at the Management Development Institute in The Gambia. Dr. Perkins has also been a consultant to the Sahel Division of the World Bank and has advised the Center for International and Strategic Studies on the politics of economic reform in Sub-Saharan Africa.

Dwight H. Perkins is director of HIID and H. H. Burbank Professor of Political Economy at Harvard University. His research has focused on economic reform and development in Asia; and he has acted as a consultant on economic policy to the governments of China, Malaysia, and Papua New Guinea, as well as to the Korea Development Institute, the World Bank, the Ford Foundation, the United States Senate, and a number of U.S. government agencies and private corporations. Dr. Perkins is the author of eleven books and more than eighty articles on issues of economic development, particularly that of Asian countries.

Thomas Tomich is an institute associate at HIID and Cambridge coordinator of the Food Security and Nutrition Unit Project for the Office of the President and Cabinet of Malawi. He has been a consultant for the United States Agency for International Development, for the Aga Khan Foundation, for the World Bank, and for the governments of Indonesia and The Gambia. Dr. Tomich also served as resident adviser and resident coordinator for the Center for Policy and Implementation Studies in Jakarta, Indonesia. Dr. Tomich's book *Transforming Agrarian Economies: Opportunities Seized, Opportunities Missed* (with Peter Kilby and Bruce F. Johnston) is forthcoming.

Ann D. Velenchik is professor of economics at Wellesley College. Her research concentrates on labor market issues in Africa, and she has carried out resident work in the Sub-Saharan African nations of Cote d'Ivoire, Ghana, and Zimbabwe. Dr. Velenchik's current research is focused on training, firm size, and wage determination in the manufacturing sector in Zimbabwe and Ghana.

Jeffrey Vincent is an institute associate at HIID and lecturer in the Harvard University Department of Economics and John F. Kennedy School of Government. He is deputy director of the Central and Eastern Europe Environmental Economics and Policy Project, sponsored by the United States Agency for International Development, and codirector of a project on international forestry economics and policy funded by the United States Environmental Protection Agency. Dr. Vincent is currently working on problems of economics and environmental resources in Indonesia, Jordan, Pakistan, and Thailand.

Louis T. Wells, Jr., is Herbert R. Johnson Professor of International Management in the Harvard Graduate School of Business Administration. He has been a consultant to HIID for the government of Indonesia and has advised other organizations, governments, and private firms on foreign investment policy and on negotiations between foreign investors and host governments. Dr. Wells has published many articles, reviews, monographs, and books, including *Third World Multinationals: The Rise of Foreign Investment from Developing Countries;* and his work has appeared in Arabic, Chinese, French, German, Japanese, Korean, Norwegian, and Spanish, as well as English.

Jennifer A. Widner is professor of government at Harvard University. Dr. Widner is affiliated with the Center for International Affairs at Harvard, where she has served as Africa Seminar coordinator, directed the Workshop on the Angola-Namibia Negotiations, and organized other conferences on development issues. She has taught at Duke University and Yale University as well as at Harvard and is the volume editor of *Economic Change and Political Liberalization in Sub-Saharan Africa,* published in 1994, and the author of other books on Africa.

Index